CW00731546

BRITISH AIRSHIP BASES

OF THE TWENTIETH CENTURY

BRITISH AIRSHIP BASES

OF THE TWENTIETH CENTURY

MALCOLM FIFE

FONTHILL

Fonthill Media Limited
Fonthill Media LLC
www.fonthillmedia.com
office@fonthillmedia.com

First published in the United Kingdom and the United States of America 2015

British Library Cataloguing in Publication Data:
A catalogue record for this book is available from the British Library

Copyright © Malcolm Fife 2015

ISBN 978-1-78155-281-0

The right of Malcolm Fife to be identified as the author of this work has been asserted by him in accordance with the Copyright, Designs and Patents Act 1988

All rights reserved. No part of this publication may be reproduced, stored in a retrieval system or transmitted in any form or by any means, electronic, mechanical, photocopying, recording or otherwise, without prior permission in writing from Fonthill Media Limited

Typeset in 10pt on 13pt Sabon
Printed and bound by CPI Group (UK) Ltd, Croydon, CR0 4YY

Contents

Acknowledgements

I give special thanks to the following for assistance with this book: Mick Davis, Editor of the *Cross and Cockade* journal, who checked for factual errors and allowed me to use his plans of airship stations; Ross Dimsey, for editing the manuscript; Brian Turpin, for validating the factual content of the text; and Bob O'Hara, for research in the Public Records Office.

Finally, I would also like to acknowledge the helpful contributions of the following: Giles Camplin, the Airship Heritage Trust; Kenneth Deacon; Andrew Dennis, Assistant Curator of the RAF Museum; George Edwards, local and family history librarian in Haverfordwest; Jim Eunson; Clare Everitt, Picture Norfolk; Jon Excell, Editor of *The Engineer*; Kevin Heath, the Aviation Research Group in Orkney and Shetland; Steve Jackson, Library and Archives Senior Assistant at the Manx Museum; Paul Johnston, Image Library Manager of the National Archives; Alan Johnstone; Nigel Lutt, Archives/Ops Manager of the Bedfordshire and Luton Archives; Julie Mather and Emily Weeks, Research Assistants at the Fleet Air Arm Museum; Guy Mather; Vinit Mehta, the RAF Museum; Derek Millis, the Airship Heritage Trust; Graham Naylor, Senior Librarian at the Plymouth Central Library; David Ratcliffe; Linda Rhodes, Local Studies librarian at the Heritage Services in Barking; Sally Richards, the Imperial War Museum Picture Library; Brian Riddle, Chief Librarian at the National Aerospace Library; Pat Roland; Sabine Skae, the Dock Museum; Peter Tamaqua, Library and Archives Assistant at the Science Museum; Paul Ternent, Senior Archives Assistant at the Northumberland Archive Service; Janet Tierney, Curator of Goole Museum; Sonya Waplington, the Cumbria Archives; Guy Warner; Peter Wright, *Cross and Cockade*.

Preface

There are few inventions that have captured the imagination like airships. First flown at the end of the nineteenth century, they evolved within a span of less than fifty years to become the largest flying machines ever seen. Some were over twice the length of the largest passenger jets of the early twenty-first century. Few of those who witnessed these leviathans of the air in flight would forget the experience.

The career of the airship was remarkably brief, lasting little more than half a century: by the end of the Second World War, the species had become almost extinct. There have been numerous attempts to revive it, but most have, at best, met with only very limited success. Airships now live on in novels, action films, and advertisements.

One of the drawbacks of operating large airships in the early twentieth century was the need for complex supportive infrastructure on the ground—large sheds to house them, hydrogen plants to supply them with gas, and workshops for construction and repairs. In fact, so dependent were large airships on accommodation to protect them from the elements, that the availability of such structures to some extent dictated airship policy. In the latter stages of the First World War, several enormous airship sheds—rivalling even cathedrals in size—were constructed in Britain. They were built in a short space of time, and mostly lasted no more than five or six years.

Far easier to house were the non-rigid airships operated in large numbers by the Royal Navy in the First World War. They were much smaller than the 500-to-600-foot-long rigid Zeppelin airships in German service, being around 200 feet in length. These consisted of a bag of gas, known as the envelope, under which was suspended a control car containing the power plant and crew. Over 200 such machines served in the Royal Navy Air Service, as opposed to only a handful of rigid airships, but it is the latter type which most people think of when the word 'airship' is mentioned.

While there have been numerous publications on airfield histories, only a small number are devoted to airship stations. Peter Wright was responsible for a three-part article on Royal Naval Air Service (RNAS) airship stations, which appeared in the First World War aviation magazine *Cross and Cockade* in 2001–2 and dealt mainly with the buildings at each location. This book is the first to detail all locations used by British civil and military airships, and is intended to give the uninformed reader a depiction of the activities at each station. Where possible, the research has been based on original records and contemporary newspaper articles. Finally, it should be noted that when the RAF was formed on 1 April 1918, it inherited the personnel and aeroplanes of the RNAS. Hence, the prefix 'RNAS' has been dropped from the names of airship stations after this date, although they still remained the property of the Admiralty.

1

The Airship Pioneers

If the more sensational claims are to be believed, airships are as old as civilisation itself. Col. Lockwood Marsh, a secretary of the Royal Aeronautical Society in the early 1920s, claimed to have discovered the earliest reference to them in an ancient Abyssinian manuscript. According to him, it describes a flying machine resembling an airship which King Solomon presented to the Queen of Sheba, 'a vessel wherein one could traverse the air (or winds) which Solomon had made by the wisdom that God had given unto him'.[1]

In the thirteenth century, Roger Bacon, a Franciscan Friar who spent much of his time carrying out scientific experiments, thought that human flight could be achieved by filling a thinly walled metal sphere with rarefied air or liquid fire. Fanciful ideas on how man could break free from his earthly domain flourished in the following centuries. Francesco Lana de Terzi, a professor of Physics and Mathematics at Brescia, Italy, detailed a proposal for a vacuum airship in his book *Prodromo* in 1670. His lighter-than-air vessel would be shaped like a small ship with four thin foil copper spheres pumped to vacuum conditions attached to it. Once the craft became airborne, a sail would be used to propel it in the same manner as a sailing ship. However, Francesco Lana de Terzi's vacuum airship never left the page. He was aware that such an invention could be used as a weapon of war and naively wrote:

> God would not suffer such an invention to take effect, by reason of the disturbance it would cause to the civil government of men ... it may over-set them, kill their men, burn their ships by artificial fireworks and fireballs. And this they may do not only to ships, but to great buildings, castles, cities....[2]

Jean Baptiste Marie Meusnier, an officer in the French Engineer Corps, is credited with creating the first practical design for an airship in 1784. It was an elongated balloon driven by propellers. Early in the nineteenth century, Sir George Cayley, the 6th Baronet of Brompton, further refined these ideas. He is regarded as one of the founders of Aeronautics, for he was the first person to understand the principles of flight. After designing and building a number of model gliders, he turned his attention to airships, and by 1816 had designed a streamlined airship with a semi-rigid structure, and later, one powered by a steam engine. While Sir George Cayley went on to construct and fly gliders which could lift a man, his airships remained firmly on the drawing board. A major drawback was that there were no lightweight power plants available at the time to transform a balloon into an airship. The only power plant available was the steam engine, and as well as adding considerable weight to any lighter-than-air craft, the sparks produced by its combustion process could set fire to the hydrogen-filled envelope.

Despite these drawbacks, Henri Giffard flew his steam-powered airship, appropriately named the *Aerial Steamer*, 16 miles from Paris to Trappes in September 1852. A 3-hp engine drove the propeller. This was the first powered flight in history, and the French continued to lead the way. Charles Renard and Arthur Krebs built an airship, *La France*, for the French Army. It was constructed in a purpose-built shed at Chalais-Meudon near Paris and was some 170 feet long, with a large propeller mounted at the front. In 1884, it became airborne for the first time and had the distinction of making the first fully controlled free flight powered by an electric motor. While *La France* has long been in the airship graveyard, the shed where it was built has survived into the twenty-first century.

At the close of the nineteenth century, Count Ferdinand von Zeppelin built a large floating shed on the shore of Lake Constance at Friedrichshafen, from which rigid airships later derived. They were larger than anything that had previously flown and soon captured people's imagination across the world. Although other countries attempted over the next forty years to copy the Zeppelin airships, none could match their engineering standards. While Germany was turning these out on an industrial scale, Britain's attempts were confined to a few individuals tinkering with limited resources. The *Dundee Evening Post* on 30 April 1903 reported one such a venture ending in disaster:

> Early on Sunday morning an airship, which had been built by Mr Robert Buchanan of Denmead in Hampshire, came to an untimely end. The inventor claimed that his aerial machine, which was practically the work of a lifetime, could travel against the wind. A model had been favourably reported to the War Office and arrangements made for an expert aeronaut to inspect the airship on behalf of the Government. Unfortunately it has now been destroyed by a fire, which reduced the shed in which it was stored to ashes. A tramp named Williams was brought before Droxford Magistrates on Monday on suspicion of causing the fire and remanded. He is said to have admitted lighting a fire near the shed because he was cold and hungry.

A small number of British airship pioneers did succeed in creating airships which managed to get off the ground. To house their inventions, the first purpose-built airship sheds were erected and sometimes referred to as 'garages'. They were occasionally also known as 'hangars', although this term now refers to buildings used to house aeroplanes. The correct term for a building in which an airship is protected from the elements is 'shed'.

Crystal Palace, London

Crystal Palace had a long association with 'lighter-than-air' flight. When Queen Victoria opened the Great Exhibition in 1851, a balloon piloted by Charles Spencer flew overhead. Fifty years later, members of the same family would make the first successful airship flight in Britain. When the Great Exhibition came to an end, the gigantic structure of Crystal Palace was dismantled and re-erected on Sydenham Hill, where it and the surrounding grounds performed a similar function to that of a twenty-first-century theme park.

Before the relocated Crystal Palace opened in 1854, Vauxhall Gardens had been the favourite London venue for entertainment and recreation. It was also a popular ballooning site, from where the *Locomotive Balloon*, built by Hugh Bell, ascended in May 1850. It was equipped with an airscrew which should have given it directional flight like an airship, but unfortunately it was ineffective.

Models of airships and various flying machines participated in the world's first air show, which was staged at the Crystal Palace in 1886. Other attempts at conquering the air were also made from here—Thomas May built an unmanned *Aerial Steamer* which was seen to lift off a track next to one of the fountains. Despite ballooning and occasionally powered attempts to take to the air, the number of visitors to Crystal Palace was on the decline by the turn of the century. Perhaps in an effort to revive its fortunes, permission was given around 1900 to construct Britain's first purpose-built airship shed on its polo grounds, the largest open space available; it was a timber-framed structure with large horizontally sliding doors.

The Spencer Brothers, who fabricated balloons inflated with hydrogen and coal gas in Highbury, London, decided to expand their activities and build the *Spencer Airship*. It was transferred to Crystal Palace for assembly, and on 23 June 1902 took to the air. It became known as the *Mellin Airship*, because it carried advertising for the Mellin Food Company. Not content with their name being branded across the sky, the company had huge advertising boards put on the doors of the airship shed itself. Airships have been used in promotional roles ever since, and in the First World War dropped leaflets over British cities exhorting the inhabitants to purchase government bonds.

Two weeks later, the *Spencer Airship* again took to the air, watched by vast crowds including colonial troops. It made about thirty flights from Crystal Palace during the next few weeks, piloted by Stanley Spencer. In the summer of 1903, the *Spencer No. 2 Airship* was assembled in the shed. It took off on 17 September 1903 with the intention of circling St Paul's dome, but strong winds carried the craft directly over the Cathedral and blew it north over Alexandria Palace. It eventually managed to land in Trent Park, 13 miles to the north of the city. A week later, watched by a crowd of 30,000 people, Stanley Spencer again took off from Crystal Palace, in his second attempt to reach the heart of London—but this had to be cut short when the airship came into contact with a telegraph wire. A third and final attempt was made on 1 October 1903, but strong winds prevented the airship from achieving its goal. The Spencer Brothers gave up flying their airships from Crystal Palace after this failure.

However, they went on to build a further airship in 1913, which flew around the country advertising Bovril.

In the years leading up to the First World War, airships continued to make use of Crystal Palace as a landing ground. On 5 October 1907, the military airship *Nulli Secundus* (Second to None), piloted by the pioneer aviators Col John Capper and F. Cody, successfully flew around the dome of St Paul's Cathedral as well as Buckingham Palace. They attracted attention during their flight by sounding a powerful siren on board. Strong winds had prevented them from returning to Farnborough, so they attempted to land on Clapham Common, only to be hampered by the vast crowds gathered on that open space. Instead, they diverted to Crystal Palace, where a successful landing was made and the airship was roped to the ground for several days. A strong wind blew up on the 10th, pulling up a number of the guy-ropes, and the decision was made to deflate the envelope to prevent further damage, but it was too late to save the *Nulli Secundus*. On 10 October 1907, the *Derby Daily Telegraph* published a description of what occurred:

> The airship lies a complete wreck on the cycle track at Crystal Palace. It was between eight and nine o'clock this morning that the accident occurred. Half a gale was blowing from the south-west and the sappers in charge of the aerostat noted with apprehension her imminent danger. She was tugging violently at her anchoring ropes when a sudden squall caught her bow and a number of stakes were pulled out under the strain, the whole contrivance keeling over. She had the appearance from a distance of a performing elephant, the huge bag resting on one end, the other being in the air. The envelope of the aerostat was at once deflated but the intricate framework lay a hopelessly confused mass of aluminium tubing and rope work.

The airship was transported back to Farnborough where it was rebuilt to fly briefly again as the *Nulli Secundus II*.

Alexandra Palace, London

Alexandra Palace was North London's answer to Crystal Palace. This landmark building, which opened its doors in 1875, was built on high ground overlooking the suburb of Highgate, and was intended as a public centre of recreation, education, and entertainment. The grounds around the base of the hill were landscaped into a public park. Some years later, the trustees of Alexandra Palace gave the inventor Dr Barton permission to erect a shed in which he could construct his new airship. No doubt this was meant to boost attendance figures, for visitors were going to be allowed to view the aircraft while it was in construction. The *Shields Daily Gazette* gave the following description of this project in August 1901:

> The machine is a combination of the balloon, screw propeller and aeroplane principles and will be, when completed, 200 feet in length. It will have a lifting capacity of between

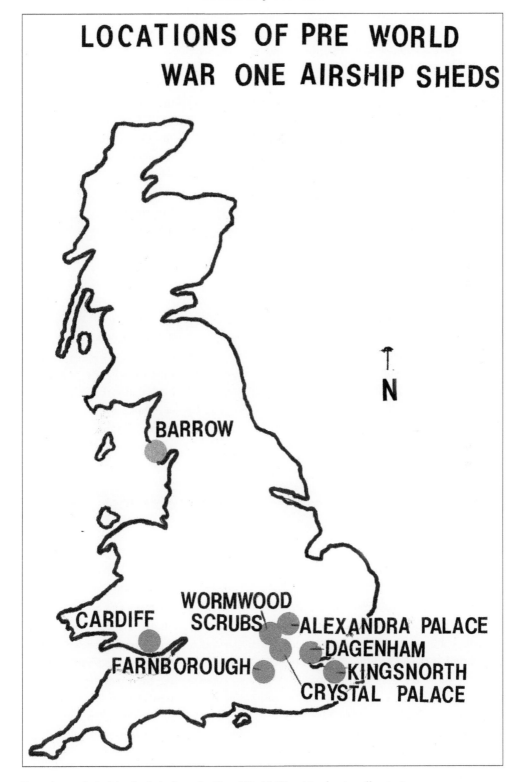

Locations of airship sheds before the First World War. (*Author's collection*)

four and four and a half tons. The crew consisting of three men, the vessel will be propelled by six screw propellers driven by two light petrol engines capable of developing 72 horse power. It is expected that its maximum speed will be thirty miles an hour. It will be equipped to remain in the air for 48 hours. According to Dr. Barton this design had been evolved after 16 years of experimenting. The War Office funded the project to the tune of 4,000 pounds.

In spring 1903, the shed was constructed next to the pond on the north-eastern side of Alexandra Palace at a cost of £450. It was reported to have been 170 feet long, 70 feet high, and 70 feet wide, and was made of timber but for its concrete foundations and floors. On 5 October 1903, a sudden strong wind blew up and seriously damaged it. Glass from the windows was sent flying, and the huge timber sides of the shed were smashed like matchwood. Dr Barton and his assistant fled from the building and remained outside, expecting to see the collapse of the roof. Luckily, the squall did not last long and the airship was not damaged, but this incident delayed the first flight. The following year, Dr Barton narrowly escaped serious injury when one of the gas bags he was inflating exploded. Four years later than intended, the airship took to the air manned by Dr Barton and three other crew. They had intended to fly over the centre of London, but the wind instead blew them eastwards over Essex. The airship came to rest at Heaton Grange near Romford, 16 miles away, where a garden party was in progress. The airship's envelope was ripped when the stern of the craft began rising back into the air:

> What had five minutes previously been a magnificent invention proudly soaring in mid-air lay across the potato patch, a complete wreck. As the ship fell she crashed over on her side, tearing the stern motor from its bearings and smashing the starboard aft propeller off close to its boss. In less time than it takes to describe, the huge balloon had fallen over. The wreckage enveloped the aeronauts, but they struggled clear in a moment and the party were able to congratulate themselves that no personal injuries had resulted.[3]

This was the first and last flight of Dr Barton's airship. The War Office was less than impressed and swiftly dismissed this project.

East Moors, Cardiff

Although most early airship flights took place in or around London, there was one major exception to this trend. Ernest Willows of Cardiff began constructing his first airship at the age of 19, and went on to become one of Britain's foremost airship pioneers. Willows built a wooden shed and a hydrogen gas plant on a large area of open ground in East Moors, close to the banks of the Severn Estuary. He began constructing his first airship, the *Willows I*, in 1905, and it took to the air in August of that year for 85 minutes.

In 1909, Willows lengthened his airship shed by 16 feet to begin work on the *Willows II*, which took to the air in November. The following year, he flew over

Cardiff and landed outside the City Hall, much to the delight of its occupants. He then flew his 86-foot-long airship back to its shed at East Moors. On 6 August 1910, he set off in the *Willows II* with the intention of flying from Cardiff to London. He stopped about twelve times *en route*, shouting down to people on the ground for directions. Five miles short of Crystal Palace, the *Willows II* ran out of petrol and drifted over the suburbs of London, eventually landing several miles from its intended destination. A group of railway men coming off a night shift grabbed hold of the trail ropes and brought the airship safely down to earth. This was the longest flight achieved by a British airship at that time. After refuelling, Ernest Willows reached Crystal Palace, and from here made several more flights, including one around St Paul's Cathedral and an ambitious return flight to Paris.

He then abandoned his premises at East Moor and moved his activities to the Midlands, establishing a balloon and airship company at Villa Road, Hansworth, Birmingham. A hangar was initially made available for his airships at Wolverhampton before Ernest Willows decided to move to the Midland Aero Club's new aerodrome at Castle Bromwich. Here he built the airship shed in which the *Willows IV* was constructed. The military had taken an interest in Willows's activities since he first took to the air, and his new creation, accompanied by its shed, was later sold to the Royal Navy for £1,050. Despite his successes, he was declared bankrupt in 1912: his airship shed at East Moors, Cardiff—which had cost £205 to build—was sold at an auction, fetching just over £12, and the 1930s expansion of Cardiff saw the redevelopment of the land with new housing. Ernest Willows was paid homage in the street name 'Willows Avenue'; in the 1960s, a new secondary school was named after him, as was a new pub on City Road as recently as 2000.

Dagenham Aerodrome, London

In 1908, Britain still lacked an aerodrome that could be used by private aviators. In an effort to remedy this, the Royal Aer*f*o Society raised funds to purchase an area of reclaimed land on the north bank of the lower Thames, immediately to the east of Dagenham Dock. In those days, most of the surrounding area was flat, low-lying countryside. The landing ground itself was almost entirely surrounded by water which gave it a degree of privacy. The River Thames demarcated its southern boundary, and a large inlet known as Dagenham Breach lay on its north-western edges. One acre of ground on the north-west side was reserved for the clubhouse and hangars. By the summer of 1909, hangars to house four aeroplanes were completed, along with a clubhouse made of iron. There was also a further shed on the banks of Dagenham Breach to house floatplanes.

A number of individuals applied to use this new flying ground, including Mr Moreing, an Australian who had made a fortune from gold mining. He had a French-built *Voisin* biplane here, but never managed to fly it further than 200 to 300 yards. The most surprising sight for visitors to the aerodrome was a moderately sized airship shed, situated a short distance from Mr Moreing's aeroplane hangar. It housed a deflated airship, some 105 feet in length, believed to have been built by the Spencer Brothers. In the summer of 1909, an attempt was made to inflate it, but this resulted in damage to the airship, which managed only to rise a few feet off the ground, its only ascent. Mystery surrounds this airship, which was believed to belong to Mr Moreing, and of which the ownership was also claimed by another Australian. The ground at Dagenham proved unsuitable for an aerodrome—one description called it 'a weed preserve'. Its brief career came to an end in 1911, when the hangars were sold and re-erected a short distance away on Handley Page's Barking Creek ground. The land was purchased by the Ford Motor Company in 1923, and a large factory erected on it.

Hendon Aerodrome, London

Ernest Willows moved to London in an attempt to re-launch his career. He undertook balloon and airship instruction at the Hendon Aerodrome in Colindale, north-west London. The area had long been used for lighter-than-air flights. Henry Coxwell and James Glaisher were the first to fly from here in a balloon called the *Mammoth* in 1862. The first powered flight from Hendon was in an 88-foot airship made by the Spencer Brothers. It took off from the Welsh Harp Reservoir in 1909, piloted by Henry Spencer and with the Australian suffragette Muriel Matters as its sole passenger. Shortly afterwards, the Grahame White Aviation Company acquired 200 acres at Colindale and constructed Hendon Aerodrome, which was used by powered

The airship shed at the Dagenham landing ground. (*Barking and Dagenham Archive and Local Studies Centre*)

aeroplanes from 1911 onwards. Ernest Willows was engaged by the owner of the aerodrome to fund the construction of a new airship, which began to materialise in a canvas shed built specifically for this purpose. At this time, Willows was the only civilian airship pilot in Britain.

On 27 November 1913, the *Willows V*, the biggest airship Willows had ever built, made its first test flight. He intended to use it to make joy flights over London, and the next day flew it over the dome of St Paul's Cathedral. Early the following year, an air display was held at Hendon, where it featured as a star attraction. On 16 March 1914, disaster struck when gale force winds blew through the front of the shed and damaged the *Willows V*—the shed required major repairs. This occurred at the end of Ernest Willows's tenure at Hendon; he returned to Cardiff, where his company made balloons in the First World War. On 3 August 1926, he was killed alongside four passengers at a flower show at Hoo Park, Bedford, while giving pleasure trips in a captive balloon.

The Spencer Brothers flew their last airship from Hendon. It was known as the *Bovril Airship*, as its prime function was to promote the famous fluid beef extract. One side of its envelope bore the slogan, 'Give Him Bovril', and the other, 'Give Her Bovril'. This small airship, just 96 feet in length, made many flights over London in the summer of 1913. On one occasion, it was joined by a biplane that performed mock attacks on it—a premonition of what was shortly to come. Hendon continued to operate as an RAF aerodrome until 1968, and part of the site now houses the RAF Museum.

Proposals for Airship Passenger Services

While Britain was still toying with small airships of little more than novelty value, the Germans were using Zeppelins on passenger flights. In 1912, plans were drawn up to establish a network of airship services from London. This was not the first time such an idea was proposed: in 1835, London newspapers printed an announcement by the European Aeronautical Society that it was going to establish a network of passenger services to other European cities, of which the means of transport would be by an airship propelled by giant oars! The public were invited to view the airship, the *Eagle*, under construction at its 'dock yard', a wooden enclosure in Victoria Road, Kensington. A *Times* correspondent reported that the body of the balloon was complete, and that the car—which could carry twenty-five people—was in the advanced stages of construction. This project had numerous critics, for instance the *Morning Herald*:

> A more unwieldy and ungraceful entity never moved on or in any element. The whale and the elephant are beaten hollow by it in point of form and grace.[4]

Count Lennox, who was in charge of the *Eagle* project, defended it, stating that the airship would reach Paris in 6 hours. Future destinations would include Vienna, Berlin, and St Petersburg. But the dock yard in Kensington never did become London's first airport, for the *Eagle* never got off the ground:

The aerial monster, instead of taking a flying trip to Paris and afterwards to the other principal cities of the Continent, has got into the very un-poetical clutches of the Sheriff of Middlesex under an execution for debt.[5]

Kensington was redeveloped in the next decade, as part of London's outward expansion, and De Vere Gardens—near Hyde Park—now stands on the site of the *Eagle*'s dock yard.

Nearly a century later, planned airship services from the capital city did not fare much better. In July 1913, the press announced that the National Airships Association had been formed. Its inspiration was D. E. L. A. G. (Deutsche Luftschifffahrts—Aktiengesellschaft, the German Airship Transportation Corporation), which organised passenger flights on airships. The British company was going to purchase semi-rigid airships to fly on services connecting London and Birmingham, Manchester and Paris, as quickly as possible. The company was also in possession of plans for revolving airship sheds which it proposed to erect on the western side of London and several other British cities. Although some sources depicted this enterprise as a serious attempt to run scheduled services to rival rail and sea transport, it was initially intended to attract only persons who wanted to experience lighter-than-air flight. The *Dundee Courier* reported on 11 July 1913:

The double airship shed at Nordholz Airship Station near Cuxhaven, Germany. Remarkably, the entire building is mounted onto a giant turntable, so it can be rotated to face the direction of the wind to facilitate the launch of airships. There were plans to build a similar example in West London shortly before the First World War, to house airships intended to operate passenger services. (© *IWM—q20640*)

The announcement is made of a great airship passenger service in England in the autumn. A capital of about half a million is already assured and even this large sum will be increased as the service is extended. The idea of the promoters of the scheme is to establish a national industry in airships. To begin with, various types of dirigibles will be constructed and as a result of their performance the best type of airship will be evolved. The semi-rigid style of vessel will be first produced but, as the size of these vessels is restricted, the rigid form of construction will be adopted in the later and larger airships.

These ambitious plans, like many others announced over the next two decades, came to nothing. Little more of it was heard after the initial blaze of publicity. The plans to build revolving airship sheds was based on an example at Nordholtz, near Cuxhaven, Germany, which was constructed on a giant turntable, so that the whole structure could be turned to face the direction of the wind when a Zeppelin was about to take off.

Ever since airships first flew at the end of the nineteenth century, there had been reports of mysterious machines seen in the skies. These sightings were not confined to Britain, but extended as far as continental Europe and North America—a gift to newspaper editors, who frequently speculated on their origin. Some tried to offer rational explanations, but few would let the facts get in the way of a good story—not unlike the outbreak of UFO sightings after the Second World War.

In May 1909, the *Morpeth Herald* reported that the Norwegian Steamer *St Olaf* encountered an airship flying low over the sea at night, narrowly missing its mast. All on board could see the airship plainly, for although the night was very dark, the airship was well lit. Paranoiac fear that dastardly plans were afoot spread through Britain like wildfire, not least in the run-up to the First World War. Matters took a sinister turn when airships were reportedly seen over Royal Navy dockyards, and were attributed to Zeppelins on spying missions in 1912—not least the *Hansa*, spotted over Sheerness, and purportedly capable of crossing the North Sea in a matter of hours in favourable weather. *The New York Times* even mentioned the incident on 17 November 1912:

> A dirigible appeared above Sheerness on the night of Oct. 14th and was plainly observed by the officers of the Royal Corps stationed there, who thinking it a British airship trying to land, lit large flares as a guide but the aerial visitor gradually disappeared and nothing more was heard of it.

Questions were raised in Parliament, because there were strategic Royal Naval installations at Sheerness, including the Chattenden magazine, at stake. At the time, there was little doubt that the area had been visited by a foreign airship, in contrast with more recent investigations that suggest that the *Hansa* was probably in Germany at the time. German newspapers made fun of the claims of phantom airships over England, and even alleged that British airships were intruding on their skies. The *Kölnische Zeitung* proclaimed that the most likely explanation was the desire of the conservative press to work up popular sentiment in favour of armament. The journal dubbed the airship scare 'the new English sickness for which the country's own common sense is the only physician'. Shortly after the outbreak of war, on 21 October 1914, the *Hull Daily Mail* printed the following:

> Alleged Attempt to Get Airship Base. Attempts to establish an airship base at Worthing had been made by a German named Hermann Houber, who was arrested there on Tuesday. He was said to be a director of the National Passenger Airship Association of London. He had been at Worthing since the beginning of the year endeavouring to establish an airship harbour near the town. He alleged that it was wanted in connection with a proposed London and Continental Airship Service. Negotiations were proceeding for the acquirement by him of a site of 60 acres on the western side of the town. He was taken by the police yesterday afternoon to the detention camp at Frimley.

Xenophobia was by this stage widespread, and it is likely that Hermann Houber was in fact innocent. On 7 November 1914, the *Manchester Evening News* printed the story of an even more audacious German plan to set up base in the capital city itself:

> German Fort in London. A well informed correspondent writes to the Standard. About a month ago an inspection was made in the London district of certain building owned by a foreign firm ostensibly as a factory. For obvious reasons the locality and precise nature of the building cannot be mentioned but much can be gathered from the opinion of a military expert who has visited the works and describes them as nothing more nor less than a terrifically strong fortification which could dominate some of the most vital points in London. All the buildings are said to be reinforced concrete of a strength and thickness altogether out of proportion to the nature of the work carried out in the factory. Every floor is of exceptionally thick concrete and flat roofs of certain buildings are of the same material, also of unnecessary thickness and strength as far as peaceable manufacturing is concerned. From these roofs, which are strongly supported, an uninterrupted view is obtained of some of the most important points in London.
>
> Other significant features are the fact that certain of the buildings could be used as aeroplane sheds whilst every facility is offered for landing and mooring of airships and the existence of powerful electrical plant on the premises would render the fitting up of wireless telegraphic apparatus an easy matter. Finally it is known that many Germans are employed on the works under the director of the same nationality. After a very thorough examination of the premises by detectives and military experts nearly a month ago exhaustive reports were sent to the War Office and Home Office with a strong recommendation for immediate and drastic action being made nothing more has been heard of the matter.

Despite these anxieties, Germany never had any plans to invade Britain in the First World War. Interestingly, the British were not alone in their paranoia: in 1909, fearing that airships may be used for criminal purposes, the Russian Minister of the Interior ordered the police to attend every ascent and placed all members of aeronautic clubs under surveillance.

2

Military Airship Bases before the First World War

European nineteenth-century industrialisation produced tremendous innovation on the battlefield. Balloons were recruited into military reconnaissance and observers sent aloft to gain information on enemy positions. Upon viewing the first ascents of the Montgolfier balloons in Paris in the late eighteenth century, Benjamin Franklin himself commented on the cost-effective potential of airships for military surveillance and intervention. Nearly a century later, when Paris came under siege, balloons were used to fly members of the French government into unoccupied parts of France. But, unlike airships, hydrogen-filled balloons were totally at the mercy of the prevailing wind. In 1862, two Royal Engineers Officers witnessed the use of balloons in the American Civil War and drew the attention of the War Office to their potential upon returning to England. In 1863, they demonstrated balloons to the British Army, but the idea was rejected on the grounds that they were too expensive. It was not until 1878 that the Royal Engineers set up a small unit to operate balloons which, ten years later, had become the School of Ballooning and was moved to Aldershot.

In the mid-nineteenth century, it was decided that there should be a sizeable military garrison close to London, but there was little land in south east England that was not being farmed. One of the exceptions was Aldershot, in north east Hampshire: here, the soil was not productive, and much of the land was still covered with trees. It was decided that this area would be ideal for stationing troops and staging military exercises, and a depot for manned military balloons was established at Stanhope, about 3 miles south of the Basingstoke Canal. When in 1880 the First Boer War broke out, the British Army made extensive use of balloons for artillery observation, for instance during the Siege of Ladysmith. The balloon factory at Aldershot, which was equipped with a small plant for making hydrogen gas, turned out two balloons per month.

After this first redistribution into the theatre of war, it was decided to greatly expand the balloon contingent in the British Army. The site at Aldershot was too small for further development, so the balloon shed and hydrogen plant there were uprooted.

> The balloon factory is at present on a piece of ground about 2½ acres in extent. The buildings are placed close together, there is no room either in the factory or on land adjoining where any new building can be erected.[1]

The need to find a new 20-acre site with good water supply became urgent, and serious consideration was given to moving to another part of the country altogether. Weedon, a village 8 miles west of Northampton, was favoured because it already had large military barracks and was in the centre of England, so there was little risk of manned balloons being blown out to sea. However, many civilian workers—including women—were employed at the existing Aldershot works, and the lack of housing in the vicinity of Weedon dictated against the facility moving there in any case. British aviation history might have completely changed course had the move gone ahead. Instead, the Balloon Factory was relocated just 2 miles north of Aldershot.

In 1903, the construction of Britain's first military airship was officially approved. But it was thought that an improvised shelter or windbreak would not give it adequate protection, and a proper airship shed became essential. This was to be erected in Aldershot, but was constructed in such a way that it could readily be dismantled and moved to a new site should the Balloon Factory moved away from the area. A permanent site was found on Farnborough Common, a large area of level ground, free of housing or other buildings. Trees and scrub had already been cleared in the northern section by the army when it was used as a camping ground, and there was sufficient space for manoeuvring an airship. In 1904, tenders were put out to twelve engineering firms for the construction of the airship shed, and it was awarded to Joseph Westwood & Co. The War Office had forgotten to include the doors in the tender, a major component of any structure used to shelter airships, so to compensate for this, the width of the shed was reduced from the original design to ensure no additional expenditure was incurred. Problems were also encountered with the foundations, for the ground underneath the superficial surface soil was almost a bog. To allow adequate foundations, the excavation was filled with old wooden gun carriages from teak warships which did not rot. Finally, a 600-yard access road turned out to be an expensive undertaking, for it too had to be built on marshy ground.

By 30 April 1905, the airship shed was almost ready for occupation, and the Balloon Factory—including the electrolytic hydrogen plant and the gas holders—was literally uprooted from Aldershot and transported to its new location shortly afterwards. Balloon and airship envelopes were manufactured inside the high-roofed shed. The entire complex now covered about 20 acres, abut would in time spread over the surrounding countryside to become the world famous Farnborough Aerodrome.

Farnborough Balloon Factory (Royal Aircraft Factory from May 1912 onwards)

Location: O. S. 1/50,000 map 186 (SU) 865542. Hampshire, 30 miles south-west of central London.

Airship Sheds: Balloon shed, re-erected in 1906 (275 feet long, 62 feet wide, and 45 feet high); Beta shed, steel frame, built in 1905 (160 feet long—extended in 1912 to 300 feet—82 feet wide, and 72 feet high, with a doorway that was 64 feet high and 32 feet wide); 'A' shed, steel frame, built in 1910 (324 feet long, 60 wide, and 75 feet high); steel framed canvas covered portable shed, built in 1911 (250 feet long, 50 feet wide, and 60 feet high); 'C' shed, steel frame, built *c.* 1912 (350 feet long, 100 wide, and 60 feet high).

Based airships with British design (1906–1913): *Nulli Secundus* (*Nulli Secundus II*), *Baby* (*Beta, Beta II*), *Gamma* (*Gamma II*), *Delta, Eta,* and *Willows IV.* Those in brackets are rebuilt versions of the original airships.

Based airships with foreign design: *Clément-Bayard II, Lebaudy, Astra Torres,* and *Parseval.*

Although work began on *Nulli Secundus,* Britain's first military airship, as soon as its shed was ready, it would be another two years before it took to the sky (10 September 1907). *The Western Times* described the scene:

> After a long time waiting for its appearance, the many interested spectators who have made Farnborough Common their rendezvous for the last three weeks were rewarded yesterday by witnessing the first open-air trial of the military airship which has been under construction in the Military Balloon Factory. Mounted police kept all spectators some distance from the factory but the view was unobstructed, so that all could see the great sausage-shaped balloon as it was gradually drawn out of the shed where it was built by groups of men of the Royal Engineers.

The airship was forced to land at Crystal Palace, where it was seriously damaged by strong winds. It was taken back to Farnborough to be rebuilt, and jocosely renamed *Nulli Secundus II*—'Second to None, the Second'.

Nulli Secundus II took off on 24 July 1908, carrying a crew of three. It made a prompt return to the ground, as its handling party failed to release all its mooring ropes. It pitched nose down and then rebounded into the air, striking one of the common's many trees. After being returned to its shed for repairs, it took to the air for the final time in August. Further mechanical problems were encountered and *Nulli Secundus II* was permanently grounded; the machine was later declared to be of no further use and accordingly broken up.

In the meantime, another British military airship was coming to life in the airship shed. Christened *Baby* because of its small size, it took to the air on 11 May 1909. It performed poorly, so was rebuilt with a larger envelope and renamed *Beta,* and in June 1910 undertook a successful night flight over London. Later that year, *Beta* took part in army manoeuvres, and was on one occasion in the air for nearly 8 hours, flown by a crew of three. A third airship, the *Gamma,* made its first flight in 1910.

At this time, the Balloon Factory was still a small establishment, consisting of only eight officers and 149 men. In addition to operating army airships and balloons, it now also undertook experimental work with aeroplanes which operated from nearby Laffan's Plain. In an effort to further boost Britain's airship fleet, the *Morning Post* launched an airship fund, whilst the *Daily Mail* ran a campaign to raise funds for an airship shed at Wormwood Scrubs. A further airship shed was constructed by the Cleveland Bridge and Engineering Company of Darlington at Farnborough to house

Britain's first military airship, *Nulli Secundus*, moored on the running track at Crystal Palace, London. It diverted here when it was unable to return to its base at Farnborough due to strong winds, after flying over London. On the night of 5 October 1907, *Nulli Secundus* was seriously damaged by an unexpected gale. (*The Royal Aeronautical Society*)

Nulli Secundus flying over Crystal Palace, London. It was 111 feet long and 18 feet in diameter. The envelope was covered with netting from which hung a long spar and the control car. (*The Royal Aeronautical Society*)

The debut of *Nulli Secundus II* on 24 July 1908 at Farnborough. It is emerging from the *Beta* airship shed built in 1905/1906. Next to it is the Balloon shed. (*The Royal Aeronautical Society*)

The *Gamma* emerging from the Lebaudy shed (a.k.a. the Alpha shed) at Farnborough. The building has a modern appearance when compared with some of the other airship sheds built around the same time. (© *IWM—RAE-O 229*)

the *Lebaudy* airship, purchased by the *Morning Post*. It was a steel-framed structure with a vaulted roof and two continuous bands of glazing. This company went on to build several of Britain's largest airship sheds. Like may early airship sheds, it was painted white, which made it easily visible to airship crews. At Scott Field in the USA, a more extreme colour scheme was adopted: the roof of the airship shed here was painted black and white in a chessboard scheme.

The *Lebaudy* should have easily fitted into the new shed at Farnborough, but its builders increased the airship's height by nearly 10 feet beyond the original specification and neglected to inform the War Office. On 26 October 1910, the *Lebauby* landed at Farnborough after a non-stop flight from Paris. A handling party of 160 soldiers then attempted to house it in the new shed, when the officer in charge realised that all was not right, and instructed his men to halt. His order was countermanded by an interfering brigadier, however, so the handling party continued to walk the *Lebaudy* through the open doors of the airship shed. The result was that the envelope tore on the edge of the building, and as the gas escaped, the deflated airship fell to the ground. It had to be rebuilt, and took to the air once more. 'Airship runs Amok' ran the headline in the *Sheffield Daily Telegraph* on 5 May 1911:

> With the propellers working at half speed a circuit was made, the airship which is 370 feet long travelled well and answered her rudder readily. After a flight of about an hour's duration, during which she was encircled by Colonel Cody and Mr. de Havilland in their aeroplanes, a descent was attempted and it was then disaster came. By the aid of her propellers the airship came down in wide circles and when some 300 feet from the ground dropped two long towing ropes fore and aft. The speed of the vessel with the propellers still working was very great and all attempts by parties of soldiers to catch the ropes failed and she drove straight down towards the Balloon Factory buildings. The ropes fouled the railings and buildings but were jerked clear. After circling over the roofs, the airship came down lower and appeared to the spectators to be quite out of control.
>
> To the dismay of the thousands of assembled sightseers, the vessel drove straight for a clump of trees on the Farnborough plateau. Women and children ran screaming from the path, the trailing ropes tripping up scores of people and then with a crash the ill-fated airship caught the topmost branches of the trees which pierced the gas envelope with a report that could be heard a mile away. The whole great structure crashed downward across the Farnborough road, tearing down telegraph wires, uprooting railings and eventually falling in a shapeless mass over a detached villa, the wreckage of the envelope completely smothering the house while the car and framework smashed to matchwood trees and shrubs in front of the house. There was a rush of helpers to the assistance of the occupants of the car and to the relief of all, the seven passengers were extracted from the wreckage little the worse for their mishap. The wreck is so complete that it is doubtful whether repair is possible.

The *Lebaudy* never did fly again. Its sponsors at the *Morning Post* agreed to pay compensation to the owner of the house damaged in the crash. The British-built *Beta* came close to crashing into Woodlands Cottage two weeks after it had been damaged by the *Lebaudy*! Another airship, the *Clément-Bayard* funded by the *Daily Mail*, fared little better, as will later be elaborated. On a more positive note, this handful of British-built airships stimulated much pioneering work in the years leading up to the First World War. They and their staff frequently trained with the army, and were often deployed away from their home base. In 1911, the *Beta* became the first army airship to be fitted with a wireless, which could successfully transmit and receive signals up to 30 miles away.

In 1912, the Army Aircraft Factory at Farnborough—as it was then known—saw the original *Beta* shed extended westwards to double its length. It had a long life, functioning until 1960. A 'portable' airship shed was erected in 1912 by the Cleveland Bridge Company, using a team of fifty men. It consisted of lattice frames completely covered in heavy canvas sections, which were laced together to provide protection from the elements. It was the predecessor of many such examples used in the First World War, but due to its lightweight construction, was particularly vulnerable to adverse weather conditions. The structure was dismantled not long after it was erected, and a more solid structure—the 'C-Shed'—was erected in its place. But this did not spell the end for the portable shed, for it was re-assembled alongside its new replacement. There were now five sheds at Farnborough: the Balloon, Beta (B), Lebaudy (A), Delta (C), and the portable—the latter did not last long, for it was again dismantled in 1914. The *Gamma* and *Beta* airships were joined by the *Delta* in 1912. Around the same time, a number of

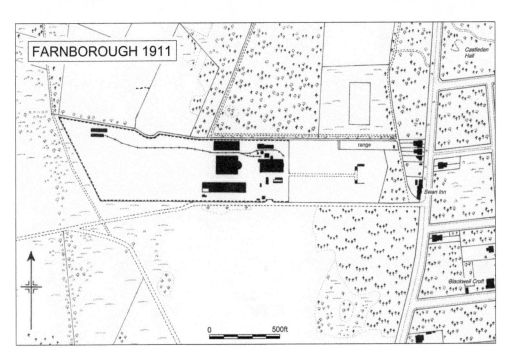

Farnborough, 1911. The long rectangular building in the plan is the Balloon Factory which originally stood at Aldershot before being dismantled and re-erected here. Next to it is the *Beta*'s shed, constructed in 1905/1906. The steel framed *Alpha* shed, built three years later, stands on the northern boundary of the site. To the east was the main workshops building. A tramway for transporting cylinders ran across the complex. (*Mick Davis*)

reports began appearing in the press that Farnborough was building an immense airship for the Royal Navy. They were entirely erroneous, and nothing more was heard of this project. There was no shed here that could undertake such an enterprise.

Maj. M. Maitland made a successful parachute jump from the *Delta* on 18 October 1913. The same year, experiments were carried out with elementary mooring masts, and as an alternative to housing airships in sheds, trials were carried out using natural features of the landscape as a form of shelter. The *Delta* and the newly built *Eta* participated in army exercises from their temporary base situated in woodland at Crookham. In addition, an old chalk pit at Odiham provided a base for the *Willows IV* airship. The ground crews and airmen slept in tents next to their craft. These exercises paved the way for the airship mooring out stations set up across Britain in the closing stages of the First World War.

Towards the end of its manoeuvres, the *Willows IV* on one occasion developed engine trouble. Rather than dismantle the airship and transport it back, first by horse-drawn wagon and then by rail, Maj. Maitland flew to Odiham in the *Eta*. On 13 August 1913, it successfully towed the *Willows IV* back to Farnborough on the end of a cable. This is the only such recorded rescue of a damaged airship by another.

Around this time, the Army Council decided to establish a new airship base at their training grounds on Salisbury Plain. Airship sheds were going to be erected at Perham Down, a point adjacent to Ludgershall Station on the Midland and South Western Railway. It was intended to dismantle some of the buildings at Farnborough, and to re-erect them on the plain. On 1 January 1914, all army airships were transferred to the naval wing of the Royal Flying Corps, which put an end to this proposed airship base. By the time the war broke out, Farnborough had become a naval air station, and the airship no longer played any role in the British Army.

Wormwood Scrubs

Location: O. S. 1/50,000 map 176 (TQ) 225818. Middlesex, ½ mile from the Wormwood Scrubs railway station.
Airship Shed: one (354 feet long, 75 feet wide, and 98 feet high).
Based airships in 1910: *Clément-Bayard II* (in 1910).

In both World Wars, the British public, private companies among other organisations raised funds to purchase aeroplanes for the armed forces; the first flying machine to be funded in this manner was an airship. The *Daily Mail* led a campaign to raise funds to purchase the *Clément-Bayard II* airship from its French designer, and it was sent to Britain for several months of tests. These proved successful. The *Daily Mail's* fund provided the balance. Both Farnborough and Salisbury Plain were initially considered by the War Office as possible sites for a shed, but Wormwood Scrubs was chosen for its closer proximity to London. Construction commenced on 15 July 1909, funded by the newspaper, and became known as the 'Daily Mail Airship Garage'. The *Clément-Bayard II's* shed was completed by August of that year; its designer was

The army airship *Beta* attached to a mooring mast at Farnborough. This airship undertook mooring trials here in 1912 and again in spring 1914. (© *IWM—RAE-O 724*)

The army airship *Willows IV* moored in a disused chalk quarry near Odiham, Hampshire. Such experiments provided valuable experience in the creation of RNAS mooring out stations in the latter stages of the First World War. (© *IWM—RAE-O 229*)

Herbert Ellis, who visited France to acquaint himself with sheds already standing there. The main contractor was R. Moreland and Sons, and 1,000 tonnes of steel were used in the structure, costing £6,000. And yet it was an aeroplane, not an airship, which first sought shelter in the shed.

In 1906, the *Daily Mail* offered a £10,000 prize to the first aeroplane to fly from London to Manchester, but it was not until 1910 that the challenge was taken up. Claude Grahame-White, an Englishman, succeeded in flying as far as Litchfield, but was forced to land because of engine trouble. While on the ground his bi-plane was blown over. He returned by train to London with his damaged machine, and permission was given for him to undertake emergency repairs at the Wormwood Scrubs airship shed. After spending two days' work on his machine, Grahame-White attempted to make a test flight, but was hampered by a huge crowd of spectators, and had to abandon his take-off. On hearing that a French rival was already on his way to Manchester, he returned to his aeroplane the same evening. Grahame-White spotted a gap among the people still gathered at Wormwood Scrubs, and successfully took to the air, flying much of the way at night. Despite his brave attempt, he lost the prize to his competitor, French pilot Louis Paulhan.

The *Clément-Bayard II* did not arrive for nearly a year after the airship shed had been finished. The craft turned out to be disappointingly slow and difficult to control when first flown in France. It arrived in October 1910. Not long afterwards, it was deflated and dismantled, never having made a single flight from Wormwood Scrubs. Its shed, however, had a much longer existence and proved to be of more value. On 29 October 1910, Ernest Willows first flew his airship *Willows III–City of Cardiff*, from here. A few days later, he set off for France and eventually reached Paris on 28 December, and the feat was celebrated with a New Year's Eve flight around the Eiffel Tower. At the end of 1910, the Wormwood Scrubs airship shed was donated to the War Office by the *Daily Mail*, and its canvas doors were upgraded to a solid sliding type. Some thought was given to the possibility of transferring the whole structure to Farnborough, but in the end it remained where it was, on the edge of open ground.

Over the next few years, the Wormwood Scrubs hangar saw little use as an airship shed, but was instead made the most of for the storage of army equipment. There were was one exception, when an army airship visited from Farnborough, as recorded in *Flight* on 27 July 1912:

> The Government airship shed at Wormwood Scrubs has been so very seldom put to the use for which it was intended, that it is interesting to chronicle the arrival of an airship there last week. *Gamma* sailed over from Farnborough on Thursday, July 18th, via Windsor, passing through a heavy storm of rain somewhere in the neighbourhood of Bagshot. After steering over Windsor and Eton, an easterly course was laid and somewhere between 4.30 and 5.00 p.m. the ship was sighted over White City. A circuit was described there at a height of over a thousand feet and while this was in operation, two officers in uniform dashed up to the airship shed in motor cars. It was evident that the airship crew had seen them, for she began to descend on an even keel and a small black pennant was observed to be flying between the frame and envelope. This, I believe, is the 'about to land' signal.

By this time a large crowd had collected and the northerly wind was blowing the smoke almost horizontally from some factory chimneys nearby. The airship made a small circuit round to the west of the shed, descending rapidly under the thrust of her propellers, now revolving in an almost horizontal plane. She was brought up into the wind over the enclosed ground on the east of the shed and from that point descended vertically until about 150 feet from the ground. A rope was then dropped, the engines stopped and a small amount of water ballast thrown over to check any tendency to fall rapidly. The crowd then swarmed over the railings and pandemonium reigned. A stiff breeze added to the difficulties of the officers in charge. Fortunately it was blowing almost straight into the mouth of the shed and after some delay while the huge doors were opened, the airship was safely housed within and the police 'persuaded' the crowd to retire outside.

No ascents were made that day or Friday owing to the bad weather but on Saturday morning early I was informed the airship returned to Farnborough. A spectator told me afterwards that the work of getting the ship out of the shed was done by not more than twelve men, of whom two were policemen. The crew then got in, a few ballast bags were removed, the engines started and at the sound of a whistle everyone let go and the ship ascended vertically into the air, quickly disappearing in the direction of Hammersmith. I learn that a large part of the journey back was made in dense fog and that in consequence steering by compass had to be resorted to. The airship squadron had a very neat gas tender, it is a motor vehicle adapted to take heavy gas cylinders and also a number of men, small stores, etc. It was used on this occasion to bring the detachment down from Farnborough.

In August 1912, a list of sites for airship stations was drawn up and the erection of two airship sheds planned in the vicinity of Chatham. One would be of new construction, and the other the reassembled Wormwood Scrubs shed depending on the cost—in the end, the latter remained where it was. In 1913, a Mr Christitch—a naturalised British citizen—approached the War Office with a design for an airship that could carry aeroplanes. He described his project thus:

> The idea is that the airship serves as the parent ship to the others. There is a monoplane at each end and a bi-plane in the centre and you can release the two monoplanes or the bi-plane by itself and retain the balance. They can be detached and re-attached while the airship is in full flight. You can send them out for scouting purposes and for attacking an enemy's Scout craft. They are suspended to the parent ship by steel ropes and once the engines of the aeroplanes are started they can slip off the ropes and fly in any direction. Each would be armed with a gun. When they wish to return, a grappling rope is let down from the airship and catches a hook in the top of the aeroplanes which are different from others in that the body is completely closed in. In the bottom of each aeroplane is a trapdoor through which to drop bombs.[2]

The War Office was not prepared to consider Mr Christitch's invention further, unless he built a fully sized machine at his own expense; he was, however, given access to the airship shed at Wormwood Scrubs for this purpose. The airship was never built, but in the latter stages of the First World War, rigid airships were converted to carry aeroplanes with a device not unlike that suggested by Mr Christitch.

'The *Daily Mail* Airship Garage' was revived at the onset of war. It formed the centrepiece of the Royal Naval Airship Station of Wormwood Scrubs. *D'Orcy's Airship Manual*, published in 1917, mentions that the Army possessed an airship shed, some 197 feet long, at Brighton, but this appears to be an error, as it does not feature in official records.

Airships for the Royal Navy—Cavendish Dock, Barrow-in-Furness

Location: O. S. 1/50,000 map 96 (SD) 215683. Cumbria, a large dock on the southern edge of the town of Barrow-in-Furness.
Size: 142 acres (including the dock area).
Airship Shed: one (600 feet long, 100 feet wide, and 70 feet high).

The success of Zeppelins in achieving record-breaking flights in the early years of the twentieth century caused considerable concern among some at the British War Office. It was decided in 1908 that the country should have a Zeppelin of its own. The proposal was set out in a memorandum to Adml Fisher, the First Sea Lord, from Capt. R. H. Bacon, who was responsible for the introduction of submarines into the Royal Navy in 1900, with the backing of Prime Minister Asquith and the Committee of Imperial Defence.

Capt. Bacon placing the Zeppelin order with Vickers, the company already manufacturing warships for the Royal Navy. Although Vickers had its origins in Sheffield, the company purchased a shipbuilding yard in Barrow-in-Furness in 1897, which became the Naval Construction Yard. This turned out all types of vessels, as well as ancillary products like marine fittings, and by the late nineteenth century, the town had the largest iron and steel works in the world. The reasoning behind Capt. Bacon's decision to commission Vickers was that submarines in many ways resembled airships; but unfortunately, Vickers specialised in making iron and steel products weighing hundreds of tonnes.

The enormous but little used Cavendish Dock was chosen as the site for the shed in which to construct the first Vickers airship, the *HMA No. 1*, or '*Mayfly*', as it became known. The dock enclosed an area of water covering 142 acres, and was nearly half a mile in length—the largest single dock in the world at the time. Designs of the Zeppelin and work on its shed commenced in 1909, both heavily influenced by developments in Germany. This would be the first and only British airship shed to be built over water—the Zeppelin Company had two floating construction sheds in Manzell, Germany. The Vickers staff had assumed that the German sheds were built on water on which airships would take off and land. They were in part correct, but failed to grasp that the sheds could themselves be rotated so that their doors faced the direction of the wind, enabling the Zeppelin to point into the wind for take-off.

Vickers built their new airship shed over water but it was immoveable, fixed to the side of Cavendish Dock. And besides, by 1909, the Germans were moving away from building over water, and began constructing their airship sheds on dry land.

The final specification for the Vickers shed was for it to be 600 feet long by 100 feet wide. The airship itself was designed to be 512 feet in length and 46 feet in diameter. Francis Morton & Co. of Hamilton Ironworks, Garston (Liverpool), were awarded the contract to build the shed. Immediately after work had started, a serious problem was encountered: the sea bed of Cavendish Dock was sand and mud up to 50 feet deep, so to ensure that the structure had sound foundations, over 400 piles had to be sunk, along with numerous cement-filled bags, only later to be covered by a layer of concrete. By April 1910, the airship shed was almost ready: the walls were of corrugated iron and the roof was covered with fibre-cement slates and corrugated iron; large glass windows, 20 feet high by 13½ feet in length, were placed at intervals along its sides; the entrance was protected by a canvas curtain above ground level, and a steel gate covered with boarding, from ground to water level. The curtain was opened and closed by means of a winch with three draw ropes, an operation which took about 15 minutes.

In addition to the airship shed, Cavendish Dock boasted a small aeroplane hangar from which an Avro Type-D aeroplane mounted on floats could carry out trials. Erecting the airship itself, the *Mayfly*, now began in great secrecy, the project guarded day and night by the Marines—one man caught inside the perimeter without permission received a

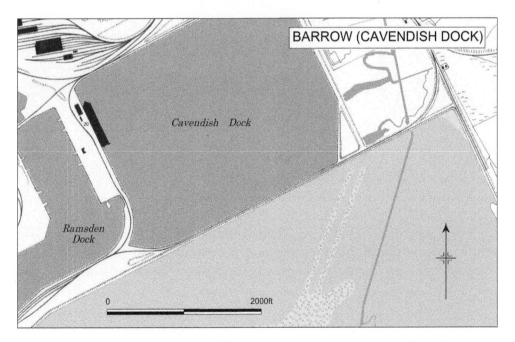

Cavendish Dock. The Vickers airship shed in which the *Mayfly* was constructed is on the western edge of the Cavendish Dock. Immediately to the north is the town of Barrow-in-Furness. (*Mick Davis*)

two-month prison sentence. By January 1911, *Mayfly* was almost ready. The distinctive triangular keel had been fitted, and after the flooring of the shed had been cut away, its two cars were floated into position and attached. There was no hydrogen-producing plant at Cavendish Dock, so the gas was delivered by rail from the Knowles Oxygen Company of Wolverhampton, and myriads of cylinders were stored close to the airship shed.

On 1 October 1910, the obsolete light cruiser HMS *Hermoine* was moored nearby, at Ramsden Dock, to provide accommodation for the airship crew and other lighter-than-air specialists. The pilots received their training aboard the Army's *Beta* airship at Farnborough. On 22 May 1911, *Mayfly* saw the light of day for the first time:

> The vessel left the shed just as the sun rose over the distant hills and presented a wonderful sight, the sun striking her silver grey sides and giving them the colour of burnished gold. The bugle sounded 'haul' and the dirigible was seen in motion. At ten minutes past four its stern came out of the shed and not an inch did the airship seem to deviate from the centre line, little by little the huge fabric emerged and in exactly ten minutes the *Mayfly* as she has been named was altogether out of the shed and her buff nose was being towed out by means of the centre rope.[3]

The *Mayfly* was attached to a small mooring mast in the centre of the dock., and the 38-foot-high lattice work structure placed on top of a floating pontoon—Capt. Bacon's idea. While Germany led the field in most aspects of airship design, this was a purely British innovation. The nose of the airship was hooked to the mast so that the craft could rotate like a weather vane to point into the direction of the wind, thus minimising the airship's exposure to the elements. It was soon put to the test, for on the *Mayfly*'s second day outside, a strong wind rose up to 45 mph. Search lights mounted on the dockside illuminated the *Mayfly* at night, so its movements could be observed. It survived the experience unscathed, but was not long after returned to the shed. The Vickers design team calculated that their airship could probably remain airborne for 12 hours, whereas the Admiralty required a flight capability of 24 hours, so major modifications had to be carried out.

Some commented that the *Mayfly* was aptly named, since it 'Might Fly'! In July 1911, the *Liverpool Echo* reported that four 'sailors' visited Harwich wearing caps with the badge 'HM Airship No. 1', and told members of the public that they were members of the crew of the airship recently launched at Barrow. They said they had flown from Portsmouth, and had arrived safely at Shotley, where their airship was quartered for the night in readiness to depart for Scotland on Tuesday. The 'sailors' gave a graphic description of the airship, and stated that no man weighing over 10 stone 10 lb was accepted on board. On Tuesday morning, a crowd gathered on Harwich Pier, Shotley, to witness the departure of the airship. At six o'clock, all eyes strained towards the quay, but at seven o'clock, there was still no sign of the airship. Only later did it transpire that this had all been a hoax.

The *Mayfly* never did leave Barrow-in-Furness. On 24 September 1911, it was towed out of its shed again, but while being manoeuvred on the waters of the dock basin in preparation for its first flight, there was a sudden squall. The sound of cracking metal

The newly completed Rigid *No.1*, the *Mayfly*, being towed from its shed to the centre of Cavendish Dock for an outdoor trial in May 1911. Later in the year, it catastrophically broke in two at the same location. It was later scrapped without ever having flown. (*The Dock Museum, Barrow-in-Furness*)

was heard, and to the dismay of the large crowd that had gathered on the dockside, the giant airship broke in two. The wreckage was nudged back into the shed, where it was found to be damaged beyond repair, and was eventually dismantled. Although the accident was later attributed to mishandling by the ground crews and not to the design, this dealt a major blow to the fledgling British airship industry. It would be a further five years before the next British-built rigid airship took to the skies, during which time the Germans had built and flown a multitude of Zeppelins.

RNAS Kingsnorth Airship Station

Alternative name: 'Hoo'.
Location: O. S. 1/50,000 map 178 (TQ) 800727. Kent, the Isle of Grain, 30 miles east of central London, and 5 miles north-east of Rochester.
Size: 570 acres (within boundaries of 2,566 x 1,700 yards).
Station Complement: thirty-eight officers, 755 men (in Jan 1918).
Airship Sheds: one rigid shed of wooden construction (700 feet long and 150 feet wide) and one rigid shed of metal construction, sometimes referred to as the iron shed (555 feet long and 109 feet wide).
Hydrogen Plant: silicol (60,000 cubic feet per hour), water gas (7,000 cubic feet per hour), and electrolytic (5,500 cubic feet per hour).

Gasholder: one (500,000 cubic feet).
Gas Tanks: sixty-six (8,000 cubic feet each).
Based Airships: Astra Torres *No. 3*; Parseval *No. 4*; Astra Torres *No. 8*; Submarine Scout *S.S.1*, *S.S.7*, *S.S.9*, *S.S.14*, *S.S.30*, *S.S.31*, *S.S.40*, *S.S.41*, and *S.S.43*; Submarine Scout Experimental *S.S.E.3*; Submarine Scout Pusher *S.S.P.1*; Submarine Scout Twin, *S.S.T.1* and *S.S.T.2*; Coastal *C.1*, *C.4*, *C.8*, *C.11A*, *C.12*, and *C.19*; Coastal Star *C*6*; North Sea *N.S.1*, *N.S.2*, *N.S.4*, *N.S.5*, and *N.S.6*; Semi-Rigid Italian M-class *S.R.1*; and an *AP.1*.

High priority was given to establishing an airship station to bolster protection of the important Royal Navy Dockyard at Chatham, at the mouth of the Thames. The catalyst for action was the formation of the Air Department at the Admiralty in 1912, after which plans were soon drawn up to establish a number of seaplane bases around the coast of Britain, along with three airship stations. One of them was to be at Kingsnorth, and by October 1912, negotiations were underway to acquire land there; in January 1913, estimates were drawn up for constructing two airship sheds, but had to be revised when it was decided that larger models were required. Two months later, Adml R. Poore, C-in-C at the Nore, detailed the unsuitability of Kingsnorth to the Admiralty. To access the site, a new road was needed to cross the marshland—an expensive undertaking— and the extensive wetlands next door made it an unhealthy location besides. This meant that, in order to reduce the chance of an outbreak of malaria, servicemen who had suffered from this disease in the past could not be sent to Kingsnorth, if the station was established. Adml Poore would have preferred the new airship station to have been built near the railway at Port Victoria, a few miles north-east, at the mouth of the River Medway, but plans were now too far advanced for the site to be changed.

From the outset, Kingsnorth airship station was an ambitious project. Hill and Smith of Brierley Hill, Staffordshire, commenced work on the steel-framed shed in April 1913, and by the summer some fifty men were employed in its erection. In July 1913, Vickers was awarded the contract for the construction of a second shed. This was required as soon as possible, so a prefabricated exemplar was imported from Germany. Not only did this include all the wood and metalwork, but it also came with all the necessary nuts, bolts, and screws. Some 300 railway-wagon loads were required to transport these items from Cory's Wharf, Rochester, to a railway siding near Kingsnorth. Two scaffolders accidentally fell to their deaths towards the end of 1913 during its assembly. Vickers was also awarded the contract to supply Kingsnorth with a silicol hydrogen plant. Work was undertaken to create a network of roads in support of operations, and approval given for the construction of an electric light and power station, petrol store, oil store, engineering workshop, garage, blacksmith's forge, and explosives store. Housing blocks were erected to accommodate the officers and men.

Kingsnorth airship station was officially commissioned in March 1914, by which time both the large timber and metal airship sheds were nearing completion, but much work still remained to be done on the buildings. A large-scale programme over the next four years saw the continued expansion of the station. It became apparent to the Admiralty that additional land was needed to facilitate the safe operation of

The two rigid sheds under construction at RNAS Kingsnorth in April 1914. The two distinct designs are apparent in this picture. The 'steel' shed stands on the left and the 'wooden' one, based on a German design, on the right. (*The Fleet Air Arm Museum*)

airships, so a further 81½ acres of marshy ground at Barton Farm was annexed in August 1914.

Wg Cdr Usborne was the Kingsnorth CO at this time. There were then less than 200 men based there, plus two petty officers and forty-eight boys 'borrowed' from a nearby depot to assist in airship handling duties. Many of the personnel lived in tents, because their barrack huts were still under construction. In order to transport the heavy hydrogen gas plant to the site, the naval tramway was extended to the Medway, where it terminated at the new Abbott's Court Jetty. On 28 June, airship *No. 3* was being inflated in the metal shed when a fire 'of large dimensions' broke out.[4] Numerous gas bottles discharged jets of flaming hydrogen, and the personnel fled the shed and took shelter behind one of its doors. The fire, later attributed to spontaneous combustion, soon burned out.

Although war was only a couple of months away, the Admiralty seemed more concerned by the suffragettes' threat to its installations than by any action from a foreign power. Winston Churchill, then First Lord of the Admiralty, wrote the following memo to the Inspecting Captain of the Naval Air Wing:

> The wooden shed at Kingsnorth would be a fine quarry for the suffragettes and it appears to me that it should be watched. The existing watchman informs me that he watches all night long and on Saturdays from 12 noon till 7 o'clock next morning. This means that he probably walks round once or twice and goes to sleep for the rest of the time. The matter should have your attention and a regular watch established pending the time when the men enter.[5]

Nevertheless, attention had turned to the threat of a German aerial attack by November 1914. Anti-aircraft guns, then a new weapon, were positioned close to the officers' quarters. RNAS Kingsnorth went on to play a major role in the First World War.

RNAS Cromer Airship Station

Location: planned only—O. S. 1/50,000 map 133 (63) TG 2--4--, Cromer, Norfolk.

In 1909, the *East Essex Advertiser* speculated that three military gentlemen were possibly looking for a suitable spot for an airship station. If they were, they obviously thought the area unsuitable for this purpose, since no airship station was ever built here. The first definite reference to the intention of locating an airship station in East Anglia occurs in August 1912, when Capt. Murray Sueter, Director of the Air Department of the Admiralty, wrote a paper setting out the future policy for naval aviation. It suggested that an airship shed be built in the vicinity of the Norfolk Broads, and the decision to construct an airship station at Cromer appears to have been finalised the following year. Due to financial restrictions placed on the expansion of naval aviation in December 1913, the Air Department of the Admiralty was instructed to 'make no progress with the Cromer airship station beyond providing the land and erecting one shed, only half the cost of the shed to fall in 1914–15'.[6]

It appears that work may have commenced on this project, but—surprisingly—by June 1914, the Admiralty did not appear to have a clue as to what was going on. Winston Churchill asked Capt. Sueter, Inspecting Captain of the Naval Wing,

> What is the position about the airship shed at Cromer? How much money is taken for it this year? What progress has been made and how far are we committed?[7]

Unfortunately, Capt. Sueter's answers to these questions have not survived. The shed was certainly never completed, and to add to the confusion, a list of airship sheds drawn up in 1914 makes no mention of Cromer, but records a proposal to build a large shed at Norwich, 25 miles to the south.

3

RNAS Airship Stations in South-East England

When war was declared in the summer of 1914, there was alarm that Germany's Zeppelins could bombard British cities to dust—some Londoners even planned to flee to the countryside. Although enemy airships did roam British skies unchallenged in the war's early stages, the physical damage they caused was very limited. This was at a time when another new weapon of war, the submarine, was not yet regarded as a serious threat. The Germans did not initially have very many of them, and it was assumed that, by the time that they were in a position to expand their fleet, the conflict would be over.

These initial assumptions by the Admiralty could not have been more wrong. In the first ten weeks of conflict, no less than five British cruisers were sunk. The first merchant ship, British registered SS *Glitra*, was sunk off the coast of Norway in October 1914. On 28 February 1915, the Admiralty issued a specification for an airship which could be used to patrol the coast of Britain, and within weeks, an improvised airship was cobbled together by a team at RNAS Kingsnorth under Cdr Masterman. It used an envelope from the *Willows IV*, to which the fuselage of a BE.2 aeroplane was attached, and became the basis of the Submarine Scout airship, sometimes known as the 'Sea Searcher'. It first flew in March 1915, and production began not long after. The basic design was refined, and in subsequent years the Submarine Scout Pusher and Submarine Scout Zero were put into production.

At the outbreak of war, Britain had only three military airship stations—RNAS Kingsnorth, RNAS Farnborough, and the little used RNAS Wormwood Scrubs. In 1915, construction work began on establishing a chain of airship stations around the coast from which the fleet of Submarine Scout airships could operate, for attacks on merchant shipping mostly took place only a few miles offshore. In spite of airships and other defensive measures taken, German submarines went on to sink some 7,700 ships of all nationalities, resulting in the loss of one quarter of the world's merchant fleet.

Although the First World War is often regarded as a conflict blundered into by the European aristocracy and prolonged by the incompetence of generals, it can justifiably be looked upon as a war of aggression in as much as German military developments provoked Western European neighbours to act. The war may well have been futile, but the sacrifice made by British RNAS airship crews, and other allied servicemen who lost their lives, should not be diminished.

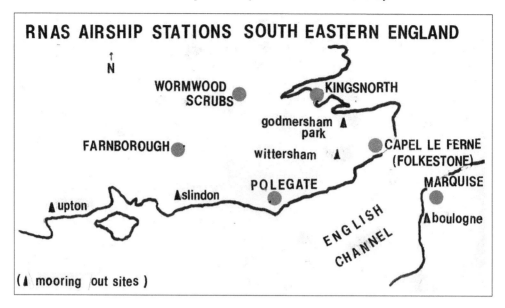

RNAS airship stations in South-East England. (*Author's collection*)

RNAS Folkestone Airship Station

Alternative names: 'Capel', 'Capel-le-Ferne'.
Location: O. S. 1/50,000 sheet, 179 (TR) 260390. Kent, immediately east of Folkestone at Capel-le-Ferne.
Size: 124 acres (within boundaries of 960 x 780 yards).
Station Complement: 19 officers, 247 men (Jan 1918)
Airship Sheds: Submarine Scout shed (308 feet long, 39 feet wide, and 49 feet high); Submarine Scout shed (312 feet long, 44 feet wide, and 51 feet high); and Submarine Scout shed (321 feet long, 70 feet wide, and 61 feet high).
Gas Plant: B. S. silicol (5,000 cubic feet per hour).
Gasholder: one (10,000 cubic feet).
Based Airships: Submarine Scout, *S.S.1*, *S.S.4*, *S.S.5*, *S.S.8*, *S.S.10A*, *S.S.11*, *S.S.12*, *S.S.13*, *S.S.26*, *S.S.28*, *S.S.32*, and *S.S.37*; Submarine Scout Pusher, *S.S.P.1* and *S.S.P.3*; Submarine Scout Twin, *S.S.T.1* and *S.S.T.8*; Submarine Scout Zero, *S.S.Z.1*, *S.S.Z.4*, *S.S.Z.5*, *S.S.Z.18*, *S.S.Z.26*, *S.S.Z.29*, *S.S.Z.36*, *S.S.Z.46*, *S.S.Z.69*, and *S.S.Z.74*; and Coastal, *C.19*, *C.21*, *C.23*, and *C.23A*.

RNAS Folkestone was situated on the edge of the cliffs between Folkestone and Dover, overlooking the English Channel, and was commissioned on 8 May 1915. Work had commenced on the site exactly two months earlier. Most subsequent airship stations were located close to the sea, but not on the coast itself, in order to prevent shelling by German naval vessels suffered at the Walney Island airship station. Initially, there was only one airship shed at RNAS Folkestone. The large and imposing Abbots Cliff House, perched on the cliff edge, was requisitioned as a temporary officers' mess.

On 7 May, Flt Sub-Lt R. S. Booth, accompanied by his navigator/wireless operator, piloted Submarine Scout *S.S.1* to RNAS Kingsnorth—the airship was to be the main attraction at an opening ceremony the following day. This was Booth's first cross-country flight, and the light was fading as the *S.S.1* approached the new airship station. A large white canvas cloth, known as the landing tee, had been laid out on the ground to indicate the direction of the wind to the airship pilot. However, the inexperienced ground crew had laid out the marker incorrectly: while the long arm of the 'T' should have been turned down-wind, it had been laid out pointing *up*-wind. The airship therefore had the wind behind it when it attempted to land, and as it approached the ground, the handling party was unable the restrain it. On the third attempt, the airship again overshot and headed towards the edge of the station.

It flew between two telegraph poles on the boundary, cutting the wires. Moments later, the airship burst into flames, its envelope ignited by a shower of sparks from the wires. It crossed the main road and hit another pole a few yards from the cliff edge, where it finally came to a halt. Flt Sub-Lt Booth suffered only minor burns, and despite this mishap, became an outstanding airship pilot and Wing Commander in the RAF. His navigator also escaped without any major injuries. The commissioning ceremony went ahead the next day, minus the attendance of an airship.

Several heavy falls of snow were experienced in the first winter of operation. It blew in under the roof of the Marshall Fox shed, and accumulated to a depth of 2 feet on top of Submarine Scout *S.S.12*. The additional weight caused the airship to keel over, with its starboard elevator touching the ground. To prevent this happening again, a gas hose was secured to the inside of the roof and slung round the envelope of the airship.

In January 1916, *S.S.12* covered a total of 1,014 miles in nearly 37 hours of flight—this was at a time when most other RNAS airship stations were still under construction. By April, *S.S.12*'s flight endurance had increased to 108½ hours. Night trials were made with *S.S.13*, the engine of which had been modified, because, prior to this, the airship had been distinctly audible at 3,400 feet—its maximum altitude—from which it was also visible, even in the dark. It appears these were early trials for developing an airship to carry out secret missions behind enemy lines, but it was RNAS Polegate that went on to create an airship for this role.

In June 1916, Submarine Scout *S.S.4*, *S.S.11*, and *S.S.32* proved their strength. They had flown 3,808 miles in 24 days, consuming 563 gallons of petrol and 69 gallons of oil in the process. The following month, *S.S.4*—one of RNAS Folkestone's longest serving airships—was on an instructional flight when it suffered an engine failure due to a fractured magneto spring. In the First World War, Britain produced dozens of different types of aero engines which were unreliable because their magnetos were liable to malfunction. In the case of airships using power plants intended for aeroplanes, these were prone to overheating because they were generally used on flights of long duration. Airship crews became skilled in carrying out repairs in mid-air, sometimes even climbing out of the car to spin the propeller to restart the engine. On one occasion, the crew of Submarine Scout *S.S.4* were unable to regain power and drifted with the wind until they dropped a grappling hook on the beach

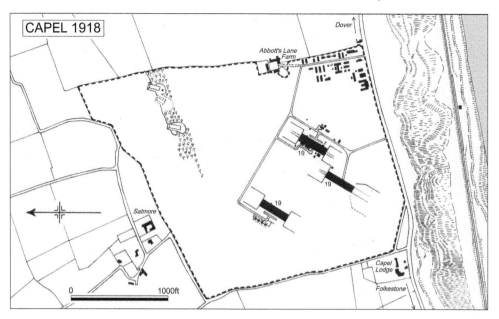

Capel, 1918. RNAS Folkestone was located on cliff tops overlooking the English Channel. In 1916 it had two Submarine Scout sheds, each over 300 feet long, plus a single portable shed, 160 feet in length. The latter shed was damaged by strong winds and replaced by another Submarine Scout shed. There were further berths for airships in the woods immediately to the north. The huts for housing personnel are located next to the Folkestone–Dover road, which ran along the cliff tops overlooking the sea. (*Mick Davis*)

near Folkestone. The airship rode in the wind, 15 feet above the ground, and it was impossible to get new supplies of gas to the seashore, so after 271 days it was necessary to let the gas escape from the envelope.

Envelopes were kept inflated as long as possible to save hydrogen, which was usually maintained at levels above 90 per cent. How long the hydrogen ratio remained at this level depended on the quality of the envelopes, which could vary greatly. The purity of the gas decreased over time, thus decreasing its lifting capacity. The station commander at RNAS Folkestone in 1916, 'Skipper' Cunningham, would carry out airship inspections on Sunday mornings to check that they were gas tight. It is said that he poked the envelope of a non-rigid airship inside shed No. 1, and that it emitted a 'blimp' sound: this machine was subsequently nicknamed 'Blimp', and in time all non-rigid airships were generally referred to as 'blimps'.

The main role of the airships at Folkestone, or Capel as it was often called, was to protect troopships crossing the English Channel, from Dover to Calais and Folkestone to Boulogne. On 3 July 1917, Submarine Scout *S.S.29* was given the honour of escorting the ship carrying King George V on one of his visits to the Front. Eleven days later, *S.S.24*, *S.S.29*, and Coastal *C.23A* provided the guard on the return journey from Calais to Dover. A more mundane task of RNAS Folkestone's was to protect the large number of ships passing through the straits of Dover, many of them on their way to the Port of London.

Although the airship station had been operating for over a year, its gas plant was still under construction in September 1916. Greater progress had been made with the accommodation for the airships, with the station now three sheds strong. A fourth one is shown on a plan dated 1916, but it was never built, and there was also a portable shed, which was transferred to Dunkirk that year. A new officers' mess was constructed out of corrugated iron on a timber frame, raised on wooden posts. Initially, this was not too popular with the officers, as they missed the opulent surroundings of Abbots Cliff House.

Although the French coast was in allied hands, RNAS Folkestone was within the range of enemy planes, so small clearings were cut in the adjoining Dawkinge Wood for airships to take refuge from an air raid. The station commander complained that the concrete roads built to serve the station could easily be seen from the air, so they were temporarily sprayed with tar that matched the surrounding ground. This required a considerable amount of labour and it was suggested that in future, the concrete be pre-emptively camouflaged with colouring in its preparation. This was not the only road problem in the summer of 1916: at Warren, the cliff collapsed into the

A near vertical view of RNAS Folkestone (Capel). Three airship sheds are visible while a fourth is under construction. While most RNAS airship stations had only two or three sheds for non-rigid airships, RNAS Folkestone for a brief period had four. One was dismantled and transferred to RNAS Mullion. (*The Fleet Air Arm Museum*)

sea, taking with it a stretch of the Dover–Folkestone main road. It would be another three years before it re-opened for traffic.

One Sunday, Victor Goddard was flying a Submarine Scout when his attention was drawn to anti-aircraft fire over Dover. As he flew across the town he looked down and saw crowds of people waving to him. Somewhat perplexed by this behaviour, he flew back to RNAS Folkestone. There, events took another curious turn: the Lord Mayor, who had arrived a short time earlier, began praising a puzzled Victor Goddard for saving Dover. What in fact had happened was that a German reconnaissance seaplane had flown off just as the airship arrived. The inhabitants had falsely concluded that the RNAS machine had driven the enemy away.

A small number of Coastals were delivered from 1916 onwards. They had a longer range than the Submarine Scouts, so were suited to patrolling areas of sea larger than the narrow Dover Straits. Coastal *C.23*, which arrived on 24 October, was written off on 21 May 1917 while heading back towards RNAS Folkestone. The airship began to lose height, and in an effort to counteract this, items of equipment were thrown overboard. One of the crew grabbed the Lewis machine gun mounted on top of the airship, but instead of bringing it down the ladder, he flung it over the side. On its way down it caught part of the gas-filled envelope, tearing a large hole in it: the airship plunged to earth, landing in a field close to the airship station. Although shocked, the crew survived the experience without any serious injury. *C.23* was rebuilt as *C.23A*, but did not return to its former base, going instead to RNAS Mullion.

In January 1916, approval was given for the improved version of the Submarine Scout designated *S.S.P.* (Submarine Scout Pusher). It was intended to establish this class of airship at RNAS Folkestone. It had a larger car, was capable of holding a crew of three, and had aluminium—rather than fabric—petrol tanks attached to the sides of the envelope. *S.S.P.1* arrived at RNAS Folkestone on 15 March 1917; the following day, *S.S.P.3* set off from RNAS Wormwood Scrubs bound for the same destination, but never arrived—it crashed near Faversham after the rudder jammed. After six *S.S.P.*s were completed, production came to a halt; most of them operated from RNAS Anglesey—which *S.S.P.1* ultimately moved to—and RNAS Caldale.

It was decided instead that RNAS Folkestone would instead receive the new *S.S.Z.* (Submarine Scout Zero) airships, a design devised by the engineering officer posted there, in response to the Vice Admiral of the Dover Patrol's request of an airship that could be towed by ships off the Belgian Coast. The prototype *S.S.Z.* was constructed at RNAS Folkestone from Submarine Scout *S.S.50*, and then used as a template for the manufacturers. Although the Admiralty was impressed with the design—which became the backbone of the non-rigid airship fleet in the latter stages of the war—Cdr Cunningham and his engineering team were rebuked for 'making unauthorised modifications to naval equipment'.[1]

Submarine Scout Zero *S.S.Z.2*, *S.S.Z.3*, and *S.S.Z.4* arrived at RNAS Folkestone in June 1917. The old Submarine Scouts *S.S.4*, *S.S.10B*, *S.S.11*, and *S.S.12* were rendered obsolete and so sent to RNAS Wormwood Scrubs. By autumn, airships *S.S.Z.1*, *S.S.Z.3*, *S.S.Z.4*, *S.S.Z.5*, *S.S.Z.18*, and *S.S.29* were performing well. Anti-submarine patrols from RNAS Folkestone were usually carried out over the English Channel one hour before sunrise and one hour after sunset, but sightings of enemy submarines were still relatively rare. German submarine captains could see airships taking off from RNAS Folkestone, perched on top of the white cliffs, and make good their escape before they were spotted. There was one encounter on 27 September 1917, but the submarine disappeared before naval vessels arrived on the scene.

Two airships were lost in the second half of 1917 while out on patrol. On 4 August, the engine of *S.S.Z.2* stopped while it was escorting transport ships to France, and it was not long before the airship came down into the sea. A strong wind then blew it in the direction of the enemy-held coast, while several Royal Navy vessels attempted to intercept it—a destroyer managed to attach a line to the mangled airship, but it came loose. The pilot and the wireless operator were eventually rescued by another destroyer, HMS *Mastiff*, and moments later, *S.S.Z.2* suddenly sprung back to life. A gust of wind caught it and it was once again airborne. But its brief flight took it over the ship's funnel and into a stream of sparks; this ignited the envelope, which promptly burst into flames and plummeted to the deck. Two crew members fighting the fire sustained serious burns; one later died. Its replacement, *S.S.Z.18*, did not survive beyond the end of the year. On 12 December, it too suffered engine failure, 7 miles from Boulogne. It landed on the water and a trawler towed it part of the way back, with a paddle mine-sweeper concluding the trip back to Dover.

S.S.29 had narrowly escaped disaster the previous month. It had set off for RNAS Cranwell, but after flying for half an hour encountered thick fog. It was subsequently given permission to return to RNAS Folkestone, but conditions were so bad that the crew decided to make a forced landing near Lyminge. A position was chosen in the lee of a wood where two old men were working. The intention was to come down close to the ground, land the wireless operator and engineer, and then—with the help of the two men—moor the airship. One of the old men caught the trail rope. The engine stopped just as two of the crew jumped off. The now lightened airship rose rapidly to a height of 1,500 feet, and there was no starting handle fitted, so the pilot—now the sole person still on board—had to climb out of the car and stand on the skids to swing the propeller, an act that needed constant repeating. The airship now rose above the fog and the sun began to heat up the gas, and continued to rise to 5,000 feet before the pilot managed to restart the engine. After waiting for a gap to appear in the clouds, it landed safely back at RNAS Folkestone.

At this time the station's gas plant needed constant attention. A coarse form of silicol had recently been delivered, which was found unsatisfactory, as it caused sudden rises in pressure. A much stronger caustic solution was necessary to initiate the chemical reaction than could the fine-grained silicol. Splinters of wood from the tubs in which the coarse silicol was supplied caused further problems by blocking the jets of the gas plant.

In February 1918, a piloted kite balloon was supplied to the station for use in fogs. It could reach a height of 2,000 feet, 500 feet above most local land fogs, and hence could act as a navigational aid for airship pilots. The following month, operations were hindered by sudden and frequent cliff mists. On one occasion, three airships were on patrol when the station became completely enveloped in fog. Every form of signal was employed to assist the pilots, including searchlights, Very pistol flares, Lewis guns, bugles, and shouting.

On 21 March 1918, *S.S.Z.5* lost its way in fog and landed near Boursin, west of Boulogne, and a group of Australian soldiers assisted with its mooring. More seriously, *S.S.Z.26* suffered engine failure at the end of February: as it drifted past Dover, it was taken in tow by HMS *Phoebe*, but the tow-rope parted several times and the crew was ordered to abandon the airship—they were picked up after spending 20 minutes in the sea. The *S.S.Z.26* rose high above them, and was never seen again.

In 1918, RNAS Folkestone's airships were pitted against German submarines. On 7 April, *S.S.Z.1*—piloted by Capt. Grabowsky—caught sight of a submarine conning tower 4 miles away. The enemy craft remained on the surface for several minutes, apparently unaware of the approaching airship, and only when *S.S.Z.1* was within two minutes' distance submerged. The airship dropped two bombs, and three minutes later, the submarine returned to the surface. This kind of action continued for several more days.

Mines were also spotted several times in April 1918, along with a waterlogged boat carrying the body of a drowned seaman. On several occasions in May, Folkestone's airships detected the possible presence of enemy submarines: at the beginning of the month, *S.S.Z.36* saw oil rising to the surface and reported the position to a drifter. The drifter dropped two depth charges, and a short time later the boat fired a signal with a Very pistol, which signalled, 'submarine ahead of me'. Further drifters arrived to patrol the area, but there was no further sign of the submarine.

On 9 May 1918, *S.S.Z.5* sighted air bubbles, and dropped two bombs. A few days later, the same airship detected more bubbles: bombs were again dropped, and this time oil was seen. Armed trawlers then dropped two depth charges, and more oil came to the surface. On 17 May 1918, oil bubbles were spotted, this time by *S.S.Z.5*, which dropped two more bombs: the second bomb caused air bubbles to rise to the surface in great profusion, so a destroyer was summoned to drop depth charges. Two days later, on 19 May, Coastal *C.21* and Submarine Scout Zeros *S.S.Z.3* and *S.S.Z.46* came across the same patch of oil, and thoroughly bombed and depth-charged it in conjunction with several destroyers. Destroyer *Kangaroo* reported seeing a submarine come to the surface for a minute then sink. On 21 May, *S.S.Z.1* detected a submarine conning tower some 10 feet below the surface: it dropped a bomb and alerted destroyers, who then arrived and depth-charged the area; they later reported that they thought the German submarine had been accounted for. While escorting a convoy on 25 May, *S.S.Z.36* caught sight of the periscope of a submarine preparing to attack. As the airship approached, the submarine disappeared beneath the waves; two bombs were dropped ahead of the swirl, and half an hour later several destroyers arrived on the scene and depth-charged the area. Folkestone's airships also located twenty-five mines while on patrol in May 1918, six of which they exploded with machine gun fire. A floating cowshed was even bombed by Coastal *C.21*!

Enemy submarines continued to be very active into the following month, and twenty-three bombs were dropped in offensive operations in June. On the first of the month, *S.S.Z.29* was instructed to search for a damaged submarine; it later observed its track, and shortly afterwards, *S.S.Z.4* appeared on the scene. *S.S.Z.4* then dropped a 100-lb bomb which failed to explode. At the same time, *S.S.Z.29* was climbing to 500 feet in preparation for an attack and also dropped a bomb, which did detonate. It then dropped a second and a large amount of oil rose to the surface. Destroyer *P.48* arrived and dropped a depth-charge which caused six large explosions over a stretch of half a mile. It was thought that they were caused by mines. The Royal Navy on this occasion confirmed that a German submarine had been sunk. While airship crews often made such claims when they dropped their bombs on suspected enemy craft, they were often erroneous. An enemy craft was attacked by Sub-Lt Davidson and his observer in *S.S.Z.1* in the Straits of Dover on 17 June. It dropped two bombs on a patch of oil, one of which failed to explode. An armed trawler arrived and dropped depth charges. There was a series of violent underwater explosions, but the German submarine managed to escape.

Earlier in the month, the crew of *S.S.Z.46* caught sight of a periscope, but the submarine vanished before an attack could be made. The following day, on 8 June, *S.S.Z.29* dropped two bombs, resulting in a large quantity of oil and bubbles rising to the surface. A few days later, the *S.S.Z.18* crew sighted 'a curious looking object with cables attached', but it disappeared before the airship could release its bombs. RNAS Folkestone's airships maintained their vigilance up until the final stages of the war. On 16 September 1918, German submarine *UB-103* was detected off Cap Griz Nez by *S.S.Z.1*, flown by an American, Ensign N. J. Learned, who had been seconded to the Royal Navy for training. Patches of oil were leaking from the damaged enemy vessel, and its fate was sealed when warships responding to the airship's wireless messages arrived on the scene.

In the summer of 1918, the number of personnel at Folkestone increased. The existing hut accommodation was sufficient only for 238 NCOs and men: over eighty now had to be housed in tents, while others slept in the lecture room. The canteen facilities were now totally inadequate as well, and more huts were requested before the winter. After the war concluded, Folkestone airship station was rapidly demobilised: by February 1919, all but one of its airships had been deflated. Plans drawn up in 1918 had envisioned four Submarine Scout Zeros and two Submarine Scout Twins based here by the summer of 1919. However, like numerous other bases, Folkestone was auctioned off, and in spring 1922, two of its airship sheds were dismantled for scrap; most of the other buildings were demolished at the around the same time. The remaining airship shed survived until 1947, when a tender was issued for its demolition. It had been used as a factory and garage for a local bus company. Today, the site is arable farmland and contains a caravan site; Capel-Le-Ferne, a suburb of Folkestone, lies on its eastern edge.

Folkestone had two mooring out stations: Godmersham Park, and Wittersham.

Godmersham Park Mooring-Out Site

Location: O. S. 1/50,000 map 179 (TR) 049504, near Ashford, Kent.

Unusually, this mooring out site was located well away from the coast, in a wooded valley. Tree-felling on the site commenced in April 1918, and the sub-station was commissioned on the 12 May 1918. Unlike most other mooring out sites established at the close of the First World War, Godmersham Park had been previously used by airships. The trees and high ground there reportedly provided excellent protection for their handling at landing, and three berths had been created for them in the woodland. In September 1914, trees were cleared here to make a temporary base for the Astra Torres airship, which protected ships ferrying the BEF to France. Four years later, Submarine Scout Zeros flew from here. The first, *S.S.Z.4*, arrived on the day the station was commissioned; it flew seventeen patrols escorting convoys in the remainder of that month, during which it sighted five mines. It also discovered a French seaplane in distress, and summoned a rescue craft.

By early summer, a workshop, bomb pit, and wireless hut were under construction, and kitchens, food stores, petrol stores, and refuse pits had been completed. Because of the nature of the ground, transport was difficult; a Crossley Tender was used to haul all stores, including the hydrogen cylinders. Construction of a light railway was proposed to overcome this problem. In June 1918, Folkestone airship station is recorded to have been six Submarine Scout Zeros, one Submarine Scout, and a further five Submarine Scout Zeros deployed at mooring out sites. At least one airship, the *S.S.Z.5*, was destroyed while based at Godmersham Park—it was consumed by a fire on 17 September 1918, caused by incessant lightning during a rainstorm. Two others managed to land safely: the first to land was *S.S.Z.1*, which was blown against some trees and chopped off a branch with its propeller—while walking towards the shelter of the trees, the handling party experienced severe electric shocks every time there was a flash of lightning. The second was actually struck by lightning while on the ground—although the airship itself was not damaged, several of the ground crew had their hands burnt by the electric current.

Wittersham Mooring Out Station

Location: O. S. 1/50,000 sheet 189 (TQ) 886281. Kent, north of Rye.
Alternative name: in some official documents, 'Rye'.

In late 1918, two portable airship sheds were under construction for the site. They were 175 feet in length, 50 feet wide, and 55 feet high. In the Houses of Parliament on 20 November 1918, Mr R. MacDonald asked the Under Secretary of State to the Air Ministry,

> [...] whether it is proposed to continue the construction of airship sheds near Rye with the Royal Air Force men working for military pay and under military conditions, or whether, in the event of these sheds being still required, the men working upon them will be demobilised and discharged and then employed as civilian workmen?[2]

Dr MacNamara replied,

> The sheds referred to are portable airship sheds, one of which is completed. The other will be completed in the course of the next few days. My Honourable Friend is under a

misapprehension as to the labour employed in the construction of these sheds. They have been constructed by civilian labour under contract and the Royal Air Force personnel are only employed in the erection and moving of the sheds after delivery.

With the rapid demobilisation of the RAF at the end of hostilities, Wittersham never saw active service as a mooring out site.

RNAS Polegate Airship Station

Location: O. S. 1/50,000 sheet 199 (TQ) 581035. Sussex, 5 miles north-west of Eastbourne, 17 miles east of Brighton.
Size: 142 acres (within boundaries of 970 x 830 yards).
Station complement: thirty seven officers and 264 men (January 1918).
Airship Sheds: Submarine Scout shed (322 feet long, 70 feet wide, and 60 feet high).
Gas Plant: B.2 silicol (5,000 cubic feet per hour).
Gasholder: one (10,000 cubic feet).
Based Airships: Submarine Scout, *S.S.5*, *S.S.6*, *S.S.9*, *S.S.9A*, *S.S.13*, *S.S.16*, *S.S.26*, and *S.S.27*; Submarine Scout Twin *S.S.T.2*; Submarine Scout Zero, *S.S.Z.6*, *S.S.Z.7*, *S.S.8*, *S.S.Z.10*, *S.S.Z.19*, *S.S.Z.27*, *S.S.Z.28*, *S.S.Z.30*, *S.S.Z.41*, *S.S.Z.42*, *S.S.Z.43*, *S.S.Z.44*, and *S.S.Z.48*; and Coastal *C.12*.

In 1914, a 142-acre site next to Polegate village was selected for the a small airship base. It was close to a railway, and the South Downs sheltered it from the west wind. However, the ground consisted of poorly drained meadowland, so although construction work commenced at the beginning of 1915, the waterlogged soil caused delay. William Arrol & Co.—responsible for erecting the first airship shed—were not able to fully complete the structure until the end of the year. On 8 May 1915, bricklayer William Body was standing 2 feet above the ground on a trestle during a winching operation on a second trestle—the trestles were 60 feet tall and weighed five tonnes—when a gust of wind caught the trestle. This snapped the cable, and as it fell to the ground, the unfortunate workman sustained fatal injuries. By July 1915, however, work was sufficiently advanced on the station to allow one Submarine Scout to be based there.

Initially, fourteen officers were housed in two thatched cottages at Wannock Village, while 137 naval ratings were accommodated around Willington, Polegate, and Wannock. In the second half of 1916, barrack huts were built on the station close to the road to Eastbourne. As the war dragged on, the ground around the barracks was landscaped with flower beds and rose gardens, in contrast to the Spartan accommodation at most other airship stations. Throughout 1916, work was undertaken on the doors of A-shed, for the entrance had to be enlarged to accommodate Coastals. This was done by excavating the ground to lower its level at the south-west doors, rather than increasing the height of the structure.

The Submarine Scout sheds at RNAS Polegate. A Coastal is poking its nose out of the far shed. (*The Fleet Air Arm Museum*)

The hydrogen gas plant near the two airship sheds had also been completed by the summer of 1916. It had not been in operation for very long before it malfunctioned, and by September, a shortage of gas had curtailed flying on a number of days. In July 1916, pioneering parachute experiments took place at RNAS Polegate: drops testing the Calthorpe Guardian Angel equipment were first made using a 12-stone dummy. On 5 August, three more parachute experiments were conducted from Submarine Scout *S.S.13*, the first two again with dummies, and the third done by Sir Bryan Leighton, who jumped out of the airship at 900 feet. He was forty-eight, and just two years earlier had passed through Upavon Flying School. This was the first time anyone had successfully parachuted from an airship.

Another unusual sight at RNAS Polegate that summer was the all-black airship, *S.S.40*, which had been assembled under guard in one of the sheds. It was intended to transport agents into enemy territory, but was never used in this role. Victor Goddard, who had captained *S.S.12* at RNAS Folkestone, carried out its first test flight to France on 6 July 1916. In the course of this journey, an oil pipe fractured and the engine stopped three times; the *S.S.12* free-ballooned towards Marquise, but eventually landed safely at its destination. Around the same time, several Submarine Scouts destined for the Italian government were assembled and test flown from RNAS Polegate. Another memorable event for this station took place on 19 July 1916, when the recently arrived Coastal *C.12* undertook an endurance flight that lasted 17½ hours. It started its flight with 240 gallons of petrol, and just 10 gallons remained when it landed. Its pilot, Sub-Lt McEwan, flew the airship as far as Land's End, where other airships were seen (probably from RNAS Mullion). The weather was

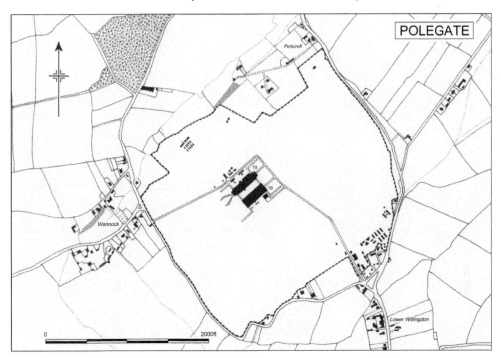

Polegate. The two Submarine Scout sheds are at the centre of the station. The silicol plant is immediately to the north of them. The main camp is located to the south-east, next to the road to Eastbourne. (*Mick Davis*)

intermittently cloudy, so McEwan had to determine his position from wireless stations *en route*.

One of the hazards for airships on long patrols was that, whilst they might take off in calm weather, conditions could drastically change for the worse upon their return. On 3 September 1916, *C.12* and *S.S.9* went in search of a reported enemy submarine: when they left the station, the wind was blowing at about 25 mph, but when *C.12* returned, it had increased to 42 mph. Three men were injured upon landing, though *C.12* was eventually housed safely inside the shed. The *S.S.9* was less lucky: its engine developed problems 10 miles out to sea, and at 2 miles off Beachy Head, a cylinder burst and all power was lost. It drifted 45 miles to Dungeness, where it hit the ground at 40 mph. By the time the airship had come to rest, it was totally wrecked. Fortunately, the crew escaped uninjured. The following year, *C.12* carried out frequent patrols in June and July. One day, after landing safely, the airship was caught by a strong gust of wind as it was being walked into its shed: the car struck the ground heavily, and its envelope was damaged. It was sent to RNAS Kingsnorth for repair, but did not return.

In the summer of 1916, the second airship shed had been completed: RNAS Polegate could now accommodate five Submarine Scouts and one Coastal. It was decided to dispose of the Coastal, *C.12*, for since most patrols were made over confined waters, its retention could no longer be justified. It also took up too much space in the airship

Coastal *C.12* in A-shed at RNAS Polegate, October 1916. Submarine Scout *S.S.16* is in the background. (*The Fleet Air Arm Museum*)

shed, and required more men to handle it on the ground than the smaller Submarine Scouts. Like RNAS Folkestone, RNAS Polegate later received Submarine Scout Zeros to replace the Submarine Scouts. The first, *S.S.Z.6*, was inflated in June 1917, followed by *S.S.Z.7*, *S.S.Z.8*, *S.S.Z.9*, and *S.S.Z.10* the following month. No longer required in France, the black-painted airship *S.S.40* made a re-appearance; after several flights it was deflated, and its envelope repainted with standard aluminium dope, giving it a silver appearance. It had been found that in sunny weather the black-doped envelope absorbed heat, causing the gas to expand and making the airship difficult to fly. It was sent to Wormwood Scrubs on 27 August. Submarine Scouts *S.S.6*, *S.S.9A*, *S.S.13*, and *S.S.16* were also sent to Wormwood Scrubs later in the year, as they were replaced by Submarine Scout Zeros.

When anti-submarine patrols were carried out in 1917, RNAS Polegate airships were usually sent out to on sea patrols one hour before dawn and coordinated with airships from RNAS Folkestone. While on one such patrol on the 24th of April, the engine of *S.S.13* stopped because of a failure in the petrol supply. It came down in the Channel, 45 miles south-west of Beachy Head; the airship *S.S.9A* located it and sent a destroyer to its assistance, which took the downed airship in tow to Newhaven. One M. J. Golightly was based at RNAS Polegate in 1917 and flew patrols in Submarine Scout Zeros. He described his experiences in *Flight* in 1960:

The armament comprised one Lewis gun and two 65 lb bombs. These ships were more comfortable [than the S.S. type] in every way for the crews but there was still little protection. Clad only in a leather flying coat, thigh boots, and leather flying cap, the crew

Submarine Scout *S.S.13* being walked out of the No.1 shed at RNAS Polegate in February 1917. A trench ran the entire length of the shed, into which the control cars of the airships could be slotted, so they did not have to sit awkwardly on the concrete floor. (*The Fleet Air Arm Museum*)

were exposed to the elements. There was no such thing as safety belts and no parachutes were supplied. Nor was any provision made for sustenance of any kind, except that a few malted milk tablets were issued for an eight-hour patrol. Crews met many hazards and adventures when patrolling in these Zero-type airships. On one occasion we went to meet and escort a convoy near the Isle of Wight. We had a following wind and arrived at the meeting point in 45 minutes from the time of leaving Polegate. Shortly afterwards, a gale blew up and in trying to keep the head to the wind, the pilot discovered that one of the rudder controls had broken. We left the convoy and began our struggle to return to base after thirteen hours in the air.

We succeeded in crossing the coast at Brighton. We were evidently being watched by local people who did not realize our danger, for one resident telephoned our commanding officer to ask if his 'blimps' or 'silver queens' [the latter was the common public's name to designate airships] had nothing better to do than stunt over Brighton for the benefit of the public! Actually we were being so buffeted by the gale that we quite expected to crash on the high ground to the north of the town and be blown up by our own bombs.... Another incident occurred during a patrol on a clear summer afternoon. We received a wireless message to proceed to a plotted area off Newhaven where an enemy submarine which had caused the loss of troopships sailing for France was thought to be lying submerged. On arrival over the spot we could see her silhouette and promptly dropped our bombs. Although we were at about 500 feet, the explosion as the bombs struck home lifted us to over 1,000 feet in what I should think was the quickest climb recorded for an airship.[3]

This is probably the incident referred to in official records concerning *S.S.Z.9*.

The shape of a submarine was marked out at the landing ground at RNAS Polegate for bomb-dropping practice. In addition, a floating target was moored out at sea for live bombing practice. A number of experiments also took place on the ground. Systematic tests were carried out with different forms of landing lights to determine the best type and arrangement for all conditions. A searchlight was tried on the landing ground with a system of port and starboard lights, and alternately fixed, flashing lights on the windbreaks and sheds. To assist with these trials, night flying was attempted whenever possible. Mooring-out tests were made with the Usborne Method using *S.S.16*.

On 6 October, the wind was gusty and blowing at about 25 mph. In part due to rust damage, *S.S.16*'s forward handling guy failed and the airship rose 200 feet into the air. It was still held by another cord secured to a mooring block, which caused the envelope to rip as it attempted to break free. With the loss of gas the airship came down about 300 yards away, and was later dispatched to RNAS Wormwood Scrubs for repair.

By August 1917, work on the heightening of windbreaks around the airship shed was underway, but was hampered by the shortage of steel; repainting the airship sheds was also delayed by poor weather. To prevent rubbish from blowing underneath the

The camp at RNAS Polegate. The roofs of the huts have been camouflaged. A parade ground lies next to the huts.

huts, wire netting was fixed around their bases. Not surprisingly, RNAS Polegate came to be associated with the saying, 'A dirty station means dirty airships and dirty airships means dirty flying'. Land was drained and ditches filled to establish a new landing ground in the second half of 1917. A visit was also made to the French airship stations on the opposite side of the Channel at Montebourg, near the Isle of Marcouf, and Guipavas, close to Brest. Both had sheds measuring 490 feet by 80 feet, and it was thought that they would make suitable emergency landing grounds for British airships based on the south coast. The commanders of these stations were reported pleased to receive English airships at any time.

In November 1917, there was a small explosion in one of the airship sheds at RNAS Polegate, originating from the car of Submarine Scout Zero *S.S.Z.7*. The wireless operator was testing his set, and a spark ignited petrol fumes; fortunately, due to the quick action of the crew of the adjacent airship, the fire was quickly extinguished. In November, both *S.S.Z.6* and *S.S.Z.7* sunk mines with their Lewis guns.

On 13 November, *S.S.Z.9* was attempting to land in fog. It dropped its trail rope which, instead of being caught by the landing party, wrapped itself around the station's telephone wires. It tore out pieces of the airship's envelope in the process, causing it to plummet to earth near the men's quarters. Fortunately, it did not fall very far and the crew survived this experience unscathed. *S.S.Z.8*, which had been on escort duties with *S.S.Z.9*, was forced to land on an area of the Downs which had not been engulfed by fog. A landing party was dispatched to retrieve it, and they literally walked the airship 4 miles back to RNAS Polegate. They stopped at a pond on the way to see how well the airship's car would float.

At the end of the year, there were further unscheduled landings which ended in a similar compromise. The 20th of December 1917 dawned fine and clear, but by the afternoon, a thick fog had formed, after which snow began to fall and a north-easterly wind sprang up. Five airships were airborne at the time—*S.S.Z.6*, *S.S.Z.7*, *S.S.Z.9*, *S.S.Z.10*, and *S.S.Z.19*. They were instructed by wireless to return to RNAS Polegate with all possible haste, but by the time they arrived overhead of the station, it was completely shrouded with fog. Two airships, *S.S.Z.7* and *S.S.Z.19*, managed to find a break in the weather and put down near Beachy Head Coastguard Station. Lt J. Havers landed his airship, *S.S.Z.6*, near Hailsham Farm. The remaining two sought refuge inland and put down near Jevington.

Once darkness fell, the easterly wind threatened to turn into a gale and the fog dispersed, so three of the pilots now decided to try and return to RNAS Polegate, rather than remain moored out all night. Landing lights back at their base were laid out to assist with their return. First back was *S.S.Z.6*, which landed safely, followed soon after by *S.S.Z.19*. The latter had taken off with *S.S.Z.7* from Beachy Head but they had lost contact with each other. The two remaining airships, which had landed at Jevington, decided to remain where they were, rather than risk flying in the adverse conditions. By coincidence, *S.S.Z.7*, captained by Lt Swallow, crossed over Jevington while attempting to return to Polegate. The two airship crews on the ground used an Aldis lamp to signal a warning to the airborne craft, but Lt Swallow unfortunately mistook the flashing light for an RNAS Polegate marker beacon. He descended, landing on top of *S.S.Z.10*, and completely ruptured its envelope. Realising his mistake, he began climbing away.

While he was executing this action, sparks set fire to the escaping gases from *S.S.Z.10*. Lt Swallow's airship was propelled to a height of 400 feet and then plummeted to earth. He was killed instantly in the crash, but his two crew members survived, seriously injured. They were pulled from the burning wreckage by Air Mechanic Harold Robinson and Boy Mechanic Eric Steer, who received the Albert Medal for their actions. *S.S.Z.10* was now an inferno, but Lt Victor Watson, believing some of the crew were on still on board the moored machine, attempted to search the wreckage. At that precise moment, its bombs exploded, seriously injuring Lt Watson's right arm, which later had to be amputated. The remaining airship, *S.S.9*, was removed from its moorings and taken to safety, and Lt Watson was also awarded the Albert Medal. Wartime censorship kept disasters of this kind from public knowledge, which gave rise to rumours—among them, that there were many unaccounted casualties on the Downs at Jevington.

Submarine Scout *S.S.9* was involved in further drama on 24 August 1918, when it ran out of petrol in the face of a strong head wind. It floated over the English Channel, and its captain, H. Mortiboy, made a forced landing near Rouen. The airship was repaired, courtesy of the French airship service, and returned to its base. Less lucky was Submarine Scout Zero *S.S.Z.6*, which developed engine trouble while out on patrol, 15 miles from Littlehampton on 16 March. A patrol boat was sent to assist, and the airship crew dropped a rope to be taken in tow. *S.S.Z.6* was descending into

Submarine Scout Zero *S.S.Z.30* at RNAS Polegate, 1918. A heavily camouflaged windbreak is visible below the airship. At this station there seems to have been no shortage of paint to create the heavily dappled camouflage scheme on the windbreak and the adjoining shed. (*The Fleet Air Arm Museum*)

position when one of the gas valves became stuck in the open position: the envelope began to deflate, and despite the crew throwing everything overboard, the airship dropped rapidly and hit the water with force. Fortunately, all the crew were safely picked up by the patrol boat, though only one of the three newly installed Perrin lifebelts functioned properly. The airship was then suddenly resurrected—freed of its load, it rose out of the sea and flew off in the direction of the English coast. It landed near Chichester practically undamaged. While being salvaged there, the envelope broke loose and flew off again, landing 12 miles to the north.

The adventures for *S.S.Z.6* were not over. It left Polegate on patrol one day in April 1918 at 3.45 a.m.; by 6.00 a.m. there was a report of bad weather, and the airship was recalled. But by the time it had arrived back, the station was covered in a blanket of fog, which *S.S.Z.6* rose to 1,000 feet to avoid. When the countryside became visible again, the crew calculated their position to be north-east of Hastings and followed a railway line south, until the proximity of hills made it impossible to trace the tracks through the fog from a safe height. A north-westerly course was then set in the hope of escaping the fog and returning to base by an inland route, but the pilot then determined that the fog overland was too thick to make it to the base, and so came down to 100 feet, hoping to pick up an army camp or aerodrome.

At Beasdon railway station, contact was established with a man on the platform using a handkerchief for Morse signalling! He informed them that there was a camp just over the hill. The pilot then rose back into the air but just missed the top of the hill, which was hidden in fog. Unable to find the camp, a course was set for Wormwood Scrubs, London, and *S.S.Z.6* again descended close to the ground in search of a railway or road, narrowly missing houses and trees. A group of men working in a hop field near Hartlipp Hill in Kent was spotted, and it was decided to land. With the assistance of the workers, the airship was walked to a spot selected for mooring. The envelope grazed a tree and tore a small hole, so the airship was sent directly to Kingsnorth airship station for repair. By the end of the month it was back in service at Polegate.

Heavy frosts in January 1918 caused the pipes to burst in the hydrogen plant. Despite this and other mishaps, RNAS Polegate's airships continued to fly a large number of missions throughout the year. In May, twenty convoys were safely escorted, and over 1,000 hours notched up, including a significant amount of night flying. A number of mines were located, and a suspicious object was seen by the crew of *S.S.Z.39* on 6 June while escorting a convoy between the Owers Light vessel and Beachy Head. The pilot thought he saw a submarine and signalled the convoy, which avoided the location. The airship remained over the spot until the ships had passed, but nothing further was seen. By July, RNAS Polegate and its mooring out stations had eleven Submarine Scout Zeros and one Submarine Scout Twin on strength. At this time, the rapid deterioration of the airship's envelopes at the mooring out stations was causing concern—in June alone, eight airships had to be re-inflated with a high volume of hydrogen. In April 1918, North Sea *N.S.6* landed with an inspection party of American officers and civilians.

To help with the running of the airship station, some fifty-four women in the

Women's Royal Naval Auxiliary Corps were employed as clerks, waitresses, drivers, and fabricators. They were housed in a large Victorian House at Willington. With the formation of the Women's Royal Air Force, new accommodation blocks were built on the airship station itself. By November 1918, Polegate was responsible for eleven airships, including those at the mooring out stations. As with most other airship stations, its demobilisation was swift: flying had ceased by early 1919, and all its airships lay collapsed in the airship sheds.

Towards the end of 1918, there were only two officers and twenty-two other ranks left at Polegate. There had been plans to have two Submarine Scout Twins and four Submarine Scout Zeros operating here, but the war had ended. Early the following year, when former RNAS Polegate was handed over for disposal, there were just two caretakers on-site. Auctioneers' notices appeared in July 1921, advertising a three day sale: the two airship sheds were listed along with wooden huts, a billiard room, kitchens, boiler houses, a water tower, gas holder, latrines, flagstaff, and wireless masts. Some of the smaller buildings escaped auction, for instance the transport repair workshop, which was taken over by an engineering company until demolition in 1995. The last surviving traces are the mooring blocks with the iron rings, which can still be found in some gardens and woodland today. Most of the land once occupied by RNAS Polegate has now been engulfed by housing—few twenty-first-century residents think of the airships that once flew from here. Willingdon Court and Thurrock Close (off the A 22 road) occupy an area where the wooden accommodation huts once stood. The site of the main entrance, the guard room, and administration blocks is now located beneath Coppice Avenue.

RNAS Polegate was responsible for the following two sub-stations.

RNAS Slindon Mooring Out Station

Location: O. S. 1/50,000 map 197 (SU) 952104. Sussex, in the foothills of the South Downs, 5 miles north of Bognor Regis.

The Slindon Mooring Out Station was commissioned in 1918. Three L-shaped bays were cut into the woods off the main drive to Norewood to berth airships. Initially, the station consisted of six bell tents and three marquees, and a nearby folly was used as a wireless station! In addition to the men enlisted in the Royal Naval Air Service, there was a camp carpenter to fell trees and build huts—instead of tents—for accommodation. They were not much of an improvement, since old airship fabric was used for their roofs! Old envelopes, too, were improvised to provide shelter for the field kitchen and stove, which according to official records made meal times a much more pleasant experience in wet weather.

In July, Submarine Scout Zero *S.S.Z.6*, *S.S.Z.9*, *S.S.Z.28*, *S.S.Z.44*, and *S.S.Z.48* were based here. Most spent only four days operating from this mooring out site, although *S.S.Z.28*'s stay lasted 20 days; it flew a particularly long mission of 26 hours and 30 minutes, manned by Lt E. J. Protheroe, air mechanic J. R. Innell, and wireless mechanic H. Bailey. It was proposed to have three Submarine Scout Zeros based here in the summer of 1919. Currently, the site remains a part of the countryside, little changed from the days when airships flew.

Upton Mooring Out Station

Location: O. S. 1/50,000 sheet 195 (SY) 990930. Dorset, Upton Heath, immediately north of Upton, a northern suburb of Poole.

This mooring out station was commissioned on 23 April 1918 under the command of Capt. D Knowles DSC. It enabled the area from the Needles, on the Isle of Wight, to Portland Bill to be patrolled by airships. The three clearings where the airships were moored among the trees had pits excavated to accommodate the cars and tails; the men were billeted in tents in a nearby clearing, and pits were dug to store the petrol and bombs. On 18 May, while operating from this station, *S.S.Z.19* bombed a suspicious oil patch, but no wreckage was observed. Examination of post-war records have found that no German submarine was lost in the area. On 3 May, *S.S.Z.30* was astern out of No. 1 bay when the wind sprang up very suddenly from the east: it reached speeds of 40 mph, and it seemed likely that the airship would be wrecked. The rudder was removed, so disaster was averted, and by evening the wind had dropped. Airships *S.S.Z.8*, *S.S.Z.19*, *S.S.Z.30*, and *S.S.Z.43* operated from here in July, but strong western winds and rain restricted flying on most days.

Nevertheless, patrols continued to be flown from here up until the end of the war and permanent hutments were built for personnel. Shortly after the armistice, the site was abandoned. Much of Upton Heath has since been extensively quarried.

4

RNAS Airship Stations in South-West England

The last major RNAS airship station to be commissioned in the First World War was located on the Lizard Peninsula in Cornwall. Since the days of the Roman Empire, its inhabitants would have been among the first in England to witness hostile fleets, such as the Spanish Armada, sailing up the Western Approaches, In 1914, it was believed that the main threat would come from German submarines operating in the English Channel and in the North Sea. Hence, many early airship stations were located either on the east coast or near the Straits of Dover. But it soon became apparent that the enemy was not going to confine its naval offensives to these waters alone, so an airship station was established near the fishing village of Mullion—named after the church of St Melans—to protect the copious cargo ships in the Western Approaches. There are few points on mainland Britain further south than this.

RNAS Mullion Airship Station

Alternative name: in its early days it was known as the 'Lizard' airship station.
Location: O. S. 1/50,000 map 203 (SW) 705210. Cornwall, 45 miles south-west of Plymouth.
Station Complement: twenty-five officers, 362 men (in Jan 1918).
Size: 320 acres (within boundaries of 1,933 x 1,100 yards).
Airship Sheds: one Coastal shed (300 feet long, 100 feet wide, and 70 feet high, with door width of 100 feet); one Submarine Scout shed (220 feet long, 70 feet wide, and 70 feet high, with door width of 70 feet).
Gas Plant: silicol (10,000 cubic feet per hour).
Gasholders: two (one of 120,000 cubic feet, and another of 20,000 cubic feet).
Gas Storage Tanks: twenty (each of 8,000 cubic feet).
Airships based here: Submarine Scout, *S.S.14*, *S.S.15*, *S.S.25*, *S.S.27*, *S.S.40*, *S.S.42*, *S.S.45*, *S.S.47*, *S.S.49*, and *S.S.75*; Submarine Scout Experimental *S.S.E.2*; Submarine Scout Twin *S.S.T.2*; Coastal *C.2*, *C.9*, *C.10A*, *C.22*, and *C.23A*; and Coastal Star *C*6* and *C*10*.

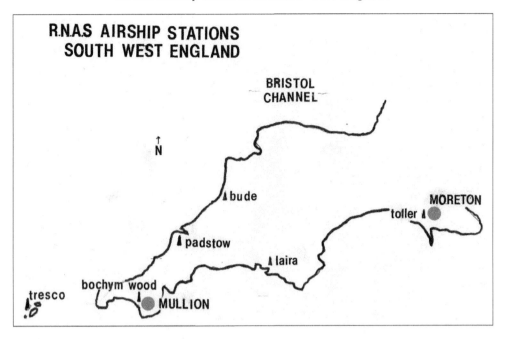

RNAS airship stations in South-West England. (*Author's collection*)

A convoy of Royal Navy vehicles including Sentinel steam-lorries employed in the construction of RNAS Mullion. Some of the men standing on them are dressed in oil skins. (*The RAF Museum*)

Although RNAS Mullion was the last of the chain of coastal patrol stations to be commissioned, its airships had more encounters with German submarines than most. Construction work commenced in March 1916, much to the discomfort of local residents, who had to endure large numbers of lorries rumbling down the narrow Cornish lanes. While local labour was hired to construct some of the more basic buildings, the airship shed was built by A. and J. Main of Glasgow. Teams of horses dragged the large girders across to two 10-tonne travelling cranes, which moved the steelwork into position. Like almost all other large airship sheds in Britain, it was built on a south-west–north-east axis, so that the main door faced the direction of the prevailing wind. This generally prevented the airship being blown into the side of the shed, but when the wind blew in other directions it could make the housing of the airship a difficult undertaking. On top of the shed was a standard observation tower to assist with manoeuvring of the airship in and out of its quarters; windbreaks mounted on concrete blocks provided further protection against the elements. Although Cornwall's coast is particularly prone to gale force winds, rising ground immediately to the west of the station formed a natural defence against the elements.

As the construction progressed, there were rumours among the local inhabitants as to the true purpose of the establishment. Some thought it was going to be used for clandestine missions behind enemy lines. By the end of the first week of June, the airship shed was almost ready, the concreting of the floor was nearing completion and the structure was being painted. RNAS Mullion's first airship was intended to be Coastal C.8. It was constructed at RNAS Kingsnorth, from where it departed on its delivery flight on 5 June 1916, only to crash inexplicably into the English Channel. Its captain, Flt Lt Dickinson, and two other crew members were drowned, the sole survivor being the wireless/telegraph operator. Coastal C.8's replacement, C.9, instead of being flown down from RNAS Kingsnorth, was sent by rail and had to be assembled when it arrived on 19 June. On 1 July it successfully accomplished its first flight and went on to make thirteen more flights over the next three weeks, covering a distance of 2,216 miles and spending nearly 27 hours in the air. On 22 July, C.9's forward engine failed after it had been airborne for no less than 19 hours, and it was taken in tow by the destroyer HMS *Foyle*. As the envelope began losing pressure, its crew had to transfer to the warship and C.9 ended up in the sea. It was beached at Mullion and eventually repaired.

Coastal C.10 also arrived the same month, but because the silicol plant was not yet operational, there was not enough hydrogen to inflate it. This was a common occurrence at many of the new airship stations in their first months of operation, making them dependent on the delivery of cylinders of hydrogen gas. By July, RNAS Mullion's silicol plant was briefly up and running, but the motor of the electricity generator soon broke down. The range of the wireless/telegraph station had also proved disappointing. In an effort to improve its performance, the hut was moved to a new position and the radio masts were heightened. On 10 August, Coastal C.6 visited Mullion from RNAS Pembroke and left Cdr Bosanquet there to give instruction to all flight officers in navigation.

The meteorological hut at RNAS Mullion. It has a tall mast with a weather vane. (*The Fleet Air Arm Museum*)

The silicol plant for producing hydrogen at RNAS Mullion. It is a small scale example when compared with some of the facilities at the major airship stations such as RNAS Kingsnorth. There is a gasholder for storing the gas as well as smaller tanks visible in front of the building. (*The Fleet Air Arm Museum*)

The first encounter with a German submarine—or the 'the Kaiser's tin fish', as they were sometimes called—took place on 9 September 1916. *C.10* spotted two large sailing ships which were on fire. As *C.10* steered towards the stricken vessels, its crew caught sight of a submarine at the surface, so flew straight towards it at 700 feet, and prepared to drop bombs. It was within about a third of a mile when the submarine suddenly submerged and disappeared from view below the choppy waves. A passing steamship was signalled by semaphore to proceed to the burning sailing ships and pick up survivors, while a Royal Navy vessel also arrived in the area to assist with the rescue. The survivors, sailors from the south of France, described how their ships had been shelled by the submarine's deck gun: the crew took to the life boats, but were forced back on board by the Germans to retrieve barometers, telescopes, and other valuables. An incendiary bomb was then placed on one of their crippled ships. The German submarine crew were taken totally by surprise by the arrival of *C.10*, and hastily fled the scene. This was the first action by a British airship against an enemy submarine in the First World War. The following day, *C.9* was requested to look for a semi-submerged schooner which was a danger to navigation presumably one of the sailing ships sunk the previous day. The airship located and hovered over the vessel for nearly 3 hours until a naval vessel arrived. It then dropped four 16-lb bombs on the schooner, but failed to sink it.

A survey was made of the north Cornish coast with the intention of establishing seaplane bases there, but no suitable site could be found in the inhospitable terrain. Instead, the airships from RNAS Mullion were given the task of patrolling the approaches to the Bristol Channel, coordinating their efforts with RNAS Pembroke. In 1917, an Intelligence Office was established at Mullion to gather information on the activity of German submarines in the Western Approaches, and predict where future attacks on shipping may take place.

A portable Coastal shed, originally intended for Airship Expeditionary Force 3, was transferred from RNAS Folkestone and erected by a company of the Air Construction Corps, so that three Coastal airships could be operated at any one time. On its completion, Coastal *C.23A* was also transferred from RNAS Folkestone. At the beginning of 1917, Coastals *C.9* and *C.22* were operational and *C.10A* was being rebuilt after an accident. For the first seven months of that year, no more than two airships were ever inflated at the same time, though the small number of Coastals were kept busy throughout the year.

Convoys were introduced to Gibraltar during the summer and a short time later to Atlantic ports. In July, *C.9* carried out several important missions, escorting ships carrying wounded troops, American troops, and special-value cargoes. On one occasion, this airship swept an area 40 miles ahead of a convoy in conjunction with *C.2* and destroyers. However, not all RNAS Mullion's airship missions had a successful conclusion. On 22 February, *C.9* escorted eight Dutch steamers from Falmouth to the Scilly Isles. Shortly before the convoy reached its destination, the airship was relieved of duty and turned for home, whereupon a German submarine immediately attacked the convoy, and sank six ships. RNAS Mullion's airships counteracted German submarines on several occasions in 1917. On 27 April, the same *C.9* received orders to search for a submarine that had been sighted and then submerged. The airship was assisted by trawlers and destroyers, and after 9 hours made a sighting, but the

An aerial view of RNAS Mullion in the summer of 1917. The Coastal shed is on the left and the one with its doors open is a semi-portable airship shed that had been transferred from RNAS Folkestone. On the ground in front of the Coastal shed are four Sopwith 1½ Strutters and a single Bessonneau hangar to house them. (*The Fleet Air Arm Museum*)

submarine submerged before the airship could reach it. Bombs were dropped on the area, and a patch of oil was seen to rise to the surface.

On 23 June 1917, *C.9* sighted a submarine submerged at depth, around 15 miles south of Start Point. A 65-lb bomb was dropped on it, and it was then depth-charged by a destroyer: wreckage came to the surface, as well as patches of oil. The airship could not linger on the scene due to an impending thunderstorm and it headed back towards RNAS Mullion. On 9 August, *C.2* was escorting a convoy when it caught sight of a submarine 7 miles away. The airship in closed on the submarine, but when it was within about 2 miles, the submarine submerged. Two 100-lb bombs were dropped less than two minutes after the conning tower disappeared, one about 300 yards and the other 200 yards ahead of the residual swirl. Four destroyers arrived a short time later and depth-charged the area. One hour later, a large patch of oil appeared at the surface. No further trace of the submarine was seen and no enemy craft were reported in the area, so it was presumed to have been destroyed.

In September 1917, *C.9* made no less than three attacks on submarines, two of which were believed to be successful. In one case, a large steamer was discovered torpedoed shortly after dawn. After a five-hour search, a submarine was sighted about 5 miles away, and the airship dropped two 100-lb bombs ahead of the swirl of the swiftly submerged vessel. Later in the day, large bubbles of air and a quantity of oil were reported seen at the surface by a destroyer. It was assumed that *C.9* had claimed another submarine.

In October, *C.9* made a further two attacks on one of Kaiser's tin fish. On the 3rd, while returning from escorting a convoy, it bombed a lurking submarine, and

The Coastal shed at RNAS Mullion. It has windbreaks on either side of the entrance. To the right of the building, work is taking place on assembling the semi-portable airship shed. (*The Fleet Air Arm Museum*)

trawlers were summoned to the spot and dropped depth charges. They later reported the submarine sunk, for large quantities of oil were subsequently seen. On 28th, a suspicious track was sighted, so a flare was dropped, which indicated something moving beneath the surface. Bombs were dropped and armed trawlers released depth charges, but destroyers later reported hearing a submarine on their hydrophones, so it probably managed to escape. C.9 continued in service at Mullion until it was deflated on 14 September 1918. It had flown a total of 3,720 hours and covered a distance of around 68,200 miles—more than any other airship in service with the RNAS. This was not the only Coastal airship at RNAS Mullion to encounter German submarines. C.5A arrived from RNAS Pembroke on 11 November at the conclusion of a twenty-four-hour patrol. It stayed several days, and on one patrol dropped four 100-lb bombs on a submarine periscope and the spot marked with a calcium flare. A trawler was informed and released depth charges. C.5A returned for more bombs, with Coastal C.23A relieving it on watch. On its return, oil was observed rising to the surface, so a trawler and two motor launches depth-charged the area. C.23A was standing by a torpedoed ship when it caught sight of a patch of oil, and bombs were dropped on it. It was not definitely established whether it came from a submarine.

The following month, on 15 December 1917, C.23A had a definite sighting of a submarine, 4 miles off Start Point. At the time, the airship was 16 miles downwind, so it took 18 minutes for it to reach the area. Two destroyers arrived on the scene and dropped depth charges without a definite result. On the 26th, C.23A was escorting a convoy leaving Falmouth when two of the leading ships were torpedoed, the first sinking in about 10 minutes, the second remaining afloat. At the time of the attack, the airship had been 5 miles away, sweeping the area. The convoy altered course after the attack, but half an hour later a torpedo narrowly missed another ship: *C.23A* dropped two bombs on the patch of sea from where the torpedo had been fired, but the submarine most likely escaped, since the vessel crippled by the first attack was torpedoed again at midnight and finally sunk.

Not all enemy submarines immediately submerged at the approach an airship. On 17 March 1918, *C.23A* sighted a submarine around 3 miles away. Almost immediately, the airship found itself under attack, with shrapnel shells bursting all around it. It climbed towards the cloud base—only 350 feet at the time. Once obscured by the clouds, the airship proceeded up-wind to position itself for an attack; the pilot then descended rapidly over the location of the intended target. At 600 feet, there was a break in the cloud, but the submarine could not be seen. Suddenly, there was a further shrapnel burst behind Coastal *C.23A*'s rudder plane: deciding it was impossible to carry out the attack in this manner, the airship re-ascended and proceeded to the windward of the submarine, when it was found that the envelope was leaking and the attack had to be called off. At first it was thought that shrapnel had done the damage, but this was later attributed to a leaking valve.

In the same month, Coastal *C.2* escorted a convoy of ten ships. Unfortunately, 15 minutes after the airship departed, one of the ships either struck a mine or was torpedoed. No trace of a submarine was discovered, but an hour after the vessel had been hit, twelve underwater explosions were seen within a 12-mile radius, indicating that a whole mine field had been set off. Two weeks later, *C.2* spotted an open boat with nine survivors from a torpedoed ship. The airship used its wireless to call for destroyers to come to the rescue.

The Cornish coast was foggy in the winter months. On three occasions in March 1918, *C.2* navigated its way back to base by following roads or railways at a height of 20 to 50 feet. At one stage, the forward handling guy-ropes trailed across some telephone wires, which the rudder plane also dangerously touched. While Coastal airships were the stalwarts of RNAS Mullion, the summer of 1917 saw the arrival of the first Submarine Scout Zeros—*S.S.Z.14* was put through trials on 28 July, and *S.S.Z.15* on 6 September. This new class of airship proved to be extremely successful here.

On 8 August, *S.S.Z.14* sighted a submarine and dropped two bombs, neither of which exploded. A destroyer then arrived on the scene, but by then the submarine had vanished. On the 21st, the same airship sighted a patch of oil and some bubbles, so two bombs were released—to no effect. While on patrol on 22 October 1917, the engine of a Submarine Scout Zero failed. The airship drifted for 10 hours, covering 300 miles along the English Channel, touching down close to trenches south of Calais, before finally landing at Montreuil, France. The envelope was deflated and transported back to England with the control car. The single-engined Submarine Scout Zeros generally suffered far fewer engine problems than the earlier classes of airship, as along with the twin-engined Coastal. S.S.Z.s they were powered by the Rolls-Royce Hawk engine, which had been designed specifically for the task and was known by pilots to stop only when it ran out of petrol.

The airships at RNAS Mullion had to patrol large expanses of open sea, and were often exposed to strong winds blowing off the Atlantic; airship crews therefore felt

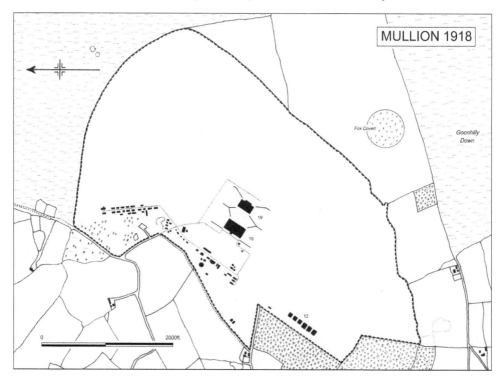

Mullion, 1918. The main airship shed at RNAS Mullion was a Coastal shed, while the smaller example is a semi-portable type. Their entrances are protected by numerous windbreaks. Bessonneau aeroplane hangars stand next to the woodland in which the Bonython mooring out site was located. (*Mick Davis*)

uneasy about flying the single-engined Submarine Scout Zero, despite its reliability. To remedy this situation, a group of officers led by Flt Lt R. Montagu used an enlarged Submarine Scout Zero envelop and fitted it with two Hawk engines. An enlarged car was constructed for it which could carry a crew of four or five instead of three. This creation, which was christened 'The Mullion Twin' and carried the designation M.T.1, crash-landed in the River Plym while undergoing trials on 15 March 1918. Although it suffered a further accident, the Admiralty was so impressed that it decided to put it into production. It was redesignated the *S.S.E.2* became the template for the Submarine Scout Twin, which was ordered to re-equip many of the RNAS airship stations by 1919. Just thirteen examples, however, were built at Wormwood Scrubs before the production line was closed at the end of the war.

Submarine Scout Twin *S.S.T.2* was the only example to serve at RNAS Mullion. At the beginning of 1918, RNAS Mullion had the following airships on strength: Coastal, *C.9*, *C.23A*, and *C.2*, and Submarine Scout Zero, *S.S.Z.14*, *S.S.Z.15*, and *S.S.Z.25*. The station's complement consisted of twenty-five officers and 302 men. New buildings, including an engine test house, were still being erected, and the old telegraph hut was also replaced. As was the case with many other airship stations, the doors of the new airship shed were giving trouble due to several broken cogs in the mechanism. All the fences were repaired and extended to keep out cattle and

RNAS personnel outside their hut at Mullion. They have made an ornamental porch leading to the front door of their accommodation. (*RAF Museum*)

sheep which had been straying onto the parade ground and around the huts. Further examples of the Submarine Scout Zero airships were received throughout the year, and another new type arrived in the form of the Coastal Star, an improved version of the Coastal. Two examples were received—*C*6* and *C*10*.

Like several other major RNAS airship stations, Mullion took on the additional role of an aerodrome in the latter stages of the war. Initially, Sopwith 1½ Strutter aeroplanes were assembled here and then flown to other bases in Cornwall. In May 1917, five machines were attached to RNAS Mullion for anti-submarine patrols. At first they were housed in the main airship shed, but in July a Bessonneau hangar was erected next to it. The following month, aeroplane patrols came to a sudden end when all the pilots were transferred to the Western Front. Although additional machines were delivered in October, they remained grounded, and flights resuming only at the end of the year. At the beginning of 1918, little flying was undertaken and five of the Sopwith 1½ Strutters departed to the Isle of Grain for experiment work. A couple of D.H.9s arrived to replace them in March, and in the next few weeks carried out many practice flights as well as photographic sorties. As further aeroplanes arrived, they were grouped into No. 493 Flight. D.H.6s also began to appear at RNAS Mullion, and served in No. 515 and No. 516 Special Duties Flights. All these flights were amalgamated into No. 236 Squadron, RAF. By the summer of 1918, the station had a total of six Bessonneau hangars in which to house their aeroplanes. They were small structures when compared with the airship sheds.

There were frequent accidents. Pilots were often either inexperienced or had been deemed unsuitable for service on the Western Front. In addition, the D.H.6s were often in poor condition and not well maintained. Among the machines lost was a D.H.6 (C7799), which crashed into the Lizard Cliffs—the pilot's body was never found. Two further machines, C7842 and C7844, made forced landings in the sea—only the former stayed afloat, and it was salvaged by a French trawler. Mullion's aeroplanes did make several attacks on suspected submarines, but without success. Despite its strategic position close to the sea lanes of the Western Approaches, RNAS Mullion was rapidly demobilised at the end of the war, even though there had even been a plan to base two rigid airships here. In the next few months some mine-spotting patrols were flown, but by early 1919 all its seven airships had been deflated. If the War had continued, the proposed airship strength by the summer of 1919 would have been one Coastal Star and three Submarine Scout Twins. In addition, there would have been a further ten airships allocated to the mooring out stations.

Aeroplanes continued to fly from here for some time after the airships left service. On 18 January 1919, D.H.9 (C1304) crashed on take-off, resulting in one fatality, and by the summer, No. 236 Squadron had it too been disbanded. A short time later dismantling of the airship station was underway. Some of the buildings were put up for auction, but the main airship shed was dismantled and transported to Padstow, where it was re-erected to serve as a bus station. In the Second World War, an experimental balloon station was set up on the site, and some of the First World War buildings still standing were put to use again. Appropriately, the station was commanded by a Mr Long, who in the previous war had been the coxswain on Coastal C.9. By the early twenty-first century, most traces of the airship station had been obliterated; a wind farm now occupies its site, a reminder of the exposed nature of the area and the inclement weather conditions that the airship crew had to endure. RNAS Mullion had several active mooring out stations, as listed below.

Bochym Wood Mooring-Out Site

This mooring out site was located in a small wooded valley immediately to the west of RNAS Mullion, and was used when there was not enough room in the sheds for all the airships. This location provided valuable experience in utilising woods to berth airships. The natural protection afforded by the trees did away with the need to construct an expensive structure in which to house the airships. Raw materials, particularly steel, were in short supply, but by using the natural environment, a small airship station could be set up in a few days.

Bude Mooring Out Station

Location: O. S. 1/50,000 map 190 (SS) 238013. Cornwall, 3 miles south of the small seaside town of Bude.

This mooring out station was commissioned on 19 May 1918, with the landing of Submarine Scout Zero *S.S.Z.42*:

> The landing ground is extremely treacherous, but with new fields taken over when the passage has been made secure by the felling of a few trees, it is hoped that the landing on this station will be made a little less difficult.[1]

It was situated south-east of Langford Woods, between Langford Hill and Langford Bridge. Trees were felled to make berths for two airships. The officers were quartered in Langford Barton House, while the other ranks had to make do with tented accommodation. The railway to Bude ran close by, so that men and supplies could easily reach this remote location. This mooring out site was ideally situated for airships to carry out patrols of the approaches to the Bristol Channel and the southern sector of the Irish Sea.

In June 1918, *S.S.Z.47* was based here and flew several patrols. At that time, few sports facilities were available to the men, so they were allowed to use a cricket pitch at Bude, though they hoped to eventually make one on the airship station itself. 'Bathing parties' also went swimming in the sea.

It was proposed to base one Submarine Scout Twin and two Submarine Scout Zero airships here by July 1919, and to erect one portable airship shed that was 175 feet long, 50 feet wide, and 55 feet high. However, like most mooring out stations, Bude was hastily abandoned at the end of the war and these plans were scrapped. All traces of it on the ground have long since disappeared. Langford Wood is still there today, surrounded by numerous small fields.

Bude Mooring Out Station with Submarine Scout Zeros taking advantage of the shelter provided by the trees. Close by are the tents which provided the living quarters for the personnel. (*The Royal Aeronautical Society*)

Laira Mooring Out Station

Location: O. S. 1/50,000 map 201 (SX) 510550. Devon, three miles north-east of Plymouth city centre, on the banks of the River Plym.

One of the criteria for this station was that it should be close to the Royal Navy barracks. A number of sites were examined, including ones at Trevol and Ensettle, but the most suitable was at Chelston Meadows, despite it being considered rather too far away from the barracks. The mooring out station established here was in use by September 1917, making it one of the first in Britain. The ships were secured to the trees and it was impossible for the envelope to move in any direction. On one occasion an *S.S.Z.15* airship rode out a gale of 60 mph, accompanied by heavy rain, and suffered no ill effects, and on four other occasions Zero ships rode out gales of 50 mph. *S.S.Z.25* was not so lucky, as it broke loose from its moorings in January 1918 and was completely wrecked.

In December 1917, an application was made for a searchlight and lighting for the mooring-out berths, so that airships could be refuelled and prepared for flight after dark and patrol before daylight. On 15 March, Submarine Scout Twin *S.S.T.2* was dispatched from RNAS Mullion to Laira to carry out speed trials. On landing, it was caught by a violent gust of wind and the guy-rope became loose. The airship began rising back into the air with one of the landing party clinging onto its skids. The crew quickly deflated the envelope and ended up in the nearby riverbed, the tide being out at the time. A new envelope had to be dispatched from RNAS Mullion.

Various improvements were carried out to the landing ground in May 1918, and additional windbreaks were built for the airships moored in the woods. In July, *S.S.Z.27* and *S.S.Z.45* were based here. At the same time, a YMCA marquee was opened at the station. Proposed strength for 1 July 1919 was one Submarine Scout and two Submarine Scout Zeros. A portable airship shed—175 feet long, 50 feet wide, and 55 feet high—was scheduled to be erected but this never happened due to the end of the War. The suburbs of Plymouth have now engulfed much of the surrounding area, and the ground that was once used as the mooring out site has been extensively quarried and more recently used as a landfill site.

RNAS Padstow Aerodrome

Location: O. S. 1/50,000 sheet 200 (SW) 902767. Cornwall, to the north of the seaside of town of Padstow.

In 1918, an aerodrome was established on the cliff tops near the settlement of Crugmeer. It served as a base for D.H.6 aeroplanes engaged on anti-submarine patrols with those from RNAS Mullion. A small mooring mast for airships was put up, which was used occasionally by Submarine Scout Zeros—such as *S.S.Z.75*—from both RNAS Bude and Mullion. When the aerodrome closed shortly after the end of

Submarine Scout Zeros *S.S.45* and *S.S.Z.47* in dense woodland at Laira, Plymouth, in June 1918. Mooring-out stations used this type of airship almost exclusively. (*The Royal Aeronautical Society*)

Submarine Scout Zero *S.S.Z.45* at the landing ground at Laira Mooring Out Station. Further airships are concealed in the woods. Artificial windbreaks have been erected between the trees to enhance the protection provided by them. (*The Royal Aeronautical Society*)

the war, the airship mooring mast was purchased for scrap by the landlord of the Farmer's Arms public house at St Merryn, and was sadly left to rust by the roadside for many years.

Toller Mooring Out Station

Location: O. S. 1/50,000 sheet 193 (SY) 540980. Grey's Farm in Dorset, west of the village of Toller Pocurum and north of Bridport.

Commissioned on 9 March 1918, this was the most easterly of Mullion's mooring out stations. There were two mooring-out bays cut into the wood, on top of a hill surrounded by farmland. The Maiden Newton to Bridport railway passed close to the southern edge of the base and the buildings at Grey's Farm were enlisted as a makeshift headquarters. Submarine Scout Zeros *S.S.Z.14* and *S.S.Z.15* were among the first airships based.

Patrols were flown over the waters between Start Point and Portland Bill. In May, four convoys were escorted by airships from this site. This activity consumed a considerable quantity of hydrogen. In the course of that month,

> [...] approximately 700 cylinders have been manhandled a quarter of a mile over rough ground. It takes six men to pull one tube up the hill to the road. The work is extremely hard and with the class of man now allocated, extremely difficult. The road to the railway is in extremely bad condition and although a party of station hands have been working on it, the road will not last more than another month without thorough repair.[2]

S.S.Z.15 was stationed at Toller the same month. It was lost at sea, 2 miles south of Exmouth, on 13 April 1918, until when it had made seven flights—totalling 61 hours—escorting convoys. There was a fall of snow on the 16th April which caused the only airship on base, *S.S.Z.14*, to sink into the ground. Additional hydrogen rectified the problem. In the summer, the farmhouse was repaired and the District Council carried out improvements to the road—piping was laid from the road to the airship berth, which did away with the need to haul hydrogen gas cylinders over rough ground. In July, a letter was sent to the Admiralty requesting two portable canvas sheds to house the airships—both Bude and Laira made similar requests—and huts to replace tented accommodation for the approaching winter. The letter argued that, while the majority of the personnel at these stations were in good health, not only the men but the spare engines and supplies were suffering from being stored in damp tents!

The Admiralty agreed with the request to house the men in huts, and that single airship sheds would be supplied to Bude and Laira, though Toller's request for a shed was turned down. The reason given was that a large airship station was currently under construction at Dorchester, not far away. When this became operational, the mooring out site at Toller would be dispensed with. Submarine Scout Zero *S.S.Z.45* made a forced landing near Toller. Its observer J. Owner was hurled through the front of the control car, but sustained only slight injuries; the pilot Lt Savage, and engineer H. Jobson, were more seriously injured. The observer managed to stagger to the nearest Post Office, were he phoned for help. Like other mooring out sites, Toller was abandoned shortly after the end of hostilities. The area is once more farmland and wood.

RNAS Tresco

Location: O. S. 1/50,000 sheet (SW) 981145. New Grimsby, on the island of Tresco, Scilly Isles.

In 1917, a large RNAS seaplane station was constructed on the western side of picturesque Tresco. Large seaplane hangars, a slipway, and many barrack blocks were built around a sandy bay. A site was set aside for mooring airships immediately to the south of the complex, off Abbey Road. The landing ground was sheltered by a bank of trees on its west side. Submarine Scout Zero *S.S.Z.14* made a trial landing at Tresco on 25 August 1917, and was handled on the ground by personnel from the seaplane station. There were plans to establish a permanent mooring out station here, but the war ended before these became a reality. While most other locations were to receive one portable airship shed, Tresco would have been allotted two for 1919. It was also planned to base a small number of Submarine Scout Zero airships on the island.

Planned Airship Stations for South-West England

Thought was given to locating an RNAS airship station at Falmouth, but it came to nothing. In September 1916, it was also suggested that an airship station should be established to protect the harbour at Poole. This was the largest man-made harbour in Europe and an important anchorage for Royal Navy warships, but was at the limit of the patrol area for airships from RNAS Polegate. The C-in-C at Portsmouth requested two new airship stations, one on the Isle of Wight and the other at Portland, with two airships allocated to each base. It was thought that the ditch of the Verne Citadel at Portland could be used to shelter airships, while Bembridge was short-listed as a possible base on the Isle of Wight. In response to this request, the Director of Air Services wrote:

> C-in-C Portsmouth has asked for 2 airship stations in addition to the 4 seaplanes now being sent to Calshot to work from either that base or Portland. We have one Coastal shed in stock and could manage to move a Submarine Scout shed from Barrow if required or obtain another at fairly short notice I think. Possibly one station somewhere in the neighbourhood of Wareham where there is heathland might be found and would suffice. The Verne is too exposed. As it is no easy matter to find a site, before any action is taken in this respect, it is submitted that a decision may be given as to whether a station or stations are to be provided.[3]

A site at Moreton in rural Dorset was short-listed, but it was almost a further two years before construction commenced. It was one of three sites approved in 1917—the others were Killeagh and Cramlington—as bases for anti-submarine patrols. There were ambitious plans for Moreton, Killeagh, and Loch Neagh, three sites where large rigid airships would be housed. Originally the list was much longer, but steel shortages dictated that only these stations were approved for construction. The Rigid Airship Committee had suggested in May 1916 that large sheds be built at Bristol and on the Devonshire Coast. In the same year, it was also proposed to build a shed at Taunton, to serve as a refuge in case weather conditions prevented a rigid airship from returning to its base on the east coast.

RNAS Moreton

Alternative names: 'Dorchester', 'Woodsford Aerodrome'.
Location: O. S. 1/50,000 map 194 (SY) 764895. Dorset, 4 miles east of Dorchester, 10 miles north-east of Weymouth.
Size: 355 acres (within boundaries of 1,930 x 1,330 yards).
Airship Sheds: Coastal shed (358 feet in length, 110 feet in width, and 75 in height).
Airship Sheds Proposed: one double-berth rigid airship shed.
Gas Plant: silicol.
Airships (Proposed for 1919): four Submarine Scout Twins.
The construction of this station caused more controversy than almost any other. On 30 August 1917, official approval was given for the construction of three new airship stations for non-rigid airships involved in anti-submarine work—at Dorchester, Cramlington near Newcastle-upon-Tyne, and Killeagh in southern Ireland. The Director of the Air Service wrote in an internal memo:

> [...] in the case of Dorchester, the Air Service had selected a site and recommended the establishment of the station over a year ago.... Had these recommendations been acted upon, airships would already have been patrolling between Start Point and the Isle of White by the summer of 1917 ... [that] unless drastic action was taken, clearly no patrols would be carried out from this station until the summer of 1919.[4]

Most of Britain's foodstuffs had to be imported by sea, so arable land had become a precious commodity. For this reason, the president of the Board of Agriculture objected to large tracts of land being converted to house airships at Moreton. Several other sites were examined between Sidmouth and Southampton, but none were judged suitable. In the end, the Air Service got its way, and on 12 February 1918, 370 acres of land were requisitioned at Woodsford. Objections were apparently withdrawn, on the grounds that only 70 acres in total would be disturbed by buildings. Presumably the remainder of the site, which served as the landing ground, could still be used for grazing or some other agricultural use. Adding to its viability as an airship station, the Bridport to Maiden Newton Branch Line (now closed) ran along the southern edge of the land at Moreton. Materials were ferried by train during construction.

Proposed sites for RNAS Rigid airship stations. (*Author's collection*)

As with most airship stations, the Coastal shed faced the prevailing—and here, south-west—wind. Some £80,000 was allocated to its construction, out of the estimated cost of £200,000 for the entire station. Immediately to the south, laid out along a new road, were all the other buildings. At the western end was the silicol plant and the gas cylinder storage site served by a railway siding. At the opposite end, on the public road that ran past the site, were the guard house, the officer's quarters, and accommodation blocks for other personnel. It was proposed to base Submarine Scout Twin airships here when the station was completed. There were more ambitious plans still: to construct a double rigid airship shed to house two Class-33 airships. This was intended to be ready by 1920, assuming that the war continued. With the end of fighting in November 1918, work on the silicol plant and other facilities was scaled down. The airship station was at this point near complete, and it was decided to focus on finishing the airship shed —a decision which would cause controversy the following year.

In May 1919, it was announced that Moreton would no longer have a role as an airship station, but that it would house large numbers of sea mines then held in storage in commercial warehouses. By this time the accommodation blocks, storerooms, and

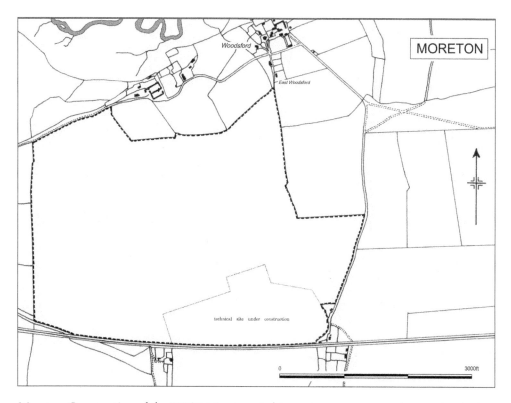

Moreton. Construction of the RNAS Moreton airship station was very nearly completed when it was deemed surplus to requirements. It stood on arable farmland, and the railway line to Dorchester ran not far from the southern boundary of the site, where the airship shed and technical buildings were. Woodsford village lay close by, and the proposed airship station was sometimes referred to by this name. (*Mick Davis*)

railway sidings were ready and little expense was needed to complete the airship shed. In August 1919, a letter by Lord Middleton was published in *The Times*. It made a number of allegations concerning how money was wasted at RNAS Moreton, some of which was inexplicable. The matter was subsequently raised in the House of Lords, and the government defended the station thus:

> [...] it was wrong to assume that the date of the Armistice was the date the war ended. The Armistice merely meant a cessation of hostilities which, however, we were prepared to resume at any moment, if that should have become necessary. It was unfair, therefore to argue as if all our preparations could have ceased after 11 November 1918.

This was not the end of the matter. Further questions were raised in the House of Commons on 28 October 1919, when Maj. Colfox asked Dr McNamara, the Under-Secretary of State for Air:

> if work is still being carried on in connection with Woodsford Aerodrome, near Dorchester, whether special trains were still being run daily to carry workpeople to their work there. What has been the total cost of the aerodrome, to what use is it to be put, and whether the land not already covered with buildings and no longer required can be handed back and used once more for agricultural purposes?[5]

Dr McNamara replied:

> I have been asked to reply, as the Woodsford Aerodrome is in Admiralty occupation. The completion of the aerodrome as an airship station has been abandoned. A few minor works are still in hand to complete the buildings required for use by the Admiralty. Special workmen's trains are not being run, they were stopped on the 13th of September. The approximate cost of the aerodrome will be £185,000. The station is to be used for the temporary storage of machinery. As regards the land, the farm tenant has never been dispossessed of the portion referred to and is still in occupation. The requisition cannot, however, be withdrawn until the question of the ultimate disposal of the station is settled.

A few days later, the first tentative steps were taken to relinquish RNAS Moreton, but the Admiralty continued to use it as a storage facility, and it was not until June 1920 that it was passed over to the Royal Air Forces Disposal Board. It remained under state ownership for another year. The land eventually reverted to agriculture. The Second World War airfield RAF Warmwell was constructed close by, but made no use of the former airship site itself. The massive concrete base of the airship shed survived into the 21st century, as have a few of the buildings, including the guardhouse and the officer's quarters, now repurposed into farm buildings. The railway line that once ran past the site closed in 1975.

5

RNAS Airship Stations in East England

Britain faced an enemy with a North Sea coastline, so the obvious response was to build a chain of airship stations and aerodromes the length of the east coast. The country's first purpose-built airship station for the Admiralty was RNAS Kingsnorth, near the Thames Estuary. In time, all the major airship stations were built in close proximity to the North Sea or, as it was ominously known in bygone centuries, 'the German Ocean'.

RNAS Pulham Airship Station

Alternative name: 'Pulham St Mary'.
Location: O. S. 1/50,000 map 156 (TM) 194836. 18 miles south of Norwich and 26 miles southwest of Lowestoft.
Size: 920 acres (within boundaries of 2,600 x 2,330 yards).
Station Complement: twenty-nine officers, 651 men (in Jan 1918).
Airship Sheds: one rigid shed 712 feet long and 151 feet wide, with the door opening 100 feet high and 151 feet wide, and one rigid shed 756 feet long and 180 feet wide, with the door opening 110 feet high and 180 feet wide; and one Coastal shed 223 feet long and 70 feet wide, with the door opening 70 feet high and 70 feet wide.
Gas Plant: one B silicol plant (10,000 cubic feet per hour), and four Water Gas units (14,000 cubic feet per hour).
Gasholders: three of 500,000 cubic feet, and one of 120,000 cubic feet.
Based Airships: Rigids *No. 9*, *No. 23*, *No. 24*, *No. 25*, *R.26*, *R.32*, *R.33*, *R.34*, *R.36*, and *R.80*; Submarine Scout *S.S.14A*, *S.S.28*, *S.S.29*, *S.S.35*, and *S.S.36*; Submarine Scout Experimental: *S.S.E.1* and *S.S.E.3*; Submarine Scout Zero; *S.S.Z.3*, *S.S.Z.71*, and *S.S.Z.77*; Submarine Scout Twin *S.S.T.14*; Coastal; *C.14A*, *C.17*, *C.26*, and *C.27*; Coastal Star *C*6*; North Sea ; *N.S.1*, *N.S.7*, and *N.S.16*; Parseval, *No. 4* and *No. 6*; and the Italian-built Semi-Rigid *S.R.1*.

As early as 1912, surveyors and land agents Thomas Gaze and Sons were given secret orders to acquire land for the establishment of an air station for the Admiralty. Five hundred acres were purchased in Pulham St Mary and Rushall, including Upper

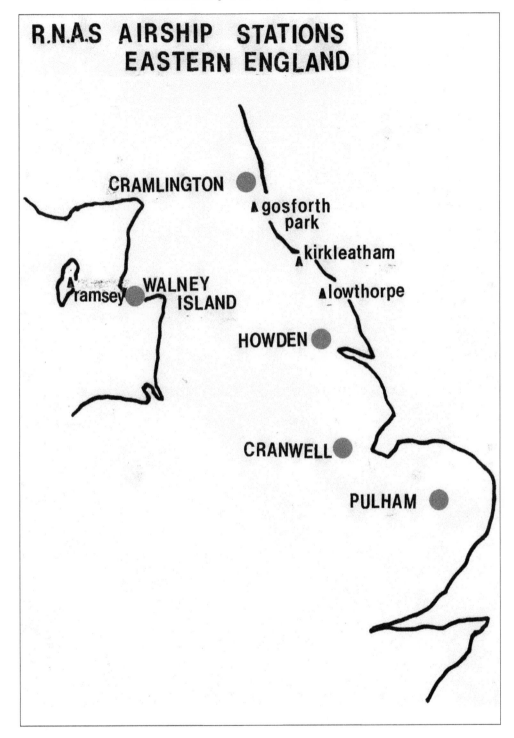

RNAS airship stations in East England. (*Author's collection*)

Vaunces Farm, Brick Kiln, and Home Farm. Civilian contractors, with the aid of the Air Construction Corps, cleared and levelled the site for 100 Royal Navy personnel to move in by 1915. To bring the construction materials to the base, a short branch line was laid into the site from Pulham Market station on the GWR Waveney Valley line. The first airship shed was a wooden structure that was 90 feet high, strutted, and stiffened with steel ropes. Its wooden doors weighed 90 tonnes and had to be assembled on the ground, before being raised into place by 200 men hauling on ropes running through pulleys at roof level.

RNAS Pulham was officially commissioned in February 1916, but the first operational Coastal airship *C.17* was not delivered until August. These airships initially had buff-coloured gas envelopes and were given the nickname 'Pulham Pigs' by the local residents. This stuck, and all the airships later based here were similarly referred to. Anti-submarine patrols extended from Margate to Dunkirk in the south, and from Mablethorpe to the Netherlands in the north. *C.17* was damaged on 1 November 1916 while carrying out experiments with a new type of grapnel. The trail rope wrapped around one of the propellers, which then came loose and damaged the envelope.

The commodore in charge of Lowestoft Naval Base was less than impressed by the role played by airships at RNAS Pulham in their first few months of operation. He wrote the following letter to Wg Cdr Maitland, in charge of RNAS Pulham:

> I do not think that the patrols as at present carried out by the airship from Pulham are of the least value. I do not want them to patrol the War Channel but when circumstances and

The 222-foot-long Coastal shed at RNAS Pulham. (*The National Archives*)

weather permit to go much further afield (20 to 30 miles from land), where they might have a chance of observing enemy vessels or submarines and should they encounter fast destroyers, to be able to escape by their superior speed. Reporting that seven merchant vessels were observed in Yarmouth Roads, steering south, and that six ships were observed riding at anchor is of no value whatever, and it is nothing but a waste of petrol and material for patrols such as these to be carried out. I fully realise in the present season of the year, when the light hours are so short, that it may not be possible to do so much as I hope they will be able to do in the summer but when they are on patrol, it is much better to go straight out to sea and remain either drifting with the wind or with the engines just moving and carefully searching the sea for mines or submarines, than it is to go North and South along the coastline which is already adequately patrolled by the patrol vessels.

RNAS Pulham began 1917 with three airships on strength. The fleet of Coastals was joined by North Sea *N.S.1*, which arrived from Kingsnorth on 8 April. On the 13th, it carried out an eight-hour patrol, in which the water in the cooling system boiled and burst both the radiators, which had to be replaced. Another far more serious incident took place a few days later: *C.17* was on patrol on the 21st near North Hinder Lightship, at the extreme edge of the patrol sector, when it had a fatal encounter with German seaplanes. Wireless contact with Flt Sub-Lt E. Jackson was lost at 9.30 a.m., and later in the day, a trawler reported witnessing a British airship intercepted by enemy aircraft off Nieuwpoort, Belgium, and being shot down at close quarters, despite putting up intense resistance with its machine guns. Royal Navy seaplanes were sent to investigate, but could find no trace of the Coastal or its crew of five. The commodore issued the following instruction to HMS *P 22* on the 25th:

> You are to proceed at daylight with all dispatch to the North Hinder Light vessel and ask if they saw anything of a British airship on Saturday, 21st April. If so, whether she appeared to be drifting or underway, if the latter, try and obtain from them a rough estimate of course and speed. Your enquiries should be made with great discretion and should indicate that we are anxious as to any possible survivors, but that we are not asking for naval information which they might possibly refuse to divulge.

No survivors were found. The Station Paymaster WO Walters was one of the crew lost, having gone on this patrol for some air experience. Victor Goddard, who flew the black airship in France, had been the designated pilot, but in a twist of fate was unwell that day. Although the worst was feared at RNAS Pulham, the fate of the airship only became clear when German radio confirmed their victory a few days later. After this, the Admiralty insisted upon the upper machine-gun being manned at all times while flying over the sea, even if it meant carrying an extra crew member. In addition, all airships out of sight of land were to communicate their position to base once an hour as a safety measure. But even in these early days of radio transmission, the enemy had monitoring stations to listen into communications, so this measure actually made the British airships more likely to be attacked.

Hydrogen gasholders at RNAS Pulham, May 1917. The largest has been painted in camouflage for storing hydrogen. (*The National Archives*)

April 1917 was a bad month for RNAS Pulham, on the ground as well as in the air. Its silicol plant was housed in a group of brick buildings with asbestos-clad roofs. Pipes from the gas plant ran into a valve house and into the control and pump house filling points near the airship sheds. It was here that the airships were filled with hydrogen. At midday on 19 April 1917, RNAS Pulham was rocked by an explosion in which two men were blown through the side of the gas house. One of them, Lt Wildman, was killed, and the other, a rating, sustained serious injuries from which he later died; gas officer Lt Mitten was covered in caustic soda and badly shocked, a civilian was also burned, and several other personnel sustained injuries.

While most airship stations had silicol plants to produce hydrogen by 1918, RNAS Pulham also possessed a steam iron plant—because of the station's size—which could produce large amounts of gas. Another type of gas plant at Pulham produced gas by the expensive electrolytic process, in which water was broken down into hydrogen and oxygen by way of an electric current. It required a large supply of electricity produced by diesel-powered generators, which were housed in a large brick building on the opposite side of the road to the gas plant.

Despite the loss of *C.17*, airship patrols were resumed over the southern part of the North Sea after a short interlude. The following encounter was reported by the captain of *C.27*, and serves as a reminder that not all submarines encountered were enemy craft:

I have the honour that while patrolling today off Kessingland Submarine *F.1* was sighted on surface, proceeded towards her and challenged but no reply was given. No Ensign was

The hydrogen plant and boiler house at RNAS Pulham, December 1917. It has the appearance of a sizeable industrial complex. (*The National Archives*)

The petrol station at RNAS Pulham, December 1917. (*The National Archives*)

flying but being so close to land it was presumed to be a British craft, nevertheless I asked by visual signal for their recognition signal. At this moment another Submarine *V.4* was observed on starboard bow which a few seconds later submerged and proceeded with the periscope only showing. Made requisite course to come up with her and circled periscope until she re-appeared. I then challenged her and after speaking to her by visual signal and a delay of 20 minutes the necessary recognition signal was given. In the meantime Submarine *F.1* had hoisted her Ensign.[1]

The following month, *N.S.1*, which had arrived in April, carried out an endurance trial. The first attempt had to be cut short when it developed engine trouble after being in the air for over 16 hours. On 26 June, *N.S.1* took off again at 6.00 a.m. and did not return until 7.22 a.m. on the 28th, having been in the air for over 49 hours and covering 1,536 miles. At the time, this was a record-breaking performance by a British airship.

With the loss of *C.17* in mind, RNAS Howden issued an instruction that their airships were to fire on all seaplanes within range, regardless of nationality:

> Experience has proved that it is very difficult to make out distinguishing marks on friendly seaplanes on a sunny day and such marks can frequently be only made out when the seaplane is quite near the airship.[2]

Not long after, Pulham instructed their airship crews to do the same.

In July, the Admiralty Office at Whitehall got word of complaints by unnamed ratings regarding the food and housing of the Air Construction Corps at Pulham:

> The complaint as regards food is that it is not as good as at the Crystal Palace, not so well served and not sufficient in quantity. Possibly this is only the case in certain messes and due to want of skill on the part of mess caterers. Another complaint is that these ratings, which are there for training, have neither overcoats nor oilskins and cannot purchase them at less than three weeks' notice. There is also no place to dry clothes when they get wet. It is also stated that the washing tables are in the open air and shaving has to be carried on in the open even if raining and blowing hard. As all these men are of a class not medically fit for active service I think that anything that can reasonably be done to lessen hardship and exposure might be done for them.[3]

An investigation was launched into these complaints. Pulham was a main base for the Air Construction Corps, with its local headquarters in the original Upper Vaunces Farm, ¾ mile from the airship sheds. The commander of the camp wrote in his defence:

> I would like to point out that this is purely a temporary camp where the men undergo about 6 weeks' disciplinary training, after which they are drafted away to different companies:

1. Ablution benches of the usual pattern have been erected at convenient locations near the tents and equipped with basins, sink, filters, etc. Each bench has water laid on. The men may shave in their tents if they like. Arrangements were made as soon as the camp was started for the men to use the bath hut in the Depot. Two parties are sent every afternoon to bathe in the Waveney River at a safe point near Needham. Every man gets a bath at least once every ten days.

2. Messing. The camp is on Service rationing. An excellent galley has been erected which is in charge of a service P.O. Cook with two qualified assistants, the necessary extra cooks being made up from the Camp and changed every week. The carving of joints is a weak spot, it being very difficult for untrained men to cut up the allowance exactly but careful supervision is kept over this and every effort is made to see that Ratings get their fair share.

A staff officer was sent from the Royal Navy base to investigate the allegations, and he came to the conclusion that there was no substance to most of them:

There are about 950 recruits in this camp. The sick list is very small, the daily attendance at the sick bay being about eighteen. The majority of these cases are sore feet and other such minor ailments. Except for the matter of drying clothes, I could see no grounds for complaint. Camp life is strange to them and no doubt it takes them a few days to shake down. The general health of the camp is so good there can be little or no hardship or exposure.

Finally, it was pointed out that the camp was due to close in August 1917 in any case. In September 1916, 656 members of the Air Construction Corps were at Pulham, including ten officers and four warrant officers, although they were housed in a separate camp. The Air Construction Corps, which became the Air Service Constructional Corps in 1917 also had men based at other airship stations including RNAS Cranwell, Howden and Polegate around this time. Although civilian workers were responsible for erecting the large airship sheds, this unit assisted with much of the work on the ancillary buildings. The Admiralty could call upon the services of the Air Construction Corps, which had its own lorries and earth-moving machinery to prepare the ground for a new airship station or aerodrome. This also undertook a diverse range of tasks which included the building of portable airship sheds, windbreaks, barrack huts, and storage buildings. Roads and paths were laid, and trees felled when required.

In autumn 1917, the loyalty of foreign-born citizens living close to RNAS Pulham was brought into question. A Dutchman, Mr A. Van Citters of the Grange, had a commanding view of RNAS Pulham and the movements of all its airships. The CO requested that this person be investigated:

Mrs Van Citters is believed to be an Englishwoman; she is, however, exceedingly talkative. Mr Van Citters has made many efforts to come onto the Station, although he has been refused more than once.[4]

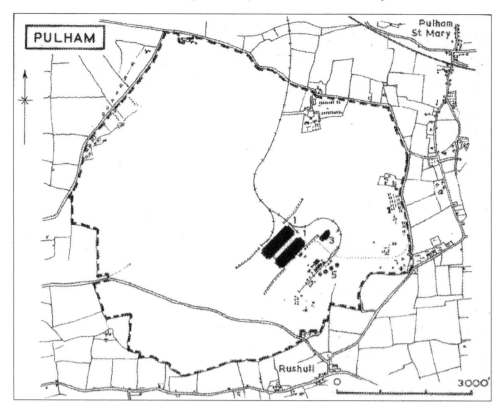

Pulham. The two large sheds for rigid airships were the dominant feature of RNAS Pulham. Next to them was a much smaller Coastal shed. All the sheds' entrances faced the south-west wind. Close by was an extensive complex of gas holders and the buildings in which hydrogen was produced. Like many other airship stations, personnel were housed at the very edge of the station, near a public road. (*Mick Davis*)

The commodore at Lowestoft was of the opinion that all foreign nationals in the district had to be removed as soon as possible. Mr Van Citters had already been investigated the previous year, and the chief constable of Norfolk had vouched for the *émigré*:

> I know this gentleman personally. He is a Dutchman and married to an English Lady. I am certain he is quite above suspicion and thoroughly loyal to the British cause. He was near Pulham Air Station almost before airships were thought of in England.

These findings were forwarded by the Intelligence Division to the commodore responsible for RNAS Pulham. Considerable paranoia was directed against foreign nationals at the outbreak of the war, but was less common by this time.

The weather dealt a blow to the airship station in July, when *C.14A* was damaged while a handling party were attempting to house it in its shed. On a more positive note, two men made successful parachute jumps from Coastal *C.26* on the 17th. Wg

Cdr Maitland had given approval for all officers and crews of Coastal airships to make one optional parachute jump from a height of no less than 1,000 feet a few days earlier. There does not seem to have been great enthusiasm for this opportunity. Experiments with parachutes continued throughout the year, featuring both dummies and men. Eventually, compact cases which could carry parachutes on airships were devised, and several Coastals fitted with them by December. A different type was developed for rigid airships.

The landing ground was visited by aircraft from time to time. An Armstrong Whitworth FK8 bi-plane *A.2730*, from the Royal Flying Corps aerodrome at Narborough, landed on 26 August. It departed again on the 29th, but crashed a mile away from its destination, killing its occupants, 2Lt N. V. Spear and mechanic S. W. Burrel.

In September 1917, experimental work on RNAS airships was transferred to Pulham, which had workshops, a landing ground, and accommodation for experimental airships. This work had previously been undertaken at RNAS Kingsnorth, but was handed over to RNAS Pulham via the Deputy Controller for Armament Production. RNAS Kinsnorth would concentrate on building airships, but experimental work would still be carried out here if it related to their construction.

Construction of the first rigid airship shed was completed in February 1917 and the second shed was almost ready for use by the end of the year. The first rigid airship to be based at RNAS Pulham was *No. 23*, which arrived from RNAS Howden on 30 October. On 13 November, it carried out two speed trials: 51.7 mph was obtained on the first, and 52.3 mph on the second. Instructional flights were also carried out, one of which went to London, via Westminster and Buckingham Palace, on 6 December. This airship had been fitted with parachutes for all the eighteen crew members.

At the beginning of December 1917, RNAS Pulham was set to become one of the principal stations of the airship service; however, this plan was about to receive a major setback. On the morning of the 11th, *C.27* left to patrol an area of sea east of the Norfolk coast. It had a crew of five on board, and was piloted by Flt Lt Dixon. Wireless signals were exchanged between the airship and Pulham for the first two hours of its flight. Contrary to the Second World War—when all the coastline facing Britain was in enemy hands—in the First, the southern part of the North Sea only had a narrow wedge of land under German control in the form of Belgium. They had a seaplane base there at Zeebrugge, Belgium. Three Hansa Brandenburg W-29 floatplanes—one flown by the base commander himself, Oberleutnant (Flt Lt) Friedrich Christiansen—caught sight of *C.17* on the horizon. They intercepted it and one machine-gunned it from above: the envelope caught fire, and *C.17* plunged into the sea, killing all the crew, in spite of their parachutes. One of the German pilots actually managed to capture the last seconds of *C.27* with his camera.

The following day, Flt Lt Kilburn persuaded his superiors to let him search for his best friend, Flt Lt Dixon, the captain of the missing airship in *C.26*, but without success. As the airship was returning home, its engines failed approaching the English coast. Now at the mercy of the winds, it was blown back out to sea, eventually

A vertical aerial view of RNAS Pulham. A large airship is about to enter one of the two rigid airship sheds, adjacent to a small Coastal shed, visible in the lower part of the picture. At the top of the picture are several large gas holders and buildings in which hydrogen was manufactured. (*Picture Norfolk*)

crossing the Dutch coast. It came down near Dordrecht, were its crew jumped out as it approached the ground. As was often the case, the now lightened airship took off again and eventually finished its journey near the Zuiderzee. The following evening, a telegram was received stating that the crew of two officers and three ratings had been interned. The Netherlands at that time was a neutral country. Fears concerning C.27 were confirmed when German newspapers stated that their seaplanes had brought down a British airship. It was consequently decided to cease operating airship patrols over the North Sea from RNAS Pulham; RNAS seaplanes would be used in this role instead.

In February 1918, RNAS Pulham had the following airships on strength: Rigids *No. 23* and *No. 9*; Parseval *No. 6*; Coastal *C.14A*; and Submarine Scout Zero, *S.S.Z.3* and *S.S.35*. A 2-lb gun was mounted on top of the nose of Rigid *No. 23*, and six shells were fired, aimed downwards at the surrounds of the station. Instead of the projectiles embedding in the mud—as was intended—they apparently ricocheted into the surrounding area. Nevertheless, at the end of January the experiment was declared a success. The main drawback was that the gun would have been difficult to fire at elevated targets, such as attacking aircraft. The second rigid airship, *No. 9*, took to the air in February, after extensive repairs. Meanwhile, on the ground, the expansion of RNAS Pulham continued. Warrant officers' quarters, officers' servants' quarters, petty officers' mess and recreation room were all under construction throughout March. Experiments to test the wind flow around the windbreaks for the airship sheds were also undertaken. At one point it was proposed to make the windbreaks for the rigid sheds moveable, using a system of a steel cables in a trench and driven by an electric motor. The idea, presumably, was to adjust the angle of each windbreak to respond to the angle of the prevailing wind, and thereby enhance its effectiveness. This innovative idea was not approved.

Unintentional damage was inflicted on one of Norfolk's historic buildings in April. The commander at Pulham received the following letter from the chapter clerk at Norwich Cathedral:

> On Wednesday morning last about 3.00 a.m. a small airship from Pulham passed over the spire of Norwich Cathedral and it is now found that in so doing some rope suspended from it became entangled with the terminal point of the lightning conductor and wrenched it off. The piece is now in my Office and can be inspected. I shall be glad to hear that the authorities will repair the damage done.

In June 1918, Britain's first rigid airship to fly was dismantled at Pulham to make more space in the airship sheds for newer machines. The remaining airships continued to fly for the remainder of the year, and undertook various experiments. The most dramatic of these involved Rigid *No. 23* being adapted to carry fighter aeroplanes by a system of trapeze and release gear attached to its underside. On 3rd November, the airship took off carrying a Sopwith Camel biplane with a dummy in the pilot's seat. While over open countryside near Pulham, the unmanned aeroplane had its engine started and was successfully released from the mother ship. Although piloted by a dummy, it landed in one piece in a field! These tests were done in conjunction with No. 212 Squadron at Great Yarmouth. Lt Keys participated in the first manned flight on 6th November in another Camel. After his aeroplane was released, it circled around the airship, before landing at Pulham. The Sopwith Camels modified for this role were referred to as 'Ship Camels'. After the Armistice these experiments came to a halt.

November 1918 also saw a new type of airship arrive at Pulham in the form of the Semi-Rigid *S.R.1*. It had been built in Italy, and reached British shores after an eventful flight across France, the only example of this type to serve with the British military. In the months following the end of the war, experimental work continued at Pulham. This, and the fact that it boasted two rigid airship sheds, saved it from immediate closure. Two days before the Armistice was signed, the Pulham-based Rigid *R.26* flew over the Lord Mayor's show in London. On 20 November, *S.R.1* and *No. 23* escorted twenty surrendered German submarines into Harwich Harbour. After completing their task, the two airships were complimented for their work by the officer in charge—to whom they dipped their bows—and flew back to Pulham. The following describes RNAS Pulham's mooring out station.

Hunstanton Mooring Out Station

Location: north coast of Norfolk, on the edge of the Wash.

By the summer of 1918, most airship stations had at least one mooring out station, but this was not the case with Pulham. Plans were drawn up at the end of 1918 to establish a site at Hunstanton the following year, which foresaw two portable airship sheds, two Submarine Scout Twins, and three Submarine Scout Zeros stationed here by the summer of 1919. However, plans for Pulham's mooring out station were abandoned at the war's conclusion.

RNAS Howden Airship Station

Location: 1:50,000 map 105 (SE) 750328. East Riding, Yorkshire, 15 miles south-east of York, and 20 miles west of Hull.
Size: 1,240 acres (within boundaries of 3,100 x 2,600 yards).
Station Complement: forty officers, 612 men (in Jan 1918).
Airship Sheds: two rigid sheds, one 704 feet long and 149 feet wide, with the door opening 101 feet high and 149 feet wide, and one 750 feet long and 2x150 feet wide, with two doors each opening 130 feet high and 150 feet wide; and two Coastal sheds, one 323 feet long and 111 feet wide, with the door opening 80 feet high and 110 feet wide, and one 320 feet long and 110 feet wide, with the door opening 80 feet high and 110 feet wide.
Gas Plant: 'B' silicol (10,000 cubic feet per hour), water gas, four units (14,000 cubic feet per hour).
Gasholders: two of 500,000 cubic feet, two of 250,000 cubic feet each, and one of 20,000 cubic feet.
Based Airships: Rigids *No. 9, No. 23, No. 24, No. 25, R.26, R.27, R.29, R.31,* (post-war) *R.33, R.38, R.80,* and *R.100*; Parseval *No. 4, No. 5, No. 6,* and *No. 7*; Submarine Scout *S.S.9.A*; Submarine Scout Experimental *S.S.E.3*; Submarine Scout Twin *S.S.T.3, S.S.T.4, S.S.T.5, S.S.T.7, S.S.T.9, S.S.T.10, S.S.T.11,* and *S.S.T.12*; Submarine Scout Zero *S.S.Z.23, S.S.Z.31, S.S.Z.32, S.S.Z.33, S.S.Z.38, S.S.Z.54, S.S.Z.55, S.S.Z.62, S.S.Z.63,* and *S.S.Z.64*; Coastal *C.2, C.4, C.11, C.11A, C.19,* and *C.21*; Coastal Star *C*2, C*4, C*9,* and *C*10*; and North Sea *N.S.4, N.S.5, N.S.7, N.S.12,* and *N.S.16*.

The River Humber had four ports, including Hull, used by both merchant ships and the Royal Navy. The high concentration of vessels waiting to access the ports made its estuary an attractive hunting ground for German submarines. In August 1915, two naval lieutenants, Burke and Flower, were sent to reconnoitre the area for a suitable site for an airship station. Much of the land through which the Humber flowed was flat and dissected by streams, ditches, and drainage channels, so the two officers had some difficulty in deciding on a satisfactory location. But in early September 1915, an area 3 miles to the north of the small market town of Howden was selected. Within the same month the necessary land had been requisitioned by the state.

Unlike some parts of Yorkshire—where hundreds of industrial chimneys presented a major problem for early aviators—Howden was an agricultural area with few hazards for low-flying airships. The initial site was some 400 acres in size, but by 1918 it had extended to 1,124 acres. It lay north of Howden village, mainly on the east side of Bubwith Road, and appears to have expanded as far west as Brindley's Plantation and far enough south to include part of Spaldington Common. Hall Farm and Mount Pleasant Farm formed its eastern and northern boundaries respectively. Another reason for building an airship station here was its close proximity to the North-Eastern Railway line from Selby to Hull. A single track branch line was laid from the main line at North Howden Junction, extending 1½ miles to the edge of the site. It was initially used to transport construction materials, with work on the station underway by the end of 1915.

Although far from complete, the station was commissioned on 15 March 1916. Three months later its first airship, Coastal *C.11*, arrived. Around the same time, *C.4* arrived by rail for assembly at the station. One of the airship sheds was just about complete, but only the north-east door could be used. The framework of the second Coastal airship had been erected by July, when the construction of rigid airship shed No. 1, by A. Findlay & Co., was in progress, with nearly a quarter of the roof finished. By the end of the year, the whole structure had been completed.

The two Coastal airship sheds were positioned in front of the rigid shed on the north-east end, so that they could protect it from unfavourable winds. In addition, projecting from each Coastal shed was a 700-foot-long windbreak made of steel framing. The completed railway branch line crossed the length of the base before terminating next to the complex of airship sheds. The huts for the ratings were mostly in use by the summer, but the mess rooms were still not ready. The newly-built silicol plant was reported to be giving a lot of trouble, with an explosion taking place on 23 July 1916.

The two Coastals made numerous flights over British military camps and anti-aircraft defences in their first month of operation, presumably to familiarise the personnel with their craft, so they would not be mistaken for Zeppelins. On the evening of 18 July, both of the airships were heading up the Humber towards their home base when they encountered thunderstorm clouds. Coastal *C.11* suddenly rose to 1,800 feet, despite the fact that its nose was pointing downwards at the maximum angle possible, with full power applied. When *C.11* reached RNAS Howden, the landing party grabbed the trail rope, but there was a sudden change in the wind direction and the airship began to drift away. It eventually dropped to the ground with some force, but by 9.30 p.m. was safely back in its shed. *C.4*, which had been following closely, was hurled to 1,200 feet by a strong up-current under the storm cloud. As the storm continued, heavy rain deluged the airship to such an extent that it became necessary to jettison 300 lbs of water ballast and 40 gallons of petrol. Then, as the airship descended towards the landing ground, the engine failed due to a faulty petrol pump. It just cleared one of the windbreaks, but then was brought under control by the landing party and touched down, none the worse for its experience.

Flying was hampered by frequent thunderstorms in August, and the hydrogen plant was still not functioning, causing a shortage of gas. Coastal *C.11* carried out two landings at Atwick as a demonstration for the Army. The landing party consisted of a company from the Durham Light Infantry, and this was the first time that most of the soldiers had seen an airship. An anti-aircraft gun and searchlights arrived at RNAS Howden, probably in response to a Zeppelin raid which had taken place a few days earlier. Airship crews were given instruction on machine-gun firing, and various methods tried to simulate a moving airborne target—the crew of *C.11* tested their marksmanship by firing at flocks of pigeons whilst on patrol. By the summer of 1916, electric lighting generated by two Campbell oil engines installed in the power house was supplied to parts of RNAS Howden. On 23 August, *C.15* and *C.16* landed to refuel while on their way to RNAS East Fortune. Airships would in future often use RNAS Howden as a staging post while on delivery flights to stations in Scotland.

The doors of the north Coastal shed were still giving trouble in September. As a consequence, *C.4* and *C.19* were housed in the south shed, although it was still in the final stages of construction. A Jeffrey lorry was employed to tow the airships in and out of the shed. At most other stations this was done by the handling party without the assistance of any machinery. The guy-ropes were attached to the lorry by means of a bridle and the airship riding head to the wind being transported on it. Just before entering the shed, the guys were tightened up; a snatch block was also fitted to the lorry so that it could be used as a landing block when airships were landing away from the usual site.

By the end of 1916, the complement was twenty-five officers and 467 men, including 139 men of the Air Construction Corps. Further Coastal airships, such as *C.19* and *C.21*, were now on strength. The first example of a Parseval airship was delivered in December: its 312-feet long envelope made it the largest non-rigid class of airship to serve with the RNAS. With four Coastals on strength in early 1917, more frequent patrols could now be flown over the Humber Estuary. It became common policy not to send more than two airships out on patrol at a time; although this reduced flying hours, it was hoped that it would allow more continuous patrols to be kept up. The rear admiral commanding the east coast endorsed a suggestion put to him on how to increase the efficiency of the patrols: this involved patrolling airships from RNAS Howden to proceed to either RNAS Pulham or RNAS East Fortune without returning to the station. They would remain there until a suitable mission required their return. The reverse would apply to airships based at the other two stations. The advantage of this scheme was that patrols could be carried out when the wind direction made it difficult to carry out an 'out and home' mission, and it was more practicable for an airship to proceed directly to a station downwind. The pilots would also be acquainted with a larger portion of the coast. The commanders of the airship stations were generally in favour of this proposal, but it was pointed out that there was no accommodation available for additional airships at RNAS East Fortune.

RNAS Howden's first rigid airship—*No. 9*—arrived on 4 April 1917. It was used initially for instructional flights for officers and crews. The first serious accident occurred on the 23rd, when *C.11*, piloted by Flt Lt Hogg, encountered low cloud near

One of the two Coastal sheds at RNAS Howden, August 1917. The silicol gas plant is visible to the right of the shed. The housing for personnel is further up the road. (*The Fleet Air Arm Museum*)

The No. 9, Britain's first rigid airship to take to the air, at RNAS Howden in April 1917. During its stay here it carried out a number of instructional flights for personnel based at this station. (*The Fleet Air Arm Museum*)

Scarborough upon returning from a patrol over the North Sea. As the airship headed overland towards RNAS Howden, the crew suddenly glimpsed a hill looming through the mist. The pilot began to take evasive action, but the controls were slow to respond, and the complete rear section of the car—including the engine, the engineer in his seat, and all the valve controls—were torn away. Now greatly lightened, the crippled airship rapidly ascended to a height of 3,000 feet. The gas valves jammed, causing the pressure to rise rapidly, and tearing off a patch in the envelope. As the gas escaped, *C.11* began buckling up in the air, and it headed back to earth at an alarming rate. Flt Lt Hogg broke his legs in the crash, as did his coxswain. The wireless operator sustained internal injuries, while the engineer who had been thrown out earlier landed on Scarborough Racecourse, around half a mile from the main crash site, with only a broken arm, and had managed to stagger to a post office in the suburb of Falsgrave. He had no money with him, and the post mistress needed some persuasion before he could send a telegram to RNAS Howden.

When airships underwent major reconstruction, the designation 'A' was usually added to their number. No sooner was Coastal *C.11A* back in the air on a trial flight over the Humber, when disaster struck again. The airship had been in the air for about 50 minutes when it became very 'heavy'; despite ballast being dropped and full power applied, its descent could not be halted. It fell into the River Humber, the car was submerged and seconds later the envelope burst into flames. Two officers—the second coxswain and the wireless telegraph operator—were trapped under the water and drowned, but the first coxswain and the engineer managed to escape from the car and reach the surface. They were rescued by a Mr Higham and his son, who swam out to the downed airship.

In June, Rigid *No. 9* carried out a ten-hour patrol over the North Sea. The following month, it remained airborne for close to 27 hours, and covered a distance of 430 miles. At that time it was a record for a British rigid airship. On 25 October, *No. 9* left for Cranwell, but was forced to return to Howden at the end of the month because of bad weather. It was seriously damaged while being taken into the shed, and was out of commission for the rest of the year. On the 29th, Rigid *No. 23* called at RNAS Howden while *en route* to Pulham. It departed ten days later. Previously, on the 14th, Rigid *No. 25* had arrived from its manufacturers, Armstrong Whitworth, who had their works a short distance to the west of Howden. Acceptance trials were carried out on 23 December the Hornsea Mere was used for bombing trials.

In the course of 1917, several more Parseval airships arrived. They were built by Vickers at Walney Island and then shipped here for assembly and trial flights. Their main role would be to train crews for rigid airships. In May, Parseval *No. 6* carried out trials and a further six-hour trial flight was made in June. Because this airship lacked lift, it was principally employed in night flying: on one occasion in July, it carried out a patrol of 16 hours; two special night flights were also made for testing anti-aircraft defences. On 6 August, it departed for RNAS Cranwell, where it was to be used for training purposes. The sole example of the Submarine Scout to be based at RNAS Howden was *S.S.9A*, which was sent here for experimental purposes. While returning from a patrol on 4 December, its engine failed and it had to make a forced landing,

MAY 11ᵗʰ/17

Above: An aerial view of RNAS Howden in May 1917. The rigid shed has Coastal sheds on either side. Construction of the second rigid shed had not yet commenced. (*The Fleet Air Arm Museum*)

Right: The R.23 inside the rigid shed at RNAS Howden. (*The RAF Museum*)

but suffered only slight damage. The Annual Report on airship stations for 1917 states:

> The greatest amount of patrol and escort work as in the previous year was carried out by the Coastal Airships. Long hours were put in, in all conditions of weather and on the whole these ships may be said to have exceeded expectations.

At the end of the year, RNAS Howden was staffed by forty officers and 612 men. The windbreak on the north Coastal shed was extended, and was experimentally covered with expanded metal instead of corrugated iron. Also, the spaces at the bottom of the windbreaks were filled in with brushwood, which enhanced their effectiveness. The tests proved very satisfactory, as no suction was caused and eddies were reduced. It was found that when the wind blew from certain directions, the windbreaks at airship stations actually increased wind turbulence, making it difficult to house the airships.

By the beginning of 1918, construction had commenced on the second rigid shed, designed and constructed by Sir William Arrol & Co.. It covered 8½ acres, was 750 feet long, and was built principally of steel and partly of timber. At the end of the war, the pace of construction slowed and it was not finished until 1 April 1919. It had the distinction of being the largest airship shed to be built in Britain, excluding the partially built example at Flookburgh.

Coastal-class airships were still flying most of the anti-submarine patrols early in 1918. On 23 January 1918, *C.19* was sent to investigate a report of an attack by an enemy surface craft, but when it arrived over the sea, a dense fog covered the surface. A further report was received of a submarine on the surface off the Yorkshire Coast, and the pilot altered course to intercept it. On arrival at the last reported position, visibility was very poor, so the airship circled over the area. A gap finally appeared in the fog, and a light grey submarine could be seen steering north-west. The airship headed at full speed towards it, but as it closed in, the submarine dived. Two 100-lb bombs were dropped: one fell short, but the second caused a quantity of air to surface. *C.19* remained in the vicinity for half an hour but nothing further was seen.

On 21 March 1918, Coastal *C.4* was informed that a surfaced submarine was attacking merchant ships off Flamborough. The airship set course and opened up both engines to full power. Five miles off the coast, a dark grey submarine was seen about ¼ mile away. As *C.4* approached, it submerged but was still visible underwater. The airship dropped a 100-lb bomb, which exploded about 3 feet astern; a second bomb was dropped, and exploded with a direct hit on the stern of the submarine which rose towards the surface and rolled. The submarine appears to have survived the encounter with *C.4*, for a cargo ship reported a short time later that a torpedo had been launched at it, but that it had missed.

New Submarine Scout Zeros began to arrive to replace the Coastals for patrol work. By April 1918, *S.S.Z.31*, *S.S.Z.32*, and *S.S.Z.33* had been delivered. A small number of Coastal Stars were delivered to RNAS Howden around the same time. On 10 May, *C*4* escorted a south-bound convoy of forty ships. The same airship protected two convoys on the 25th, the first composed of thirty ships, five drifters, and two torpedo boat destroyers, and the second of thirty ships, six drifters, and a pair of destroyers. In May, the following based airships all notched up many hours in the air: Rigid *R.26*; Parseval *P.5*; Coastal Star *C*2* and *C*4*; Coastal *C.4*; and Submarine Scout Zero *S.S.Z.23*, *S.S.Z.31*, *S.S.Z.32*, *S.S.Z.33*, *S.S.Z.38*, *S.S.Z.54*, *S.S.Z.62*, *S.S.Z.63*, and *S.S.Z.64*.

In July 1918, numerous thunderstorms hindered the amount of flying that could be undertaken by RNAS Howden's airships. The armament officer for the station, Maj. Alderson, died that month from pneumonia after a bout of influenza. In the summer months, the first members of the Women's Auxiliary Air Force began arriving at Howden, as well as other airship stations across the country. They were housed in their own accommodation on the west side. Howden managed to escape the fate of most other airship stations after the end of the war, on the basis that it had a large rigid shed in the final stages of construction, which was able to house recently completed machines such as *R.33* and *R.34*.

As the huge twin-berthed airship shed took shape, disaster struck the No. 1 shed. On 16 August 1918, it not only housed the Rigid *R.27*, but a number of smaller machines including *S.S.Z.38*, *S.S.Z.54*, and a new unnumbered *S.S.Z.* type. In addition there was *S.S.Z.23*, which had been packed for delivery to the US Navy. An American crew were working on the unnumbered *S.S.Z.* airship, which they had built from spare parts and were intending to present to their British colleagues. As they were applying the finishing touches, the wireless telegraph operator began checking his equipment. Most messages sent at that time were transmitted in Morse code, which involved tapping a metal key, and thus sometimes generated sparks—petrol fumes in the airship's car were immediately ignited by just such a spark, and within no time, the inside of the airship shed was an inferno, and a hole blown in the roof by the exploding gases. Much of the internal air pressure was relieved because one of the main doors had been left open. However, the explosion flaps failed to work, and as a result, all subsequent sheds were built without them. A man, who was on look-out duty in the observation tower on the roof, attempted to run down the stairs, but was tragically seared to death. All the airships in the shed were consumed by the flames.

The damage done to Howden's rigid shed in August would indirectly lead to the loss of a second Rigid, the *R.31*, which had recently been completed by Shorts Brothers at Cardington. Unusually, its framework was wooden, rather than metallic. On 6 November 1918, it departed Cardington for East Fortune; on the journey, some of the wooden girders began to fracture and it made an emergency landing at Howden. As the second rigid airship was under construction and not ready for use, *R.31* was housed in the damaged rigid shed. Although most of the roof steelwork in this shed was not seriously damaged by the previous hydrogen fire, the hole in the roof had not been repaired, so as the *R.31* lay there month after month, rainwater dripped down onto her, causing the glue which held the wooden structure together to soften and the airship to begin to literally fall apart. A Court of Inquiry was held early in 1919, but no one present could explain why this airship was still at Howden. It was decided to

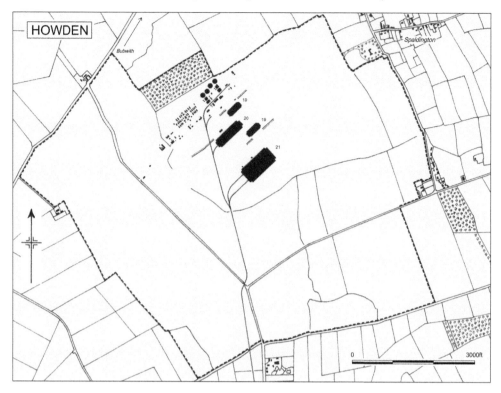

Howden, *c.* 1919. RNAS Howden was one of the largest airship stations in Britain. The plan shows what it when the large double rigid airship shed was completed. The other large building is also a rigid airship shed, completed at the end of 1916, with a large windbreak on its western side. The two smaller Coastal sheds at the opposite end provided protection from the wind for the other entrance. A railway line running across the station terminated at the gas plant, with a siding extending into the double rigid shed. (*Mike Davis*)

dismantle *R.31*, and its remains were sold for firewood. Unfortunately, it was later found that the wood had been fireproofed and did not burn.

Mooring-out sites for RNAS Howden were Gosforth Park, Lowthorpe, and Kirkleatham.

Gosforth Park Mooring Out Station

Location: 1:50,000 map 88 (NZ) 247707. North of Newcastle-upon-Tyne city centre and immediately north of the suburb of Gosforth.

Established in 1917, this was probably the first mooring out site on mainland Britain, since most other sites were not commissioned until 1918. The practice was for airships to land here at night at the end of a patrol, moor out, then return to RNAS Howden at dawn the next day. The airships were moored in the open, secured to a landing block or a Jeffrey lorry, and a supply of gas and petrol was stored here. Whilst moored at

Gosforth, *C.19* broke her propeller, which pierced the envelope a number of times. The Coastal rapidly lost pressure and the tail lurched upwards, breaking off the after-skid and three struts. The airship was deflated to prevent further damage being done to the car. This sub-station was closed on 1 October 1917, because the soldiers who assisted with the mooring of airships were moved from the district.

Lowthorpe Mooring Out Station

Location: 1:50,000 map 101 (TA) 070610. East Riding, Yorkshire, between Bridlington and Great Driffield.

This mooring out station was commissioned on 6 May 1918. Two berths were carved out of Church Wood, close to Lowthorpe Village, and the landing ground was a field of buttercups. American Ensign Phil Barnes wrote to his parents that he had [5] 'landed in England upon a field of gold'.[5] Lowthorpe was only a few minutes' flying time from the sea, being close to Bridlington Bay—RNAS Howden, on the other hand, was situated far inland, 30 miles from the North Sea, greatly reducing the time an airship could spend on patrol. In April 1918, the first airships to arrive here were *S.S.Z.32* and *S.S.Z.38*, one of which was captained by Lt George Meager.

Very few records which directly relate to the mooring out sites survive, as paperwork was usually the preserve of the parent station. However, Lt George Meager devoted a chapter of his book, *My Airship Flights 1915–1930*, to his time at Howden's mooring out sites. He was later promoted to captain, and served aboard the *R.100*. While he was giving ground crew ten-minute flights over Lowthorpe on 19 May 1918, when another airship, *S.S.Z.23*, came into land and momentarily distracted his attention. He failed to notice a clump of trees on the north-east side of the landing ground, making contact with the branches and badly damaging the control car. The envelope deflated, and the airship returned to Howden.

The entrance to Lowthorpe Woods was narrow, which made it hazardous for airships moving into their berths in strong winds. In such conditions, they could often not land, and had to fly on to Howden. *S.S.Z.54* got caught in the trees at the entrance while being walked out for her first patrol and had to be deflated. After this, the entrance was made more funnel-shaped by the additional felling of trees. The minimum duration of the patrols flown from here was 9 to 10 hours. One flight made by Lt Barnes in *S.S.Z.23* lasted nearly 26 hours, a record at the time for this type of airship. On one occasion, Lt Meager landed at the new RAF aerodrome at Driffield to take its CO, his friend Capt. Harold Balfour, up in his airship. Balfour was renowned for his low-level flying in Sopwith Camels, and Meager wanted to impress him with some low-level airship flying. He flew down the main street of Driffield at around 20 feet above the roof tops. On returning to the Driffield, the airship cut the aerodrome's telephone wires, much to the delight of its passengers. Later that day, two officers from the Royal Engineers at Driffield arrived at the mooring out station requesting that they be taken up in an airship, having missed the earlier flight. George Meager obliged, just clearing the chapel spire and at one point flying through a gap in a hedge—more telephone wires were severed.

Two portable airship sheds were intended for construction here by 1 July 1919, each 175 feet long, 50 feet wide, and 55 feet high. Although the main accommodation was in bell tents, there were also a few wooden huts in Church Wood. The planned complement was two S.S.T. and two S.S.Z. airships. These plans were not implemented, however, and the site abandoned. The landscape in the early twenty-first century is much as it was when airships flew from here—a mix of woodland and open fields. In the 1920s, fresh trees were planted at the edge of the woods, removing the last traces of the mooring out site.

Kirkleatham Mooring Out Station

Location: O. S. 1/50,000 map 94 (NZ) 590220. Cleveland, near the mouth of the River Tees, immediately south of Redcar.

Kirkleatham was officially commissioned on 4 June 1918, as a base for Submarine Scout Zero airships. Unlike many other mooring out sites, it was not in a wood but to the lee of a wood. Airships were simply moored to screw pickets under the shelter of a belt of high trees. There was no opening through which to take the airships in and out of the clearing. In June, S.S.Z.62 was damaged in a gale while moored here. A few days later, on the night of the 21st, George Meager—the CO at the site—had his airship S.S.Z.55 damaged in a storm and flown back to Howden for repair. Early in July, Meager escorted a convoy from Whitby to the mouth of the Tyne while operating from Kirkleatham. Like almost all other mooring out stations, Kirkleatham had no airship sheds, and all maintenance had to be done in the open. On one occasion, an engineer used a ladder to climb up onto the envelope of an S.S.Z. airship to change a valve. While on top, the envelope suddenly gave way, trapping him inside with only hydrogen to breathe. The engineer managed to cut his way out of the bottom of the envelope, by which time he was almost unconscious. Envelopes had a much shorter life-span at mooring out stations, as a result of exposure to the elements and puncture by tree branches while being handled in their berths. One portable airship shed—175 feet long and 50 feet wide—was allocated here for the summer of 1919, as were two S.S.T.s and three S.S.Z.s. The end of the war put paid to these plans. Kirkleatham, however, was listed as a mooring out site for Cramlington in the RAF monthly Lists of Units and Stations for early 1919. In June of that year, it was still officially a mooring out site under direct control of NW Area.

In 1917, an ambitious programme of new rigid airship bases was proposed to the War Staff of the Admiralty: building large sheds both in Northumberland and North Yorkshire. A lack of funds and shortage of raw materials ensured that such ideas never materialised, but a modest plan was approved to create three additional stations from which anti-submarine patrols could be flown by the smaller non-rigid airships—these were Killeagh (Ireland), Moreton, and Cramlington. The conflict ended before any of them could become operational.

RNAS Cramlington Airship Station

Alternative name: 'Newcastle'.

Location: O. S. 1/50,000 map 88 (NZ) 254782. Northumberland, 9 miles north-east of Newcastle-upon-Tyne.

Size: 57 acres (within boundaries of 870 x 680 yards), excluding the landing area.

While some aerodromes—such as East Fortune—doubled up as airship bases, a new site was selected for the operation of airships, as opposed to using the already established RFC landing ground. RNAS Cramlington was positioned immediately to the north-east of the aerodrome, with the Great North Eastern railway separating the two.

RNAS Cramlington's single Coastal shed was painted a shade of brown. No windbreaks were built to accompany it, although it lay in a fairly exposed position. The station's complement was to be twenty officers and 281 men to operate four Submarine Scout Twins. The conflict ceased before any airships were permanently based here; in 1929, the airship shed was used briefly by a civilian airship.

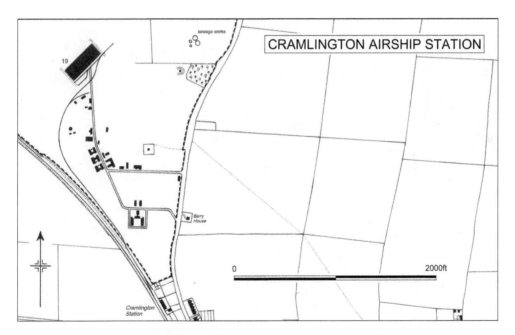

Cramlington. Construction of the Cramlington airship station, north of Newcastle, commenced in 1918, but the end of hostilities made it redundant. The London–Edinburgh railway ran along the southern edge of the site with a siding leading to the airship shed. On the opposite side of the mainline railway was Cramlington Aerodrome. (*Mick Davis*)

6

RNAS Airship Stations in Wales

Akin to Scotland, there were few Royal Navy facilities in Wales in the Victorian era. Two of three major train ferries, which carried mail and passengers to Ireland across the Irish Sea, left from Welsh ports—Fishguard in the south and Holyhead in the north. Although sections of the Irish population were hostile to the British, over 200,000 Irish men fought in Britain's armed services in the First World War; and the only way of transporting them to the Front was by sea, often on the ferry boats that plied the crossings. To safeguard these important shipping links, two airship stations went under construction in Wales as early as 1915. The first was on the Island of Anglesey where, many centuries before, the Druids made their last stand against the armies of Rome.

RNAS Anglesey Airship Station

Alternative names: 'Llangefni', 'Bodfordd', and 'Gwalchmai'—after hamlets in the vicinity of the base.
Location: O. S. 1/50,000 map 114 (SH) 437768. Isle of Anglesey, 12 miles south-east of Holyhead, and 8 miles north-west of Caernarvon.
Size: 242 acres (within boundaries of 1,600 x 1,200 yards).
Station Complement: eighteen officers, 157 men (in Jan 1918).
Airship Sheds: Submarine Scout shed (302 feet long, 70 feet wide, and 50 feet high).
Gas plant: silicol water gas plant (5,000 cubic feet per hour).
Gas holders: one (10,000 cubic feet).
Gas tanks: eight tanks (each of 8,000 cubic feet).
Based airships: Parseval *No. 4*; Submarine Scout *S.S.18*, *S.S.22*, *S.S.24*, and *S.S.25*; Submarine Scout Pusher *S.S.P.1*, *S.S.P.5*, and *S.S.P.6*; Submarine Scout Zero *S.S.Z.31*, *S.S.Z.33*, *S.S.Z.34*, *S.S.Z.35*, *S.S.Z.50*, *S.S.Z.51*, *S.S.Z.72*, and *S.S.Z.73*.

RNAS Anglesey was commissioned on 26 September 1915. As was often the case, it was located close to a railway—the branch line to Amlwch, off the mainline to Holyhead. It was built in an area of low-lying ground, surrounded by undulating landscape on all sides. Three miles to the east was the small market town of Llangefni,

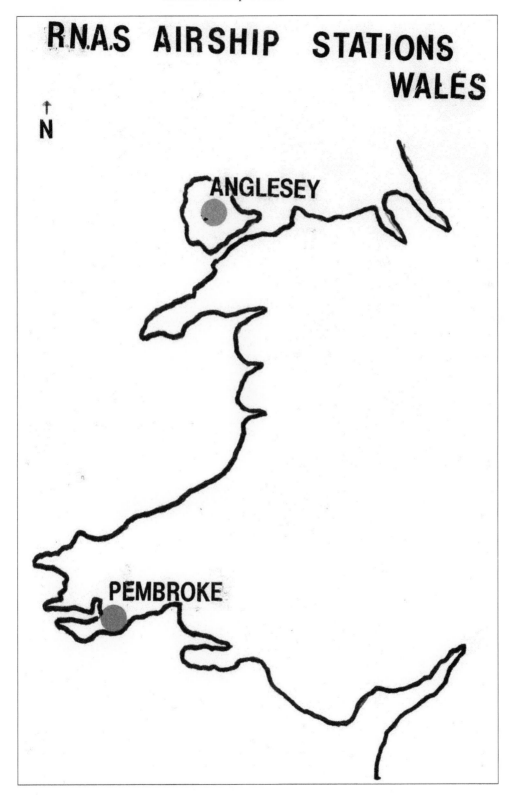

RNAS airship stations in Wales. (*Author's collection*)

'church on the River Cefni', with a population of around 1,700. When the base was constructed, dislocation of the local inhabitants was minimal. Small holdings within its boundary were generally left intact and fields near its boundary were grazed by livestock as airships flew overhead.

The first commander of RNAS Anglesey was Maj. G. H. Scott, who became the Deputy Director of Airship Development and commanded the *R.34* on its crossing of the Atlantic in 1919. He later perished in the *R.101* crash. In addition to escorting the passenger and mail boats sailing to Dublin, RNAS Anglesey's airships patrolled the central part of the Irish Sea—from the Isle of the Man in the north to Bardsey Island in the south—and the mouth of the River Mersey. Large numbers of merchant ships rounded the island of Anglesey on the final stage of their voyage to Liverpool, then one of the largest ports in the world. The waters to the north were under the protection of airships based at RNAS Luce Bay, and to the south covered by RNAS Pembroke.

In late September 1915, Submarine Scout S.S.18 was the first airship to arrive here, by rail. It first flew on 26th September. By 5 November 1915, Submarine Scouts *S.S.22*, *S.S.24*, and *S.S.25* had also arrived. In a biography of Ernest Johnston, *Airship Navigator*, RNAS Anglesey at this time is described as 'a cluster of creosoted weatherboard huts nestling in the lee of a large airship shed on the edge of a wide, desolate field'.[1]

The Submarine Scout B-shed at RNAS Pembroke in the final stages of construction, *c.* early 1916. (*The Fleet Air Arm Museum*)

Submarine Scout *S.S.24* in flight over RNAS Pembroke. *S.S.42A* is in the background, being handled by its ground party. (*The Fleet Air Arm Museum*)

RNAS Pembroke viewed from the north-west. The camp extends along the road leading to the two airship sheds. There are large windbreaks either side of each shed. (*The Fleet Air Arm Museum*)

RNAS Anglesey was still under construction in the winter of 1915–16. There was no operational gas plant, so low pressure hydrogen cylinders had to be used. Great difficulty was experienced in moving them into position due to the muddy state of the ground. By February 1916, the airship shed had been completed at a cost of £19,220; it was protected by four windbreaks, each 160 feet long and 40 feet high. Almost as soon as the shed was completed, the doors refused to work properly—these were the Achilles heel of these structures. Even though the construction of huge buildings to house airships was a major undertaking in itself, it was made even more demanding by the need to have huge moving doors at either end, sometimes weighing hundreds of tonnes. In the case of the Anglesey airship shed, one of the small rail wheels supporting the door had broken in half and the door could not be closed. A makeshift repair was undertaken it was necessary to rig a canvas screen across the entrance. These doors were still giving problems many months later. The total cost of the station was £58,700.

Enemy action was at a low ebb during this winter, so airship crews practised their bombing skills on the nearby landing ground, where a dummy target the same size and shape as a submarine would be laid out. The airships used 16-lb bombs, which made a loud bang but did not do much damage. Capt. Williams, who wrote *Airship Pilot No. 28*, mentions that once when he was dropping bombs on the 'submarine', a sheep walked across the target. A bomb exploded close by, lifting the animal high into the air, but after landing, it walked away, apparently none the worse for wear. The weather in February 1916 was recorded to be poor, and although flights were made as far north as the Isle of Man as possible, flying was only possible on eight days that month. Two airships broke down while on patrol, the first managing to land successfully in a wind of 40 mph, before being deflated while being blown backwards with its engine running at full revs.

Another airship broke down while over the sea and drifted for an hour before putting down on the water. A trawler responded to its distress signals and towed the stricken craft 15 miles to Holyhead. On 22 October 1916, the station suffered its first and only fatal airship accident. While attempting to land, *S.S.18* struck a cow, which dislodged the undercarriage and damaged the car—the animal was not as lucky as the sheep, for it was fatally injured. The airship's observer then either fell or jumped out the airship, resulting in a rapid ascent. *S.S.18* was blown far out to sea, and eventually came down near the Irish coast after the pilot managed to release some gas. The car hit the water with force, splitting in two and throwing out the flight engineer, who drowned, weighed down by heavy flying clothes. The pilot managed to cling to the wreckage until he was picked up by a passing ship.

Before the war was over, several more of RNAS Anglesey's airships suffered similar fates. In 1917, the station received a number of Submarine Scout Pushers to replace their Submarine Scouts. After thirteen months' service here, Submarine Scout Pusher *S.S.P.6* was forced to put down on the Irish Sea because of engine trouble. A passing ship rescued its crew, but before it could be taken in tow, the ailing craft—now relieved of much of its load—rose back into the air and disappeared in a south-easterly direction. After floating across much of Wales and England, it eventually fell back to

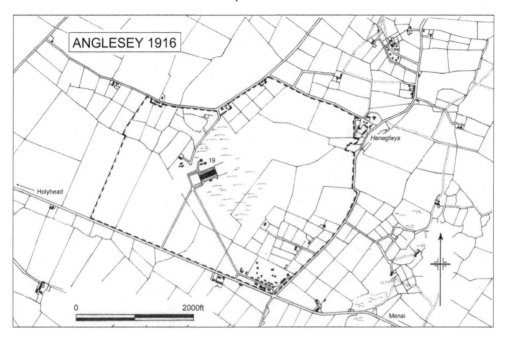

Anglesey, 1916. RNAS Anglesey shortly after it was commissioned. The single Submarine Scout shed stands isolated in a patchwork of small fields used for pasture, some of which are inside the boundary of the station. The huts for the personnel lie some distance away from the airship shed, clustered on the southern edge of the perimeter next to the road to Holyhead. (*Mick Davis*)

An aerial view of RNAS Anglesey (Llangefni) from of 3,000 feet, April 1917. The Submarine Scout shed is in the centre of the picture. Despite its camouflaged paint scheme, the building does not exactly merge with its surroundings. The silicol plant is on the left of the shed. (*The Fleet Air Arm Museum*)

RNAS Anglesey from the south, 1917. In the foreground are the accommodation huts for personnel. Beyond it is the airship shed with two airships on the landing area; one of them is Submarine Scout Zero *S.S.Z.51*. Small fields are enclosed within the boundary of the station. (*The Fleet Air Arm Museum*)

earth in a wood near Chichester, Sussex, from where it was salvaged by personnel from the airship mooring out station at RNAS Slindon. *S.S.P.6* was repaired and returned to service at RNAS Anglesey. On 12 April 1918, it was dispatched to RNAS Cranwell to take up a training role there, but it never arrived. The engine failed, and it was forced to make an emergency landing near Blackburn, Lancashire, and was severely damaged.

S.S.Z.35 had an equally chequered career. On Friday 26 April 1918, it was patrolling the approaches to the port of Liverpool in the company of several other airships. They were providing escort to an inbound convoy, after which they were to guard a troopship sailing for Ireland. *S.S.Z.35* was sent to investigate a report of a submarine near Formby lightship. Just as the crew spotted the tell-tale signs of oil and bubbles on the surface, the airship's engine failed and it was forced to put down 32 miles off the coast. The crew were quickly rescued and their airship towed by a trawler to Llandudno Bay, where it was beached in front of crowds of curious onlookers. Emergency repairs were carried out by a party from Anglesey, assisted by the local fire brigade. In the evening, *S.S.Z.35* managed to make it back to its base. Later in the year, on 17 October 1918, the airship was lost at sea when it suffered a tear in its envelope, and it eventually sank 15 miles north-west of Holyhead. Fortunately, the crew was saved.

Despite the efforts of RN Anglesey's crews, numerous merchant ships were sunk by German submarines off the northern coast of Wales. Convoy escort was an important task, and the Submarine Scout airships would guard departing Liverpool convoys sailing south through the Irish Sea. Once it reached the Skerries, the convoy would become the responsibility of RNAS Pembroke's airships. On certain occasions, Anglesey's airships would make a round trip much further south and land at RNAS Pembroke, where they would refuel. Conversely, the Coastal airships from RNAS Pembroke would rendezvous with a convoy at Wexford heading north, and once relieved of their responsibility, would head for RNAS Anglesey, where they would refuel or await an outbound convoy. One such mission was related in the Daily Airship Report on 2 April 1918:

> S.S.Z.51. 5.30 a.m. Left Base. 8.15 a.m. W.N.W. Holyhead Harbour. Sighted large cargo ship W.N.W. and escorted her until 9.25 a.m. W.N.W. Holyhead. 8.45 a.m. Fired Lewis Gun (practice). 9.10 a.m. Sighted Irish Mail course east. 10.00 a.m. W.N.W. Holyhead. Sighted troopship *Mauritania* escorted by 4 American destroyers, Nos. 25, 50, 68 and another steering east. Escorted this convoy until 12.00 p.m. 10°N Puffin Island. Sighted a large convoy steering west. 6 large cargo steamers escorted by 2 A.P. vessels and British destroyers Nos. H.C.1, H.C.5, H.17 and H.19 escorted until 1.00 p.m. 3°N Lynus Point. 2.00 p.m. Landed. *S.S.Z.51* then took off again at 5.45 p.m. with a new crew. Visibility at that time was above 32 miles. The airship went in search of a submarine reported twelve miles north of the Skerries. Later at 7.05 p.m., an eastbound convoy was escorted with *S.S.Z.51* returning to RNAS Anglesey at 8.30 p.m. It hit the ground heavily, the propeller tore the envelope necessitating immediate deflation.

In 1918, RNAS Anglesey's airships had several encounters with suspected enemy submarines. At that time the station had the following craft flying patrols: Submarine Scout Pusher *S.S.P.1*, *S.S.P.5*, and *S.S.P.6*; Submarine Scout *S.S.25*; and Submarine Scout Zero *S.S.Z.50* and *S.S.Z.51*. A streamlined patch of oil was spotted by the crews of *S.S.Z.34* and *S.S.Z.35* 8 miles off Amlwch, then bubbles of oil were observed coming to the surface. Two 230-lb bombs and one 100 lb bomb were dropped, after which a trawler dropped depth charges, and some wreckage was seen. Bubbles of oil continued to rise to the surface. Some time later, *S.S.Z.34* was patrolling the mail route from Kingstown, Ireland, to Holyhead when it caught sight of what appeared to be a periscope. It dropped a 100-lb bomb, but this failed to explode; nonetheless, the airship crew heard a distinctive clang. A second 230-lb bomb was then dropped and exploded on an object close to the surface, lifting the airship from an altitude of 1,200 feet to 2,000 feet. With fog closing in, nothing further was seen of the suspected enemy submarine.

The following month, *S.S.Z.50* was investigating a reported sighting of a submarine on May 4, 10 miles north of Holyhead. It came across a suspicious patch of water and signalled for *S.S.Z.34* to come and assist. Both airships dropped bombs on a very dark brown object travelling under the water so cruised over the area until darkness fell, but nothing further was observed. *S.S.Z.50* landed back at base at 11.30 p.m. On 10 May 1918, *S.S.Z.34* saw a suspicious object 8 miles west-north-west of South Stack. It dropped a 230-lb bomb which exploded without visible effect on the object. An armed trawler arrived, shelled it, and then proceeded to ram it. *S.S.Z.34* then opened fire with its Lewis gun. Upon closer examination by the trawler, the target turned out to be a buoy!

A submarine was reported in the vicinity of the Skerries on 17 May 1918. *S.S.Z.50* was sent the next day to investigate and dropped a bomb on a moving oil patch. It was joined by *S.S.Z.35* and a destroyer. A search was made of the area, but nothing further was seen. The following day, surfacing oil bubbles to the south-west of Caernarfon Bay Light were observed by *S.S.Z.51*. A destroyer was called in to investigate and a periscope was seen. The airship climbed to a height of 1,400 feet and dropped a bomb on a dark shadow beneath the surface. Large quantities of oil rose up. A US navy ship then dropped multiple depth charges. Two more American destroyers and two patrol boats arrived and dropped more depth charges.

S.S.Z.34 spotted oil bubbles 15 miles to the north-west of Bardsey Island on 28 May. A destroyer dropped depth charges and more bubbles came to the surface. The previous day, the same airship had had a similar encounter 5 miles south-east of Carnarvon Bay Lightship. On 5 June, *S.S.Z.50*'s crew caught sight of a submarine, some 200 feet long and painted light grey, about a mile away. The submarine opened fire with four rounds in quick succession; the airship's Lewis gun was brought into action, and the submarine fired about eight more rounds. The airship was astern and chasing at full speed when the submarine suddenly submerged. A 230-lb bomb was dropped ahead of the swirl, but there was no further sign of the submarine. While on patrol on 27 June, *S.S.Z.35* observed a wake in the sea and followed it for 4 miles. The wake suddenly stopped and air bubbles were seen rising to the surface. The airship dropped a large bomb which failed to explode, so armed yacht *Vanessa* was summoned to the spot to investigate.

RNAS Anglesey's airships detected few traces of enemy submarines after late June, although they remained active in the Irish Sea up until the end of the war. In 1917, Submarine Scout *S.S.33*, in conjunction with an armed launch from Holyhead, carried out trials with an early version of sonar. It involved unravelling a long cable with a hydrophone attached from the airship into the sea. These experiments produced encouraging results and were continued into the following year, but the war ended before this invention could be used operationally. Like with several other airship stations, planes were deployed to RNAS Anglesey to assist the airships with the anti-submarine patrols. They flew what were often referred to as 'Scarecrow Patrols', the main purpose of which was to deter enemy submarine attacks by their appearance alone. The idea was that upon seeing a plane, an enemy craft would submerge, inhibiting its ability to attack shipping.

On 7 November 1917, six Airco DH.4s of 19TS Hounslow left Hendon for RNAS Anglesey. The two-seat bombers encountered bad weather over North Wales so four of them turned back and diverted to Shotwick Aerodrome. One landed on Lavan Sands and was destroyed by the incoming tide, despite attempts to pull it clear using farm horses. The final plane pressed on and attempted to land at RNAS Anglesey, but was caught by a strong wind and crashed, killing the pilot and seriously injuring the observer.

Despite twenty-nine more ships being sunk in RNAS Anglesey's patrol area over the next four months, the next deployment of planes was not made until the following summer. June 1918 saw the arrival of DH.6 aeroplanes of 521 and 522 Flights, No. 255 Squadron. They were housed in the open and serviced by the airship crews. Much of the ground at RNAS Anglesey was poorly drained and the only suitable area for landing and taking off was located on the north-east side of the airship shed—far from ideal. The aeroplanes departed for the newly commissioned Bangor Aerodrome in mid-August. The day before they were due to depart, an Airco DH.6 (B3021) suffered engine failure while on patrol, crashing and killing its pilot, Lt J. R. Johnstone, while another Airco DH6 (C2021) failed to return from patrol over the sea. Before the arrival of planes for anti-submarine work, RNAS Anglesey had a single Sopwith Scout for communications purposes.

By September, new WRAF accommodation blocks were almost ready to house the eighteen women at Anglesey airship station. The transport section at this time had the following vehicles on strength: one motor car, three light tenders, five heavy tenders, one steam wagon, and two motor cycles. By late 1918, the station had 237 personnel, including eighteen officers.

The worst loss of life in Welsh waters came only weeks before the Armistice. It took place on 10 October 1918, when the morning mail boat from Kingstown to Holyhead, RMS *Leinster*, was struck by two torpedoes from German submarine *UB-123*. The ferry was often escorted by an airship, but on that day strong winds had prevented flying. Of the *Leinster*'s 771 passengers and crew, over 500 perished. This was the last ship lost to enemy action in the Irish Sea in the First World War.

The end of the war was celebrated by *S.S.Z.73* flying under the Menai suspension bridge, a feat devised at an Armistice party! Two or three mornings after the party, when the weather was calm and the tidal conditions amenable, the airship headed for the centre of the bridge at 40 mph, the high speed giving full elevator control. It successfully passed under the span, a feat all the more remarkable given that the crew's upward view would have been obscured by the envelope. A bag dangling on a cord was used to measure the airship's height above the water.

RNAS Anglesey's airships continued to operate until late 1918. The mission now was to deal with the menace of enemy mines which had been released in large numbers by German submarines. By February 1919, however, all its airships had been deflated, and by the autumn the station had closed. There had been plans to base four Submarine Scout Zeros here in mid-1919, had the war persisted. The following year, the site was passed to the Government Disposal Board, since the newly formed RAF had no further use for it. Anglesey County Council purchased some of the buildings and converted them for use as a small local hospital; the airship shed was demolished. In the Second World War, the RAF Mona airfield was built on the site. Although it has not hosted any permanent flying units since 1945, it has served as a relief landing ground for the nearby training airfield at RAF Valley since 1951, and retains this role in 2014.

RNAS Pembroke Airship Station

Alternative name: 'Milton'.
Location: O. S. 1/50,000 map157 (SN) 054030. Pembrokeshire.
Size: 272 acres (within boundaries of 1,700 x 1,100 yards).
Station Complement: twenty-two officers, 281 men.
Airship Sheds: one Coastal shed (302 feet long and 100 feet wide), one Submarine Scout shed (301 feet long, 46 feet wide, and 52 high).
Gas Plant: silicol (10,000 cubic feet per hour).
Gasholder: one (10,000 cubic feet).
Gas Tanks: eight (each of 8,000 cubic feet).
Based Airships: Submarine Scout *S.S.15*, *S.S.37*, *S.S.42*, and *S.S.42A*; Submarine Scout Zero *S.S.Z.16*, *S.S.Z.17*, *S.S.Z.37*, *S.S.Z.52*, *S.S.Z.53*, *S.S.Z.56*, *S.S.Z.67*, and *S.S.Z.76*; and Coastal *C.3*, *C.5A*, and *C.6*.

RNAS Pembroke was commissioned in January 1916 and was located on agricultural land south of the Carew River. In the Middle Ages, this ground had been divided between the demesne of the Manor of Carew in the west and Sageston in the east. A few miles to the west of the station lies Milford Haven, a large sheltered anchorage formed by a valley flooded at the end of the last Ice Age.

The station received its first airship, Submarine Scout *S.S.15*, from Wormwood Scrubs in April 1916, and housed it in the partially erected portable Submarine Scout shed. In the early morning of the 19th, the airship was being rigged and prepared for its first flight when a sudden strong wind—gusting between 40 and 60 mph—tore the canvas doors facing south-west. They were patched up but ripped again. The airship was hurriedly re-housed in the partly built steel Coastal shed in extreme difficulty but without further complication.

The first flight from RNAS Pembroke took place six days later on the 25th, when *S.S.15* flew for 35 minutes and covered a distance of about 16 miles. A month later, the first Coastal arrived—this had a longer range than the Submarine Scout and was thought appropriate for this station, which was responsible for the open seas of the Western Approaches. RNAS Anglesey, on the other hand, never received Coastal airships, as its patrol area was confined to the relatively narrow waters of the Irish Sea.

By July, *S.S.15* had notched up over 25 hours on patrol, covering 534 miles over the sea and a further 231 miles over land. Coastal *C.6* had flown 21½ hours, of which 552 miles were over the sea and 118 miles over land. Included in this mileage was a trip to RNAS Anglesey, where it landed for half an hour. Another flight of 10 hours' duration went as far as Dublin. In fact, several British airships appeared in the skies over the city in the months after the Easter Uprising 'to show the flag'.

In May 1916, the airship sheds were still not complete. While every inducement was made to get the contractor to complete the work as quickly as possible, he complained that there was difficulty in obtaining sufficiently skilled labour. It should also be noted that throughout the First World War, most construction work was forbidden on Sundays for religious reasons.

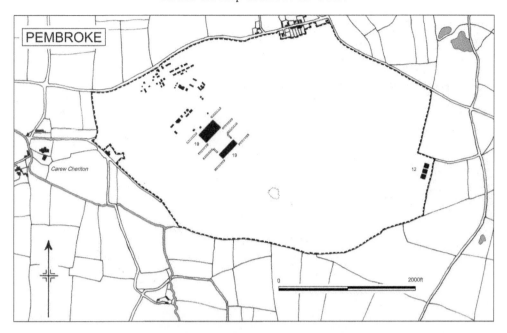

Pembroke. The smaller airship shed in the plan is for a Submarine Scout, while the larger example is a Coastal shed. The huts housing personnel were situated close to a public road on the northern edge of the station. There are several Bessonneau aeroplane hangars near the eastern boundary, well away from the other buildings. (*Mick Davis*)

The officers' quarters at RNAS Pembroke in June 1916. (*The National Archives*)

The vehicle garage in the final stages of construction at RNAS Pembroke in June 1916. (*The National Archives*)

The newly built Coastal shed at RNAS Pembroke in June 1916. It was just over 300 feet in length and cost £25,000 to build. (*The National Archives*)

A men's accommodation hut at RNAS Pembroke. The walls are of corrugated iron. This building is typical of the basic quarters for airship station personnel throughout Britain. Asbestos was sometimes used in place of iron. (*The Fleet Air Arm Museum*)

By June 1916, the Coastal shed was finished but for the concreting of its floor and the windbreaks, which were in the final stages of construction. There was a major setback on the 5 August 1916, when there was an explosion in the gas generator house. It was powerful enough to lift the heavy generator more than 2 feet off the ground; the roof rafter fractured, and dislodged both tanks of soda and ruptured all the pipes as it fell. Three men were seriously injured and seven others received minor injuries. By September, the structural damage had been repaired, a new plant was in the process of installation, and electric lighting had been installed for the steel Coastal shed.

It was not long before disaster struck RNAS Pembroke again, this time in the air. *S.S.42* was dispatched on 15 September 1916 to investigate a report of a submarine off Lundy Island in the Bristol Channel. The weather began to deteriorate, so a radio message was sent instructing the pilot, Flt Lt E. Monk, to return to base. Three hours after take-off, the airship began its final stages of descent over RNAS Pembroke. The handling party was assembled on the landing ground a short distance below, when there was a sudden gust of wind, which lifted the airship 30 feet into the air before dashing it back to the ground. The port suspension wires had snapped, resulting in the car almost inverting itself, with all the crew still on board. As *S.S.42* rose back into the air, the wireless operator fell 20 feet to the ground. Now relieved of most of its load, the damaged craft climbed rapidly away. Flt Lt Monk, the sole crew member remaining on board, managed to clamber on to the top of the inverted car as the Submarine Scout drifted across the Bristol Channel and back towards Lundy Island.

Further wires snapped and the car now hung vertically below the envelope. By this time, Flt Lt Monk was clinging onto the undercarriage. The airship continued to drift south, crossing almost the entire length of Devon before crashing in a field near Ivybridge, just shy of the English Channel. Flt Lt Monk injured his back as he jumped clear, but both he and *S.S.42* would fly again.

Coastal *C.6* made an involuntary landing not far from Devon, when it was forced down at Germag, near RNAS Mullion, on 2nd December 1916.

In March 1917, it was returning from an 11-hour patrol when it experienced double-engine trouble and crashed into the sea. The crew, however, survived. Mr H. Gamble, who served at the RNAS Pembroke as an airship engineer and observer in 1917, left valuable insight into the patrol work carried out there:

> We operated from near Milford Haven in South Wales and our work was mainly to patrol the Irish Sea, St Georges Channel and the South Coast of Ireland. A typical patrol was from St David's Head, across Bardsey Island to Black Rock on the Wicklow coast down to Tuskar Rock, the extreme south-east corner of Ireland, from there across the Bristol Channel and homeward via Lundy Island. These patrols were carried out each day, except when fog or gales prevented them. The average daily patrol was from ten to fifteen hours per day. We used to welcome a change in this programme especially when told off for escort duty, that is to say we would escort a convoy of merchant ships laden with valuable cargo for America, from Bristol Channel ports right out into the Atlantic, zigzagging in front and then circling above the ships whilst naval surface craft patrolled near each flank. After leaving an outward convoy we would usually pick up American troopships and would escort them around the south of Ireland right up to Anglesey, this of course was not as dreary as patrol work. Patrolling at 400 feet when visibility was good we could easily survey fifty square miles of sea so that you could keep your eye on surface craft to prevent them from being attacked.[2]

One of the first actions by an RNAS Pembroke airship against a possible enemy submarine took place in November 1916, when *C.6* dropped two small bombs on what the crew suspected was a periscope east of Cork. One of the most dramatic encounters between a submarine and a British airship took place the following year. On 7 December 1917, *S.S.Z.16*—flown by Flt Lt Barrs—sighted a hostile submarine 20 miles from the Smalls. It was about 240 feet long and painted light grey, and the weather and visibility at the time were poor. The airship altered course towards the submarine, climbing to get above the angle at which the submarine's deck gun, just forward of the conning tower, could fire. The submarine unexpectedly altered course and headed towards the airship, firing a round at it. In response *S.S.Z.16*'s wireless operator swept its deck with machine gun fire. The submarine quickly submerged, but was still visible 20 feet below the surface. Two bombs were dropped, but one failed to explode, and the submarine soon disappeared. In fading light and increasing wind, Flt Lt Barrs set course for home, while two destroyers made for the location where the bombs had been dropped. The following day, *C.5A*—flown by Flt Lt Hart—was escorting a convoy near the Smalls when a periscope was sighted. The airship changed

The sick bay at RNAS Pembroke. The hut is similar to those used for accommodation purposes. (*The Fleet Air Arm Museum*)

The canteen building at RNAS Pembroke. It is distinguishable from the other huts on the station by its tall chimney. Like other examples, its floor is raised above the ground on short stilts. (*The Fleet Air Arm Museum*)

course to investigate, but lost sight of the suspected hostile submarine. Three bombs were dropped on its suspected position and warning flares were fired to attract naval drifters. At 3.25 p.m., a periscope was sighted 400 yards south-west of the previous position; *C.5A* dropped a fourth 100-lb bomb and the naval drifters surrounding the spot launched numerous depth charges. A large patch of oil appeared followed by bubbles. The oil patch increased in size, but although naval drifters remained in the vicinity all night, nothing further was observed.

Flt Lt Barrs was in action with his Coastal *C.3* again a few days later: on 19 December 1917, a submarine was sighted near the Smalls, and when the airship was still 3 miles away, it dived without giving any recognition signal. The pilot therefore decided that it was hostile, and dropped one 100-lb and one 130-lb bomb approximately 100 feet ahead of the swirl where the submarine had submerged. Nothing further was seen, but the amount of oil for miles around this spot was noticeable. Some trawlers were sighted shortly afterwards, and Flt Lt Barrs altered course to communicate with them, only to discover that they were fishing trawlers. In late 1917, modifications were made to RNAS Pembroke's airship sheds, including a trench dug into the floor of the portable shed to enable it to accommodate larger airships.

On 22 January 1918, disaster struck. The crew of Submarine Scout Zero *S.S.Z.17* were working on its car in this shed when it suddenly burst into flame. They were unable to extinguish the fire and fled the building for fear of a gas explosion. Shortly

A winter's day at RNAS Pembroke. Coastal *C.3* is being walked out of its shed by the ground handling party. (*The Fleet Air Arm Museum*)

afterwards, the airship's envelope burst into flames, and 10 minutes later, the 100-lb bombs on the airship exploded. Fortunately the effect was largely confined to the concrete trench in which the car was sitting. The wooden framework of the shed caught fire and was not extinguished until 9.00 p.m., six hours after the fire had started. About half the building was destroyed as well as *S.S.Z.17*. This caused an immediate problem housing the airships. The commander wrote to the vice admiral at Milford Haven:

[...] so far as anti-submarine and convoy work is concerned this would seem to be one of the most important airship stations and it is desirable to keep as many airships for service as possible. At present it is just possible to house the two Coastals and one Submarine Scout in the steel shed. It is not possible to inflate S.S.16A and there is not room for S.S.Z.39 which ship is under orders to proceed to Pembroke when completed.

He went on to suggest that the two remaining Coastal ships be exchanged for Submarine Scout Zeros, which would enable four airships to be housed in the shed, instead of three. On the night of 17 March, Coastal *C.3* and *C.5A*, and Submarine Scout Zero *S.S.Z.16* and *S.S.Z.52*, were all housed in the Coastal shed. Potential mooring out sites to house the Submarine Scouts were examined in the disused quarries close to the station. Tenders for reconstructing the shed were accepted on 19 April, with a time scale of three months stipulated, and a quarry near St Florence was selected as the mooring out site. The new Submarine Scout Zero airships had begun arriving at RNAS Pembroke in August 1917. The first example was transported by road and assembled at the station on the 7th. Due to a shortage of this class of airship, *S.S.42* was rebuilt after its accident and returned to service as *S.S.42A*, but its career was short-lived. On 12 September 1917, it was attempting a night landing when it collided with a farm building. The airship then drifted out to sea in the direction of Carmarthen Bay and was wrecked near Bull Point. Flt Sub-Lt Cripps and the wireless operator were lost at sea.

In the last year of the war, Submarine Scout Zeros were the main type at RNAS Pembroke. One of their duties was to escort American troopship convoys carrying soldiers to fight in France. *S.S.Z.46* was instructed to protect one such group. On its arrival on station, it was mistaken for a Zeppelin and one of the escorting vessels opened fire on it. Fortunately, it survived the experience. On the night of 25 March 1918, *S.S.Z.46* carried out an all-night patrol just outside Milford Haven, for there was a bright moon and a submarine had been reported lurking in the vicinity. In April, all eight outward-bound convoys from Milford Haven were escorted by two or three airships. On 12 April, *S.S.Z.16* was ordered to search for a submarine reported 10 miles north of St David's. After patrolling the area for 4½ hours, a patch of oil was discovered and the airship dropped a 100-lb bomb on it. Later in the month, *S.S.Z.37* heard gunfire, and shells were seen to explode half a mile from the coast near a merchant ship. It was believed that an enemy submarine was the source of the gunfire, but despite ten-mile visibility, no trace of it could be found.

In June there was a report of gunfire off Lundy Island, and *S.S.Z.52* was sent to investigate. The culprit turned out to be a merchant ship firing at drift wood. In May 1918, enemy submarine activity was mainly confined to the North Cornish Coast and the Irish Sea west of Bardsey Island. A total of seventy-one patrols were flown in June 1918, of which thirty-nine were over 7 hours' duration. The following Submarine Scout Zeros were involved: *S.S.Z.16*, *S.S.Z.37*, *S.S.Z.52*, *S.S.Z.53*, *S.S.Z.56*, and *S.S.Z.57*. The next month, the number of patrols flown was curtailed because of weather conditions: the portable airship shed was still under repair at this time, and work at the station was further hampered by a serious outbreak of influenza—which had passed its worst by the end of July. RNAS Pembroke still managed to hold a sports day at that time, and for the less energetic, films were shown in the YMCA building.

On 11 August, *S.S.Z.37* had an attention-drawing accident, making a forced landing on the seashore at Mumbles near Swansea. On long flights, airship crews would sometimes beg for fresh fish from passing boats by lowering a bucket on a long rope. RNAS Pembroke also acted as an aerodrome for aeroplanes flying anti-submarine patrols close to the coast. In July 1917, a hangar was erected in the corner of the station:

> This is of great convenience as it is now possible to take the machines off the ground just outside it, instead of having to bring them over from the airship shed. The hanger has been provided with a telephone so that it is now possible to have an aeroplane in the air within a very short time of an emergency call.[3]

Initially, there were five Sopwith aeroplanes on strength at l;g Pembroke—*5215*, *5214*, *5234*, *5613*, and *6919*. In June, *519* and *529* Flights were based here. The following month they were merged to form No. 255 Squadron, which remained at Pembroke until it was disbanded in January 1919. Airship flying ceased around the same time and the station was decommissioned. The land was sold off in lots and most of the buildings were demolished not long after the closure. Any surviving traces of RNAS Pembroke airship station were swept away when construction work began on a new RAF aerodrome (Carew Cheriton) occupying the same site. In the early stages of the Second World War, aeroplanes from here flew patrols over the sea to protect shipping in the Atlantic, just as airships had done in the First. The aerodrome closed at the end of the war, and much of the land returned to agriculture. Most of the buildings have been demolished and a bypass road has been constructed across the northern part of the site.

7

RNAS Airship Stations in Scotland

Scotland had no significant naval bases until the late eighteenth century. All of Great Britain's naval bases were located on the South Coast of England. With an emergence of Germany as a major power, the Royal Navy undertook a major re-orientation of its warship bases. To confront the German threat, a new naval base was constructed at Rosyth, near Edinburgh. This was not yet ready by the outbreak of the First World War, so the Grand Fleet initially made use of the sheltered waters of Scapa Flow in the Orkney Islands. As many as 100,000 naval personnel wound up stationed in this remote part of Britain.

The first airship station in Scotland was in fact at the other end of the country, near Stranraer. This was RNAS Luce Bay, the main role of which was to protect the vital sea crossing between Scotland and Ireland.

RNAS Luce Bay Airship Station

Location: O. S. 1/50,000 map 82 (NX) 120550. Dumfries and Galloway, 5 miles south-east of Stranraer Harbour railway station.
Size: 444 acres (within boundaries of 2,270 x 1,530 yards).
Station Complement: thirteen officers, 155 men (on 1 January 1918).
Airship Sheds: one Submarine Scout shed (302 feet long, 70 wide, and 50 feet high).
Hydrogen Plant: B.2 silicol (5,000 cubic feet per hour).
Gasholder: one tank of 10,000 cubic feet, eight tanks of 8,000 cubic feet.
Based Airships: Submarine Scout *S.S.14A*, *S.S.17*, *S.S.20*, *S.S.23*, *S.S.33*, and *S.S.38*; and Submarine Scout Zero *S.S.Z.11*, *S.S.Z.12*, *S.S.Z.13*, and *S.S.Z.20*.

This station was situated on a low-lying area at the head of Luce Bay, and was protected from the worst of the winds by rising ground both to the east and west. In May and June 1915, its airship shed was under construction. It was designed to hold four Submarine Scouts, and—typically of an airship shed—offices and workshops were situated in annexes attached to the outside walls. RNAS Luce Bay was officially commissioned on the 15 July 1915. The Director of the Air Department wrote:

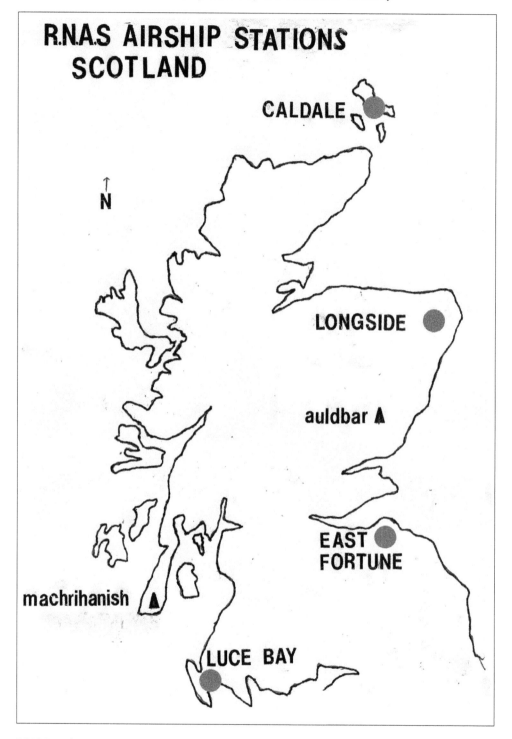

RNAS airship stations in Scotland. (*Author's collection*)

The airship shed at RNAS Luce Bay, 1918. Large windbreaks protect both of its entrances. An airship is just visible to the right of the shed. (*Scran*)

With reference to the approval to establish airship patrols in the North Channel and Irish Sea, a shed has now been completed at Luce Bay and an airship of the S.S. type has been sent there and others will follow. A small portable shed has also been approved at Larne for emergency use of these ships and this will be erected shortly. The shed approved for Anglesey is also completed and a portable shed will eventually be erected on the Irish Coast opposite. An S.S. type will be sent to Anglesey in the near future. Submitted to inform the SNOs concerned and to place those ships under orders for submarine patrol.

It would be a long time before the shed at Larne was erected. The commander of RNAS Luce Bay was George Cyril Colmore, who walked with a limp—a legacy of his service at RNAS Polegate when, a few months earlier, he failed to stop his car when challenged by soldiers on patrol. They opened fire on his vehicle, and one of the bullets passed through the engine and hit him in the leg. The first airships to arrive at RNAS Luce Bay were Submarine Scouts S.S.17 and S.S.23, which could not be inflated until the doors were finally fitted to the airship shed on the 1 August 1915. At night, the Duty Officer slept in the building, so he was readily available for any emergency; outside, four sentries stood guard, changing duty every two hours; and a motor launch patrolled the coast, as the station—only a mile from the seashore—was considered vulnerable to seaborne attack.

By September, there were three airships on strength and live bomb practice was carried out on targets at sea. Work was continuing on the station in early 1916, for the concreting of the airship shed floor was yet to be completed and left nowhere to inflate the airships' envelopes. The state of the roads that winter was so bad that lorries could not reach the airship shed, and the only method of getting hydrogen cylinders to and from it was by horse and cart.

Like all other airship stations, RNAS Luce Bay had its own wireless station. In its first year of operation it intercepted messages from a German submarine thought to be about 100 miles to the north. Answering signals emanating from a considerable distance away were also intercepted, and the information was immediately passed on to the Naval Centre. Night flying was inaugurated in early 1916. Ground lighting was provided by two Blanchard lamps placed 300 feet apart, forming the extreme edges of an arrow point. Ratings holding torches pointed towards a landing airship made up the rest of the sign. The Blanchard lights were left on around the clock.

One new recruit recorded his feelings upon arriving at RNAS Luce Bay, in the October 1916 edition of the station's own newspaper, the *Freugh Gazette*:

> My first impression of the station was that of a shed placed in a field and the quarters to the west neatly arranged. My memory had not led me astray, and with the exceptions of a few additions, the station was the same as when in November last year I passed over the station in Naval Airship Number 4. The station is, in my opinion, quite a model one but one thing is its distance from any place of amusement. I won't say too much on this point, however, as I may hurt the susceptibilities of the real inhabitants of the district.

At RNAS Pulham, the station commander requested that additional trains be laid on to take his personnel to local towns in the evening for recreation, but the railway company turned down his request.

Flying from RNAS Luce Bay in the first half of 1916 was restricted by poor weather and a hydrogen shortage. It was not until 13 October that all four of the based airships were airborne together. The following month, *S.S.23* had to make a forced landing near Girvan. Only a small number of patrols were flown towards the end of the year—two in October and four in December. Luce Bay's airships were responsible for patrolling the North Channel and a section of the Irish Sea as far south as the Isle of Man, as well as the approaches to the Firth of Clyde and the northern coast of Ireland. The total number of flying hours for the year was only 411.

By 1917, flying hours had increased dramatically—to 1,300—as the pace of operations stepped up a gear. The Stranraer ferry to Larne, Northern Ireland, was escorted as often as possible, so a mooring out station was established there too. A new class of airship arrived in the shape of the Submarine Scout Zero in the summer. The first example flown from Luce Bay was *S.S.Z.11* on 21 July, shortly followed by *S.S.Z.12* and *S.S.Z.13*. It was fortunate that they arrived when they did, as a visit by the Admiralty Board of Survey at the beginning of the month condemned the control cars of two of the older Submarine Scouts. This left the station with only one operational airship.

In August, the airships conducted forty patrols and numerous practice flights. *S.S.Z.11* had a run of bad luck during the month. On returning from its fourth patrol, it landed back at RNAS Luce Bay with its control car entangled with telegraph wires. Worse followed on the 20th, when the same airship suffered complete engine failure upon returning to base, after completing a patrol over the southern sector. At the time, the uplands were shrouded in mist, so visibility was poor, and when the airship

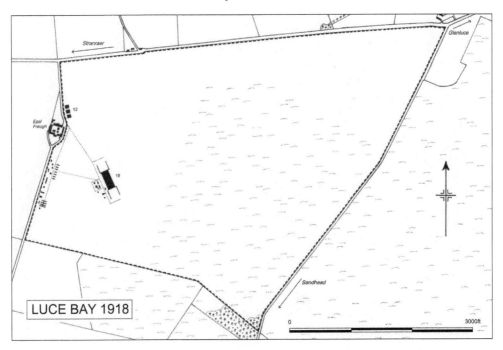

Luce Bay. The single Submarine Scout shed stands in a large open area of grassland and sand dunes. It is one of a handful of sheds in Britain to face the north-west rather than prevailing south-west winds. The domestic quarters and technical buildings are strewn along the road on the western boundary of the station. (*Mick Davis*)

drifted in a northerly direction, it struck the face of Larg Hill in the wilds of the parish of Minnigaff, Kirkcudbrightshire. It touched down in a hollow of the hill about 500 feet from the summit, and part of the wreck was carried over the hilltop into the next valley. Some of the crew were badly injured, but help did not arrive for several hours, for there were no roads in the area and the nearest inhabited house was 4 miles away across a boulder-strewn moor. The wreckage was later removed on the back of horse-drawn sledges.

In September 1917, the new airships were able to fly thirty operational patrols because RNAS Luce Bay now had its own silicol hydrogen gas plant. For almost two years, it had been dependent on hydrogen cylinders transported from England. Further improvements were made, including a new wireless hut with two tall masts. Despite the efforts of the airship crews, enemy submarines still frequently sank ships in their patrol area: one of the most notable losses was HMS *Drake*, an armoured cruiser that was torpedoed in the North Channel—luckily, the entire crew survived. The airships were sometimes requested to fly missions to look for mines laid by submarines. On Thursday 20 December 1917, *S.S.Z.13* experience total engine failure due to mechanical issues. It was fortunately only 3 miles away from the station when this occurred and managed to land safely. At that time of the year, the crews of airships had to endure extreme cold: the surrounding hills, some nearly 2,000 feet high, were now covered in snow and chilled the winds which blew across them. By the end of

1917, RNAS Luce Bay had Submarine Scout Zeros—*S.S.Z.11, S.S.Z.12, S.S.Z.13*, and *S.S.Z.20*—and one Submarine Scout—*S.S.23*—on base.

Bad weather continued to restrict flying into 1918. It was decided that the purity of the hydrogen should not be allowed to fall below 90% for the Submarine Scout Zero airships, for below this level the airship would not leave the ground when the atmospheric pressure was low and the air temperature normal. Meanwhile, searchlights were installed to act as night landing aids, an engine test house was also constructed at the beginning of the year, and the airship shed received additional protection in the form of two Airedale terriers!

The only flying undertaken in February 1918 was a reconnaissance flight to investigate a Russian cruiser anchored in shallow water in the Solway Firth. In March, there was a dramatic improvement in the weather—over 328 hours were flown, the highest total for the station since it was commissioned. RNAS Luce Bay airships escorted ten convoys consisting of upwards of 130 ships. But not all vessels sailed in groups, and the airships also escorted sloops and hospital ships sailing between Scotland and Ireland. On 18 March 1918, *S.S.Z.11* dropped a bomb on a suspicious track; an armed yacht then dropped depth charges on the same spot, and differently coloured oils came to the surface.

In May 1918, patrols were flown on twenty-five days, but airships several times had to be recalled on account of mist. Oil bubbles were seen rising to the surface by the crew of the patrolling *S.S.Z.12*, so a trawler in the vicinity was directed to the location and dropped depth charges. The airship remained over the position for a further 4 hours but nothing more was seen. May was fraught with a number of inconveniences: delivery of gas cylinders by rail was inexplicably discontinued, and food rations—which were transported by cylinders—now had to come from ASC Gailes, a rail journey that lasted 5 hours.... Still worse, the bread supplied was of poor quality and were no means provided for refrigerating meat. An application for a recreation hut was submitted to compensate for the mess hut which was now too small.

Aerial patrols over the shipping routes were re-enforced with the arrival of D.H.6 aeroplanes of 'A' and 'B' flights of No. 255 Squadron in July 1918, followed by a further flight from No. 272 Squadron. These were eventually combined to form No. 258 Squadron and based at Luce Bay. By August, the station had at least eight aeroplanes on strength, the main task of which was to survey the shipping lanes along the coast and deter enemy submarines—such duties became known as 'scarecrow patrols'. The D.H.6s flew in pairs for up to 2 hours, sometimes covering distances of up to a 100 miles—an extremely boring exercise for the pilots.

On 30 September 1918, the first combined patrol—consisting of two Submarine Scout Zeros and four D.H.6s—was flown. The aeroplanes were housed in six Bessonneau hangars and the airmen lived in tents or in Armstrong huts. On the ground, the station had a fleet of support vehicles—one motor car, seven tenders, two motorcycles, and one ambulance. Airships fared less well in the month of August. While returning from patrol, the pilot of *S.S.Z.12* decided to perform a low-level run to impress the (numerous) residents of Stanraer out for a stroll. The airship flew across the end of the pier, but the pilot failed to see a large flagpole mounted on it. This pierced and immediately deflated the envelope—the control car, with its engine still running, fell into a boat lying alongside the pier. The empty envelope spread itself over the pier, and *S.S.Z.12* completed the remainder of its journey to RNAS Luce Bay by rail. It was not unusual for deflated airships to be transported around the country by train.

There was another, far more serious accident that month. While on patrol in the southern sector, *S.S.Z.13*—piloted by Lt Astley—suffered engine failure. The engine would not restart, so the crew began throwing a great variety of items overboard to avoid putting down in Solway Bay. Now entirely at the mercy of the wind, the airship drifted towards the cliffs near Rockcliffe, south of Dalbeattie. Grappling hooks were dropped as it approached the shore, but this only made matters worse—when they caught fast, the airship suddenly plummeted earthwards. It disgorged its crew of three into shallow water before being blown back out to sea, and was later dashed to pieces on the rocky coast. However, the crew's problems were not over: a bag containing top secret Admiralty code books had been left on board. An armed guard was placed on the shoreline, and personnel from Luce Bay scoured the coast for many days without success. In late September, a member of the public discovered the bag and handed it in.

Although the end of the war was only a few days away, RNAS Luce Bay's airship crews did not let their guard down. On 3 November, *S.S.12* was summoned to investigate reports of gun fire to the south of Aisla Craig Lighthouse. Oil was spotted on the surface of the sea near Maidens Tor Head. Bombs were dropped and armed trawlers summoned to depth charge the area. Hydrophones later confirmed it was a submarine but it appeared to have escaped. In fact, the Germans did not lose any submarines during the war to Luce Bay's airships. With the end of hostilities saw the station rapidly demobilised and flying ceased by December 1918. The two remaining airships, *S.S.Z.11* and *S.S.Z.20*, were laid up in their shed. The anti-submarine No. 258 Squadron was disbanded the same month and its aeroplanes departed for the last time.

A government meteorological station continued to make use of the site for another year. The end came when the buildings were auctioned off in December 1921. Bidders came from all over the country. The airship shed was sold for scrap for £2,750 and each of its four windbreaks for £196. Many of the smaller wooden buildings were re-used by the local inhabitants. With the threat of another conflict on the horizon, the site was turned into a training aerodrome for the RAF in the late 1930s. It was given a new name—West Freugh—and saw continual use for the remainder of the century. Although little used in the twenty-first century, the aerodrome still occupies the land on which RNAS Luce Bay once stood.

RNAS Luce Bay was responsible for Machrihanish Aerodrome and Mooring Out Station, Ramsey Mooring Out Station, and RNAS Larne and RNAS Doagh Island, Ireland (see Chapter 8).

Machrihanish Aerodrome and Mooring Out Station

Location: O. S. 1/50,000 map 68, (NR) 682201. Argyll, Strathclyde.
Size: 65 acres (within boundaries of 600 x 500 yards).

In the closing stages of the First World War, a small 65-acre aerodrome was established 2 miles to the west of Campbeltown. The Campbeltown–Machrihanish light railway ran along its northern edge. It was intended that the aerodrome also serve as a bolt hole for airships from RNAS Luce Bay, but there is little evidence of them making much use of this facility. Unlike most other mooring out sites, which were in woodland, there was no shelter here from the westerly winds. It was proposed to erect two portable airship sheds here for two Submarine Scout Twins in 1919. D.H.6 aeroplanes of No. 272 Squadron flew anti-submarine patrols from here to protect the approaches of the Firth of Clyde. Conditions were primitive, with canvas Bessonneau Hangars and Armstrong Huts being the only buildings. After the Armistice, the aerodrome reverted to farmland. Campbeltown aerodrome was later constructed a short distance to the north-west.

Ramsey Mooring Out Station

Location: O. S. 1/50,000 map 95 (SC) 417962.

This mooring out station was situated about 2 miles to the north-west of the coastal town of Ramsey on the Isle of Man. A range of high hills immediately to the south and rising ground on the north would have provided protection for the site. Official records have it as still being under construction on 31 October 1918, and it does not appear to have been used before the end of hostilities. Two Submarine Scout Twin airships were also planned to be based here by the summer of 1919, along with two portable airship sheds, each 175 feet long, 50 feet wide, and 55 feet high.

RNAS East Fortune Airship Station

Location: O. S. 1/50,000 map 55 (NT) 550785. East Lothian, 4 miles south of North Berwick, 18 miles east of Edinburgh.
Size: 1,330 acres (within boundaries of 4,000 x 2,700 yards).
Station Complement: thirty-two officers, 580 men (on 1 Jan 1918).
Airship Sheds: rigid shed to fit two (700 feet long, 180 feet wide, and 100 feet high); and two Coastal sheds (320 feet long, 120 feet wide, and 80 feet high).
Hydrogen Plant: 'B' silicol (10,000 cubic feet per hour), water gas plant (14,000 cubic feet per hour).
Gasholders: two of 250,000 cubic feet, one of 20,000 cubic feet.
Tanks: sixty-six (each of 8,000 cubic feet).

Based Airships: Rigids *No. 9*, *No. 24*, *R.29*, and *R.34*; Submarine Scout Zero *S.S.Z.3*, *S.S.Z.59*, and *S.S.Z.60*; Coastal *C.5A*, *C.15*, *C.16*, *C.18*, *C.20*, *C.24*, and *C.25*; Coastal Star *C*1*, *C*3*, *C*7*, and *C*8*; North Sea *N.S.1*, *N.S.3*, *N.S.4*, *N.S.5*, *N.S.7*, *N.S.8*, *N.S.11*, and *N.S.12*.

At the beginning of the twentieth century, a large new naval base was under construction at Rosyth, and in 1912, it was proposed that an airship base with one shed should be established near here. A further two locations were raised—the Norfolk Broad area with one shed and Teapot Head at Chatham with two sheds. In the period leading up to the First World War, plans to expand the airship fleet were curtailed due to financial restrictions. To protect Edinburgh and Rosyth from Zeppelin attacks, priority was giving to establishing an aerodrome that could house fighter aeroplanes. East Fortune, close to the mouth of the Firth of Forth, was selected as suitable for this role. The name appropriately means 'fort town' and possibly refers to the farms which once supplied provisions to a nearby fortress in ancient times.By August 1915, a site for an aerodrome and airship station had been selected, and in the autumn a small number of aeroplanes arrived. As there were no hangars, they were housed in a Piggot tent, but this was soon blown down in a gale. Many of the personnel lived in the neighbouring farm buildings. Upon visiting the aerodrome, Adml Lowry was less than impressed:

> It is presumed that the aeroplanes at East Fortune are supplied for the defence of Edinburgh and the Forth against attack by airships. For this purpose it appears to me that the machines capable of rapid climbing are essential and their armament should be suitable, e.g. small bombs with sensitive fuses rather than heavy ones, light automatic machine guns and possibly inflammable darts to ignite gas bags. All the above were wanting when I visited the Station in November last.[1]

An airship station was constructed alongside the aerodrome and commissioned on 23 August 1916; one Coastal shed was completed, and a second almost finished. Foundation work had also begun on a large rigid shed. A siding was laid into the northern part of the airship station from the main Edinburgh to London railway, which skirted the northern boundary. The line ran in a westerly direction past the living quarters, before dividing into two branches—one which ran a short distance to the south with a round loop and terminated beside the large airship shed—and another which continued west and ended by the hydrogen plant with a short run-round loop.

As with RNAS Longside, East Fortune's first airships were Coastal-class, capable of long range patrols. The first two, *C.15* and *C.16*, were delivered by air from RNAS Kingsnorth via RNAS Howden on 23 August. A week later, *C.16* set off on its first patrol. After two hours, one of its engines failed due to a faulty magneto. As it turned back to base, the second engine's magneto also failed. The wind was in the crew's favour, blowing the airship towards the shore, where it force-landed on the beach at Coldingham Bay, Berwickshire. The crew abandoned the airship and it drifted out to sea, later to be found by a destroyer which took it in tow—but it broke free, and rose

A Submarine Scout Zero from RNAS East Fortune carrying out landing trials on the aircraft carrier HMS *Furious* in the summer of 1918. Ship-based airships would have greatly expanded sea patrols, but were never employed in this role in the Royal Navy. (© *IWM—Q 20640*)

to 6,000 feet. Locating it was difficult in the dark, but it was eventually found 20 miles out to sea. *C.16* was dragged up on the beach the following day, by which time it was a total wreck. It later became the practice for airship crews to carry spare magnetos which they could change in the air if needed.

For a month *C.15*, the other surviving Coastal, stood alone at the station. A replacement for *C.16* arrived in the form of *C.20* on 22 September 1916, and a further two, *C.24* and *C.25*, were delivered by rail in November. Adml Sir David Beatty was anxious to provide the Grand Fleet with some form of long range reconnaissance aeroplane. It was thought that the Coastal-class airship could undertake this role, particularly if its range could be extended by towing it behind a warship and refuelling it at sea. The admiral was also of the opinion that when rigid and North Sea airships became available, they could help fulfil a large number of duties undertaken by light cruisers. On 20 November 1916, *C.20* carried out towing trials with HMS *Phaeton*. These were less than successful, ending with the airship making a zigzagging dive into the sea. Fortunately, the trail rope was released, so after suffering some minor damage, *C.20* became airborne again. The towing trials were extended into the following year using HMS *Phaeton* on 3 May 1917. *C.15* was hauled behind it on a rope at a height of a 100 feet. The crews were then exchanged and 35 gallons of fuel delivered to the

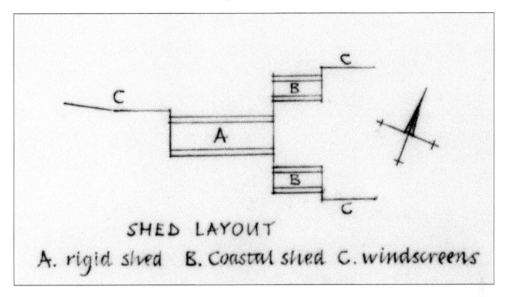

SHED LAYOUT
A. rigid shed B. Coastal shed C. windscreens

This plan shows the layout of airship sheds at RNAS East Fortune. The sheds face into the prevailing south-westerly wind. There is a large windbreak on the north side of the entrance to the large rigid shed but none on the opposite side. This is because the most damaging winds usually blew from the north-west and rarely from the opposite direction. Several other airship stations, including RNAS Howden and RNAS Longside, had their airship sheds laid out in a similar manner. (*Scran*)

airship. Further trials took place in the following months.

On 16 July 1917, all airships based at RNAS East Fortune were ordered to proceed to sea with the Battle Cruiser Force. One of them was to be refuelled at sea and the rest back at base. After being airborne for 4½ hours, C.24 and C.25 headed back towards East Fortune, only arriving 8 to 9 hours later after encountering 40 mph headwinds. C.15 then flew north and made contact with HMS *Phaeton*, 75 miles off Peterhead, where it dropped its trail rope and was taken under tow for refuelling while still airborne. Then things began to go wrong. One of the airship's engine stopped, then restarted, firing on only four of its six cylinders. The decision was then made to haul the Coastal down onto the deck to repair it, but the pressure of the envelope began to decrease and the airship became unmanageable. To prevent it completely going out of control, C.15 was 'ripped' (the ripping panel was pulled) and it rapidly deflated. Much of the deflated envelope draped over the ship's stern. Part of the envelope was cut adrift, while the rest—including the control car—remained on board. Not long after, the idea of refuelling Coastal airships from warships was abandoned, as there was little doubt that this could only be undertaken in perfect weather conditions.

An unusual role was assumed by Coastal airships in the winter of 1916. C.20 acted as a target tug, by towing a drogue for aeroplanes to shoot at with their Lewis guns. By the end of the year, the two Coastal sheds were complete and ninety-eight of the 104 concrete foundations for the rigid shed laid. RNAS East Fortune's airships now escorted numerous convoys entering and leaving the Firth of Forth or steaming along the east coast. The station's area of responsibility extended from the Bell Rock Lighthouse in the north to the Farne Islands in the south, at a distance of 30 to 40 miles offshore. An official memo written in March 1917 stated:

> In regard to patrols seaward East Fortune is probably the most important station as the enemy submarines which operate off N.E. of England are believed to cross the North Sea on approximately the 56th parallel of N latitude, it is therefore suggested that two North Sea ships should be sent to this station for the double purpose of Fleet reconnaissance and extended submarine patrols.

It appears this recommendation was heeded, since two North Sea airships were delivered to RNAS East Fortune a few months later—until then, Coastals had been the station's sole digest. On 23 April 1917, *C.24* was 10 miles east of St Abb's Head when it sighted a German submarine about 4 miles away. The submarine fired a torpedo at a merchant ship and then submerged. A search that lasted 5 hours was made, but nothing further was seen of the enemy. On 15 July, *C.15* spotted a string of bubbles, 25 miles east of May Island. Two 65-lb bombs were dropped ahead of the bubbles, resulting in a precipitation of air coming to the surface. Oil then followed, leaking into the sea for the next 1½ hours and it was presumed that an enemy submarine was either badly damaged or destroyed.

By October 1917, there were three new North Sea airships based here—*N.S.1*, *N.S.3*, and *N.S.4*. They were 252 feet long, had floats so that they could land on the sea, had berths and cooking facilities, and carried a crew of up to ten men. Coastals *C.24* and *C.25* and Rigid *No. 24* were also on strength at this time. North Sea airships escorted the Grand Fleet in September 1917, while also exercising with anti-aircraft batteries around Edinburgh and the Firth of Forth. December 1917 proved a troubled month for RNAS East Fortune's airships. *N.S.1* suffered engine failure while on patrol off the Farne Islands on the 15th. It was unable to make any headway on its other engine and had to be brought down in a field near Fenwick with farm workers assisting with its landing. It was later moored to a hedge. The wind strengthened, breaking the mooring rope and damaging the control car. To prevent further damage, the airship was deflated.

Each airship station had dedicated meteorological officers on site. In autumn 1917, these officers conducted an investigation into the nature of the winds around the mouth of the Firth of Forth, and concluded that when a westerly wind blew, the valley of the Forth acted as a funnel through which wind at heights of 500 feet and upwards gained greater velocity on reaching the Firth. This increase in wind speed was believed to occur in a triangular zone between Inchkeith Island (at the apex) and the north and south coasts of the Forth (at the sides). Along its edges, the winds were sometimes found to blow in opposite directions:

> This creates severe bumps off St Abb's on account of the high land at that point, and on occasions the bumpy region has extended as far as five miles from the coast between St Abb's and the Bass Rock. To avoid the bumps, airships approaching RNAS East Fortune

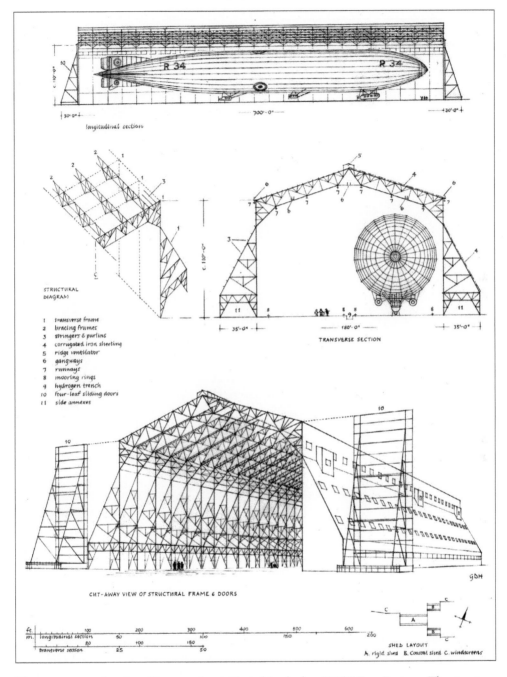

R 34

R 34

longitudinal section

STRUCTURAL DIAGRAM

1 transverse frame
2 bracing frames
3 stringers & purlins
4 corrugated iron sheeting
5 ridge ventilator
6 gangways
7 runways
8 mooring rings
9 hydrogen trench
10 four-leaf sliding doors
11 side annexes

TRANSVERSE SECTION

CUT-AWAY VIEW OF STRUCTURAL FRAME & DOORS

SHED LAYOUT
A. rigid shed B. Coastal shed C. windscreens

These cut-away drawings illustrate the rigid airship shed at RNAS East Fortune. The structure was 700 feet long and 180 feet wide. It was designed by A. J. Main & Co., and was very similar to the original No. 1 shed at Cardington before it was extended. (*Scran*)

East Fortune Airship Station viewed from the north-west. In the foreground are gas holders and the plant for manufacturing hydrogen. Behind it is the rigid shed bearing a camouflaged paint scheme, with two smaller Coastal sheds beyond it. The group of buildings in the centre of the picture is a farm which appears to be still in use, as there are numerous haystacks close by. (*The Fleet Air Arm Museum*)

from the south sometimes avoid the coast and flew inland over the Lammermuir Hills instead. It, however, had the disadvantage of flying over high ground.[2]

The turbulence of the air along the south coast of the Firth of Forth was of some concern to the CO at RNAS East Fortune, and was the subject of a number of reports. It was referred to as a 'wind barrage', and airships flying over the Dunbar area were often buffeted by strong updrafts. On 12 December 1917, the newly-built *N.S.5* departed RNAS Kingsnorth headed for RNAS East Fortune. When the airship was within 2 miles of its destination, both engines failed. After free ballooning for about 10 miles, the engines were started, but then again failed. It was decided to put the airship down near Ayton in Berwickshire and to deflate it.

North Sea airships were not the only type to suffer mechanical failures. On 22 December 1917, *C.20* left to patrol with the Grand Fleet. East of St Abb's Head, one of the engines ran out of petrol and the airship attempted to make a landing behind St Abb's Head. The trail rope was dropped but *C.20* was blown out to sea. Then the second engine ran out of petrol and it was discovered that there was a leak in one of the fuel pipes. HMS *Oriana* made an attempt to take it in tow in the North Sea, but the rope parted and the airship rose to 1,500 feet. The crew released gas from the envelope and put down in the water. HMS *Oriana* rescued the crew but were unable to save the airship. It was deliberately rammed and then finished off with gunfire.

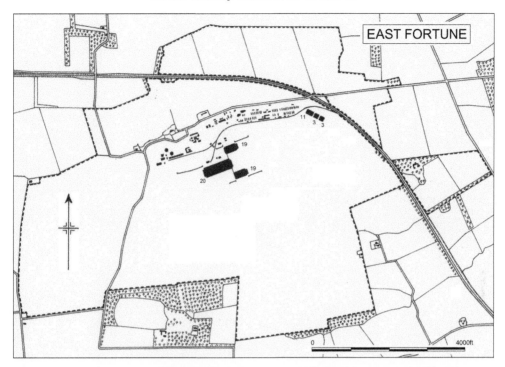

East Fortune. Located on arable farmland in East Lothian, this large airship station possessed one rigid shed and two smaller Coastal sheds. Near the Edinburgh–London railway to the east of them were several aeroplane hangars. A branch line from the mainline served the hydrogen plant and airship sheds. Unlike many other bases, the accommodation huts were in close proximity to the operational buildings. (*Mick Davis*)

By the end of 1917, RNAS East Fortune had a complement of thirty-two officers and 580 men. There was also a sizeable force of aeroplanes housed in canvas hangars. Pilots for the Royal Navy were trained here and it acted as a depot for machines normally based on warships. The night-flying fighter aeroplanes on guard to intercept Zeppelins were withdrawn, as the accompanying searchlights they needed to illuminate their targets were not available near here. The aeroplane hangars were located to the east of the rigid shed which had been completed in the summer of 1917, the last roof truss having been put in place in May. Like other airship sheds, its main door faced the prevailing south-westerly wind. The two smaller Coastal sheds either side of it were also built on a south-west–north-east axis.

The first rigid airship to land at RNAS East Fortune was *No. 9*. It arrived unexpectedly on 7 August 1917, having run short of fuel and encountering thick mist. It flew over the Grand Fleet on the 12th and returned to its base at RNAS Howden on the 13th. The first Rigid to be permanently based at RNAS East Fortune was *No. 24*, which arrived at the end of October 1917. *No. 24* flew twice before the year was out, but only performed poorly with a top speed of only 30 mph. The following year it made a number of flights escorting convoys, but on one occasion was caught in strong winds near the Bass Rock. The airship struggled for several hours with one engine not

The Rigid *R.29* at RNAS East Fortune, July 1918. Two months later, it bombed and crippled the German submarine *UB-115*, which was later sunk by Royal Navy warships. The following year, the *R.29* made flights over Edinburgh and south-east Scotland accompanied by the *R.34*. (*The Fleet Air Arm Museum*)

An aerial view of RNAS East Fortune. In the foreground is the rigid shed accompanied by the two smaller Coastal sheds. Beyond them is the Rigid *R.24* with a large group of men holding onto its ropes. (*The Fleet Air Arm Museum*)

operating, but could make no headway. It was later damaged while being taken into its shed, and in May 1918 went to RNAS Howden for repair.

The following month, Rigid *R.29* was delivered and on the night of 3 July 1918, it made a flight lasting over 32 hours from here. Its main claim to fame was made on 29 September 1918. On patrol over the North Sea, it engaged three German submarines off Sunderland. The first escaped, the second struck a mine while being pursued, and the third (*UB-115*) was hit by a 230-lb bomb. HMS *Ouse* then depth-charged the submarine, while *R.29* dropped a further bomb. Large amounts of oil and bubbles came to the surface and *UB-115* sunk 4½ nautical miles off Beacon Point, Newbiggin-by-the-Sea (Northumberland), with the loss of its crew of thirty-nine. This was the first and last time a British rigid airship was in action against an enemy vessel.

A new class of non-rigid airship arrived in 1918 in the form of the Coastal Stars. This was an improvement on the Coastal type on all fronts: it was slightly faster, more stable, and easier to handle in the air and on the ground. The Coastal Star's improved control car was also more comfortable for the crew of five, and a parachute was supplied for each man. The first model, *C*1*, arrived at RNAS East Fortune on 17 February 1918. Just over two months later, yet another new class of airship appeared—the Submarine Scout Zero. This was the smallest of all the airships flown from RNAS East Fortune, and was often deployed to the mooring out site in Northumberland at Chathill.

In the summer of 1918, Submarine Scout Zeros *S.S.Z.59* and *S.S.Z.60* carried out several landing trials on the flight deck of the Royal Navy's first aircraft carrier, HMS *Furious*. Although these were encouraging—the conclusion being that basing airships on an aircraft carrier would greatly enhance both their range and capabilities—the experiment was not repeated. Even with the now frequent airship patrols and numerous Royal Navy warships patrolling the North Sea Coast, German submarines still roamed these waters. In July, Coastal Star *C*7* was patrolling near the Bell Rock when it observed a suspicious submerged object approaching the last ship of the convoy. A bomb was dropped and a large object appeared on the surface. It was not a submarine, but a badly injured whale. Another bomb was released to shatter the carcass and a signal sent to warn ships of the potential hazard.

A large patch of oil was seen rising from a position 2 miles east of May Island on 2 August. North Sea *N.S.8* dropped three bombs on it at 3.45 p.m. and then circled the vicinity until 7.05 p.m. An armed yacht proceeded to the scene and dropped a depth-charge. The airship then left to escort a convoy of forty ships, protected by five destroyers and trawlers. While zigzagging ahead of the convoy, it sighted a submarine 5 miles off Dunbar. *N.S.8* searched the area unsuccessfully and then returned to the convoy 20 miles east of May Island at 2.05 a.m. About an hour later, fog obscured the ships and the airship spent a further two hours searching for the submarine without success, before landing back at East Fortune at 6.15 a.m. A daily report of airship flights for 7 August 1918 gives a good indication of the work being carried out from RNAS East Fortune in the last year of the war:

Coastal Star *C*1*, patrol over northern sector, 10 hours 15 minutes.

North Sea *N.S.7*, engine and water recovery, 3 hours 15 minutes, trials, middle sector.

Rigid *R.29*, patrol over southern sector, 11 hours 10 minutes.

Coastal Star *C*7*, patrol over middle sector, 7 hours 20 minutes.

Submarine Scout Zero *S.S.Z.3*, instruction, 2 flights, 3 hours 35 minutes.

Submarine Scout Zero *S.S.Z.60*, operating from Chathill.

Earlier in the summer, North Sea *N.S.3* was given the task of escorting a Scandinavian convoy off Aberdeen. At 9.00 p.m., oil was spotted rising to the surface around 5 miles off Bervie Bay. Two 230-lb bombs were dropped and a destroyer released depth charges. More oil came to the surface, but it was later concluded that it had come from a sunken ship. *N.S.3* then flew south until it reached May Island at the entrance to the Firth of Forth. Here it encountered a 40-knot off-shore wind, which made it very difficult to reach the coast. On the fifth attempt, the airship was carried up to 1,500 feet, then suddenly plummeted into the sea, wrenching the car containing the engines and two engineers from the airship. The remaining crew struggled to put on their life jackets, as the airship plunged again, submerging the crew car. Three of the crew managed to escape through the windows and two other men also made it to the surface. There was no sign of the five other crew members. The survivors lay on the partly inflated gas bag until they were picked up by a destroyer. Fortunately, this was the only fatal airship accident to be suffered by East Fortune.

Perhaps the proudest moment for the airship crews based here came when, in late November 1918, they photographed and filmed the surrendered German fleet anchored in the Firth of Forth before the ships proceeded to Scapa Flow. Only a few months earlier, Sopwith Cuckoo torpedo bombers had begun arriving at RNAS East Fortune for a top-secret mission, in which 200 aircraft were to attack the German fleet while it was anchored in the harbour. While airship flying had ceased at most RAF stations by the end of 1918, East Fortune was given a brief respite, operating for another year.

Chathill Mooring Out Station

Location: O. S. 1/50,000 map 75 (NU)193273. Northumberland, a short distance to the east of Chathill railway station, 3 miles south-west of Seahouses.

East Fortune's mooring out station, Chathill, was commissioned on 31 July 1918. Submarine Scout Zeros from East Fortune escorting convoys as far as Holy Island would often land at Chathill before returning to base. On 2 November 1918, *S.S.Z.59* had to be deflated here when a gale blew up. By this time, airships were frequently based here for patrols of the Northumberland coast. Men and supplies could easily access the mooring out site for it was close both to the Great North Road and the main east coast railway line to Scotland. In late 1918, it was planned to considerably expand the site. There would have been three Submarine Scout Zeros and two

Submarine Scout Twins detached here by the following summer, and two portable airship sheds—175 feet in length and 50 feet wide—to house them.

An order for sixteen timber-framed sheds had been placed with Dalacombe Merechal and Hervieu Ltd. for use on mooring out sites throughout Britain including Bude, Laira, Lowthorpe, and Ramsey. It was also intended to erect no less than six at RAF East Fortune in 1919. Although these sheds required a great deal of skill to manufacture, they could be easily erected. An ingenious design allowed the A-frame trestles to be erected first. Each was fitted with a winch for raising the roof. The central portions of the roof trusses were assembled on the ground, including the rafters and canvas covering; the roof section was raised by winches and the complete shed was canvas clad. No airship sheds of any type were ever erected at Chathill. Trees now stand where airships were once sheltered.

RNAS Longside Airship Station

Alternative names: 'Lenabo', sometimes 'Aberdeen' in official reports.
Location: O. S. 1/50,000 map 30 (NK) 030421. Aberdeenshire, 7 miles south-west of Peterhead, 26 miles north-east of Aberdeen.
Station Complement: twenty-five officers, 520 men (on 1 Jan 1918).
Size: 950 acres (within boundaries of 2,730 x 2,330 yards).
Airship Sheds: one rigid shed (711 feet long, 151 feet wide, and 105 feet high), one Coastal (323 feet long, 113 feet wide, and 80 feet high), one Coastal shed (323 feet long, 114 feet wide, and 80 feet high).
Hydrogen Plant: 'B' silicol (10,000 cubic feet per hour), water gas plant (14,000 cubic feet per hour).
Gasholders: two of 250,000 cubic feet, one of 20,000 cubic feet.
Based Airship: Submarine Scout Zero *S.S.Z.57*, *S.S.Z.58*, *S.S.Z.65*, and *S.S.Z.66*; Coastal *C.4*, *C.*, *C.7*, *C.10A*, *C.14*, *C.18*, and *C.25*; Coastal Star *C*4*, *C*5*, and *C*7*; North Sea *N.S.1*, *N.S.4*, *N.S.6*, *N.S.9*, *N.S.10*, *N.S.11*, and *N.S.12*.

Longside airship station was located on the Buchan Peninsula, so it was well placed to guard North Sea shipping around the peninsula. Its situation some distance inland from the coast protected it from shelling by German warships. Tawse of Aberdeen began construction work in 1915. A small village of huts was erected to house their workers and became known as 'Tawsetown'. While much of the surrounding land was used to grow crops, the site selected for the airship station was a peat bog. In fact the area is named Lenabo, also spelled 'Lanabo'—after the Gaelic 'lannam bo'—meaning 'wet meadow of the cows'. Draining the waterlogged ground proved a major undertaking. An army of Scots and Irish labourers assisted by primitive steam scoops and bucket cranes tore away at the layers of peat, some of which was even used to fire the US-made steam shovels. Work continued through the night by the light of naptha flares. A fleet of steam lorries carried construction materials along the narrow roads from Aberdeen, while horse-drawn carts were used for shorter journeys. Later, a branch line of around 4½ miles was laid from Longside railway station to transport men and materials, though this was not fully operational until 1918.

The scarcity of civilian labour delayed completion. Over £500,000 was spent on the airship station, compared with around £59,000 for RNAS Anglesey. Many of the accommodation blocks were built of Cruden brick, while out-stations had to make do with wooden huts. A high fence encompassed the whole base. At the main gate stood two pseudo-classical pillars mounted with large stone balls. They were allegedly cast by a rating called Yorky and were referred to as 'Yorky's Balls'.

The station was officially commissioned on 16 March 1916, and the first airship arrived on a railway wagon a few weeks later. By July, the two Coastal airships C.5 and C.7 were on strength. Due to adverse weather, just 78 hours were flown that month. At this time, the north Coastal shed was complete and was in the process of being splash painted, whereas the south Coastal shed was in the final stages of construction, with its metal sheeting still being attached. The Air Construction Corps undertook the work on these buildings, and by the summer of 1916, the erection of steel work for the rigid shed was well underway. After some teething problems, the silicol plant was also commissioned, but produced gas of a low purity only. Much of the station had electricity and the telephone network was coming into use. Gas mains were installed in the airship sheds, enabling airships to be inflated while in them. Work on a hydrogen plant using the water gas method commenced the following month, but its construction was delayed due to difficulty in obtaining the necessary steel.

On 22 April 1920, the *Aberdeen Journal* published the following account of life at the station, based on the accounts of anonymous RNAS serviceman who signed it 'Battle Bag':

> The drawbacks of life at Lenabo were countless but there were compensations. Yet it wasn't all monotony and exile. These boys made discoveries and amongst their 'finds' one might mention the Pitfour Arms, Henry Gilmore's, Gray's Farm and the North-Eastern at Peterhead. Were there not newly laid eggs galore, butter from real cows and glorious creamy milk—not to speak of those tasty fresh herrings? And then there was the hero worship of the natives—wonder of wonders, we are to have airships and those men are to fly them! In the course of time muddy roads gave way to second Regent Streets; floral borders sprang up everywhere, the Church Army erected a huge hut and placed billiard tables in it, the RNAS boys bought a cinema machine and gave shows, a canteen blossomed forth and sold good beer made in Peterhead, liberty cars commenced to run to and from the seaport town and airships crept out of their resting places, rose gracefully into the air and sailed off over the North Sea, to return to their base with nightfall.

But British airships did not have the skies entirely to themselves. On the 2nd and 3rd of May, a Zeppelin was seeing flying over Aberdeenshire. It had earlier dropped bombs on Edinburgh and then strayed off course. Believing that RNAS Longside might be next in the bomb aimer's sights, two B.E.2C bi-planes arrived to carry out anti-Zeppelin patrols. Around the same time, the commander of the Grand Fleet requested that RNAS Longside airships fly patrols between Cromarty and Rattray Point to look for mines that may have been sown by a German submarine.

By November 1916, there were four Coastal airships on strength. *C.18* suffered engine failure on patrol, an almost daily occurrence at this time, due to the unreliability of the magnetos. This was compounded by the fact that 'the ratings available for working the machine tools are very unsatisfactory, not a single man having any experience worth mentioning'.[3] Motor launches came to the rescue of *C.18*, towing it 18 miles to the Peterhead Fishmarket where the crew managed to restart the engines and were able to fly the final stage back to RNAS Longside.

At both the beginning and end of 1917, the weather was abnormally and continually lousy for airship work, for instance strong gales and fog. The only good weather was in late June and July. On the night of 5 June 1917, *C.7* was on patrol and was warned to return to base by wireless because of fog—while on patrol duty, Coastal airships were now in wireless contact with their base. The wind did not prove very obliging, increasing in strength to 30 mph. The airship made hardly any headway and took 3 hours to reach the coast, where it managed to land safely with only 5 gallons of petrol in its tank. On 25 October, gale force winds caused considerable damage to the airship station itself.

An aerial view of RNAS Longside. The Coastal shed functions as a windbreak for the eastern entrance of the large rigid shed. Beyond them is the hydrogen gas plant and the huts for housing personnel. (*RAF Museum*)

The roof of the south Coastal shed had large portions torn off, but fortunately there was no airship in it at the time. The following report for airship patrols on 21 April 1917 gives a good insight into the work of RNAS Longside's airships:

1. All four ships *C.7*, *C.10A*, *C.14* and *C.18* left the ground between 07.30 and 08.05. *C.7*, *C.14* and *C.18* to proceed on the North Moray Firth patrol and *C.10A* to carry out trial flight after rigging.

2. The wind at the time of leaving was N.N.W., 12 mph, and afterwards veered to N.N.E. and rose to 16 to 20 mph.

3. *C.18* set course for Brora Point and 4 miles north of Troup Head met trawler *CX1010*. A fleet of ten trawlers was passed 7 miles N.N.E. of Banff steering west at 09.15. At 09.20 investigated a Danish steamer *Vendyssel* passing west. A convoy of one Russian and four Norwegian vessels, escorted by destroyer *D. 64* and four trawlers, were met four miles N.E. of Lossiemouth passing east. At 11.12, the Commander in Chief was informed of *C.14*'s position, 6 miles north of Tarbat Ness, the course was then N.E. Between this position and Wick, which was reached at 13.20, one Norwegian vessel, twelve trawlers and a vessel *H947* were met and investigated. The course was then set for Kinnaird Head owing to engine trouble and the ship landed at 15.40.

4. *C.14* left at 7.30 and arrived off Banff at *08.45*. Here trawlers were sighted steering west. At *09.00* the after engine carburettor float punctures and trouble was experienced with the air pressure. Course was set for Longside at 10.20 when off Port Knockie and before landing at 11.30 further engine trouble was experienced. *C.14* resumed patrol at 17.30 and at 18.00 sighted Norwegian steamer *Bramse* and escort steering west. Soon after the forward engine failed due to magneto trouble and the ship landed at 20.35.

(5) *C.7* left at 8.00 and at 08.40 passed one mile east of Troup Head. Eleven trawlers minesweeping westward were passed at 09.25 and Danish steamer investigated at 00.40. The ship returned at 12.50 to examine valves. At 07.40 the ship resumed patrol and proceeded as far as 09 NMB. Norwegian steamer *Baisf* was met at 17.52. Troup Head was passed on the return journey at 19.45 and the ship landed at 20.30.

(6) *C.10A* left for trial flight in the vicinity of the Aerodrome at 07.35 and landed at 8.20. The trial was successful. The ship left the ground again at 14.30 to carry out Lewis Gun practice and photographic experiments but was compelled to land with engine trouble at 15.40. The total flying for the day amounted to 23 hours but was greatly curtailed owing to continuous engine trouble.[4]

On 1 July 1917, a signal was received stating that a submarine was attacking a merchant vessel. An attempt was made to dispatch Coastal *C.14*, but owing to the high wind its forward skid was damaged and it was returned to its shed. *C.7* was taken out instead and, it too damaged its forward skid, but managed to get airborne. There was no sign of the submarine. A few days later, on the 8th, *C.14* was escorting a convoy when a submarine periscope was sighted, 2 to 3 miles ahead of the convoy. Coastal *C.7* and *C.10A* were ordered by wireless to investigate. The submarine escaped by diving, but it was acknowledged that the presence of the airship undoubtedly saved the convoy from attack. A further encounter with an enemy submarine took place on 16 November when a motor launch reported a periscope off Kinnaird Head. *C.14* was ordered to proceed to the location. The crew caught sight of some bubbles and dropped three 100-lb bombs without obvious result.

In 1917, RNAS Longside's airships—or 'Lenabo Sows', as they were nicknamed by the locals—took part in a number of exercises with the Grand Fleet. *C.10A* and *C.14* spent 13 hours flying alongside warships on 16 July. North Sea *N.S.1* and *N.S.2* from RNAS East Fortune departed at dawn with Coastal *C.10A*, *C.14*, and *C.18* from RNAS Longside to participate in exercises with the Grand Fleet. By the time they returned to RNAS Longside, the weather had deteriorated and great difficulty was experienced in landing.

By the end of 1917, the station had a complement of twenty-five officers and 520 men, along with four airships—Coastal *C.7*, *C.10A*, *C.14*, and *C.18*. The rigid airship shed and the water gas plant were finished and a new wireless station was built, complete with new masts. A further Coastal airship was received early the following year—RNAS Longside was now the main base for Coastals.

But further types arrived in 1918, in the form of North Seas and Submarine Scout Zeros—though these were mainly based at Auldbar. In February the weather was so

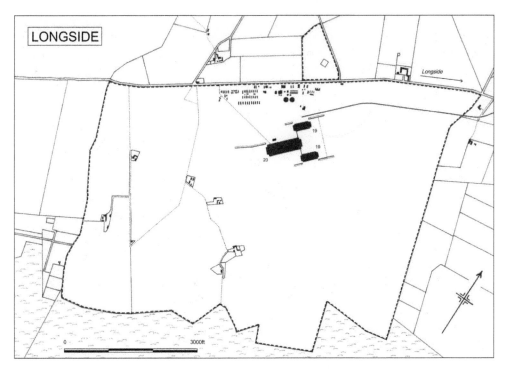

Longside. The largest building in the plan is the rigid shed which was completed in 1917. On either side are Coastal sheds. The silicol plant and accommodation huts stood close to the road to Peterhead. Within the station boundary fell a large area of moorland. Despite the marshy nature of the ground, there were several small holdings in the area, some of which survived until 1918, when they were demolished as part of improvements to the airship station. (*Mick Davis*)

bad that patrols could only be carried out on four days. There was some compensation for this, for instance in the brilliant displays of the *Aurora Borealis* observed over the station at night. When patrols could not be flown, bomb and gunnery practice was the order of the day. The station continued to grow with the construction of a blacksmith's workshop, hospital, and miniature rifle ranges. The Coastal airship sheds were repainted a smoke-grey colour, replacing the previous splash colour scheme.

As spring approached, an anticyclone formed over Scandinavia, which generated a long spell of calm weather. In March, the RNAS Longside airships flew 76 hours of escort duties and protected some 200 vessels. On the moonlit evening of the 20th, *C.10A* was instructed to escort a valuable convoy through the area. April also saw airships escort many further convoys steaming off the waters of north-east Scotland. With the formation of the RAF on 1 April 1918, the aircrews came under this new jurisdiction; however, airship stations remained the responsibility of the Admiralty. Some examples of the work undertaken by airships of Longside at this time are related in the report below:

4th April, 1918 *C.7* and *C.10A* received instructions to pick up and escort as far as possible a large south-bound convoy consisting of 40 ships. When off Tod Head, HMS *Hopeful* signalled *C.7* to stand by a mine about a quarter of a mile off the convoy. The convoy altered course and the mine was sunk by gunfire by HMS *Vehement*. *C.10* and *C.10A* then continued in company with the convoy to St Abb's Head from which position the ships returned to base. On the same day orders were received from the Commander in Chief, Grand Fleet, for an airship to pick up and escort until dark two south-bound ammunition ships, in the charge of two destroyers. *C.14* (Capt. MacColl) who was escorting the north bound coastal convoy was detailed for this duty and at once proceeded to the rendezvous and picked up the ammunition convoy. Remaining in company with it until 20.00 hrs (8.00 p.m.) a period of six hours. Then she returned to base and made a night landing.

8th April, 1918. *C.7*, *C.10A* (Capt. Jelliffe) and C.14 (Capt. MacColl) left the ground during a calm, *C.7* under instructions to escort a large south-bound convoy, *C.10A* and *C.14* to proceed on a northerly patrol. Weather conditions suddenly changed and the wind rose rapidly to 20-30 mph before it was possible to recall the ships. It was therefore considered advisable for them to remain on patrol in the hope of the wind abating. *C.7* picked up the convoy and escorted it for 10 hours, the ship having difficulty at times in keeping pace owing to the direction and force of the wind. After escorting the convoy to a position off Fife Ness, the ship returned to base. Owing to strong gusts she was slightly damaged whilst being taken into shed.[5]

In April, Longside's airships were called on to investigate six possible submarine sightings. The following month, a record amount of flying was undertaken—eighty-five patrols, thirty-six by Coastals and forty-nine by Submarine Scout Zeros. Some eighty convoys were escorted in May 1918, totalling over 950 ships. Many flying hours were spent searching for mines and, with the onset of short nights, a considerable amount of night flying was also undertaken. At the request of Rear Adml Peterhead, fishing fleets in No. 5 area were also protected by airships. July was heralded by an epidemic of influenza, with 250 cases recorded at Longside. The entire medical staff came down with the infection, but fortunately not simultaneously. Seven of the men's sleeping huts were used to house the sick; convalescent patients were employed as orderlies; and nurses and canteen staff assisted with the feeding of patients. The flying efficiency of Longside declined markedly, but this was hardly remarkable for most affected British airship stations at the time.

And yet, the number of personnel at Longside was increasing. Such was the shortage of accommodation that many of the men had to live in tents. These were totally useless in wet weather, as they leaked and did not protect from the cold: given the local climate, sleeping under canvas was totally inappropriate after September. While the station was still awaiting the construction of additional huts, a caterpillar tractor was used to pull down abandoned crofts and remove trees to improve the landing ground. At the beginning of 1918, four Coastal were flying most of the patrols.

By the summer, Longside was home to the following airships: North Sea *N.S.4*, *N.S.6*, and *N.S.9*; Coastal Star *C*5*; Coastal *C.5A*, *C.7*, and *C.25*; and Submarine Scout Zero *S.S.Z.57*, *S.S.Z.58*, *S.S.Z.65*, and *S.S.Z.66*. On 29 July 1918, several Coastals were engaged in a search for a damaged German submarine. One of them, *C.25*, commanded by Capt. Hopperton, transmitted a last message at 6.40 p.m. then lost contact. When the airship did not return a search was mounted, but the only trace found was a propeller at its last known position, 60 miles east of Aberdeen. The most plausible explanation for its mysterious disappearance was that it came across a German submarine and was brought down by its deck gun. The next day, North Sea *N.S.9* was on its first patrol under the command of Capt. Maitland when it stumbled across an enemy submarine on the surface, which opened fire on the airship. *N.S.9* fortunately survived the encounter. After the war, attempts were made to trace the submarine involved to uncover the fate of *C.25*, but the suspected culprit never returned to its home base either, vanishing in the waters of the North Sea.

All airships were hard to handle on the ground in gusty conditions, with the Coastals and North Seas reckoned to be the most difficult. It took 500 men—almost the entire complement of RNAS Longside—to restrain a North Sea airship by ropes on a windy day. On calm days, landing parties for smaller airships—like the Submarine Scout Zero—would consist of around fifty men. Official records bemoan the necessity to increase numbers to over seventy in the final months of the war, due to the low medical status of the men posted here—a complaint not restricted to RNAS Longside.

In the closing stages of the war, two D.H.6 aeroplanes flew a number of patrols from Longside. Three airships were on patrol on 21 September 1918, but were recalled when the weather began to deteriorate. Coastal *C.7* managed to land safely with the assistance of a 300-strong landing party. While being walked to its shed, turbulence around the building meant the envelope had to be 'ripped' to ensure a rapid deflation. As the wind rose to 40 mph, North Sea *N.S.9* managed to touch down safely, but on approaching its shed it also had to be deflated to prevent it becoming out of control. The last airship down was *N.S.10*, but it also had to 'ripped'. This was the only time that three RNAS airships simultaneously had to be deflated in such a manner—none of them flew again, the end of the war being close at hand. On 14 November, a detachment of D.H.9s of No. 254 Squadron arrived from Prawle Point as part of preparation for a final action against the German fleet. The attack never went ahead.

Even after the Armistice was signed, Longside's airships continued to shepherd convoys through the waters of the North Sea in November; mine-hunting patrols continued in the first few months of 1919; and although the station was now in its twilight days, one of its few remaining airships—*N.S.11*—still managed to achieve a record-breaking flight. There were plans to considerably expand the airship fleet at Longside, but the end of the war intervened. By mid-1919, when flying had all but ceased, it was still four North Seas, one Coastal Star, and no less than nine Submarine Scout Twins strong. Nevertheless, in 1920 the station was put up for disposal. There were proposals to set up a canning factory or a peat processing plant on the site, but they came to nothing. The large airship sheds were sold for scrap and demolished.

Alfred Brundell, the Depot Manager at RAF Longside, realised that he had no future here so decided to make the most of the situation—he stole items including railway sleepers, linoleum, and mineral grease. For this he was sentenced to three months in prison. The railway, which had seen little use since it was completed, was in the process of being dismantled in August 1923 when the lead wagon of a goods train struck and killed a middle-aged couple in their car. They had been driving over a level crossing, and the view of the railway track at this point had been obscured by a wood.

After many years of lying abandoned, the ground on which the airship station once stood was planted with conifers by the Forestry Commission. The area is now sometimes referred to as 'the Forest of Deer', with some of the original camp roads serving as footpaths. Interspersed among the trees are remnants of the old station— mooring blocks and ruined walls.

Auldbar Mooring Out Station

Alternative name: initially 'Montrose', the name was changed to 'Auldbar' in July 1918 to avoid confusion with Montrose Aerodrome.
Location: O. S. 1/50,000 map 54 (NO) 570560. Angus, 4 miles from the site of Auldbar Road railway station and east of the Auldbar–Brechin Road. Auldbar is spelled as 'Aldbar' on some maps.

Auldbar was commissioned as a mooring out site for Longside on 31 July 1918. The location is unusual for a mooring out station, as it was around 10 miles from the sea in the Montreathmont Forest. This location answered the need for a large area of woodland—an essential feature of most mooring out stations—as the trees provided shelter without the need to build sheds to protect airships on the ground. The forest was not far from Dundee and from there airships could be deployed to protect the approaches to the Firth of Tay. Trees were felled to create four berths, and pits were dug into the ground where the control cars could sit, so that the airships would fit more snugly. Most of the tree-felling took place in May 1918, but the work was hampered owing to a number of the ratings from Blandford developing rubella, many of whom had to be put in quarantine. A landing ground was adjoined to the road to Brechin by further felling of woodland.

Tents for housing the personnel at RNAS Auldbar Mooring Out Station, 1918. Among them is the commanding officer's quarters, located on the left side of the footpath lined with whitewashed stones. (*The Royal Aeronautical Society*)

Submarine Scout Zero *S.S.Z.58* on the landing ground at Auldbar Mooring Out Station, September 1918. (*The Royal Aeronautical Society*)

Submarine Scout Zero *S.S.Z.57*, *S.S.Z.58*, *S.S.Z.65*, and *S.S.Z.66* were deployed here. Their operation was far from uneventful: *S.S.Z.57* had to be deflated after breaking away from its moorings on 2 November 1918; and *S.S.Z.58* made an emergency landing at Johnshaven in August, as did *S.S.Z.66* at Arbroath. The planned allocation of airships for 1 July 1919 was two Submarine Scout Zeros. Unlike most of the other mooring out stations, no portable airship sheds had been ordered for this base—perhaps the forest was thought to provide sufficient protection.

RNAS Caldale Airship Station

Alternative name: 'Kirkwall'.
Location: O. S. 1/50,000 map 06 (HY) 417105. Orkney Islands, between the Old Finstown Road and a farmstead called Longhouse, 2½ miles south-west of Kirkwall.
Size: 146 acres.
Station Complement: six officers, eighty-five men (in Jan 1918).
Airship Sheds: Coastal shed (220 feet long, 70 feet wide), Submarine Scout shed (150 feet long, 45 feet wide).
Based Airships: Submarine Scout *S.S.41* and *S.S.43*; and Submarine Scout Pusher *S.S.P.2* and *S.S.P.4* (only six of this class of airship—so named for the placement of the engine at the back of the control car—were produced).

There could be few more challenging environments in which to operate airships than the Orkney Islands. There are few trees, which allows the prevailing winds to sweep over the landscape directly from the Atlantic Ocean. RNAS Caldale overlooked Scapa Flow and the Grand Fleet anchored there. In April 1916, Cdr Roland Hunt was sent to select a site in the vicinity of Scapa Flow for a Coastal airship station. Previously, Col. Harris—who was in command of the Orkney Defences—had examined all possible locations and reported that only two would be suitable. The better was in a hollow, 2½ miles west of Kirkwall, and was well protected from the winds from the west. With the exception of low barbed-wire fences, the surrounding countryside was clear for a considerable distance, and there was suitable dry level ground for the foundations of an airship shed. The main drawback was, rather surprisingly, the water supply, which in the summer months was practically non-existent. The only source of water was a stream used by a whisky distillery near the shore.

The C-in-C of the Grand Fleet informed Cdr Roland Hunt that unless an airship could be provided before September 1916, it would be of little use after that date because of the strong winds. He was of the opinion that if a Submarine Scout rather than a Coastal shed could be used, it would be operational sooner, because these sheds could be erected within twenty-eight days of the arrival of materials. The C-in-C also argued that rigid airship sheds should not be placed this far north, as it was improbable that a fleet action would be fought in northern latitudes: the vicinity of the Firth of Forth would be more suitable. If a site further north was necessary, he thought Cromarty Firth would be most appropriate, because it was sheltered from the wind.[6] According to Royal Navy accounts, £13,265 was spent on purchasing land for an airship depot there in 1915, but nothing ever came of it.

The Director of Air Services arranged for the dispatch of a portable airship shed at short notice to Caldale, and a month later (May 1916) the airship station was commissioned. It was also suggested that a Coastal shed originally intended for Mudros, Greece, could be dispatched here as soon as possible, but this part of the plan was delayed. The first airships to arrive were Submarine Scout *S.S.41* and *S.S.43*, which were dispatched from RNAS Kingsnorth by rail in late July 1916. *S.S.41* made its first flight here on the 20th of August, followed by *S.S.43* on the 24th.

As winter approached, things were not looking good at RNAS Caldale. The 'Items of Information' report from the Admiralty for November 1916 is full of woe:

> The S.S. Shed is being fitted with doors and until these are complete it will not be possible to re-inflate the ship. Very high winds with heavy rain have been experienced lately and these have swept right through the shed, thoroughly soaking the aeroplanes and cars stowed there, in spite of every effort made to protect them with deck cloths. Work on the Coastal Patrol Shed, other than clearing away the wreckage of the portion which was blown down, has been abandoned. Most of the other buildings included in the plan of the station are approaching completion but the Petty Officers hut has not yet been delivered and there is no provision for a petrol store, magazine, garage, workshops or office. The general store is a cramped and rough building and is liable to be flooded during heavy rains. The workshop lorry has arrived but owing to the state of the ground, it has not been possible to remove it from the high ground. The hydrogen mains and electric circuits are being delayed owing to non-delivery of material. The Station is occupied by one officer and one hundred men of the Aircraft Construction Corps, in addition to the Care and Maintenance Party. The work of construction is badly hampered by the weather and the working hours are being curtailed. It is barely daylight by 8.00 a.m. and quite dark again by 4.30 p.m.[7]

It is no surprise that airship operations from the station were suspended, or that RNAS Caldale was operated on a care-and-maintenance basis. Happily, by April of the following year, the situation had improved: a submarine bomb target had been laid out on the ground, the Submarine Scout shed was nearly complete, and material had arrived at the dock for the erection of a second shed. However, the 3½ miles from pier to base proved difficult for the motor lorry, which was always breaking down, so for the final ½ mile it was carried on a light railway. At the end of May, Submarine Scout Pusher *S.S.P.2* flew north from RNAS Kingsnorth to its new home. Its journey took it via RNAS Howden, where it arrived on the 11th, but it did not depart until the 26th because of difficulty in obtaining permission to fly further north. Two weeks later it was joined by *S.S.P.4*. Two patrols were flown on the 29th, but visibility was hampered by low cloud and mist.

On the ground, around 100 men from the Grand Fleet assisted in the construction of the new airship shed. Even in August, thick fog and high winds limited the number of patrols that could be flown; however, a minefield was still swept and one floating mine observed—the surface of the sea here was too rough to spot moored mines. The

A Royal Navy construction party transporting timber on the narrow gauge railway built to transport materials to RNAS Caldale. Much of the work was done by naval ratings based at Scapa Flow. (*Jim Eunson Collection*)

following month, strong winds blew over the islands. Despite difficulty in keeping up with the warships due to the wind, *S.S.P.4* managed to escort the Grand Fleet to harbour. All pilots complained of the difficulty of remaining out on patrol for more than 4 to 5 hours, because of the extreme cold. In addition, there was no land to the east of the Orkney Islands on which they could seek safety in the face of fierce westerlys, which put a further strain on aircrews. It was only a matter of time before an accident occurred.

S.S.P.2 left RNAS Caldale on the morning of 26 November 1917. The wind strengthened after its departure, and after an hour in the air, the pilot decided to return to base. Soon after, the airship signalled that its engine had failed and it was going to make a forced landing. A lookout station later reported that it had seen *S.S.P.2* come down in the sea and explode off the Island of Westray. HMS *Leopard*, which had been close by, could find no trace of the wreckage or survivors. Its crew—Flt Lt S. Devereux, AM1 A. E. Scott, and L. M. W/T J. Wilson—were all lost.

On 21 December 1917, the remaining Submarine Scout Pusher *S.S.P.4* undertook a night flight. An hour after take-off, it reported that it was snowing heavily and that it was attempting to return to RNAS Caldale. Over the next few hours the airship reported that it could make no headway against the strong wind. The crew requested that ships with searchlights be sent to the area so they could determine their position, after which radio messages from the airship ceased. The remains of *S.S.P.4* were located on the Island of Westray the following day. There was no sign of the crew, Flt Cdr W. Horner, L. M. Anthony, and AM9 R. Behn.

The winter weather was so bad that the workshop lorry had to be covered with sheet iron as the canvas covers provided little protection. In January, blizzards closed

The Submarine Scout shed at RNAS Caldale. (*Jim Eunson Collection*)

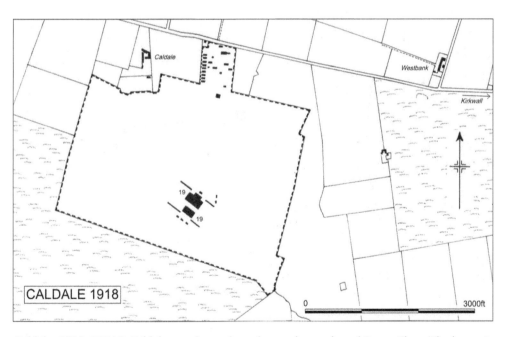

Caldale, 1918. RNAS Caldale was located on the northern edge of Scapa Flow. The larger is a Coastal shed, while the smaller is a Submarine Scout type. Both of their entrances face into the north-west wind. The accommodation huts are on the edge of the site next to the road to Kirkwall. (*Mick Davis*)

all the roads to the station and all essential supplies had to be delivered by sledges pulled by ratings. By this time there was only one deflated airship here—Submarine Scout *S.S.41*.

The Coastal shed had been completed by the end of 1917, although the windbreaks—no less than six of them—were still being worked on. Perhaps as a consequence of the loss of two airships, the Admiralty gave orders on 22 January 1918 for RNAS Caldale to be closed. But this was not quite the end of its association with the lighter-than-air machines. A short time later, it re-opened as a kite balloon station: these were manned balloons which were towed behind warships to direct the gunfire of the fleet. But by 1920 the former airship station was derelict. In the Second World War, it housed a vehicle repair yard and was used to store barrage balloons. One former serviceman recalled two large sheds surrounded by large areas of impenetrable concrete on the site. The buildings may have been RNAS Caldale's airship sheds. Extensive reconstruction took place in the latter stages of the Second World War, which swept away many of the original structures. Most of the buildings from both wars have since been demolished, and the Royal Navy base at Scapa Flow is now only a memory.

Proposed Airship Stations

There were ambitious plans to expand the rigid airship fleet in early 1916. 'Scottish lakes' were suggested as possible locations for future bases, as was Dumfries for the site of a rigid shed. In the summer it was decided that there should be provision for six Rigids of 'the largest size' and new airship stations to house them, each with two double sheds, at Glasgow, Chester, Taunton, and in Northern and Southern Ireland. None of these projects went ahead, but had the resources not been lacking, these would have been among the largest airship stations in Britain. RNAS Howden, for example, had only one double rigid shed and one single rigid shed.

8

RNAS Airship Bases in Ireland

Ireland was still part of Great Britain in the First World War, despite its rising clamour for independence. Resentment came to a head in the Easter Rising in 1916, which centred on Dublin, the island's administrative heart. The Irish rebels were eventually crushed by British troops, but their aspirations soon became a reality when Southern Ireland declared its independence in 1919.

Ireland's geographic position made it important in the war on German submarines: merchant ships ferrying vital supplies had to navigate around its coastline to reach major ports such as Bristol and Liverpool. Northern Ireland also possessed important industries, including shipbuilding yards in Belfast. Concerns that the Germans might covertly support Irish insurrections prompted Britain to heavily guard its military installations there, unlike on the mainland. Prior to the First World War, airships had been notable for their absence from the Emerald Isle—unlike in England and Wales, no airship sheds had been erected either by the military or enthusiastic amateurs.

The first airship crossings to Ireland were unintentional. The French airship *La Patrie* came loose from her moorings at Verdun on 29 November 1907, and was blown north-west. It briefly came into contact with a hill near Belfast, but rose back into the air and was last seen off the west coast of Scotland. Fortunately, there was no one aboard when it began its involuntary voyage. The first manned arrival of an airship in Ireland was equally unplanned. In the summer of 1915, Submarine Scout *S.S.17*, flown by Flt Lt Elmhirst, suffered a rudder failure. Although the engine still functioned, the craft had no directional control and was unable to return to its base at RNAS Anglesey. The easterly wind carried the airship further out to sea, where it briefly touched down—the crew pleaded for assistance from a nearby fishing boat and later another vessel, but were twice ignored. As they approached the Irish coast, the compass and wireless were thrown overboard, less essential parts having already been jettisoned. This gave Flt Lt Elmhirst just enough lift to clear the 300 feet sheer cliffs near Larne. The airship finally landed a short distance inland. Some time later, the crews of the fishing vessels were questioned by the Royal Navy as to why they did not assist. Their answer was, 'We did observe a British airship manoeuvring, it was a very pretty sight'.[1] Clearly, the sympathies of the crews lay with the Irish nationalists.

At the outbreak of war, there was a small naval base at Queenstown (now renamed Cobh) near Cork, home to four old motor torpedo boats. Initially, it was thought that the naval war would be confined to the North Sea and the English Channel, but this idea was soon revised. The first German submarine to enter the Irish Sea sank three ships at the mouth of the River Mersey, close to the Port of Liverpool, in January 1915. Matters went from bad to worse on 7 May, when the passenger liner *Lusitania* was sunk off the south coast of Ireland with heavy loss of life.

On 4 February 1915, Germany responded to British blockades by declaring the waters around Great Britain and Ireland part of the war zone. From 18 February 1915 onwards, the German submarine blockade would commence—every merchant ship in these waters was fair game. The Royal Navy reacted by enlisting hundreds of drifters equipped with special nets to literally fish for enemy submarines. The naval base at Queenstown now had a dozen steam trawlers on strength, as well as a number of torpedo boats for patrolling the south and south-west coast of Ireland. Despite these measures, the situation deteriorated rapidly, and scores of merchant ships were lost.

In June 1915, the position of Senior Officer on the Coast of Ireland was created and given to Adml Sir Lewis Bayly RN. He had several hundred trawlers, drifters, and armed yachts under his command operating from Ireland, the Scilly Islands, and Milford Haven in Wales. A watchful eye from the air was provided by airships then operating from bases on the British mainland, and in 1916 there were proposals to establish a rigid airship base at Queenstown. The shores of Loch Neagh, a large expanse of water out of reach of hostile submarines, would in addition be an ideal site for an airship-building dockyard for the Royal Navy. And yet, despite Ireland's propitious strategic position, by the end of the war just a handful of minor airship bases had been established there, all of them on its east coast only.

Doagh Island Mooring Out Station

Mooring-out station for Luce Bay Airship Station.
Alternative name: 'Ballyliffin'.
Location: 55 17'25" N, 05 23'00" W. County Down, close to the northernmost tip of Ireland in County Donegal, 15 miles to the north of Londonderry (Derry).
Airships known to have used this base: Submarine Scout *S.S.20*, *S.S.23*, and *S.S.35*; and Submarine Scout Zero *S.S.Z.11*, *S.S.Z.12*, and *S.S.Z.20*.

Doagh Island was established as a mooring out station for Luce Bay and was the northernmost of British bases in Ireland. From this location airships could provide protection for convoys rounding the north coast. The base was still under construction on 31 October 1918 and appears to have been little used before it was abandoned. Had the conflict continued, it may have been greatly expanded: it was intended to have two small steel airship sheds at Doagh Island to house two Submarine Scout Twins by the summer of 1919, and tented accommodation was due to be replaced with huts. That four of the seven windbreaks on order for mooring out stations in Britain were allocated to this base gives some insight into the inclement weather conditions experienced here. Doagh Island's location made it particularly vulnerable to gales from the north-west. Further south, near the coast facing Scotland, Larne was the only airship base in Ireland to have its own shed in the First World War.

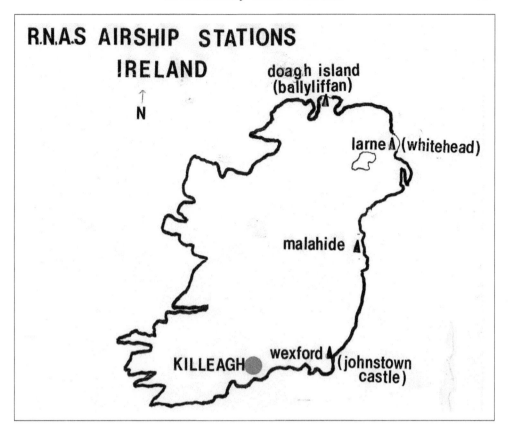

RNAS airship stations in Ireland. (*Author's collection*)

A Submarine Scout airship being handled by its ground party at RNAS Larne. (*D & N Caldwell Collection*)

RNAS Larne Mooring Out Station

Mooring-out station for Luce Bay Airship Station.
Alternative names: 'Bentra', 'Whitehead'.
Location: 54 46' 00" N, 05 43' 35" W. County Antrim. The actual site was 8 miles to the south of Larne, near Whitehead on the southern end of the Loch Larne.
Airship Shed: portable type Submarine Scout shed (150 feet long, 45 feet wide, and 50 feet high).
Airships known to have used this base: Submarine Scout Zero *S.S.Z.57*, *S.S.Z.58*, *S.S.Z.65*, and *S.S.Z.66*; Coastal *C.4* and *C.5A*; Coastal Star *C*5* and *C*7*; North Sea *N.S.6*, *N.S.9*, *N.S.10*, and *N.S.11*.

Each morning, the steamship *Princess Maud* left Stranraer, Scotland, bound for Larne carrying passengers and mail. Weather permitting, it was escorted by an airship from RNAS Luce Bay. Around midday, the prevailing wind often made the return journey of the airship difficult, but by the evening the wind had usually dropped, enabling the return trip to be undertaken with ease. As early as autumn 1915, land near Whitehead belonging to farmer James Long of Bentra was acquired for a mooring out site. This had few, if any, facilities until 1917. The first proposal for a shed here dated back to July 1915, but like much else concerning RNAS airships, there was a long delay before plans came to fruition. Eventually, an airship shed was constructed with a steel frame covered in canvas, and wooden huts raised on brick and concrete foundations. This was unusual for a mooring out site, for personnel usually made do with bell tents. Drainage ditches at RNAS Larne were filled in to improve the landing area.

The first airship to use the new shed was Submarine Scout *S.S.20*. On 5 June 1917, deteriorating weather conditions forced its pilot Flt Sub-Lt W. Parry to seek refuge here. He had to wait for four days before being able to return to RNAS Luce Bay. Later that month, *S.S.23* limped to Larne with engine trouble; the following day, another airship arrived carrying a mechanic to make repairs. When autumn came, the small airship shed served as a hay barn for the local farmer. On 25 November, autumn gales tore apart the canvas door curtain. The Army was called upon to affect emergency repairs, soldiers arrived in horse-drawn wagons, ate all the available rations, and departed with the repairs not made! The shed remained out of commission for a further month, until a sail-maker made good the damage. Submarine Scout Zero *S.S.Z.12* made emergency landings on 3 March with engine trouble and on 9 April with a damaged elevator.

In 1918, aeroplanes became such a familiar sight at RNAS Larne that locals sometimes referred to it as Whitehead Aerodrome—although no aeroplanes were based there. Its complement then consisted of nine officers and 139 men. Airships continued to operate: six patrols conducted in July went as far north as Rathlin Island, and as far south as Dundrum Bay. But by December 1918, all airship flying had ceased and the buildings were handed over to the local farmer. Some of the accommodation huts were turned into holiday homes. As late as November 1918, plans were devised to erect two steel airship sheds and two windbreaks, and to base two Submarine Scouts here by the following summer. Further down the coast at Malahide (near

This picture gives a good depiction of the location of RNAS Larne, set in a patchwork of small fields. The hills visible in the background would have provided some protection from the westerly winds. Submarine Scout *S.S.23* is hovering over the landing ground with the airship shed to the left of it. The building is surrounded by haystacks. (*D & N Caldwell Collection*)

Dublin), another airship station was established. A memo written on 7 June 1917 by a senior naval officer first submitted this idea thus:

> I have the honour to forward a suggestion for the consideration of Their Lordships, with regards to establishing a Sub Station in the vicinity of Dublin or Kingstown, to be worked in conjunction with and under the immediate orders of the Llangefni Air Station, Anglesey. By recent reports, it is evident that hostile submarines operate more often along the Irish Coast and should a portable canvas airship shed be erected in the area suggested, an excellent patrol could be carried out from Tuskar to Skulmartin, without the airship having to return to Llangefni every night. The requirements would be as follows:
>
> 1. Portable Canvas Airship Shed to accommodate S.S. Airship.
> 2. Flight Officer
> 3. Chief Petty Officer or Petty Officer
> 4. L.M. (E) and C
> 5. 30 Aircraftsmen
>
> The men would be housed under canvas.[2]

A note attached to the memo explains that it was customary procedure for a completed shed to be delivered within six weeks of its order, assuming the order was despatched in good time. But while a mooring out station was established at Malahide, it never received its airship shed.

Malahide Mooring Out Station

Mooring-out site for Anglesey Airship Station.
Location: 53 26' 40" N, 06 09" 00" W. County Dublin, the northern edge of the City of Dublin, close to the coast.
Airships known to have used this base: Submarine Scout *S.S.18*, *S.S.24*, *S.S.25*, and *S.S.33*; Submarine Scout Zero *S.S.Z.31*, *S.S.Z.33*, *S.S.Z.34*, *S.S.Z.35*, *S.S.Z.50*, *S.S.Z.51*, *S.S.Z.58*, *S.S.Z.72*, and *S.S.Z.7*.

The Malahide Mooring Out Station was commissioned on 2 July 1918. In contrast to Larne—which was situated in open farmland—Malahide was located in the densely wooded grounds of the ancestral home of the Talbot Family. 'Nests' for the airships were hollowed out in the edge of the woodland and the personnel were housed in rows of bell tents on the open ground. Officers were accommodated in Malahide Castle, parts of which date back to the twelfth century. By September 1918, the airship station's complement consisted of around ten officers and 120 men. It was proposed to erect a wooden airship shed here in 1919 with one Submarine Scout Twin and three Submarine Scout Zeros operational, and high priority was given to the provision of huts for housing the men. The end of the war put paid to these plans. The Irish state purchased Malahide Castle and the eighteenth-century landscaped parklands from the Talbot family and opened them to the public in 1975.

Wexford Mooring Out Station

Mooring-out site for Pembroke Airship Station.
Alternative name: 'Johnstown Castle'.
Location: 52 17' 30" N, 6 30' 50" W, 3 miles to the south-east of Wexford, County Wexford.
Airships known to have used this base: Submarine Scout *S.S.14*, *S.S.15*, *S.S.37*, and *S.S.42*; Submarine Scout Zero *S.S.Z.16*, *S.S.Z.37*, *S.S.Z.52*, *S.S.Z.53*, *S.S.Z.56*, and *S.S.Z.67*.

The last base in the chain of airship station on the Irish Coast was at Wexford. This coast proved fatal to a high volume of merchant ships, especially from 1915 to 1917—the area around Tuskar Rock came to be known to as 'the Graveyard'. Several German submarines also met their end in these waters: one was *UC-55*, which struck a mine off the Hook Peninsula on 4 August 1917, and whose only survivor was the commander in the conning tower at the time. In the winter of 1917, Flt Lt Hoperton and twenty men were engaged in preparing a mooring out site for RNAS Pembroke at Queenstown, near Cork, but reported that it would not be suitable for use until the leaves were back on the trees. Excavation work was undertaken but the site was never completed. It seems to have been abandoned in favour of somewhere closer to Wexford: like Malahide, the airship base was established in the grounds of

Submarine Scout Zero *S.S.Z.33* flying over the mooring out site of Malahide near Dublin. Tents which provide accommodation are pitched in front of the area of extensive woodland. (*The Fleet Air Arm Museum*)

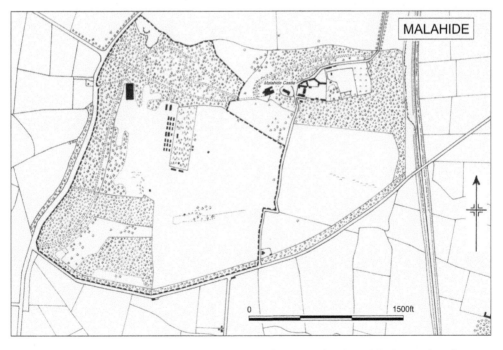

The Malahide mooring out site was situated in the grounds of Malahide Castle. Clearings were felled in the surrounding woods to house the airships, as there was no shed to shelter them. Most of the personnel were housed in tents on the edge of the landing ground (the black rectangles on the plan). The Dublin–Belfast railway ran close to the eastern edge of the landing ground. (*Mick Davis*)

a large country house, Johnstown Castle. This impressive building, with turrets and battlements of gleaming silver-grey ashlar, was built for the Grogan Morgan family between 1810 and 1855 and incorporated a part of an ancient castle. Close by lay a large ornamental lake.

The airship base was commissioned on 18 May 1918. As with Larne and Malahide, an airship from the British mainland would operate a patrol over the Irish Sea, then come down at one of these mooring out sites for the night. After provisioning and servicing, it would operate further patrols before returning to its home base. Airships from Wexford also watched over the waters on the southern edge of Ireland. The first airship to arrive at RNAS Wexford was Submarine Scout Zero *S.S.Z.56*, followed by *S.S.Z.52* at the end of the month. It was reported that the cover was good and the ships were well protected.

Mr H. Gamble related his experiences as an engineer/observer on RNAS airships at the station to Birkenhead Rotary Club in 1936:

I think the most adventurous part of my life with the airship was spent in Ireland from early 1918 until August 1918. We were sent across to near Wexford to make ourselves a nest of our own, for in a huge park many trees had been felled and instead of a shed we tied the ship up in this avenue, the wood being its only protection. To fill the petrol tanks I had to scale the trees on either side while the landing party pulled the ship over to me. Unable to get much gas sent over to us we had to wait until the sun shone on the envelope to swell the gas and give us lift before we could get out on patrol. In the cool of the evening, of course, when we returned to land, we would be very heavy and landing

A Submarine Scout Zero moored in woodland in the grounds of Johnstown Castle, which had been requisitioned for use as the airship sub-station Wexford. The ornamental lake is visible in the top of the picture. (*The Royal Aeronautical Society*)

was difficult. To assist us on our journey home one night, three German submarines gave us a good shelling. The cheeky bounders were only about 2 or 3 miles from Tuskar Lighthouse and the lighthouse keeper watched them, needless to say we did not go after them because we were such a good target.

It was on patrol from here that we bagged our second submarine off the Saltese Island off Waterford harbour. We spotted a nice little oil track moving slowly on the surface and bombed just in front of it and holed her. We invited, by signals, an American destroyer to come over to us, which she did, and when she saw the objective proceeded to finish the job by dropping seventeen depth charges and disturbing the ocean a bit with pieces of submarine and crew.

The only time we would return from Ireland would be to have a newly overhauled engine fitted, as after 150 hours of flying it was necessary to change the engine. The envelope of the ship was fitted with a ripcord, by means of which one could rip open the gasbag and deflate it in case of emergency. Unfortunately, this emergency arose one night in Ireland, for when a terrific gale sprang up suddenly the ship was torn from its moorings. I had a painful necessity of scuttling her by this process. This resulted in packing up the damaged outfit and returning to Pembroke by tramp steamer.

Mr H. Gamble was ordered to remain at Pembroke airship station and temporarily take over one of the two ships in commission. Between the 1st and 8th of June, two Submarine Scout airships were based at RNAS Wexford and carried out several patrols; a portable silicol plant was delivered and a bomb dump was constructed, too. The following month the wireless station was commissioned, but the radio masts gave a great trouble because of water on the guy-ropes. Eventually, wire replacements were fitted.

1918 also saw four large seaplane stations established on the Irish coast, including one at Wexford. These were staffed by 3,000 personnel from the US Navy, which now had a large fleet of warships based at Queenstown. In November 1918, it was planned to erect a wooden airship shed in the grounds of Johnstown Castle, which one Submarine Scout Twin and three Submarine Scout Zeros would be assigned to. With the cessation of hostilities, these plans too were abandoned, and flying ceased by the end of the year.

All mooring out stations in Ireland were relinquished swiftly. Johnstown Castle was handed over to the Irish state in 1945, along with its magnificently ornamental grounds, and is now a major tourist attraction. Few of its visitors would imagine that it once played a military role.

In 1916, the impetus to create rigid airship bases all over the British Isles came to an anti-climax due to a shortage of construction materials and coolness on the behalf of members of the Cabinet and the Admiralty. Only three sites were eventually approved—Dorchester in England, and Killeagh and Loch Neagh in Ireland. It was intended to establish an airship station on the eastern shores of Loch Neagh (54 34'28"N, 06 16'15"W), because airships could fly patrols out into the Atlantic Ocean from there, and should an operation demand it, they could also fly eastwards to undertake missions over the North Sea. The go ahead was given in 1918, but little if any work appears to have been carried out. Another large airship station was envisioned but never realised at the opposite end of Ireland, near Cork—from here, both rigid and non-rigid airships would have hunted German submarines far out into the Atlantic. Most merchant ships were sunk close to the British coastline, but increasingly effective anti-submarine methods would have driven enemy actions further out to sea had the First World War continued beyond 1918.

RNAS Killeagh Airship Station

Alternative name: 'Ballyquirke'.
Location: 51 55' 52" N, 09 56' 30" W. About 20 miles east of Cork, the village of Killeagh.
Size: 361 acres (within boundaries of 650 x 500 yards).
Airship Sheds: one rigid, double-berth shed, partially completed (840 feet long, 150 feet wide, and 130 feet high); one Coastal shed, partially completed (356 feet long, 160 feet wide, and 75 feet high).
Based airships: none (planned: two Rigid 33s and two Coastals).

The land around Killeagh was flat and had access to abundant water supplies, ideal for an airship base. It was close to the Royal Navy base at Queenstown, but the deciding factor in its selection was probably that it was close to the Cork–Youghal railway line. 365 acres were commandeered under the Defence of the Realm Act. Surprisingly, no local labour was employed: most of the tradesmen came from the British mainland, as did much of the building material, transported from Cork harbour by rail. A special siding and platform was built at Killeagh to facilitate delivery. Red brick manufactured locally in Youghal was, however, used in most of the station's buildings. Work on this large facility continued for nearly a year after hostilities had ended, but was brought to an abrupt halt on 20 August 1919. The same year saw the first and only aeroplane land here. A contemporary Irish newspaper article details the state of the station at the time that it was terminated:

> By order of the Admiralty all work at the Killeagh Aerodrome has been suspended. A wire from the Admiralty Authorities was received at the Aerodrome offices on Wednesday night, directing the officer in charge, Commander Williamson R. N., to close down the works and yesterday, of the 500 men employed there, between 360 and 400 were paid off. The remainder will be retained for some time longer in connection with the removal of the building plant of the contractors and the painting of the steel works. A large staff of riveters ceased work on Thursday and left for England yesterday. These were employed in the erection of what was to be the largest shed at the station, the dimensions of which were to be 840 feet long by 120 feet high and one side of this has been practically completed.
>
> Messrs. Cleveland Bridge and Co., Darlington, were the contractors and their order now is to paint what has been erected and leave it as it is. Work in connection with it was impeded by strikes in England, the contractors having great difficulty in obtaining the

necessary material. A cargo of cement has just arrived in Cork for this firm in connection with their contract. Messrs. F. Morton and Co., Liverpool, who were building another shed ceased about a month ago and they have removed their building plant from the station. A large water tank which was to supply the entire station was also in course of construction, the contractors being Messrs. Dove Bros, London, and it is in connection with this work the strike of carpenters took place. The strike, however, had nothing to do with the decision of the Admiralty, as it is understood that it is for reasons of economy the work has stopped.

The order caused something like consternation amongst the large number of men employed there and its consequence will also be felt by the people of Killeagh, Mogeely and the surrounding districts. The building of the aerodrome was started in February 1918 and it is stated that it would take two years more to complete. The first work was to make a road through the grounds that had been taken over from the farmers and to lay rails and up to yesterday a special train had been run daily from Cork on to the grounds with material for the contractors. A large number of huts for workmen were built by Messrs. Thos. Moran and Co., London and there is now housing accommodation for 800 men as well as a very fine building for the officer in charge and other Admiralty officials. A school has also been built on the grounds and it is hoped that after such a large outlay of expenditure these buildings will not now be left derelict but will be used for the purposes for which they were erected.

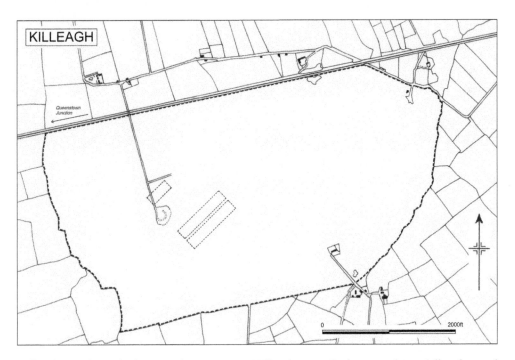

Killeagh. Work on the large airship station at Killeagh, near Cork, was substantially advanced when construction was halted. The large double rigid shed was located near the centre of the site, and the much smaller Coastal shed immediately to its north. The Cork–Youghal railway line ran along the domestic and technical buildings on the northern boundary. (*Mick Davis*)

One shed was half finished while the other was about one-third complete when construction ceased and the station was transferred, from the Admiralty to the Air Ministry, in 1919. No further work was undertaken after that. In 1919, Irish Nationalists attempted an unsuccessful raid on Killeagh to obtain arms and ammunition. Parts of the large airship shed were earmarked for Cairo, Egypt in connection with the plan to establish an airship service across the British Empire, though some components had yet to be delivered and were in store at Liverpool. The Canadian government refused an offer of the smaller Coastal shed, so this was sold in 1921 and dismantled. At independence, the site was handed over to the Irish Free State government. The site lay derelict for many years—locals pilfered materials from it, corrugated iron in particular. In 1938, it was short-listed as a site for the new Cork Airport—Killeagh was favoured by experts, but they were overruled by a politician who had it built in his constituency! A few of the buildings and a large concrete water tower have managed to survive, albeit in a ruined state, into the twenty-first century.

There was also a proposal to build an RNAS airship station at Killarney, County Kerry (Location 52 04'00"N, 09 30'00"W), but construction was never started.

9

RNAS Overseas Airship Bases

The First World War broke out at a time when the British Empire had reached its apex. Yet the era of embarking on the conquest of new lands was over, and for many British subjects overseas, foreign rule left much to be desired. In the 1920s, RAF aeroplanes were used to suppress rebels in Africa, the Middle East, and the North-West Frontier Province (now part of Pakistan). The first deployment of air power in a counter-insurgency role was considered in early 1914. Sir Geoffrey Archer, the Acting High Commissioner of Somaliland, had the previous year sent forces against 'The Mad Mullah' (Mohammed Abdullah Hassan) in response to the massacre of the Somaliland Camel Corps. But tensions in this territory continued to simmer and well outlived the war in Europe. In the early twentieth century Winston Churchill conceived the idea of using air power to enforce British rule, and had this plan gone ahead, it would have been the first overseas deployment of Royal Navy airships. Details of the planned expedition were drawn up in a Cabinet paper by Churchill:

The proposal of the Colonial Office to use aircraft in Somaliland has been carefully considered. An expedition should be capable of rendering valuable services. It is understood that the whole wealth of the Mullah is in camels and livestock and that very considerable damage could be inflicted on him, apart from actual offensive operations, by stampeding his stock and keeping them from the wells.

1. It is proposed to fit modified cars to two ships of the Parseval type now completing for the Admiralty.
2. Effect alterations to the smaller Army airship Eta so as to enable her to carry stores to the advanced base, to assist with a photographic survey of the trade routes and to be available as a spare ship in case of necessity.
3. Order one portable and two canvas sheds.
4. Order suitable hydrogen plant.
5. Arrange for armament, and in conjunction with Ordnance Department,
6. Order airship spares.
7. Order petrol and oil.
8. Order photographic gear and equipment.

Officers and Complement, 8 Officers, 40 Petty Officers and men, 6 Wireless Telegraph operators, 3 Royal Aircraft Factory Staff. Handling parties can be provided from the Indian troops at Berbera ... the experience of the Italians with airships in Tripoli is encouraging, as the temperature of Tripoli in summer is about the same as that of Somaliland in winter and both countries have a sandy soil. The question of sending out a flight of aeroplanes cannot be considered until a full report is received from officers who will be sent out to consult with the local officers on the spot as soon as general approval is given to these proposals should it be found that aeroplanes could be usefully employed on messenger work, etc., in connection with the airship.[1]

The fractious excitement of European politics in the months preceding the war meant that military priorities lay closer to home, so the expedition did not progress beyond the planning stage. The first overseas deployment of a British military airship took place on 28 August 1914. The Astra Torres, naval airship *No. 3*, arrived at Ostend, Belgium, from RNAS Kingsnorth. It accompanied a force of British troops supported by armoured cars in the defence of the town. The airship spent three days moored out in the open here before the British troops abandoned Ostend and retreated to Dunkirk; the Astra Torres flew over Ostend to see if the German forces had entered the town. At Dunkirk, it operated alongside RNAS planes flying further reconnaissance flights before returning to Britain, and the following year, a second RNAS airship was sent to operate from Dunkirk. By now the trenches on the Belgian front were only 20 miles away. From here, the airship *Beta II* flew anti-submarine missions and carried out artillery spotting duties.

In France—RNAS Dunkirk Airship Station

Location: 3 miles east of Dunkirk, on the main Dunkirk–Nieuwpoort road and canal, 1 mile from the coast.
Airship Shed: one (167 feet long and 55 feet wide).

Most British airship bases on foreign soil consisted of a portable airship shed and a few flimsy buildings. In contrast, RNAS Dunkirk was a substantial complex with solidly built structures. The premises were requisitioned from a French engineering firm for the duration of the war by both the RNAS Airship Section and the French War Office. The works had previously made shell cases for field guns and wheels for railway rolling stock. A new airship shed was constructed, built of steel girders and with brick walls on three sides, though it was not large enough to house Parseval or Astra Torres airships. The earth floor was covered with wooden sleepers on which tarpaulins were placed. The shed faced north–south, with the entrance facing the sea at the north end. A canvas windbreak was brought from Farnborough airship station and erected over the entrance. The shed was lit by electricity with ten wandering leads, which enabled inspections to be carried out at night; but there was no electric heating, and the building was said to be 'very cold and draughty'.[2] About twenty ratings were accommodated in a small lean-to building on the south side of the shed, whereas officers were housed in the company directors' quarters—which had both electric lighting and central heating!

The airship shed at RNAS Dunkirk, constructed with steel girders and bricks. It may owe its factory-like appearance to being built in the grounds of a large industrial complex. It was handed over to the French at the beginning of 1915. (*The National Archives*)

The Astra-Torres *No. 3* attached to a small mooring mast at Dunkirk, France in August 1914. The aeroplanes—from RNAS Eastchurch—were used to harass the advancing German Army. (*The Fleet Air Arm Museum*)

The landing ground was at the foot of a gentle slope with a large chalk marking in its centre. There was no gas plant here, so cylinders had to be transported across the Channel from Farnborough. Precautions were taken against a possible air raid, even though—at this stage of the war—planes were primarily used for reconnaissance. One pom-pom gun was mounted on the water tower and two Maxim guns were placed on the north-east and southern boundaries, bolstered by searchlights in case of a night attack. Ammunition was stored in an underground magazine, well away from all buildings; 'this was considered necessary,' according to a 1915 booklet, 'owing to the daily expected attack from German aeroplanes'.[3]

The RNAS had an agreement with the French that it would vacate the airship shed after a period of three months, but that after 1 January 1915, the RNAS would still be able use the landing ground and station personnel to handle airships for the remainder of the war. The following year, the RNAS established a new base at Dunkirk, this time at St Pol aerodrome, next to the harbour.

RNAS St Pol (Dunkirk) Aerodrome

Alternative name: 'Dunkerque'.
Location: On western edge of Dunkirk and immediately south of the harbour.
Airship Shed: one portable airship shed (150 feet long, 45 feet wide, and 50 feet high).

In July 1916, a portable shed at RNAS Folkestone was dismantled and transported to St Pol aerodrome, where it was re-erected. Designated as 'Airship Detachment No. 5', a complement of one officer and thirty four men was dispatched to this base in August 1916. Submarine Scout Zero *S.S.Z.1* arrived the following month and remained there until it returned to England in October. No RNAS airship used the station in 1917 and Airship Detachment No. 5 withdrew its personnel in May. Later in the year, the shed was dismantled and the parts placed in storage.

RNAS Marquise Airship Station

Alternative name: 'Gris Nez'.
Location: 8 miles north-east of Boulogne.
Airship Sheds: one shed provided by French government (361 feet long, 66 feet wide, and 46 feet high), one RNAS portable airship shed (150 feet long, 45 feet wide, and 50 feet high).
Based Airships: Submarine Scout *S.S.10*, *S.S.26*, *S.S.27*, and *S.S.40*.

RNAS Marquise was commissioned on 22 June 1915. Submarine Scout *S.S.27* arrived here on 8 July, but was written off on 5 August after it collided with a church steeple at Marquise. *S.S.10* came a few days later, but was subsequently wrecked in the Channel on 10 September. Marquise, along with the portable sheds and Submarine Scout *S.S.2*, was handed over to the newly-formed French naval airship service on 1 January 1916.

The same year, further airship stations were established along the Channel coast at Le Harve, Montebourg (Cherbourg), and Guipavas (Brest). By the end of 1916, the French naval airship service had six airships on strength, four of which were supplied by Britain. Initially, most French airship stations had only one airship shed, but in 1917, many were supplemented with a second shed that was 492 feet long, 92 feet wide, and 79 feet high. While there were allied aerodromes close to the network of trenches cutting across the French landscape, airships were noted for their absence, on account of their vulnerability. In the case of the British military, the exception to this rule was Airship Detachment No. 4, housed at Boubers-sur-Canche.

Boubers-sur-Canche Airship Station

A special airship shed was constructed by the Royal Flying Corps in this farming village, close to the Western Front and around 24 miles west of Arras. It stood alone in an open field next to a wood and was described as a 'cathedral of wood and wire covered by camouflaged canvas'.[4] In the spring of 1916, Lord Trenchard, Commander of the RFC in France, requested an airship for 'secret service in enemy territory'.[5] In a guarded shed at Polegate, work began on converting Submarine Scout *S.S.40* for this assignment. Almost all British airships were distinctively silver-coloured due to the aluminium dope applied to the envelope, but what emerged from the shed on a breezy moonless June evening was drastically different. An all-black machine was walked out to the landing ground and took to the air. The effect of its new coating was potent:

> The ship became invisible as soon as she took off, seemed to go round and fade away. Never saw her again until she landed. Very good show.[6]

The black *S.S.40* was also fitted with an especially silenced engine, and undertook several trial flights before flying to France. Forty experienced soldiers were sent from England to act as the handling party at Boubers-sur-Canche. Its pilot Victor Goddard recalled,

> [...] against a cloudy night sky fitfully lit with flickering flashes of continuous rumbling gun fire the black ship landed, old soldiers fell on the ropes and following me and my megaphone, dragged the black ship stern first into the hangar and bagged her down.[7]

Maj.-Gen. Trenchard then informed the *S.S.40*'s crew of the purpose of this unusual airship. Allied agents or spies could no longer reach the Netherlands—then a neutral territory—on the ground from France, because German-occupied Belgium now had an electric fence along its border. The black airship would overcome this obstacle by flying agents into the Netherlands under cover of darkness. However, it was soon realised that the airship could not reach its required altitude of 10,000 feet (considered the safe minimum to cross enemy lines). It was therefore flown back to RNAS Kingsnorth in Britain to be fitted with a larger envelope for greater lift. But upon *S.S.40*'s return to France, yet another embarrassing problem was discovered: enlarged—the airship could now reach altitudes of 13,000 feet—it got stuck in the entrance to its shed. When the envelope was partially deflated, it then became too tall. The situation was eventually resolved by a group of soldiers, who spent all night digging a deep channel in the floor of the shed.

After all this effort, *S.S.40* never once ferried an agent behind enemy lines. Instead, it made reconnaissance flights over the German positions at night while the Battle of the Somme raged below. The crew were amazed they never fell victim to German guns, but on several occasions the black airship was hit by rifle bullets fired by British infantry. To ensure that they were not mistaken for a Zeppelin, its occupants sang bawdy British songs as they returned from a mission. The Army dubbed it 'Bertha, the Black Blimp'. A couple of other airships were in the process of being adapted for night flying missions before the idea was eventually dropped. *S.S.40* was returned to Britain in October 1916, and resumed anti-submarine patrols. Both pilots were mentioned in dispatches (MiD) in General Haig's report on the Battle of the Somme. While the allied forces used manned observation balloons on the Western Front throughout the First World War, this was the only time a British airship operated over the trenches. In 1918, there was a plan to use Coastals in a casualty-evacuation role under the protection of an escort of fighter planes.

Boulogne Mooring Out Station

A mooring out station at Boulogne for RNAS Folkestone was planned by the summer of 1919. Two Submarine Scout Zeros would have been based here.

RNAS Airship Stations in the Mediterranean

The political geography of Mediterranean countries in 1914 was unrecognisable from that of today. Both France and Italy were firmly in the allied camp, and their colonies extended almost the entire length of the North African coastline. The Austro-Hungarian Empire had access to the Mediterranean on the Adriatic, and was joined in its alliance with Germany. Most early British airship activity was concentrated around the coastline of the home country, but with the conflict locked in stalemate in France, an audacious plan was drawn up—to land troops on the Turkish coast and strike directly at the enemy. The objective became to secure the Dardanelles, which would give access to Russia—a British ally—by way of the Black Sea. Allied troops landed at Gallipoli in April 1915 supported by the RNAS, which operated its planes from the Greek islands Tenedos and Imbros. The Turkish Army put up fierce resistance just as the allies' campaign on the Western Front ground to a standstill. Further landings were made in Turkey, but the allies' mission remained as distant as ever.

The advance party of an Airship Expeditionary Force sent to the Dardanelles arrived at Imbros to erect an airship shed on 2 August 1915. The island was equipped with a hospital, stores, and administrative buildings, so played a vital role as a staging post for the allied invasion of Gallipoli.

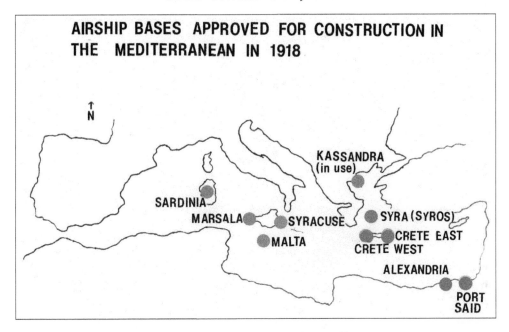

RNAS airship bases in the Eastern Mediterranean. (*Author's collection*)

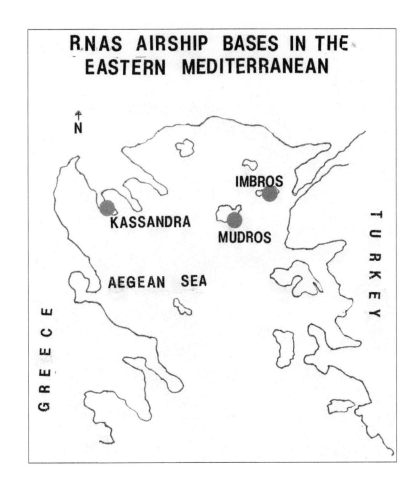

RNAS airship
bases in
the Eastern
Mediterranean.
(*Author's
collection*)

RNAS Imbros Airship Station

Location: 'Island of Imbros', 'Aegean Sea'.
Airship Shed: one portable airship shed (150 feet long, 45 feet wide, and 50 feet high).
Based Airships: Submarine Scout *S.S.7* (*S.S.3* and *S.S.19* not inflated).

RNAS Imbros was manned by fourteen officers and seventy-three men under the command of Flt Cdr E. H. Sparling. It was perched on the edge of a sheer cliff overlooking the sea, and a detachment of the RNVR Anti-Aircraft Corps provided protection against enemy air raids. Unlike the airships based in Britain, it was initially intended that those operating in the Aegean would act as spotters for land and sea-based guns, in addition to their role as submarine hunters. Submarine Scout *S.S.3* was the first to operate here. Several of its missions involved directing the fire of naval artillery, but this could only be effectively done when in range of ground-based enemy guns.

In September 1915, *S.S.7* attacked an enemy position in conjunction with HMS *Venerable* and HMS *Talbot*. Despite good visibility and a bright moon, the airship crew had difficulty distinguishing the target. This failure lead to airships being abandoned as the 'eyes' for big guns and reverting to their usual anti-submarine service. On 10 October 1915, *S.S.7* left its shed at Imbros at 8.00 a.m.; it carried out five trial flights, then at 11.25 a.m. filled up with petrol and oil and proceeded on patrol to Cape Hellas, where there was report of a submarine, but nothing was seen. While flying over Cape Irene, Lemnos, its engine began to falter, failing completely for a short time, but the airship managed to reach its base safely. In fact, it had just been fitted with the engine of another Submarine Scout, *S.S.3*—which had been gutted for parts. Flt Cdr Sparling wrote a detailed report concerning the problems of establishing and operating Imbros airship station:

The shed as originally designed was absolutely useless for the safekeeping of a ship except in flat calm for the following reasons,

1. No means were provided to keep the wind from entering the shed under the doors.
2. The doors were secured, guyed and braced so badly that there was very little to prevent the first strong wind blowing them from one end of the shed and out through the other.
3. The arrangement of the fitting of the canvas was bad there being nothing to prevent it moving in and out over a large area whenever there was the least wind blowing.
4. None of the sharp corners of the shed, edges of the plates securing the framework, bolts or nuts, were protected in any way to prevent them chafing the canvas. I have made a number of pads and have also used the pads supplied for the purpose of preventing the envelope of the ship touching the roof of the shed, to cover all these sharp edges and so have prevented the canvas from being chafed more rapidly than it has.
5. The Shed with the extra guys, the pads placed on the canvas, the cross bracing wires of the two doors, the extra widths of canvas on the foot of the doors, pads on all the sharp edges which have been fitted out here, is suitable for real summer conditions but no more.

The first blow with a continuous wind of 25 mph or over and lasting four days or more will absolutely ruin the ship and reduce her to such condition that she will have to be deflated. The wind experienced here from October 17th to October 22nd was of this force and although at first there were no apparent large crevices for the wind to enter and the motion of the ship was so large and the friction on all the rigging and guys was so much, that in this period I had to practically fit a whole new set of rigging.

6. Silicol Plant. All plants in future to be housed in a shed because in wet weather when the plant is not in a shed the silicol becomes wet and so cakes and chokes in the silicol feed valve and at the same time the shed would provide comfort to the hands working the plant who will frequently be working long hours.

7. Cars for Stations abroad. The following cars are suggested as being absolutely necessary,

A. Jeffrey truck fitted with canvas top and detachable sides for transporting heavy gear. A detachable water tank, capacity about 200 gallons with pump complete would be very useful.

B. Two 25-hp cars of the same pattern fitted with open long body as used for w/t sets at home with especially strong back axles.[8]

Flt Cdr Sparling attaches extensive notes about the number of men needed to operate the airship station and their training, and recommends that, for overseas bases, the staff for the sick bay be doubled. He deemed the provision of a photographer essential for aerial work, as well as for recording any repairs and modifications to airships. Sparling is equally critical of the number of personnel sent to establish the airship station on Imbros, pointing out that the Expedition arrived with sixty-eight men, almost all of them ratings from the RNAS Depot. In the first month, it was necessary to employ over 100 Greeks to assist them, and Sparling warns that future circumstances may not permit local labour to be available. Their duties included filling fire buckets, drawing water for washing, working pumps on the gas plant, maintaining roads, drawing coal from colliers, etc. By the following month, the number of Greeks was down to fifty. Sparling's report, while intended to provide advice for future overseas airship operations, was not well received by his superiors. Vice-Adml J. Robeck wrote the following in response to one of his subordinates:

Apart from such remarks as 'absolutely useless' the tone of Flight Commander Sparling's criticism of the disposal of RNAS personnel on the station—which is carried out by you acting under my instructions—is contrary to naval service procedure and subversive of discipline. I request you will inform Flight Commander Sparling accordingly.

In December 1915, the Director of Air Services concluded that the deployment of airships to the Aegean paved the way for a bigger expedition—Airship Detachment No. 3, which was in the process of formation to provide a Coastal airship station at Mudros, but the project was cancelled in February 1916. The personnel and stores, together with the sheds, were allocated to other purposes as required. Some of assets of Airship Detachment No. 3 were transferred at the end of 1915 to establish a less ambitious airship base at Mudros on the island of Lemnos. A portable airship shed, which had remained unassembled at Imbros, was transferred here along with un-inflated Submarine Scouts *S.S.3* and *S.S.19*.

RNAS Mudros Airship Station

Location: east side of large bay on the Greek island of Lemnos, the Aegean Sea.
Airship Shed: one portable airship shed (150 feet long, 45 feet wide, and 50 feet high).
Based Airships: Submarine Scout *S.S.3* and *S.S.19* (transferred from Imbros).

The base at Imbros was mainly abandoned for its close proximity to the Turkish coast and its vulnerability to air attack. Conversely, Lemnos was 35 miles to the west of Imbros, and from here, long daily patrols for submarines and mines at the entrance to Mudros Harbour could be undertaken. Airships were particularly well suited for spotting mines, for the waters of the Aegean were usually calm and clear, unlike around Britain.

On one occasion in the summer of 1916, an object thought to be a mine turned out to be a turtle asleep beneath the surface. Later that year, Submarine Scout *S.S.8* was carrying out a patrol of the entrance channels to Mudros Harbour when it was attacked by a Turkish seaplane. The hostile plane dropped bombs on it—incendiary ammunition had yet to be invented—but these all missed the airship, hitting the water astern. Trawlers opened fire on the enemy machine and fighters were sent in pursuit,

The portable airship shed at RNAS Mudros on the Greek island of Lemnos in the Aegean Sea. A Submarine Scout is being walked into the shed by its ground handling party. A partially completed windbreak stands in front of the shed. (*The Fleet Air Arm Museum*)

but the seaplane vanished into a hazy sky. It was subsequently decided that airships would only operate from RNAS Mudros if they had a fighter escort.

Airships continued to operate patrols from here, but were often confined to the harbour area. In addition, RNAS Mudros acted as the airship depot for the Aegean and carried out repairs to RNAS Kassandra's machines. In mid-1917, the Admiralty hatched a plan to use one of airships at RNAS Mudros in an offensive role. It was fitted with bomb racks, the intended target being Constantinople (Istanbul), no less. In the warm climate of the Mediterranean, airships could not operate very efficiently as they had reduced lift. With a payload of bombs it would almost be impossible for the craft to get airborne, so the plan was abandoned. Instead, an early Handley Page 0/100 twin-engine bomber—introduced into service in 1916—was enlisted. It attacked the Ottoman capital for four months before being destroyed in an accident on 30 September 1917.

RNAS Mudros itself was also on the receiving end of numerous air raids. The shed had so many holes from bomb splinters that it acquired the name 'Pepper Pot'. One such raid took place on 21 November 1917. A Friedrichshafen seaplane and an LVG bomber made coordinated runs from opposite directions and dropped a total of five bombs. One from the seaplane missed the landing ground altogether, but the four from the LVG only narrowly missed the entrance to the airship shed, with fragments piercing both the structure and the envelope of Submarine Scout *S.S.8*. A Sopwith Schneider took to the air in hot pursuit and succeeded in hitting the enemy with rounds from its Lewis gun. The seaplane managed to evade its attacker eventually, but was forced to land in Yukeri Bay, where it was destroyed by Royal Navy guns.

S.S.8 was repaired and continued to fly missions from RNAS Mudros until the spring of 1918, when after giving several years of good service, it was deflated for the last time. *S.S.8* was the sole occupant of this base for much of the time it was there. With its withdrawal came the end of airship patrols from the island, although the harbour continued to figure prominently in the blockade of the Dardanelles. It was here that the Armistice between the Ottoman Empire and the Allies was signed in late October 1918.

Around the same time that RNAS Mudros airship station was commissioned, a further base was established at Kassandra on the Halkidiki peninsula. It was the most active of the three RNAS airship bases in the Aegean. While there were a total of five Submarine Scout airships in this region, often only two were operational. Other airships were held at the depot at Mudros, either under repair or as a source of spare parts.

RNAS Kassandra Airship Station

Location: Kassandra is at the westernmost tip of Halkidiki, close to Thessaloniki. It is worth mentioning that Kassandra was previously named 'Flegra', which means 'land of fire' in ancient Greek. According to Greek mythology, the area was home to giants and became a battleground when they tried to banish the gods from Mount Olympus.
Airship Shed: one portable shed (150 feet long, 45 feet wide, and 50 feet high).
Based Airships: Submarine Scout *S.S.7*, *S.S.8*, *S.S.17*, *S.S.19*, and *S.S.40*; Submarine Scout Zero *S.S.Z.68* and *S.S.Z.70*.

Submarine Scouts *S.S.7* and *S.S.8* arrived here in late 1915. By this time, the last of the allied forces were being evacuated from Gallipoli. Priorities had changed and there was now an increasing threat posed by German submarines, particularly in the Western Aegean. Mudros was located too far away to operate airships to counter this, hence the choice of Kassandra. Its airship shed came from Imbros, its brief career as an airship station now at an end. Regular patrols were made as far south as Skiathos and Pelago Island, embracing the whole of the entrance to the Gulf of Salonika.

In August 1916, a German submarine was spotted on the surface in the Gulf of Salonika, but submerged as the airship steered a course toward it. Later that year, the crew of *S.S.17* detected a group of six mines. Naval trawlers were dispatched and discovered many more. At this stage, the airship had to cut short its mission because of a fault in its envelope. A Submarine Scout was shipped out from Wales and took over the mine hunting role until, on 20 December 1916, engine trouble forced it to come down on the sea, 20 miles to the west of Kassandra. It was towed back to Salonika by a trawler and sent to RNAS Mudros for repairs. It was then replaced by *S.S.8*, but in mid-1917, the latter required a major overhaul, which left the Aegean Sea without a single operational RNAS airship. Once back in the air, *S.S.8* resumed patrols from Kassandra. It was not long before disaster struck again. Storm-force winds caused the ripping panel to open while in flight, and the airship plunged into the sea. Its crew, though injured, survived. *S.S.8* was repaired using parts from other machines. On 8 August 1917, the envelope of this ill-fated machine was badly damaged when winds blew the airship against the beams of the windbreak at the station, and it was a further three weeks before it was back in commission.

This picture conveys the somewhat primitive conditions at RNAS Kassandra on mainland Greece. In the centre is the sole portable canvas shed at this location. It had been previously deployed on the island of Imbros. Inside it is a Submarine Scout. An aeroplane stands guard at its entrance. (*The Fleet Air Arm Museum*)

In September, *S.S.8* flew to the RNAS station at Salonika, where its personnel were trained in the mooring of an airship. If the weather deteriorated at RNAS Kassandra while an airship was on patrol, it could divert to Salonika until conditions improved. RNAS Kassandra was out of range of enemy air attack, but this did not necessarily make it safe. In late September 1917, suspicious signal lights were observed on a hill to the east of the station and an intruder attempted to enter the airship shed but was chased off by an armed sentry.

On 1 October 1917, *S.S.8* was on patrol over the Gulf of Kassandra and Monte Santo but had to be recalled owing to increasing wind speed. During the night, a patrol flew south of Cape Drepano. Strong easterly winds accompanied by thunderstorms and rain prevented flying on the 2nd and 3rd, but on the 4th—even though the weather was still unsettled—patrols of the entrance to the Gulf of Salonika were resumed. These continued over the shipping channels to Salonika in 1918. The formerly black airship *S.S.40*—now in a more conventional colour scheme—arrived here in the spring to assist with anti-submarine patrols. More modern airships, such as Submarine Scout Zeros *S.S.Z.69* and *S.S.Z.70*, arrived in August to relieve the long serving Submarine Scout machines, which were now relegated to training. While many bases in Britain ceased operation shortly after the Armistice, the airships at RNAS Kassandra soldiered on until the middle of 1919, spotting a large number of mines in the Aegean. Abandonment of this base marked the end of overseas operations by British military airships.

Toward the end of 1918, plans had been drawn up for a huge increase in the numbers of RNAS anti-submarine airships to patrol the Mediterranean. The British C-in-C in the Mediterranean suggested that there should be one shed in Crete and another at Port Said, Egypt. These bases would each have four Submarine Scout Twin airships on strength. In addition, right across the Mediterranean, about fifty double portable sheds were going to be required to house a force of sixty-seven Submarine Scout Twins and Submarine Scout Zeros, at mooring out stations. Approval was given for the plan, which would have seen airship bases at the following locations by 1 July 1919 (all the portable sheds were 175 feet long, 45 feet wide, and 56 feet high):

Kassandra, Greece: one airship shed, one Submarine Scout Zero plus one in reserve.
Alexandra, Egypt: three portable airship sheds, three Submarine Scout Twins.
Crete (East): two portable airship sheds, two Submarine Scout Twins.
Crete (West): two portable airship sheds, two Submarine Scout Twins.
Malta: two portable airship sheds, one permanent airship shed, six Submarine Scout Twins.
Marsala, Sicily: two portable airship sheds, two Submarine Scout Twins.
Sardinia: two portable airship sheds, two Submarine Scout Twins.
Syra, Greece: three portable sheds, three Submarine Scout Twins.
Syracuse, Sicily: three portable sheds, three Submarine Scout Twins.
Port Said, Egypt: three portable sheds, three Submarine Scout Twins.

By autumn 1918, the construction of the airship station at Malta had begun and its commander had been appointed. A base here was first proposed three years earlier by the Admiral of Malta:

A small airship station at Malta would be very valuable for scouting for submarines and would help me better to control the area around Malta. If the idea is approved I will have a site for the airship shed selected immediately, so that the airship and the shed and the telephonic communications may all be ready by the time the weather becomes suitable for the airship to get to work.[9]

Despite being heavily cultivated, an area in the proximity of Rabat, Altard, and Naxxar in the northern part of the island was thought most suitable. It was also close to the 7-mile railway that then traversed the island. Malta possessed impressive fortifications from bygone conflicts, so it was suggested that instead of erecting a shed, an airship could be housed in one of its deep moats—these would also conceal the airship from enemy aeroplanes. The Director of Air Services was less than enthusiastic about this scheme, stating the following in a memo dated 29 January 1916:

There appears to be no difficulty in obtaining a suitable seaplane base. This will be of value in any case for training purposes in the future, owing to weather conditions, and it appears desirable to proceed with this work. As regards airships—this is a very difficult subject. The Admiral Superintendent, Malta has a strong leaning to airships but does not appear to have considered the question by COS [Chief of Staff] as to the submarine attacking the airship. We happen, however, to have in stock sheds for two Coastals, a type which is superior to the Submarine Scout as they have two engines. They are fitted with wireless, bombs and machine guns. Speed 55 miles per hour, radius 150 miles and further they have the advantage of a steady platform and would probably be of more use in the clear waters of the Mediterranean than elsewhere and be a deterrent to submarines. It is not disputed that sea craft would be of more value for submarine searching but if no more suitable use is likely to be found in the near future for these airships, none of which must be regarded as a makeshift for rigids, they might be used in this way. One thing appears certain; these ships are of little use to work against anti-aircraft guns in daylight.[10]

Not surprisingly, the seaplane station was approved, but the plan for an airship station was put in abeyance until late 1918. By this time, a different location was chosen, in the centre of the island, to the west of the Grand Harbour and close to Zebbug. The RAF had control of the site until 1924, when it was leased to local farmers. The Director of Air Services also contemplated that Alexandria should receive no less than three portable airship sheds. There had been an earlier, more ambitious plan to erect a double berth airship shed there—presumably for the 33-class of rigid airships—to which 3,100 tonnes of steel were allocated, but this idea was dropped because of a metal shortage. At one stage, steel too was set to one side for an airship shed at Port Said. These projects came to an abrupt end after peace was declared, and what work had been done was hastily jettisoned. British military airships would never again fly over Mediterranean waters.

10

RNAS Training and Airship Construction Stations

The Admiralty decided early in the First World War that the training of RNAS personnel left a lot to be desired. Initially, RNAS Wormwood Scrubs, RNAS Kingsnorth, and (to a lesser extent) RNAS Barrow oversaw the instruction of potential airship crews. But it was not long before a hugecentral training establishment for RNAS personnel was opened at Cranwell in a bid to improve standards. The Admiralty readjusted the focus of Kingsnorth and Wormwood Scrubs onto non-rigid construction. By the end of the war, these two stations concentrated on little else.

RNAS Farnborough Airship Station

Until 1914, the Army had been responsible for military airships. Yet this was transferred to the Royal Navy, together with occupancy of the base at Farnborough. This was a political decision only: contrary to appearances, the Army did value its airships. Sir Sefton Brancker, who later became Director of Civil Aviation, related:

> The General Staff were furious and the Military Aeronautics Directorate threw up their hands to heaven and called down curses on the heads of the politicians. We soldiers loved our little airships and our Eddie Maitland, and fought hard to retain them, they were small but lead the world in efficient handling and we felt that they were the germ of the future.[1]

Farnborough and airships *Beta*, *Eta*, *Delta*, and *Gamma* were allotted to the Naval Wing and all airship-related training was continued there by six officers and thirty-eight men, supplemented by a civilian repair staff. The station was capable of training fifteen officers and sixty men a year, in two concurrent classes of four officers and sixteen men per three-month course. This was followed by six months on probation at the station. The station diary records the following activity on 27 March 1914:

> Parade at 6.00 a.m. The Parseval No. 4 left its shed for a 65 minute flight. This was following by Willows No. 2 which undertook a 20 minute flight. Beta was housed in C-shed for refuelling with hydrogen. There was a further parade at 10.00 a.m. Willows No. 2 then

left its shed for a second flight. There was yet another parade at 4.00 p.m. after which Parseval No. 4 made another flight but returned after 70 minutes with cracked cylinders.[2]

1 July 1914 saw the formation of the Royal Naval Air Service. On the first day of war, *Eta* made a one-hour flight but had a bad landing due to engine failure, and *Delta* returned from Dover. In early October most of the personnel were involved preparing the *Parseval*, *Beta*, and *Eta* for the Expeditionary Forces. On the 14th, fifty rifles arrived from Chatham, and over the next few days, rifle drill came into practise. At the end of the month, the Expeditionary Force left for Dunkirk. A few days later, *Eta* followed but encountered a snowstorm and was forced to land at Redhill, just 40 miles away. It was moored out there, but overnight a strong wind sprang up and it was severely damaged. *Beta* was dispatched to Dunkirk in its place.

By early 1915, flying at RNAS Farnborough had dwindled, since most of the airships had moved to RNAS Kingsnorth. The *Willows No. 2* was the last airship to make this transfer. On 3 March, RNAS Farnborough closed and the airship sheds thereon used to house aeroplanes—two by the Southern Aeroplane Repair Depot and the others for storage. Farnborough went on to become a centre of aeronautical research and experimentation, and one of Britain's most illustrious aerodromes. It has been the venue of one of the world's leading air shows for over half a century. Both the A-shed and C-shed were dismantled in 1925. The lattice steel framework of the portable airship shed, built in 1912, has been re-assemble in 2004 and preserved on site. The day of RNAS Farnborough's closure in 1915 was also the day of RNAS Barrow-in-Furness's inauguration.

RNAS Barrow-in-Furness Airship Station[†]

The RNAS Station at Barrow-in-Furness shared the site at Walney Island with the Vickers Rigid Airship Construction Works. Its importance waned in the latter stages of the war, when its activities were restricted to experimental work. Many of the RNAS personnel displaced by the Farnborough closure were posted here. In March and April 1915, they were involved in transporting stores from the Barrow Goods Station. Engineers and carpenters repaired airships, and some of the personnel constructed a hydrogen plant.

On 24 May 1915, the well-travelled *Beta* airship made a number of flights from here. The following month, Submarine Scouts *S.S.2* and *S.S.3* were tested and Parseval *No. 4* was used for training. By the end of July, the hydrogen plant was in operation and used to inflate *S.S.20*. A number of this class of airship were built or worked on here by the RNAS, utilising the old rigid airship shed at Cavendish Dock, for instance *S.S.24* and *S.S.25* in August 1915. A new portable airship shed arrived at Walney Island, followed by furniture and ammunition delivered to the local railway station. By mid-September, the portable airship shed was ready for use. Submarine Scouts continued to be built at Barrow until early 1916, but production of newer classes to replace them was

---

[†] See Chapter 8.

concentrated at RNAS Kingsnorth and RNAS Wormwood Scrubs. The opening of RNAS Cranwell meant that Barrow-in-Furness ultimately lost its role in training personnel.

RNAS Kingsnorth Airship Station[†]

RNAS Kingsnorth was one of three military airship stations in the country when Britain went to war—the other two were RNAS Farnborough and RNAS Wormwood Scrubs—and was the only one that had been purpose-built for the Admiralty. It would be another year before there would be another operational airship station in Britain. The night before war was declared, airships Astra Torres *No. 3* and Parseval *No. 4* were flying patrols over the English Channel from RNAS Kingsnorth. On its way back to base, Parseval *No. 4* came under rifle fire from a Territorial Army unit mistaking it for a Zeppelin, despite the large white ensign it was displaying. Around the same time there were reports of a Zeppelin flying up the Thames. The Parseval was, admittedly, German-built.

The troubles for *No. 4* were just beginning. On 15 August 1914, it encountered strong headwinds as it headed towards home; a propeller detached, and the airship began to drift out to sea. Two crew members managed to replace the propeller, but then another was found to be lopsided and had to be replaced with the second spare carried on board. By the time the Parseval had been restored to full airworthiness, Capt. J. Fletcher and his crew were over Belgium and could see gun flashes on the Western Front.

The two airships based at RNAS Kingsnorth continued to escort troopships carrying the British Expeditionary Force to France in the summer of 1914. Astra Torres *No. 3* was deployed to Ostend at the end of August. The admiral in command and the general on the ground initially concluded they had no use for it and applied for it to be sent back, but were in time persuaded otherwise and put it to use scouting for suspicious vessels and monitoring the movement of enemy troops. In fact, *No. 3* was found so useful for directing the guns of Royal Navy ships that the general wanted it to do nothing else. That said, the airship was extremely vulnerable to hostile fire from the ground, and a few days later it returned to RNAS Kingsnorth. Parseval *No. 4* landed at Dover on 11 August 1914, where it was supplied with petrol and ballast and arrangements for future landings were discussed by its commander. Earlier plans to set up a small airship base here were soon abandoned.

In December 1914, an additional Astra Torres was delivered to RNAS Kingsnorth. It took over the role of *No. 3* in the eastern Channel Approaches until May 1915. By then the new airship stations at RNAS Polegate and RNAS Folkestone were coming into operation and their new Submarine Scouts took over the patrolling role. RNAS Kingsnorth was the base for a motley collection of airships which patrolled the English Channel, and as the war dragged on, its function as a base from which to guard the approaches of the Thames gradually diminished. For such a strategic location,

---

[†] See Chapter 2.

it is astonishing that it was given such low priority. A letter requesting additional airships was sent to the Admiralty from the C-in-C's office at Chatham in early September:

> I have the honour to submit for Their Lordships consideration that three S.S. airships may be permanently appropriated to Kingsnorth Air Station for patrol work in connection with the Estuary of the Thames in searching for mines and submarines, observing that the enemy are very active in laying mines off the Lightships at the entrance to the Thames and these craft are particularly suited for this purpose. Much good work might be done by these airships in locating mines at low water and also possibly in harassing the submarine craft which lay them. A daily patrol would be carried out, at or near low water, over The War Channel and in the vicinity of the Lightships. There are at present no seaplanes at any of the air stations in my command, nor on board the *Vindex*, and it is submitted that these deficiencies may be made good as soon as possible.[3]

This request was turned down by the Director of the Air Service on the grounds that it was not considered practical. It would interfere with the building of Coastals, which required all the space available in the airship sheds at RNAS Kingsnorth, and airships off the Thames would probably require the protection of aeroplanes to ward off attacks by German seaplanes. This last argument proved to be a prophetic statement for two airships patrolling the eastern approaches from RNAS Pulham. Still, even though this petition for additional airships was turned down, there was one Submarine Scout at RNAS Kingsnorth that could be called on for patrol duties.

In early 1915, less than a hundred British men could fly an airship. RNAS Kingsnorth's primary function was to turn pupils who had completed the free ballooning course and ground instruction at RNAS Wormwood Scrubs into airship pilots. Occasionally, the initial stage was omitted and pilot candidates found themselves being given immediate instruction at an operational airship station. In any case, intensive training was given in both theory and practice at Kingsnorth. There were lectures in aeronautics, navigation, meteorology, engineering, and of course flying lessons. Victor Goddard, who later flew the 'black airship' in France, described the training he received here:

> You were then allowed to fly the airship under instruction. The instruction consisted not of the formal dual instruction that we've all grown used to. The instructor would sit in the captain's seat in this two-seater fuselage and he would fly the airship and you would experience what he was doing. You would sit in the front seat and you wouldn't have any part in the control of the thing at all. Then after you had done one or two landings with this instructor he would say, 'All right, now you do a flight'. He would get out and might sit in the front seat and you in the back seat and you would fly around doing a few circuits ... and when he thought you were OK he would say, 'Right, well you're an airship pilot'.

In the summer of 1916, Submarine Scouts *S.S.14* and *S.S.31* were on strength, while Coastal *C.1* was used for training purposes. In his book *Airship Pilot No. 2*, Capt. T.

B. Williams relates that, after successfully graduating as an airship pilot, he undertook a test flight in *S.S.14*. It had been fitted with a new type of engine, a water-cooled Curtiss. At around 5,000 feet it failed and would not respond to attempts to restart. The airship landed at Hoo, where the radiator was replenished with water from the village pump and Williams purchased some chewing gum to plug a leak in it. The pilot then flew *S.S.14* back to RNAS Kingsnorth minus Williams, who had decided to walk back, as the airship had lost some of its lift.

The other training airship, Submarine Scout *S.S.31*, also doubled up as an experimental platform for any innovation which needed testing. It was called 'the Flying Bedstead'. In August 1916, the official fleet for training and routine flying consisted of two Submarine Scouts and two Coastals. A year later, *S.S.14* was the only airship permanently based here. Just as it had previously done with its patrol role, RNAS Kingsnorth lost its function as a flying school for airship crews by 1917. Prospective applicants were posted to the newly opened RNAS Cranwell instead.

Kingsnorth clung on to its experimental work until the end of 1917, the best known example of which was the *A.P.1*. In the early days of the war, Zeppelins could roam across the skies almost invincible to interception by British aeroplanes, because it could take over half an hour for a fighter to take off and climb to the height of the enemy airship. In an effort to position aeroplanes such that they could go into action quickly,

Coastal *C.8* at RNAS Kingsnorth. This class of airship was assembled in the rigid sheds here. (*RAF Museum*)

the envelope of a Submarine Scout would be used to lift a B.E.2 aeroplane into the air, which would then detach itself at high altitude. The first such flight was meant to be carried out in the summer of 1915, but a number of faults were discovered and the test was delayed until 21 February 1916. Wg Cdr Neville Usborne and Sqn Ldr de Courcey of Ireland volunteered to test-fly the aeroplane/balloon combination. As the airship pilot, Usborne was responsible for the take-off, and the aeroplane pilot, Ireland, would handle the landing. Lift-off went as planned but at the moment of the aeroplane's release at some 4,000 feet above Strood, things began to go wrong. The envelope deflated and began to descend, and whereas the three independent hooks holding the aeroplane should have detached simultaneously, one failed to disengage: thus, the aeroplane became entangled in the descending envelope. In an attempt to free the aeroplane, Ireland tried to crawl along the fuselage but lost his grip and fell to his death. Usborne's body was later recovered, still strapped into his seat. A similar craft, the *A.P.2*, had been completed but never flew, for the Admiralty decided to discontinue any similar experiments with non-rigid airships. Two years later, an aeroplane was successfully dropped from a rigid airship at RNAS Pulham. Although the loss of Usborne and Ireland was a tragedy, accidents involving experimental flights from RNAS Kingsnorth were rare.

In November 1914, airship *No. 3* was employed in towing experiments behind a Royal Navy Vessel. Similar trials were carried out with Coastals in March 1916 to see whether their range could be increased by this method. A large area of the landing ground at RNAS Kingsnorth was marked out to represent the afterdeck of a destroyer. A Coastal crew practised their skills at accurately dropping a trail rope onto the mock ship and being attached to it. On 12 May 1916, Coastal *C.1* flew to Harwich Harbour where it was attached to a cruiser before being towed to the open sea. Commander of Harwich Naval Force R. Tyrwhitt declared his approval at the handling of the airships and the skill of the pilots.

Other experiments carried out at RNAS Kingsnorth involved *S.S.14*, which was used to test a new grappling hook. When dropped from 250 feet, this hook could penetrate hard turf to a depth of 12 inches and soft ground to a depth of 6 feet. Mooring experiments were carried out with a Coastal airship using both the Usborne method and, more successfully, a mooring mast. Various trials were carried out with bombs and different types of machine guns to give airships a more lethal edge.

Another role of RNAS Kingsnorth was in the design and construction of non-rigid airships. As German submarines began to exert a heavy toll on British shipping at the end of 1914, the Admiralty urgently began looking for solutions. Within three weeks of the Admiralty issuing the requirement for a small airship to carry out coastal patrols, Cdr Masterman had built and flown the first example of the Submarine Scout. It is sometimes also referred to as the 'Submarine Searcher', and consisted of a control car adapted from a B.E.2 aeroplane, attached to the envelope. There were two crew members and it could remain airborne for about 8 hours. The Admiralty was pleased with the result and decided to immediately put the Submarine Scout into production at Kingsnorth, Wormwood Scrubs, and Barrow. Other airships designed at Kingsnorth were the Coastal and North Sea classes, all the prototypes of which were also constructed here. Some of the smaller Submarine Scout Zeros were also assembled here.

The RNAS was not the only party in the market for airships—foreign governments were as well. The Russian government purchased a small number of Coastals and sent officers to Britain for training on them. C.6 was badly damaged while being flown by a Russian pilot: it rose to 5,000 feet then became very heavy and plunged, destroying its envelope and badly damaging the control car. The French were given an old Coastal, the C.4, which was rigged and refurbished in just 44 hours before being flown to Le Havre by French naval officers.

The Kingsnorth personnel were assisted by a large number of civilians, mainly women, in the production of various airship components. Some of them were instructed to wear boots so they could be called on to assist in the mooring operations if the number of naval ratings available was insufficient. This duty was not without danger. In April 1915, a Submarine Scout was coming in to land and leading mechanic Standford was the only member of the mooring party to get a strong grip on one of its trail ropes. When the airship suddenly rose back into the air, he was still holding on—at 700 feet, Standford was no longer able to maintain his grip and fell to his death. It was not uncommon for ground crew to find themselves lifted slightly off the ground, and this was probably why Standford did not let go immediately. It is just as well that such fatalities were rare—just six RNAS personnel perished in this manner during the war.

Another hazard of airship stations was hydrogen gas. Serious accidents were surprisingly uncommon, but RNAS Kingsnorth was among the few to witness fatal consequences. On 27 May 1917, a leak in one of the gas holders caught fire. Lt P. Armstrong discharged a considerable quantity of gas from it to allow the fire to burn itself out. An examination of the holder seemingly confirmed that the flames had been extinguished, but 20 minutes later it blew up. Armstrong and Leading Mechanic Charles Harris were killed in the explosion, and two other men seriously injured. An investigation concluded that a spark must have ignited the leaking hydrogen. As leaks could also cause suffocation, workers at the Kingsnorth gas plant kept canaries as sentinels.

In spite of the somewhat amateur appearance of some of the early Royal Navy airships, a prolific amount of research and development was dedicated to improving their performance. Detailed drawings were made of every part used in the construction of an airship, which were then forwarded to outside firms contracted to build the specific item on their premises and deliver them to Kingsnorth. The Drawing Office started with just a single draughtsman at the onset of the war, but by 1916 employed a staff of forty-nine. Kingsnorth's airship sheds were used as an assembly line in which to gather parts commissioned from many different sources. Shop fitters, agricultural machinery makers, and several waterproof garment manufacturers all adapted their output to the manufacture of small parts for aeronautical use. A civilian workshop on the station checked the balancing of Coastal propellers delivered by outside contractors, and in many cases made good the defects. A chemical research laboratory carried out tests on the strength of fabrics, varieties of dopes, and methods of waterproofing—it was this facility that came up with the fabric petrol tank. The performance of various engines could be monitored in the engine test house, and Kingsnorth even had a separate workshop to deal with miscellaneous instruments and experiments.

RNAS Kingsnorth viewed from the south in September 1917. The two rigid sheds are visible, with the workshops and hydrogen gas plants behind them. (*The Fleet Air Arm Museum*)

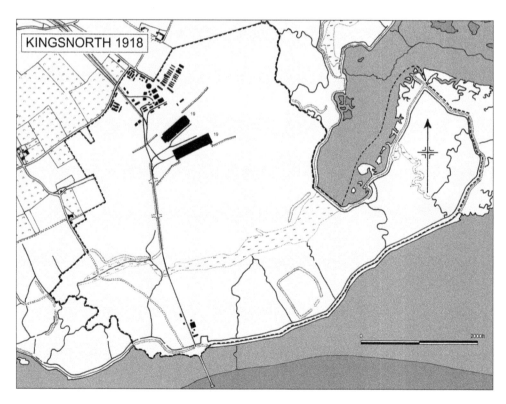

Kingsnorth, 1918. Situated on the north bank of the River Medway, RNAS Kingsnorth extended over considerable marshland. The largest building was the extended 'wooden' rigid shed which stood next to the 'steel' rigid shed. Windbreaks as long as the sheds themselves, protected their entrances. A narrow gauge railway ran from the airship sheds to a jetty on the banks of the river. Abundant workshops and hydrogen gas plants were clustered together a short distance to the north of the sheds. (*Mick Davis*)

By 1918, the extensive facilities at RNAS Kingsnorth were almost entirely involved in airship assembly. With the exception of test flights by newly assembled craft, there was little other activity in the air.. In May, Submarine Scout Zero *S.S.Z.55* was used for experimental purposes. A new Submarine Scout Twin *S.S.T.6* was delivered here in August, which, while taking off on its trial flight, developed engine trouble. The envelope was set on fire and the control car fell from 400 feet, killing the entire crew—Captains Righton, Barlett, and King, Sgt Cameron, and Airman Cowan. It happened so quickly that witnesses at the Court of Inquiry had difficult explaining exactly what had occurred.

Although the RNAS Kingsnorth airship sheds were complete in 1914, a programme of continuous expansion during the next four years attached a large number of structures to the original complex. In early 1916, a new dope laboratory, another gas holder, new stores and drawing offices, an experimental rubber-proofing laboratory, and additional accommodation for officers and men were all in various stages of construction. An essential part of any major airship station was its access to the rail network. A branch line was built in 1915 which connected with the railway line to Hoo. It ran directly to the airship sheds and sidings split off to the boiler house and hydrogen plant. The standard gauge railway at RNAS Kingsnorth even had its own locomotive, the *Lord Fisher*. Inside the station itself was a narrow gauge line, which ran south from the stores and across the Damhead Fleet Pools to a pier on the River Medway, where cargoes were delivered. Finally, a length of track with a gauge of no less than 10 feet ran through one of the airship sheds and extended to the exterior, turning to clear the windbreaks. This was laid for a power trolley useful in experiments for moving airships in and out of the shed mechanically—rather than by manpower, the traditional method.

In the summer of 1916, RNAS Kingsnorth also accommodated construction of a landing ground for aeroplanes. Aeroplanes from RNAS Eastchurch aerodrome would sometimes perform various stunts over the airship station to impress the airship pilots. On one occasion, a two-seat bi-plane flew too low and crashed into one of the windbreaks. Both crew members were found sitting on the ground in their bucket seats, escaping with only minor injuries! Despite the large investment that had been made and the numerous experimental facilities, the station was rapidly demobilised after the war. In 1919, it became a repository for live mines—4,400 of which were stored in the 'iron' airship shed—and deactivated naval mines—an unknown quantity of which were stored in the timber airship shed. The decision to close the base appears to have been taken in March and by the end of August the drawing office had been closed. There was originally discussion of retaining the base for passenger airship services, but by 1920 the whole complex—two airship sheds and 107 other buildings—was put up for sale.

In the 1920s, the sheds and a number of the former technical buildings were used for wood-pulping. The accommodation blocks were converted into workmen's housing, and Berry Wiggans & Co. set up a bitumen manufacturing plant in the former RNAS structures in 1930. Industrialisation of the area does not seem to have immediately affected at least one of the airship sheds, which was reportedly still standing as late as 1939. In the second half of the century, an oil refinery bearing upon some the land

An aerial view of some of the technical buildings at RNAS Kingsnorth in April 1917. They include gas holders for storing hydrogen produced in the surrounding buildings. To the right is a dark cooling tower, and behind it the electricity-generating station. The low buildings in the foreground include the drawing office and rubber dope laboratory. (*The Fleet Air Arm Museum*)

swept away many of the station's remaining traces. A large coal-fired power station with a 600-foot chimney was also built on the site in the late 1960s. This stopped generating electricity in 2012, and will soon too be nothing more than a memory.

RNAS Wormwood Scrubs Airship Station

Alternative name: 'HMS *President*'.
Location: O. S. 1/50,000 map 176 (TQ) 225818. London, half a mile from Wormwood Scrubs railway station, 6 miles west of central London.
Size: 30 acres (within boundaries of 666 x 286 yards).
Station Complement: eleven officers, 245 men (in Jan 1918).
Airship Sheds: *Daily Mail* airship shed (354 feet long, 76 feet wide, and 98 feet high); and the Barking airship shed—transported and re-erected here in 1918, with extensions added (300 feet long, 45 feet wide, and 55 feet high).
Hydrogen Plant: B2 silicol (5,000 cubic feet per hour).

Gasholder: One (10,000 cubic feet).
Gas Tanks: 12 (8,000 cubic feet each).

Associated Sites:
RNAS Hurlingham Free Balloon School
Location: O. S. 1/50,000 map 176 (TQ) 249761. Royal Borough of Kensington and Chelsea, London.
RNAS Roehampton Kite Balloon Training Station
Location: O. S. 1/50,000 map 176 (TQ) 218746. Borough of Wandsworth, London.

Wormwood Scrubs Common has had a long association with the military. In the early 19th century, it was used for exercising cavalry horses stabled in the centre of London, and 135 acres of ground were eventually purchased by the military, though no buildings construction was permitted. The public could use the open land for recreation, provided soldiers were not training at the time. Wormwood Scrubs is best known for its prison on the southern edge of the open ground. The *Daily Mail* airship shed was assembled but a short distance to the east of it (see Chapter 2). This shed became War Office property in 1910, and three years later, questions were raised in Parliament as to its function, for it was then being used to store the guns of a Territorial Army unit. The shed was nonetheless available for emergency use by airships based at Farnborough, and in 1913 was offered to the Admiralty, which continued to use it for storage—of cars and armoured lorries—for the first year of hostilities. RNAS Wormwood Scrubs was also the home to No. 20 Squadron Armoured Car Division, an experimental unit that participated in developing the tank.

In the summer of 1914, the few airships in RNAS service undertook numerous flights over London, particularly at night, in preparation for the expected Zeppelin bombing raids. Airship *Beta* was kept busy here in the autumn by routines such as the following:

> On the 22nd September, on a calm but foggy night, this ship ascended from Wormwood Scrubs to examine the lighting [of London] under these conditions. She quickly lost her bearings and was unable to find her way back. She cruised at 500 feet and found it impossible at times to determine whether she was over London or out in open country. She eventually located her position by sighting the name of Golder's Green Underground station picked out in electric light. By this means she was able to return to Wormwood Scrubs by a circuitous route, keeping at about 300 feet or lower over main thoroughfares and landed safely after 2½ hours in the air.[4]

But Beta flew equally regularly over London by daylight and dusk. By 1915, potential airship crew members received their initial training at RNAS Wormwood Scrubs. The course consisted of lectures on all aspects of airship operation and flying. There were also practical lessons. Pupils would often have their first taste of flight in a small man-lifting kite balloon, whereupon they would sit on a plank seat under a hydrogen balloon and be lifted into the air. At the end of the 'flight' the balloon would be winched back to the ground.

Hurlingham Polo Ground on the banks of the Thames was used for free ballooning. Pupils would be launched into the air in a basket attached to a large balloon. They could then be blown to all points of the compass, depending on what direction the wind was blowing on the day. Most Hurlingham balloons had a 60,000-cubic-foot capacity, and individual names such as *Plover*, *Seahorse*, *Shrimp*, and *Swallow*. While most flights took place across open countryside, it was not unknown for balloons to be blown across central London. One over-zealous pupil decided to bombard buses with buns as he floated overhead! The favoured place to put down a balloon was the lee of a wood, but it was not unknown for flights to be terminated in the grounds of a large country house, where the trainee airship pilots would often receive a warm welcome and be invited in for tea. At the end of the flight, the balloon was typically packed up and taken to the nearest railway station for transport back to Wormwood Scrubs.

In 1917, 3,645 officers and men made 833 balloon trips by day and twenty-seven by night. 172 officers and men combined qualified as balloon pilots that year. At the end of November, all balloon training was transferred from Hurlingham Polo Ground to Roehampton in south-west London, an open ground used by airships operating in proximity to the capital. In October 1914, airship *Eta* was detached from Farnborough to observe London from the air: it made one trip at dusk, but owing to strong winds did not remain at Roehampton for long. After the Second World War, council houses were built on the Hurlingham Polo Ground.

On completing their initial training, trainee airship pilots were transferred to RNAS Cranwell. In the early days of war, pupils could familiarize themselves with airships by access to a Submarine Scout based at RNAS Wormwood Scrubs, and were later posted to RNAS Kingsnorth for instruction (before RNAS Cranwell opened). While the training role occupied a small portion of the airship shed at Wormwood Scrubs, from the summer of 1915 onwards, much of its floor space was given over to the construction of Submarine Scouts. Unlike aeroplanes—which were generally the domain of private manufacturers—the Royal Navy built non-rigid airships on its own premises. The Kite Balloon Experimental and Testing Section left for Crystal Palace in July 1916, and thus freed up more space.

The Submarine Scout was the first of several types of small patrol airships to serve with the RNAS. A number of this class of airship were built for foreign governments, including the Italians. While piloted by Italian Cdr Dente, *S.S.44* crashed into trees at Wormwood Scrubs. His passenger, Lt Baldwin RNVR, was thrown out, whereas he himself was trapped in an inverted position in the control car. As often happened, the much lightened airship now shot upwards to 6,000 feet and flew for about an hour. It then gently descended onto some suburban roofs at Walthamstow. Not long after, the rescue party, who had been following in cars, arrived on the scene. They rescued Cdr Dente from the wreckage and deflated the envelope. Despite this incident, in the autumn of 1916 the Italian government took delivery of their airships, including the repaired *S.S.44*.

The most serious accident at RNAS Wormwood Scrubs occurred on the ground. In July 1915, a gas explosion and fire in the airship shed occurred while an airship was being filled with hydrogen. It killed mechanics George Haydon and F. Westerman and five other men suffered burns. At the inquiry, Flt Lt Dunville said the men were under

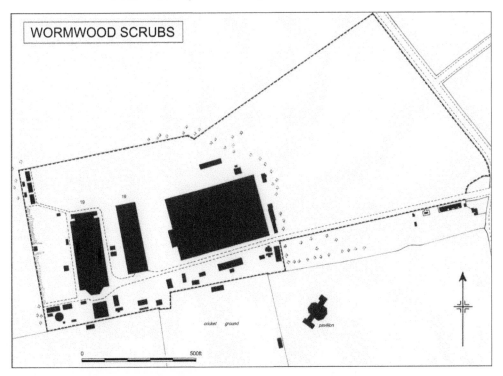

Wormwood Scrubs. Although most RNAS airship stations encompassed vast expanses of open ground, Wormwood Scrubs was compact and did not extend far beyond its principle building, the former Daily Mail shed. It was surrounded by workshops and storage facilities, and small airships flew from the open ground next to the station. A short distance to the west was the notorious Wormwood Scrubs Prison, which has long outlived the airship station. (*Mick Davis*)

his command and that a hydrogen gas cylinder was being turned off when it exploded. Sabotage was ruled out as 'there were sentries on duty and it would not be possible for anyone to pass them'. Wg Cdr F. Boothby said that when he reached the shed, it was full of smoke and that a party of officers and men had the fire under control. Some of the gas cylinders were still burning. He said he had previous experience of cylinders catching fire spontaneously, but it was a rare occurrence. There were four cases known to him in Great Britain and two in Germany, in which airships had been destroyed in similar incidents. Boothby added that he was satisfied there was no carelessness or negligence on anybody's part. The verdict of the jury was accidental death. According to the Fire Brigade, about a quarter of the airship shed, which was being used principally for storage at the time, had been damaged by the explosion.

When production of the Submarine Scouts finished, RNAS Wormwood Scrubs personnel turned their hands to building the more advanced Submarine Scout Zero and five of the six Submarine Scout Pushers were assembled here. In addition to test flights, airships were sometimes used for experiments, although these was normally carried out at RNAS Kingsnorth. In August 1916, Submarine Scout *S.S.47* made sixteen flights which included speed trials, climbing and steering tests. Assisted by *S.S.36*, it also performed anti-aircraft range-finding tests. A prisoner peering out of his cell window at the nearby prison would sometimes see a less familiar shape in the sky, as Coastals and other classes of airship were also repaired at RNAS Wormwood Scrubs. If possible they would be flown here, sometimes breaking their journey at other airship stations. Those unable to take to the air were often delivered on railway wagons. The Royal Navy had another facility close by at White City, where parts for airships were stored.

While some airship stations notched up more than 2,000 hours of flying in 1917, the total at RNAS Wormwood Scrubs came to a mere 35 hours. In the final year of the war, a further airship shed was nearing completion. It had been transferred from Barking to house workshops, and was 300 feet long, 45 wide, and 55 feet high. Chemicals were moved from here to Kingsnorth for storage in January 1919, and the station was rapidly demobilised and closed later in the year. The original *Daily Mail* airship shed was dismantled in 1924. The ground in its vicinity was designated as an emergency landing ground during the interwar years. Linford Christie Sports Stadium now marks the site where one of Britain's first airship sheds once stood. The open ground found immediately to the north is Wormwood Scrubs Park.

RNAS Cranwell Central Training Establishment

Alternative name: 'HMS *Daedalus*'.
Location: O. S.1/50,000 map 130 (TF) 010510. Lincolnshire, 13 miles south of Lincoln.
Size (entire complex): 2,446 acres (within boundaries of 4,200 x 2,800 yards).
Station Complement: forty-seven men including twenty-one officers under instruction (for airships), 203 men in total (in Jan 1918).
Airship Sheds: rigid shed No. 1 (700 feet long, 150 feet wide, and 100 feet high), rigid shed No. 2 (site cleared but construction abandoned), Submarine Scout shed (152 feet long, 45 feet wide, and 50 feet high), Coastal shed (220 feet long, 70 feet wide, and 70 feet high).
Hydrogen Plant: B silicol (10,000 cubic feet per hour), water gas plant (14,000 cubic feet per hour).
Gasholders: four of 500,000 cubic feet, one of 120,000 cubic feet.
Gas Tanks: sixty-six (8,000 cubic feet each).
Based Airships: Rigid *No. 25*; Parseval *No. 6*; Submarine Scout *S.S.28A*, *S.S.29*, *S.S.30A*, *S.S.31A*, *S.S.37*, *S.S.39*, and *S.S.39A*; Submarine Scout Pusher *S.S.P.1*, *S.S.P.5*, and *S.S.P.6*; Submarine Scout Zero *S.S.Z.23*, *S.S.Z.60*, and *S.S.Z.61*; Coastal *C.13*; Coastal Star *C*8*; and North Sea *N.S.11*.

In November 1915, the Lord Commissioners of the Admiralty decided that the Air Department should centralise its pilot, airship crew, and balloonist training programmes into a single establishment. Up until this point, instruction was scattered across the country. The results were at times unsatisfactory and did not produce the numbers of pilots needed. One young naval pilot was supposedly briefed to fly

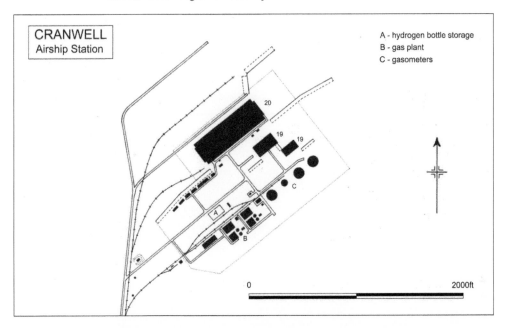

The three airship sheds at RNAS Cranwell. The largest was 700 feet long and housed rigid airships. Next to it was the 220-foot-long Coastal shed. The smallest of the three was a portable Submarine Scout shed. An extensive complex of hydrogen plants using both the silicol and water gas process are located close by. (*Mick Davis*)

around until he found a piece of land that was both large enough and flat enough for the purpose of establishing the station. He flew over Cranwell and 'thought it quite admirable'. The truth is probably more mundane, as the area had been extensively surveyed shortly before the war. Cranwell, which means 'crane's spring', was easily accessible from London and many other parts of England.

A branch line was laid from Sleaford, 5 miles away, to ferry construction materials to the site. Such was the haste to get the station up and running that the railway sleepers were laid directly on the ground. Trains were running by early March 1916, around a month after work had started. The track was later rebuilt to a higher standard and a passenger station was opened at the heart of RNAS Cranwell, with the airship base to the north and the aerodrome to the south. Construction of the accommodation huts and the aerodrome commenced in December 1915, although a severe winter hampered their progress. The first plane landed in January 1916 and the establishment was officially commissioned in March. During that month, a canvas kite balloon shed was put up to house six coal gas balloons from RNAS Wormwood Scrubs, but the first airship shed was not ready until November. This was a portable Submarine Scout shed which had to be rebuilt after it was blown down by a gale. This was followed by the Coastal shed built by Sir William Arrol & Co., finished in December 1916. The third and last shed, for rigid airships, was built by Francis Morton & Co. using 1,915 tonnes of steel. It was ready for operation in June 1917.

Some of the more daring Sopwith Camel pilots tested their skills by landing on the sloping roof of the rigid shed. They would then let their aeroplanes slide down

The three airship sheds at RNAS Cranwell. The smallest, a portable Submarine Scout shed, is on the right, immediately behind the windbreak. Sandwiched between it and the rigid shed is the Coastal shed built by Sir William Arrol & Co. (*The Fleet Air Arm Museum*)

sideways before taking off. It was planned to erect a second rigid shed at RNAS Cranwell, but this was cancelled in May 1917. The first airship was delivered at the end of 1916, but it appears that the first pupils did not arrive until May 1917. The course for airship pilots ran nine weeks but was often longer, as poor weather conditions restricted flying. At first, the pupil would be given dual instruction followed by 10 to 15 hours flying solo. Cross country flying and one night landing were also on the syllabus, and there were also examinations on theory, rigging, weather, and seamanship.

Not only were aircrew trained at RNAS Cranwell, there were also courses for riggers and other trades which were required to keep airships operational. Serious accidents involving airships here too were rare, but they did happen. On 11 July 1917, *S.S.31* was being walked out of its shed when a gust of wind caught the envelope and wrapped it over the building. The control car, complete with its crew, was left hanging precariously on the roof. One man clambered out, at which point the now lighter airship soared up into the air. A ladder was sent for by the officer of the watch to rescue the stranded crew member. But his troubles were not over, for waiting at the bottom was the Master of Arms who had been instructed to arrest him for abandoning his post without orders!

The most serious accident occurred only a few days later, on 20 July 1917. *S.S.39* had just landed and was being walked back to its shed when a gust of wind blew the airship back into the air. Unfortunately, three of the handling party held on to the ropes and were carried up to a height of about 500 feet. No longer having the strength to hold on, they fell back to earth and were killed. The airship flew on for just over a mile and was recovered virtually intact. One of those who died was Lt-Col Clive Waterlow, who was in charge of the aeroplane wing. He had previously been in command of the training of airship crews at Wormwood Scrubs and was a pioneer airship pilot. Ironically, 'Never hang onto the guy-ropes if lifted off your feet' had been his mantra, and he had always instructed his men to 'Let go immediately'.[5] In wartime, most accidents on British military bases were censored, or simply went unreported. The *Hull Daily Mail*, however, did mention Waterlow's death, if mysteriously incorrectly. It stated that he had been on his first solo flight in an aeroplane and had lost control, diving through the roof of a hanger, dying 'two hours latter from burns'.[6]

In late November 1917, twenty-six probationary flight officers went under instruction, two lieutenants from the US Navy and a flight officer having just graduated. Americans were trained here because the USA had purchased a number of British Submarine Scouts and North Seas. The following airships were being used for training purposes at that time: rigid airship *No. 9*; Parseval *No. 6*; and Submarine Scouts *S.S.37*, *S.S.39A*, and *S.S.30A* (being rigged). The first rigid airship to be delivered was *No. 9* on 15 October 1917. At the end of that month it had to divert to RNAS Howden because of bad weather. While entering the airship shed it was damaged, and remained here for two months for extensive repairs. March 1918 saw no less than fifteen American cadets graduated and one Japanese officer under instruction. By this time the airship fleet had grown to a considerable size, the following airships making this number of flights in March 1918:

Submarine Scout *S.S.28A*, 41 flights.
Submarine Scout *S.S.29*, 40 flights.
Submarine Scout *S.S.30A*, 73 flights.
Submarine Scout *S.S.31A*, 57 flights.
Submarine Scout *S.S.39A*, 31 flights.
Submarine Scout Zero *S.S.Z.23*, 5 flights.
Submarine Scout Zero *S.S.Z.50*, 1 flight.
Submarine Scout Zero *S.S.Z.51*, 2 flights.
Submarine Scout Zero *S.S.Z.33*, 1 flight.
Submarine Scout Zero *S.S.Z.31*, 1 flight.
Coastal Star *C*2*, 1 flight.
Coastal *C.19*, 1 flight.

While at an operational airship station, most airships would generally make a maximum of a dozen or so long duration flights. Many at RNAS Cranwell undertook several flights each day, but of a much shorter duration, lasting only an hour or two. By the time of the Armistice, some seventy-five airship pilots had been trained at

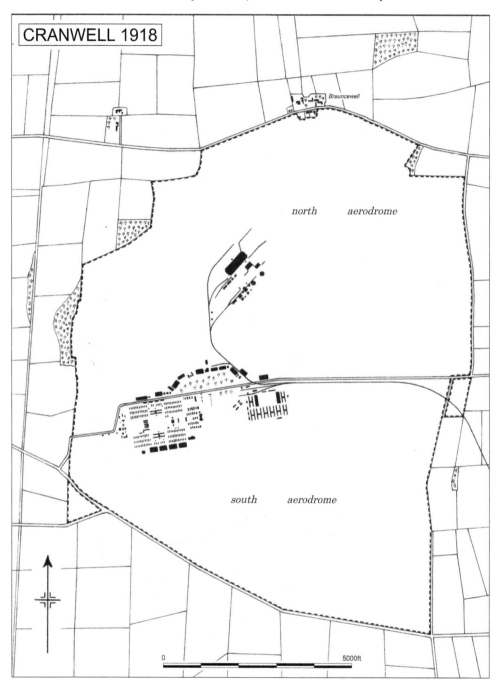

Cranwell, 1918. RNAS Cranwell was an enormous training station for both aeroplane pilots and airship crews. The north aerodrome was reserved for airship flying, while aeroplanes operated from the south aerodrome. Lying between the two was an extensive complex of barracks. A railway ran through the centre of the site, terminating at the airship sheds. (*Mick Davis*)

RNAS Cranwell, or RAF Cranwell as it became known after 1 April 1918. It should be noted that when the Royal Air Force was formed, all RNAS aeroplanes, airships and personnel came under its authority. The actual airship stations, however, still remained the property of the Admiralty. By the time Cranwell was transferred to the RAF, fifty-seven officers and other ranks had been killed in training accidents involving aeroplanes here   and its associated aerodrome at Frieston. Despite criticism of airships, only one was involved in a fatal accident—the incident with the handling party detailed above. One newly graduated aeroplane pilot, Arch Whitehouse, claimed that he came close to shooting down a rigid airship operating from Cranwell (possibly R.25), which he mistook for a Zeppelin in poor weather.

Although there was a rapid contraction in the number of airships in RAF service at the end of the war, the last one did not leave Cranwell until 1921. Over the next few years, the airship sheds and the hydrogen plant were demolished and replaced by married quarters. In the early twenty-first century, Cranwell was still home to the RAF College, where all potential officers and aircrew are trained and future military pilots gain their skills. So although lighter-than-air machines have long gone, the aerodrome still functions in its original role. There is one reminder of the airships—the road to the officers' mess, named 'Lighter Than Air Road'.

11

Rigid Airship Construction Works

At the outbreak of the First World War, the German Army had seven rigid airships in service, and the Navy one. By the end, a further two civil airships had gone to the Army and one to the Navy. Britain, on the other hand, had no rigid airships, either military or civil. In the early months of the conflict it was thought there would be little point in ordering them, since it was felt that by the time they would be operational, the war would be over.

In June 1915, there was renewed interest in rigid airships in the Admiralty. Vickers were instructed to design an improved version of their rigid airship *No. 9*, then still under construction. This was to be the known as the 23-class and was constructed by Vickers in their shed at Walney Island. A total of four examples of this new class of airship were ordered. The second example was also to be constructed in the Vickers rigid shed at Walney Island, which had the capacity to construct two airships side by side. The Admiralty also awarded contracts to Beardmore and Armstrong Whitworth of one airship each. State funding was made available to these companies to establish large airship works at Inchinnan and Barlow, because at the time Vickers had the only construction facility capable of building rigid airships. A further factory was later built by Short Brothers at Cardington.

Barrow-in-Furness Airship Constructional Station

Alternative name: 'Walney Island'.
Location: O. S. 1/50,000 map 96 (SD) 175700. Cumbria, 1½ miles to the north-west of Barrow-in-Furness town centre.
Size: 325 acres (within boundaries of 1,730 x 1,186 yards).
Airship Sheds: one rigid shed (539 feet long, 148 feet wide, and 95 feet high) and one Submarine Scout shed (300 feet long and 45 feet wide)—original destroyed in gale was 150 feet long.
Airships constructed: Rigids *No. 9*, *No. 23*, *R.26*, and *R.80*.
Parseval airships (non-rigid): *No. 5*, *No. 6*, and *No. 7*.

In 1915 there were only four rigid airship sheds in Britain—two at RNAS Kingsnorth, one at Vickers Walney Island and one at Cavendish Dock. By the following year, the

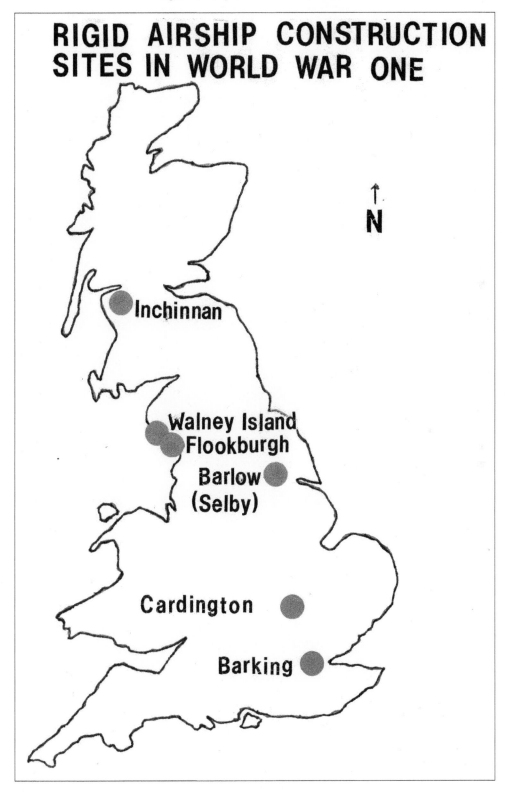

RIGID AIRSHIP CONSTRUCTION SITES IN WORLD WAR ONE

N

Inchinnan

Walney Island
Flookburgh

Barlow
(Selby)

Cardington

Barking

Rigid airship construction sites. (*Author's collection*)

Admiralty had ambitious plans to build a network of sheds where an entire fleet of rigid airships could find shelter across the country. These plans were curtailed by the lack of funds and particularly the shortage of steel. In official records, the airship works are referred to as constructional stations. Although many, such as Cardington, were large sites operated by independent companies, they are referred to as 'sub-stations' of Walney Island, the Vickers site. This emphasises the importance the Admiralty placed on Vickers as the leading designer and builder of rigid airships. Mooring-out sites were also referred to as sub-stations of their parent base.

Going back to January 1912, the wreckage of Britain's first airship, *Mayfly*, was still languishing at the back of its shed at Cavendish dock at Barrow. Despite this setback, early the next year the Committee of Imperial Defence submitted a proposal for an airship of the latest type which could be used for evaluation as well as train rigid airship crews. Despite the failure of the *Mayfly*, the order for the new airship—to be designated *No. 9*—was placed with Vickers in June 1913. One of the first problems the project encountered was that the airship shed at Cavendish Dock was too small. It was decided to build a new shed, this time on dry land, at the north end of Walney Island. On its east side lay a narrow channel separating the island from the mainland. To the west was the Irish Sea. The German firm of Arthur Muller, Ballonhallenbau of Charlottenburg (near Berlin), which designed and built sheds for Zeppelins, was contacted by Vickers for technical advice and assistance. When the airship shed was finished, it resembled many of the early German examples.

Construction did not start until late 1914, although work on the parts for Rigid *No. 9* were already taking shape in Vickers workshops. Further German technology was imported in the form of the Parseval. Britain had at one stage been interested in purchasing a Zeppelin, but were unable to do so. Despite members of the German public writing to their newspapers to protest about the sale, a smaller, non-rigid Parseval was delivered to Farnborough in June 1913. An agreement was also reached with Vickers to manufacture them under licence. Three examples were eventually built at Walney Island, but they were not completed until 1917. According to a 1914 article in *Aeronautics*, the new airship shed was

A structure of modern design with sloping sides and arched roof and guaranteed to withstand the fiercest gales that are likely to be experienced on the West Coast of England from time to time. In many ways the site chosen for the erection of this shed possesses many advantages, not the least being that a ship can be free from obstructions of any kind for several miles' radius. The internal dimensions of the shed are Length 540 feet, Breadth 150 feet, Height 98 feet. The breadth enables two of the largest ships to be built side by side. The foundations of the shed consist of solid reinforced concrete blocks of special design with foundation bolts set in. Inside the shed is a 6 inch layer of concrete ensuring a dry and level floor. The main columns, of which there are 34 on each side, suitably braced with timber and bound with steel rods each upright forming a rigid column.

The walls and roof coverings consist of pine boarding, tongued and grooved, the walls being creosoted outside and inside, the roof covered with a layer of approved waterproof felt. Efficient lightning and ventilation are embodied in the design. In order that the work may be carried on efficiently when hydrogen gas is being used, all secondary arc lights will be enclosed in air-tight lamp boxes built into the sides of the shed, ensuring complete safety against explosion or fire. At each end of the roof are fitted towers from which the work of taking out the ship when completed can be directed. These towers are in communication with each other by gangway running the whole length of the shed under the ridge of the roof, from which a staircase leads to the ground. A runway capable of lifting two tons extends the full length of the building being situated beneath the gangway. A special feature of this shed is the fitting of double hinged doors at both ends instead of the curtains usually fitted. These door are of special construction, consisting of a strong metal framework, suitably stayed and covered with pine boarding tongued and grooved and are designed to withstand the pressure of the highest winds when closed....

For the safe handling of a ship when being warped in and out of the shed, three lengths of rails are fitted extending the full length of the shed inside and about 450 feet outside at both ends. By this means the ship is 'tied' to trolleys on the underside of the rails and run out 'at the double' in the hands of the Marines. The system of fitting three sets of rails wide apart and the extra width of the shed enable the ship, if necessary, to be placed diagonally, in order that it may be taken out head to the wind. As the winds in these parts are least in the early mornings and assistance may be required to take a ship out at short notice, accommodation for 200 men is provided by wood buildings beside the main shed. In order to facilitate the handling of ships when in the open air, mooring masts are provided, as required, clear of the flying area and strong ring-bolts mounted in concrete blocks in the ground are fitted throughout the aerodrome. A complete system of fire-extinguishing is embodied in the equipment of the shed and enables eight jets to be brought to bear on the building, the water being pumped from a reservoir on site.[1]

Vickers wooden rigid airship shed at Walney Island, Barrow-in-Furness. (*The Fleet Air Arm Museum*)

Another contemporary newspaper article predicted that two new airship sheds would be erected in connection with the scheme, but only the above was built. The RNAS also had a small non-rigid airship shed at Walney Island. It was claimed at the time the airship factory would employ 1,500 men and

> [...] several sheds will also be erected for the building of aeroplanes, water planes and other descriptions of aircraft. There is plenty of room for expanding the business on Walney Island should the necessity arise.[2]

The Walney Island airship shed was completed in early 1915 and parts of *No. 9* which were being built elsewhere were transferred here for final assembly. By now, however, the rigid airship programme was in trouble again.

Unlike aeroplane manufacturers—which at that time could operate with little plant and capital—the construction of rigid airships required large expenditure, often underwritten in part by the British government. This was why the Admiralty and the Royal Navy were frequently at loggerheads with politicians. At the beginning of 1915, the First Sealord, Winston Churchill, ordered that work on *No. 9* be suspended. It was thought the war would finish that year, before the airship had flown, so he proposed that the airship wing be reduced to five—two Parsevals and three Astra Torres. Two of them were then on to be based at Barrow and the rest at RNAS Kingsnorth, and the steel airship shed here to be used as an aeroplane hangar. One part of Churchill's plan was implemented—handing RNAS Farnborough to the Army and transferring the airship repair facility to Walney Island.

But it was not only politicians who were taking pot-shots at the British airship programme. The Germans decided to have a go themselves. In an audacious attack on 29 January 1915, the German submarine *U-21* surfaced off Walney Island and opened fire with its deck gun on the Vickers airship shed. The workers began fleeing from the building, but the attack ceased as suddenly as it had begun, for the Walney Island gun battery had opened up in response to the threat, and the submarine dived and vanished into the Irish Sea. There were claims that it had been sunk, but this was just wishful thinking, for it went on to harass several vessels in the vicinity over the next few days.

Although little damage was done to the shed, the attack had a profound effect on airship policy. Other sites away from the coast were considered for relocation, as Walney Island was no longer thought a secure place to construct airships. Most operational airship stations built from then on were situated at least a few miles inland. Another consequence of the scare was that the Admiralty took over control of Walney Island, where it wished to make an operational airship base. A few anti-submarine patrols were flown from here, but they had ceased by 1917. The RNAS undertook much work to expand the facilities. It was submitted that, if the rigid airship programme was abandoned, the RNAS could take over the Vickers shed. At that time it already housed several RNAS airships

Parseval *No. 4* arrived in March. A hundred soldiers were sent to assist the naval ratings with its landing. All went well until an attempt was made to house it in the shed. With the wind gusting at speeds of up to 50 mph, the airship broke loose from its moorings with five of the handling party still clinging onto ropes. Two let go at a height of 20 feet, suffering a few broken bones. Three more were still hanging onto the ropes, but fortunately were hauled into the control car by the pilot.

In June 1915, the destructive regime enforced by German submarines over allied shipping was worsening. A programme to build four rigid airships and thirty Coastal types was launched, and work began once more on rigid airship *No. 9*. The first Barrow-built airship to fly successfully was Submarine Scout *S.S.17*—most Submarine Scouts were built at RNAS Kingsnorth and Wormwood Scrubs, but a small number was assembled here too. Another Submarine Scout airship, the *S.S.20*, was converted from a standard two-seater to three-seater for pilot instruction.

On 15 August 1915, a surfaced German submarine attacked the coast from the Irish Sea once more. It fired fifty-five shells from its deck gun at the Harrington Chemical Works, located near Whitehaven. Airships were ordered to be dispatched from Walney Island, and *S.S.20* took off and searched for the raider, but without success. In response to the attack, a senior officer of the Admiralty Department was sent to inspect the airship base at Walney Island. After visiting the Vickers rigid airship shed, he reported it to be in 'a state of hopeless congestion', probably because Submarine Scouts were then under construction, as were two new Parsevals—*No. 6* and *No. 7*.

It had been planned to erect the recently delivered 150-foot-long portable airship shed on a site near Conishead Priory, 2 miles south-east of Ulverston. Instead, it was put up next to the Vickers Rigid shed in October 1915. The old airship shed at Cavendish Dock was also in use at the time to construct Submarine Scouts. A careless workman left his blowtorch next to the envelope of the *S.S.33*, burning a large hole in it. Fortunately, there was little damage to the airship shed itself.

Aeroplanes sometimes flew from Walney Island. A Bessonneau hangar was erected next to the Vickers shed to house a Bristol Boxkite which was used to give flying experience to the airship crews. The portable airship shed had not been standing long before it was blown down in a gale on 16 February 1916 and written off. The wind also blew open a door of the nearby Vickers airship shed, damaging Submarine Scout *S.S.34*. Despite these setbacks, the RNAS carried out extensive works to upgrade the airship station. Over the following months, seventeen Royal Navy lorries—assisted by Vickers—transported material for levelling the landing ground next to the airship shed and to construct access roads. Some 47,000 tonnes of material had been transported by August 1916.

In 1917, Walney Island ceased to be designated as an RNAS flying station, but airships from other stations continued to use it to break their journey. In December, Anglesey Submarine Scout Pusher *S.S.P.5* was weather-bound here for several days. Its mission had been to take photographs of the coast defences around Barrow-in-Furness. The portable Submarine Scout shed, which had been blown down in 1916, was re-erected, complete with concrete foundations and wooden doors; ratings based at the station painted it, too. After modification, Rigid *No. 9* was completed on 17 March 1917, and carried out her trials on the 23rd. These proved satisfactory and the airship left for RNAS Howden early the following month. In the book *British*

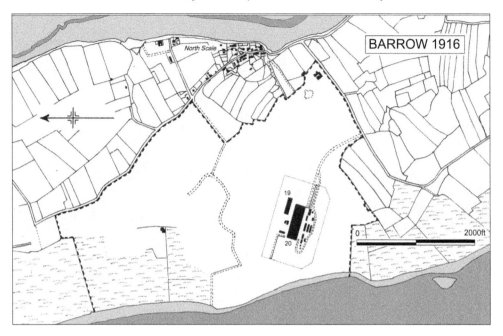

Barrow, 1916. The Vickers rigid airship shed at Walney Island, Barrow-in-Furness, was a short distance from the Irish Sea. The smaller RNAS airship shed is located next to it. They both face north-west which is unusual, since most airship sheds were orientated towards the prevailing south-west wind. (*Mick Davis*)

Airships, Past, Present and Future—published shortly after the First World War—*No. 9* received a favourable appraisal:

> In many ways she was an excellent ship, for it must be remembered that when completed she was some years out of date, judged by Zeppelin standards. Apart from the patrol and convoy work which she accomplished, she proved simply invaluable for the training of officers and men selected to be crews of future rigid airships. Many of these received their initial training in her and there were few officers or men in the airship service who were not filled with regret when orders were issued that she was to be broken up.[3]

Long before the days of the aircraft preservation movement, the author laments that it should have been preserved 'as a lasting exhibition of the infancy of the airship service but unfortunately rigid airships occupy so much space that there is no museum in the country which could have accommodated her'. The same applies to all other British-built airships, rigid or not.

On 17 May 1917, King George V and Queen Mary visited Walney Island and were shown around Vickers rigid airship shed. On 19 September 1917, *No. 23*—Walney Island's second rigid construction—took to the air and the following month was delivered to RNAS Howden. Extensive mooring-out trials were also undertaken in the last two years of conflict. On 23 April 1917, Submarine Scout *S.S.34* was fitted with a Nieuport seaplane float under its skids. It was flown from Walney Island to

Cavendish Dock, where it was secured to a mooring raft in the centre of the dock. On 4 and 5 May, the wind speed increased to 30 mph, forcing the nose to repeatedly make contact with the water, resulting in the airship being wrecked.

In July, further trials were carried out in Cavendish Dock with Submarine Scout *S.S.32A*. Experiments were then moved to the airship station at Walney Island. During November, *S.S.32A* was buffeted by strong winds. It broke away from its mooring and had to be deflated. These experiments continued into the following year when in April, *S.S.32A* was joined by *S.S.36*. The knowledge gained by these trials lead to the development of the iconic tall mooring mast. Vickers produced a tall steel mast structure which, when fitted with a masthead, could respond to any changes in the direction of the prevailing wind. It was designated the *Vickers Patent Mooring Gear No. 6533*, and possessed an automatic coupling through which an airship could be supplied with petrol, oil, water, and hydrogen. It could be operated by just six men and underwent its first major trial on 1 September 1919, when Rigid *R.24* successfully moored to it at Pulham.

The *R.26* made its first flight at Walney Island on 20 March 1918. Just over a month later it was delivered to RNAS Howden. Unusual weather conditions were experienced on 17 March 1918 when the Snowdon mountain range, around seventy miles away could be seen clearly from Barrow. Throughout 1919, work on the *R.80* continued, although at a slower pace due to a shortage of skilled labour. At one stage it looked as if its construction may be abandoned, as the Air Ministry took the view that it would have no military value. Finally, it was decided that the *R.80* may have a future as a commercial transport, so the project continued. In the autumn, a national railway strike saw a brief burst of activity at Walney Island. Vickers ran a company mail service to London using an Avro 504 biplane. To help deal with the large backlog of mail at Barrow, an airship thought to have been a Submarine Scout Twin used for mooring trials was enlisted to help. A thousand letters were loaded on board on 5 October 1919, which Flt Lt Victor Goddard flew to Whitehaven. He landed in a meadow near the town, handing the mailbags to the head postmaster. Mail flights were also undertaken to Sheffield before the strike was resolved.

On Monday 19 July 1920, the *R.80* was walked out of its shed by a 250-strong handling party composed of Vickers personnel, Royal Navy submarine crew members, and a small number of female workers. By the time of its release, the airship had been standing in the sun for some time and it rose rapidly into the air. Unknown to the onlookers on the ground, the crew were struggling to gain control of the airship, as its rudder had jammed. By flying *R.80* in a series of circles, its crew managed to land safely back at Walney Island, but not before a number of its internal steel structural members had been broken. The airship spent the rest of the year confined to its shed for repairs.

At a time when airship construction was in rapid decline across Britain, the Vickers design team were still hoping for a revival. It was thought that Orient and Cunard shipping might be interested in using the *R.80* on passenger services. It was even thought that there may be a market flying people on tours of the battlefields of the Western Front. At the other end of the scale, designs were produced for a small airship

Submarine Scout *S.S.32A*, testing the new type of mooring mast developed by Vickers at Walney Island in May 1918. (*The Royal Aeronautical Society*)

The Rigid *R.80* emerging from the Vickers shed at Walney Island. Although it was ordered during the First World War, it did not make its first flight until 19 July 1920. It was designed by Barnes Wallis, who went on to invent the 'bouncing' bomb for the RAF Dambusters. (*The Dock Museum, Barrow in Furness*)

for the affluent which could carry four people. This was not as absurd as it sounds. In 1925, a press article reported that Henry Ford was on the verge of building 'one-man dirigibles.[4] He was planning to produce these craft *en masse* and to fill the sky in the same way he had filled the streets with cars. But like Vickers' ambitions to popularise the airship, this came to nothing.

At one stage, it was hoped that Rigid *R.80* could be sold to the US Navy, but it was deemed too small to be useful. On 24 February 1921, *R.80* left its shed at Walney Island and took off for RAF Howden. It flew low over Barrow, its departure marking the end of the town's connection with rigid airships. Vickers would go on to be involved in the design and building of the *R.100*, but due to the limitations of the Walney Island shed, it had to be built elsewhere. This was not quite the end—a Submarine Scout Zero built for the Japanese government made its maiden flight on 27 April 1921.

The same year, Britain's first rigid airship shed at Cavendish Dock was dismantled. There was a plan to turn the Walney Island shed into a film studio but it came to nothing. In 1925, it suffered the same fate as most others across the country—it was sold for scrap and pulled down by a company owned by the then popular theatrical impresario, Jimmy Brennan. The RAF built an aerodrome on the former airship landing ground which has survived into the twenty-first century, used by British Aerospace transport aircraft and General Aviation. A post-war housing scheme was built on the grounds where the Vickers airship shed once stood. Appropriately, the site is marked by Airship Shed Road, off Mill Road.

Barlow Airship Constructional Station

Alternative name: 'Selby'.
Location: O. S. 1/50,000 map 105 (SE) 660294. West Riding, Yorkshire, 15 miles south-east of York, 3 miles south-east of Selby.
Size: 880 acres (within boundaries of 3,760 x 2,260 yards).
Airship Shed: one rigid shed (700 feet long, 150 feet wide, and 100 feet high).
Gas Plant: silicol (60,000 cubic feet per hour).
Gas Holders: one (250,000 cubic feet).
Airships built: *No. 25*, *R.29*, and *R.33*.

Although Britain's first attempt to build a large rigid airship ended in disaster when the *Mayfly* broke in two, there was renewed interest in reviving the programme two years later. The Second Rigid Airship Programme was initiated in 1913. Not only were Vickers to build another rigid airship, but Armstrong Whitworth & Co., an armaments manufacturer centred on Elswick, Newcastle-upon-Tyne, had also been contracted to construct several airships, including one sometimes referred to as the *Elswick Zeppelin*. Due to a reduction in the Air Department's budget, the orders were postponed. When the programme was revived in 1915, Armstrong Whitworth & Co.—along with Vickers, Shorts, and Beardmore—successfully bid to participate in the programme to build a fleet of rigid airships for the Royal Navy.

In 1913, a site had been purchased by Armstrong Whitworth near Selby, where it intended to set up a base for its aviation activities, including the building of aeroplanes. Although somewhat remote from its factories and shipyards, which were in the densely populated area around the River Tyne, the site was close to the mainline railway network. During the First World War, consideration was given to building and housing airships in dry docks enclosed with a roof, while another plan proposed excavating tunnels in the hillsides.

A more conventional approach was adopted by Armstrong Whitworth at Barlow (Boars Wood). A large airship shed was erected on land acquired from Lord Londesborough in 1913, close to the River Ouse. Like the other new airship works, it was funded in part by the Treasury. The main contractor for its construction was A. J. Main & Co., and a short branch line was built from the Doncaster–Selby Line. When the airship shed was partially built, it was decided to enlarge it so it would be able to meet the requirements of future generations of airships. By the end of 1916, the 700-foot-long airship shed was nearing completion. There were lean-to workshops along the side walls and few other buildings in the immediate vicinity.

Hagg House stood on the eastern boundary and was demolished in the latter stages of the First World War, when the airship station was expanded. Vickers supplied both parts and knowhow for the construction of the first Rigid, *No. 25*, which began to take shape in spring 1917. Workers were sent from Barrow-in-Furness to assist

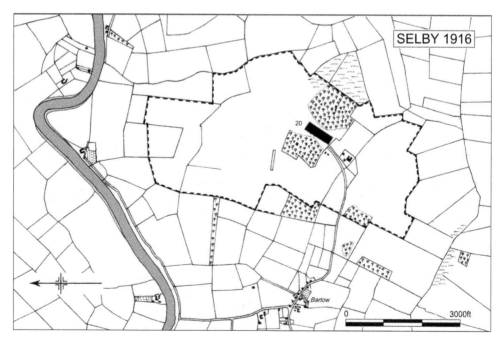

Barlow, 1916. The Armstrong Whitworth & Co. site for constructing airships was located close to the River Ouse. The low-lying landscape was dominated by the single 700-foot-long rigid airship shed. It had a single large windbreak at both its entrances. There was woodland either side of the shed when it was built in 1916, but within two years it had been completely cleared. (*Mick Davis*)

The Armstrong Whitworth & Co. rigid airship shed nearing completion at Barlow, June 1916. It was built by A. J. Main & Co. (*The National Archives*)

in its assembly. Unlike at Cardington and Inchinnan, where many of the airship components were manufactured in the immediate vicinity, Armstrong Whitworth transported the components from their works at Newcastle-upon-Tyne. There was a special railway siding, complete with unloading platform, next to the Barlow airship shed. In the spring of 1917, the hydrogen plant was commissioned, and the final work to the airship landing ground in full swing; trees were felled and ditches filled in in anticipation.

Originally, the shed was built in the centre of a wood with the intention that the trees would act as windbreaks. Later, the surrounding woodland was completely felled and artificial windbreaks constructed to protect the building's entrances. Numerous wooden huts provided office space and accommodation for the workers. The shape of things to come was sighted on 4 April, when Britain's first rigid airship, *No. 9*, flew overhead. At the end of the year, *No. 25*—Barlow's first airship—took to the air on a flight lasting 2 hours 35 minutes. It developed a bad reputation and was disliked by its crew because it tended to surge in flight. This was at first thought to be caused by impure hydrogen gas produced at Barlow, but the problem persisted after the gas was changed. *No. 25* spent much of its career at RNAS Cranwell, training crew for rigid airships. The shed at Barlow had room to construct two rigid airships side by side and, by the time *No. 25* had made its first flight, the *R.29* was already taking shape. In December 1917, a large number of additional workers—mainly women—were hired and trained in skills such as riveting, since the *R.29* incorporated many improvements over its predecessor. It finally took to the air on 29 May 1918, and was delivered

Women assembling a car for an airship in an Armstrong Whitworth & Co. workshop. In the First World War, women played a crucial role in the manufacture of airships. (*The National Archives*)

the following month to RNAS East Fortune. Despite having a short career, it was considered to be Britain's most successful wartime rigid airship, being the only one to attack and sink a German submarine.

After airship *No. 25* had vacated its place in the shed at Barlow, work began on the *R.33*. A sister ship, the *R.35*, was almost complete when the Armistice was signed. Armstrong Whitworth had high hopes that there would still be a market for airships at the end of hostilities, and there were plans to construct a second large airship shed next to the first. Work continued on the *R.33*, and in 1919 it was walked out from its shed by 500 troops sent from York especially for this purpose. It made its trial flight in March 1919. On 8 March 1919, *The Scotsman* described the scene:

> The monster British airship built by Messrs Armstrong Whitworth & Co., made its trial trip in Selby district on Thursday. A large crowd of spectators was present when the doors of the great shed were swung open and the giant aerial craft, held down by numerous workpeople, was brought out half an hour later. Captain Hicks, who was in command, waved the order, 'Let Go', and the airship gracefully ascended to a height of about 500 feet and carried out evolutions over the district for three hours and a half. She made a successful descent and was safely berthed in her shed. The vessel responded

readily to the tests and the spectators were delighted with the ease with which she was manoeuvred.

It was proposed that this airship make a trail-blazing flight to Newfoundland from here, but the Admiralty intervened—it did not want the *R.33* returning to Barlow at the end of its journey, since this was not an operational airship station. The *R.34*, too, was about to embark on a journey to North America, so this may have caused a conflict of interest. In any case, the *R.33* flew to Pulham where in April 1920 it was given the civil identity G-FAAG, and conducted numerous successful test flights. Despite its achievements, it was the last airship to be constructed by Armstrong Whitworth & Co. The orders dried up and the works closed down. At the end of August 1919, the workers received the following notice:

> Owing to the cancellation of all airship contracts the management regrets that your services are no longer required and on application to the cashier you will receive one week's pay in lieu of notice.[5]

A final meeting of the workforce was held in the airship shed. Management expressed their hope that the works would not be closed for long and would soon be opened in another form to meet the needs of the Admiralty. Mr Golightly then made a brief speech of thanks to the workers. A call went up for three cheers for the popular manager and these were given with vigour. The workforce then sang 'He's A Jolly Good Fellow,' and as they departed, 'For Auld Lang Syne'. On that day, some 560 people lost their jobs.

Barlow works never did re-open and the double airship shed was dismantled in the 1920s. Without costly extensions the shed would have been too small for the next generation of rigid airships. The heavy gauge, corrugated sheeting was sold to the public for £8 a tonne. In 1929, there were plans to turn the site into the largest silk mill in northern England, and several hundred acres into a garden city. Nothing came of these ambitious schemes. The accommodation blocks were given a new lease of life when the site was used as a Royal Ordnance munitions depot. When this closed, ash from the nearby Drax power station was dumped over the remains. The area has since been turned into a nature reserve.

Inchinnan Airship Constructional Station

Location: O. S. 1/50,000 map 64 (NS) 476682. Strathclyde, 6 miles to the west of Glasgow city centre.
Size: 413 acres (within boundaries of 1,830 x 1,400 yards).
Airship Shed: rigid shed (700 feet long, 153 feet wide, and 100 feet high)—second rigid shed planned.
Hydrogen Gas Plant: silicol (60,000 cubic feet per hour).
Gasholders: One (250,000 cubic feet).
Airships built: *No. 24, R.24, R.34*, and *R.36*.

With the revival of the rigid airship programme, the armaments firm Beardmore bid successfully to build them at Inchinnan in 1916. Based at Dalmuir, on the western side of Clydebank, the company was the Scottish equivalent of Vickers, specialising in building warships and armaments. Although it had experimented with aeroplanes as Shorts and Armstrong Whitworth had done, the company had no previous experience in building airships. The *Sunderland Daily Echo* of 20 February 1901 has one of the earliest references to a British airship allegedly under construction by another Scottish shipbuilding firm, also located on the River Clyde:

> Messrs William Denny and Brothers, the Dumbarton shipbuilders, have a 'vessel' in hand about which there is, if possible, even more secrecy maintained than about Sir Thomas Lipton's America Cup Challenger which is being built in the same yard. The new 'vessel' is an airship and it is connected to the order of a Spanish gentleman. What the plan of this latest flying machine is or when it is likely to be finished, has so far been kept of profound secret. This, however, is known before the actual construction was commenced. There was a great deal of experimental work done, then results of which made the inventor very hopeful of success.

Like many other airship projects, nothing more was heard of it. In 1913, Beardmore was reportedly involved in negotiations with the Admiralty—along with Vickers and Armstrong Whitworth & Co.—to build rigid airships, but seems to have dropped out at an early stage. While orders were placed with the other two companies later in that year, none were forthcoming for the Scottish contender. Nevertheless, Beardmore did go on to construct some of Britain's largest airships. In October 1915, it received the order for airship *No. 24* and began work on manufacturing its parts in the seaplane sheds at Dalmuir–there was no room for an airship shed in this already heavily built-up area. In contrast, the land on the south bank of the Clyde was still open countryside and sparsely populated. A site immediately opposite to Beardmore's works at Newshot Island was considered, but ultimately a location about 1½ miles south of Dalmuir was selected. Under the Defence of the Realm Act, 413 acres were requisitioned for the new airship construction station. The Treasury gave Beardmore a grant towards the cost of the new airship works.

In January 1916, Sir William Arrol & Co. started work on the airship shed. It was 700 feet long and required 2,300 tonnes of steel. The windows were all glazed with tinted glass and fitted with blinds so it could be blacked out at night. At both ends of the shed were huge sliding doors, counter-balanced with several hundred tonnes of concrete to stabilise them when opened. It took a party of workmen armed with a capstan an estimated 13 minutes to open the doors. Both of the two entrances to the airship shed were sheltered by large steel windbreaks but the northern side only. By August, it was almost finished. It was probably one of the most impressive of all the airship sheds built in Britain.

A large hangar was later built immediately to the south of it, in which Handley Page *V/1500* bombers were assembled. They were then test-flown over the aerodrome which shared the airship site. A second airship shed was planned but never built.

Work on the foundations for the Beardmore Inchinnan rigid airship shed commences at the beginning of 1916. (*The National Archives*)

The foundations with erection staging being assembled at the west end. (*The National Archives*)

The first steel arch stands over the construction site. (*The National Archives*)

The steel framework takes shape. The window frames have already been placed in position at this early stage of construction. (*The National Archives*)

The airship shed is nearly complete in the summer of 1916, having taken around nine months and 2,300 tons of steel to build. A small cottage near its entrance is dwarfed by the massive structure. (*The National Archives*)

The interior of the Beardmore Inchinnan shed with the framework of Rigid *HMA 24*. Note the many windows in the walls to allow in as much natural light as possible. (*The National Archives*)

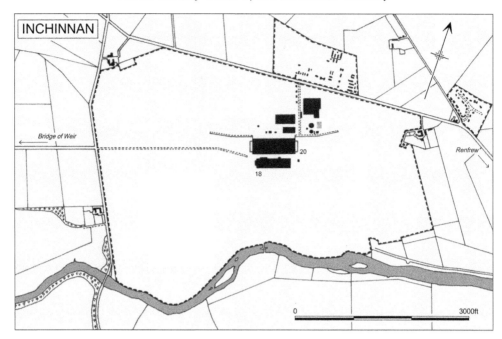

Inchinnan. The Black Cart Water, a tributary of the River Clyde, formed the southern boundary of Beardmore's Inchinnan airship works. The large rigid shed loomed over the surrounding landscape. Next to it stood a hangar in which Handley Page V/1500 bombers were assembled. The accommodation huts were on the opposite side of the road, while the houses built by Beardmore for its workers are located just outside the north-eastern boundary of the station. (*Mick Davis*)

Although Inchinnan Airship Works was not far from Dalmuir, it was on the opposite bank of the Clyde and not readily accessible, making it necessary for many of the workers to be driven each morning from Renfrew. To solve this problem, Beardmore built fifty-two houses for its key workers just a short distance from the site. It was described in the company newspaper:

> A village has been erected near the Inchinnan Works for the accommodation of a number
> of the workers and this village is looked upon as a model as it gives to the working man all
> the comfort and convenience of self-contained houses and that at very moderate rents.[6]

Even before the airship shed was finished, the first frames of the airship *R.24* had been moved into it for assembly. On 25 October 1917, 200 naval ratings arrived from Barrow-in-Furness to act as the ground handling party for its first flight. This took place on the 28th, but not until *R.24* had spent six months in the open, testing mooring techniques. It was much heavier than other airships of the same class because Beardmore had used extra strong rivets and fastenings. There was room in the airship shed to construct two large airships side by side. Work on the *R.27* started in March 1917, and it took to the air in June 1918. Like many of its counterparts, it had a short life: it was destroyed in a fire at RAF Howden on 16 August 1918.

The best known airship built by Beardmore was the *R.34*. Ground trials were

The newly completed *R.34* airship emerges from Beardmore's Inchinnan Shed in 1919. (*Scran*)

carried out in December 1918. It was scheduled to make its first flight at the end of the same month, but bad weather confined it to its shed until 14 March 1919. At the end of its second trial flight, some of the ballast bags iced up and the crew found they could not dump enough water to lighten the *R.34* as it came into land at Inchinnan. The airship came down too fast, hitting the ground with a bump, and damaging some of its girders and the propeller. When the *R.34* was first walked out of its shed a few months earlier, some of the women workers had pinned a black cat soft toy to the control car as a good luck mascot. On the evening of the bad landing, this was removed and consigned to a fire. By the end of May, the damage had been repaired and the *R.34* was ready to be delivered to the RAF at East Fortune. Two months later, it became the first airship to fly non-stop across the Atlantic. Although the war was over, Sir William Beardmore was optimistic about the future. He gave a speech at the staff victory dinner on 24 April 1919, in which he voiced the opinion that airships were 'to be the most interesting and important development of all'.

There were many proposals for establishing passenger airship services but all came to nothing. The *R.36* was the last airship built by Beardmore. It was converted for the civil market with accommodation for fifty passengers; this delayed its first flight until 1 April 1921, whereupon it took to the skies sporting the civil registration G-FAAF. After undergoing mooring mast trials at Pulham, it was damaged and spent the next four years in an airship shed here. It was proposed to use it on an experimental flight to Egypt in 1925 but this did not occur. It was broken up for scrap shortly thereafter. In September 1921, the Air Ministry announced that Inchinnan Aerodrome was to close, leaving the nearby Moorpark at Renfrew the only remaining Scottish civil aerodrome.

In autumn of the following year, the land and buildings of the Beardmore Airship Works were handed over to The Disposal and Liquidation Commission. During April 1923, the works were sold to Murray McVinnie & Co., ship chandlers and metal

The Rigid *R.34* taking off from Inchinnan. It was the first airship to fly the Atlantic. (*Glasgow University Archive*)

merchants. Later that same year, the airship shed that had loomed so large over the surrounding countryside was demolished. The giant Handley Page hangar that stood close by fared somewhat better—it was purchased by India Tyres and survived until 1982, and is sometimes mistakenly referred to as the airship shed. The houses built for the Inchinnan workforce still stand, and Glasgow Airport is located a short distance to the south of the former aerodrome and airship shed. Appropriately, Rolls Royce opened a new factory for repairing aero engines on the site of Beardmore's aeronautical aspirations in 2004.

Cardington Airship Constructional Station

Alternative name: 'Bedford'.
Location: O. S. 1/50,000 map 153 (TL), 085465. 3 miles south-east of Bedford, 45 miles north-west of London.
Size: 1,064 acres (within boundaries of 3,150 x 230 yards).
Airship Sheds: one rigid shed (700 feet long, 180 feet wide, and 110 feet high)—extended to 812 feet long and height increased to 145 feet in 1926. Rigid shed No. 2 was transferred from Pulham and erected in 1928.
Hydrogen Gas Plant: water gas (7,000 cubic feet per hour).

Airships built (including in 1920s): *R.31*, *R.32*, *R.38* (for U.S. Navy), and *R.101*. Based airships: *R.33* and *R.100*.

Cardington is considered the spiritual home of the British airship. The station was conceived shortly after the other airship works at Barlow and Inchinnan. Vickers did not have the facilities to construct rigid airships in the numbers that the Admiralty required, therefore the Short Brothers were awarded the contract for the *R.31* and *R.32*. The Treasury gave the company a grant of £110,000 towards establishing new airship constructional works, the total cost of which the company estimated at £230,000. Until then, the activities of Short Brothers had concentrated around Rochester in Kent. The Company had been founded in 1897, when Eustace Short bought a second-hand gas balloon, and with the help of his brothers went on to develop and manufacture them himself. Their first factory was under a railway arch at Battersea, London, near the gasworks. Later, the brothers abandoned balloons in favour of aeroplanes and indeed airships.

By March 1916, a site about 1 mile from Cardington village had been selected. It was within easy travelling distance of London, the ground here was reasonably flat and had few hazards for large airships, and the nearby market town of Bedford had a workforce with light engineering skills. A report to the Director of Air Services on 24 March 1916 presents a balanced assessment:

> This site has been inspected and it presents many advantages including good road and rail approach though the latter [Bedford and Hitchin Branch] is only a single line, water and electric light mains are within a short distance and the river affords a means of disposing of the effluent from sewage disposal works if such are established. The subsoil is stated to be clay which will present no difficulties as regards foundations but it will probably be necessary to improve considerably the land drainage and also cover over the water courses and ditches crossing the landing area at considerable cost. A serious defect of the site is its narrowness. It is very desirable to place the Shed on the higher ground on the northern part of the area which has the advantage of giving the maximum space for landing and also minimise the cost of railway connection, also water supply, electric mains and drainage.[7]

Regarding the criticism of the narrowness of the ground, it was pointed out that flights from it would not be very frequent as it was going to be a constructional works and not an operational station. Also, the nature of the ground to the west made it unnecessary to have a large landing area. The area required for the new airship works was valuable arable land. One of its farmers, a Scotsman, objected to losing his land for this enterprise. When construction got under way, a short branch line was laid into the site from the Midland Railway line, which formed the eastern boundary. Another siding was also laid in 1916 from Cardington station. Work started on the airship shed in August 1916 and was completed by April 1917. It was a steel girder structure with a cantilever roof, covered with painted but un-galvanised corrugated sheet iron. Both ends had sliding doors covering the full width and height of the airship shed, which took around half an hour to open using capstans powered by strong workmen. It was flanked by two large windbreaks at each end, 70 feet high and 700 feet long, as long

The hydrogen plant under construction at Cardington, 5 June 1917. (*Bedfordshire and Luton Archives*)

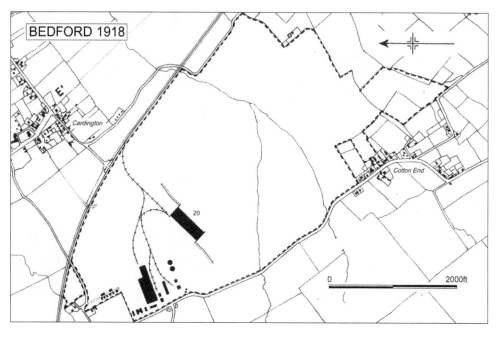

Cardington, 1918, or the Bedford Constructional Station, as it was then known. It was established by the Short Brothers for producing rigid airships for the Admiralty. Cardington is associated with two large airship sheds, but the second one was not erected until 1928. The single airship shed is flanked by large windbreaks at either entrance. The Hitchin–Bedford railway demarcates the eastern boundary of the site. (*Mick Davis*)

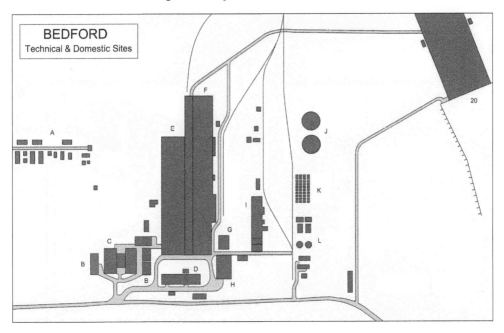

Cardington (Bedford), the technical and domestic site. The main building in this plan is the large workshop in which parts for large rigid airships were manufactured. The workshop was served by its own railway siding, which ran into the building.

A street of recently completed houses at Shortstown built for workers at the nearby Cardington Airship Works. (*Bedfordshire and Luton Archives*)

as the airship shed itself. Although Cardington is traditionally associated with its two large airship sheds, for the first decade of its existence it had only one.

An extensive compound of airframe and engineering workshops were built close by. The whole complex was run from an impressive red-brick office building. For the production of hydrogen, Humphreys of Glasgow fitted their Ranes water gas plant in 1917. This worked on the iron contact system, where steam was passed over red-hot iron ore to produce hydrogen gas.

Shortstown, a 'company town' along the lines of Lever Brothers' Port Sunlight, was created to house the airship workers. Its houses were influenced by the Arts and Crafts Movement, which was based on an 'ideal' English cottage concept that included ornamental brickwork and steeply pitched and tiled roofs. A passenger station was also constructed on the mainline for workers who lived in Bedford. It was known as 'Cardington Factory', or 'Workman's platform'.

The first airship built by Shorts was the *R.31*, which was 615 feet long and had a maximum speed of about 70 mph.

Barking Airship Constructional Station

Location: 161/177 (51) TQ450830. Creekmouth in the London Borough of Barking, Essex, north bank of the Thames, 10 miles east of central London.
Airship Shed: rigid shed (266 feet long, 50 feet wide, and 60 feet high, with door opening 40 feet high).
Airships built: (not completed) MacMechan airship.

Barking was perhaps the most enigmatic of all the airship stations in Britain, consisting of little more than a single airship shed. This timber-framed structure, clad with corrugated iron sheeting, boasted tracks for an electrically powered trolley to move an airship in and out of the building. Located near the Thames and only a short distance from the site of the former Aeronautical Society's grounds at Dagenham, this was to be the construction site of a revolutionary airship, funded by American investors. The project was the brainchild of Thomas R. MacMechan, a journalist from Baltimore. He supervised the construction of the airship shed for a 'Pigmy Zeppelin' with a basket-work wooden frame. One of the chief aims of its prominent designer, American engineer Walter Kamp, was to construct a lightweight rigid airship: laminated wood would substitute the aluminium in the framework; the airship would be 237 feet; and there would be a crew of four—navigator, engineer, and two gunners.

Rather surprisingly—since this was a military project—Thomas MacMechan gave an extensive interview about his plans for Barking in the New York newspaper *The Sun* on 3 March 1915. He was of the opinion that the German Zeppelins were coming and would deal a spectacular blow to England and the world at large:

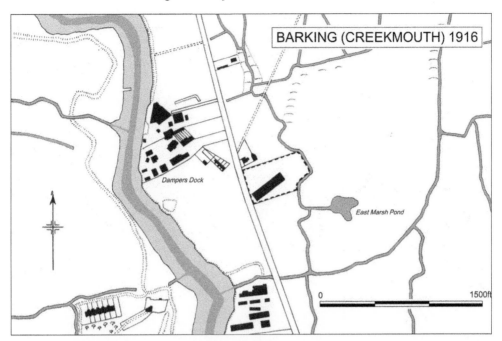

BARKING (CREEKMOUTH) 1916

Dampers Dock

East Marsh Pond

0   1500ft

Barking. The large building in the centre of the plan is the airship shed in which it was intended to build the small MacMechan rigid airship, sometimes known as the 'Marshall Fox' airship. The shed was located on the north bank of the River Thames and was flanked by one of its tributaries on the west side. The works consisted solely of the 266-foot-long airship shed—there were no ancillary buildings. (*Mick Davis*)

> The British Admiralty know this. The people of England are not afraid because they do not know the danger and the Admiralty is not telling them.

He added that if the British military had taken the Zeppelin threat seriously five years ago, the country would by now have thousands of aircraft and hundreds of huge airships. The measures taken to protect London from Zeppelin raids did not much impress him either: he criticised the decision to place searchlights around the city, as he said they acted as navigational aids to the Germans. He also voiced concern that the shells fired from the anti-aircraft guns would fall back to earth and set fire to buildings across London upon impact.

Thomas MacMechan's answer to this threat was to construct a fleet of 'Zeppelin destroyers'—little rigid airships, each armed with a gun. They would engage the enemy in the air, not unlike the way naval vessels fought each other. His airship would have a short range of action but a top speed of 70 mph, and could apparently remain stationary in the air to protect potential targets.

> These little rigid dirigibles we are building can stay in the air watching for an enemy, say 75 miles from their base for ten hours. Each of the Zeppelin Destroyers will be equipped with one torpedo gun firing a torpedo that will explode on contact.

Thomas MacMechan had no shortage of opinions on a wide number of aviation matters, including types of airmen in accordance with their nationality:

> The British aviator is possessed temperamentally with the best requirements. You jar him. He is dogged. Like a bull terrier, he never lets go. He has fine physique, endurance and he has the heart. He is the best aviator among the allies. His drawback is that he is so smug that you can't talk to him. Any civilian had better get right back and sit down. He is not scientific and he knocks a machine to pieces in short order. He mounts an aeroplane and rides away like a jockey. When he comes back he jumps out and leaves the machine to the care of a half dozen mechanics.... The German aviator is daring. He will take just as much chance as his English enemy but has a better conception of the scientific principles of his machine. He will not take reckless chances. He runs away and lives to come back again.... The French aviator, like the French nation, thinks and lives on applause. He is a poseur. He is all daring and he has a high scientific value. He handles his machine better than the others. He has a natural quickness of mind, followed by instantaneous action that means fine, accurate rapid decisions in the air. And he does it all neatly with finesse.

Construction work on the revolutionary airship began at Barking in May 1915. According to Thomas MacMechan, he would have five of them completed within the next few months. The US Naval attaché even paid a visit. Work was still underway in November of that year, but the project seems to have been abandoned not long after that date. None of these wooden airships ever flew, and some sources suggest that the whole enterprise was a business scam. The project was sometimes referred to as the 'Marshall Fox' airship, possibly after a designer, but the origin of this name is not clear.

The design of the airship shed at Barking is also accredited to Thomas MacMechan. Although his airship never saw the light of day, his shed may have been somewhat more successful. MacMechan claimed that the design was so good that the Admiralty was erecting his sheds in other locations. One of the airship sheds at RNAS Cranwell was built along the same lines as at Barking. In June 1916, after work on the MacMechan airship was abandoned, the Admiralty took over the shed and used it for storage. It was later dismantled and transferred to RNAS Wormwood Scrubs, where it was re-erected and enlarged in the spring of 1918. The area in which the Barking shed once stood is now home to numerous industrial and commercial developments, although none house airships. Thomas MacMechan's premises stood at 55 River Road.

Flookburgh Airship Constructional Station

Location: O. S. 1/50,000 map 96 (SD) 374745. Cumbria, 12 miles to the north-east of Barrow-in-Furness on the Cartmel Peninsula on the edge of Morecombe Bay.
Size: approx. 1,600 acres.
Airship Shed: rigid shed (900 feet long, 2 bays each, and 150 feet wide).
Airships planned: R.37.

Vickers did not consider its recently completed airship shed on Walney Island as suitable for further expansion, and the Admiralty agreed that the shed could not be usefully extended to build the larger airships which were to be laid down over the next few years. The landing ground at Walney Island would also not be large enough to handle them. In spring 1916, Vickers were given approval by the Admiralty to proceed with the construction of a new airship construction station at Flookburgh, a few miles to the east of Barrow-in-Furness. The ground on which it was to be built was situated on the edge of Morecombe Bay—it was thought that the extensive mudflats there would prevent shelling by German submarines. The Director of Air Services had stipulated that all new airship works should be near a military camp or at an existing station so that there would be a large reserve of manpower available at short notice to form handling parties. Flookburgh was in sparsely populated countryside, so Vickers undertook to build houses for its workers on a slope to the west of the intended airship works. The settlement was initially referred to as the 'Model Aero Village' and the streets named after First World War battles.

The design and materials were very different to the existing local architecture, the contract stating that some houses should have red tiles and others, grey slates. Construction by J. Parnell and Sons (of Rugby) and the Rainey Brothers started in

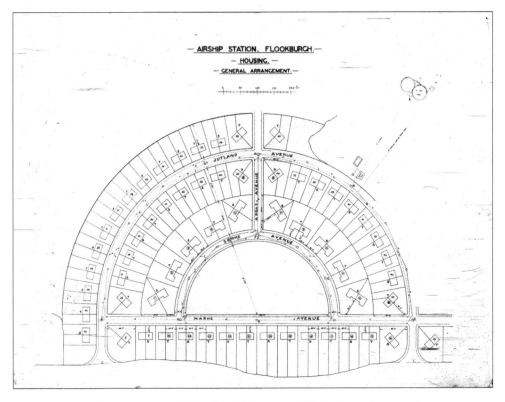

Flookburgh. A plan of the Flookburgh Model Aero Village (later known as Ravenstown) built to house the workers from the nearby Vickers airship works. Whereas the houses were completed, the rest of the facility was abandoned in the early stages of construction. (*The Dock Museum, Barrow-in-Furness*)

March 1917, and the first residents moved in at the end of the year. Around 1,000 acres of good farmland, 247 acres of salt marsh, and 350 acres of sand and mud beyond were acquired for the airship constructional works and landing ground. It was estimated that 45,000 tonnes of material would be needed for the new airship works, so a small branch line was constructed from the Barrow-in-Furness railway to facilitate its transport. By May 1917, the line was ready for use by the main contractor, Sir William Arrol & Co., which had recently completed the airship shed at Inchinnan. The Flookburgh shed, located just south of Willow Lane, was going to be much larger than anything previously built in Britain—some 900 feet long and 150 feet high. Windbreaks of equal length and height at each end meant the structure would be 2,700 feet long in total.

A military guard of ten men, three NCOs, and a lieutenant arrived in May. Construction began in July, although some preparatory work had been undertaken earlier in the year. The contractor had its own locomotive to work the branch line and its goods yard. By September, the steel framework of the giant airship shed was beginning to take shape, but work came to a sudden halt due to steel shortages—for at this stage in the war, the government thought the material would be better put to use on warships than on airship sheds. Flookburgh required around 10,000 tonnes of steel, of which 7,000 tonnes were for the shed alone, and only approximately 170 tonnes had been delivered when work ceased. There had also been issues concerning

The giant airship shed at Vickers Flookburgh Airship Works in the early stages of construction in the summer of 1917, shortly before work on it was abandoned. (*The Fleet Air Arm Museum*)

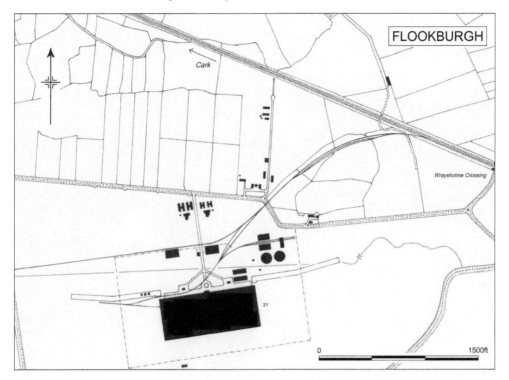

Flookburgh. This plan depicts what the Vickers site for the construction of rigid airships here would have looked like had it been completed. Its main feature was the giant airship shed, 900 feet long, which would have been the largest in Britain. Construction was abandoned at an early stage, but the railway, which branched off from the main line to Barrow-in-Furness, was completed and extended as far as the Model Aero Village, later known as Ravenstown. (*Alan Johnstone/Mick Davis*)

the foundations, for the shed was on damp ground. An alternative plan was drawn up to complete the shed using only 3,000 tonnes of steel, but despite resistance from Vickers, it was decided to abandon the project altogether.

By the time of its abandonment, over £792,000 had been already been spent on Flookburgh, compared with an estimated cost of £230,000 in total for building the Short Brothers' airship works at Cardington. Sir William Arrol & Co. continued to occupy the site until November 1919. The following year an auction was arranged by the Disposal Board. It included 300 concrete piles and numerous wooden huts used by the contractors. The railway was dismantled in 1922, by which time only 120 houses of the planned 300 had been completed. The settlement was subsequently renamed 'Flookburgh West' and later 'Ravenstown', and after being passed around various government departments, was sold off in the early 1920s. The houses are still occupied in 2014, and are the only evidence of this ambitious project left. In the Second World War, RAF Cark aerodrome was constructed on the land set aside for Flookburgh airship station, but closed in 1945. The land has since been returned to agriculture.

12

The Early Post-War Years

Civil Airship Bases

The curtailment of military aviation at the close of the First World War was as rapid as Icarus's fall from the sky. The RAF had amassed over 22,647 aeroplanes by the end of hostilities, but this had fallen to around 3,500 by late 1921, many of which were based overseas. The reduction of Britain's airship strength was equally dramatic. At the beginning of 1918, five rigid and eighty-seven non-rigid airships were in commission; but by early 1919, only a dozen were still in operation. Beardmore, Shorts, Armstrong Whitworth, and Vickers were all still working on rigid airships ordered during the war. The first scheduled aeroplane passenger air service from Britain began in 1919 (between London and Paris) and these companies thought that there would soon be a demand for passenger airship services to distant destinations.

Great faith was placed in large airships for civilian voyages, as it was believed that aeroplanes would never have the range to undertake intercontinental flights with large numbers of passengers, particularly across wide expanses of water. Airships would become the new argosies of the skies! 'Selby Airship's Great Trip' was a major feature in the *Hull Daily Mail* on 15 July 1919:

> The great airship, *R.33*, built by Messrs Armstrong Whitworth and Co. of Selby, will be brought to the Admiralty airship station at Howden within the next few days, coming from Pulham St Mary's in Norfolk. She is going to undergo a gas expansion test prior to her journey to the East which will be the greatest airship test yet carried out. She is the premier airship in the service and first in her class. Her journey will be several thousand miles and will take from 15 to 20 days. It is stated at Selby that she will start within a week for a tour of many countries. First she will go to France, then Italy, calling at Rome, and then to Switzerland. From there she will voyage to Egypt, calling at Cairo as she makes her way to India.

But such over-confidence was soon brought down to earth with the cancellation of the *R.33*'s exploratory flight. Unfortunately, over the next few years numerous other ambitious plans also failed to come to fruition. The Great Northern Aerial Syndicate put forward an early proposal for a worldwide passenger airship network as early as

1919, which—rather surprisingly—had Southport, Lancashire, at its centre. Nothing more was heard of it after the initial announcements.

What looked to be another most promising scheme was spearheaded by Mr A. Ashbolt, the Agent General for Tasmania, the southernmost state of Australia. It had its origins at the Conference of Dominion Premiers in 1921, when many expressed an interest in improving links with the mother country. At the conference, it was forecast that the first passenger airship would reach Australia and New Zealand within 18 months and that a regular service would commence 6 months later. But although the British government was more than happy to offload all its rigid airships onto virtually any company interested, it was far less keen to subsidise ensuing, costly enterprises such as this.

In 1922, Shell partnered up with Sir Dennis Burney and Vickers to put forward a proposal to run a passenger service to India. Their airships would carry 200 passengers, and the journey would take about 3½ days. All airships and equipment at Cardington and Howden would be made available to the new company. However, a change of government in the autumn put these plans into abeyance and no funds were made available.

Not all proposals for airship services involved distant destinations. Some lesser-known schemes aimed to forge links with Europe. As early as March 1918, a company formed in Norway was flying routes between its towns, and a passenger airship service linking Stavanger with Aberdeen envisaged. There were further proposals for airship services across the North Sea, and in March 1920, Howden was nominated to become the starting point of an airship service to Scandinavia and the Netherlands. The following month, representatives from a company intending to establish a route to Norway visited aerodromes in the Edinburgh area, looking for a suitable site. The former airship station at Cramlington (Northumberland) was also considered. Nothing came of even these more modest plans.

Croydon Aerodrome

O. S. 1/50,000 map, 176 (TQ) 306635

Although grandiose plans for the development of civil airship bases in the early post-war years came to nothing, one of the few positive steps taken was the erection of a tall airship mast at Croydon Aerodrome. The first passenger plane flight in the world had taken place as recently as 1914, and by the early post-war years, there was a growing route network radiating from London across Europe. Ten miles to the south of the capital's centre, Croydon became the focus of this expanding business, the equivalent of Heathrow Airport today. Work began in the early summer of 1921 on the construction of the Croydon mooring mast, situated at the western end of the aerodrome. Though it superficially resembled the tall example at Pulham, there were some major differences. It was constructed out of wood, which was unusual for a structure of this type. There was also an internal zig-zag staircase, a big improvement on the precarious climb up a vertical steel ladder at Pulham. On 30 June 1921, *Flight* featured the following description of the Croydon mooring mast:

> Though the work on the airship mast is not now so spectacular, an enormous amount of detail construction has been done this week. The power house at the foot of the mast has developed from being merely a concrete base into a mass of dynamos, motors, pumps and switch gear. A hut has been built round this electrical plant, the steam 'Rocket' or 'Puffing Billy' (a large portable steam engine with a long chimney) occupying a concrete base of its own outside the power house. The pipes for the water ballast are now in position up the mast and electricians are swarming over the outside, fixing obstruction and other lights all the way from the base to the top. The iron frame work for the revolving-head which arrived in sections has been riveted together and is now waiting to be hauled to the mast.

Not long after this article was written, electrician Herbert Tilley fell 100 feet to his death from the mast—he had temporarily unhooked his safety harness. This did not deter the *R.33* from flying low over Croydon on 18 July, and becoming the first airship to use the mast. It departed after only half an hour as the weather was deteriorating, but returned three days later and this time stayed overnight. Some problems were encountered and modifications of the mooring mast undertaken before it was used again. Once these were complete, it was hoped the *R.33* would return and possibly give pleasure flights to members of the public. The *R.36* was also considered to demonstrate passenger flights to the Mediterranean from Croydon. However, after the departure of the *R.33* on 22 July 1921, no airship ever called at Croydon Aerodrome.

The rigid airship *R.33* attached to the wooden mooring mast at Croydon Aerodrome in the summer of 1921. (*Croydon Airport Society*)

The 140-foot-tall mast was frowned upon by airline pilots, as it was in their direct line of flight. To add to its problems, it had been erected on private land without the owner's consent. A Breguet airliner crash-landed near the mast in the summer. Fortunately, all on board survived.

The Croydon mooring mast nearly met another untimely end when the grass beneath it was set on fire by a motorised lawnmower. The summer had been hot and dry, and the fire quickly threatened aeroplane hangars and the mast before it was brought under control. Not long afterwards, the government decided that the mast should be dismantled and put into storage. *Flight* reported its demise on 6 October:

> The airship mast is now about half-way down. Since Thursday night red obstruction lights have been placed at the top of what is left of it. Several local dealers have been asking if they can buy the wood of the mast and its gear which are, of course, to be stored at Cardington.

This looked to be to end of Croydon aerodrome's association with airships. On 8 February 1926, the *Dundee Evening Telegraph* made a small announcement on the possible revival of airship activity in Southern England,

> [...] on the part of the newly established London Airship Club that its members can if they so desire actually purchase their own small airships at the comparatively modest price of a couple of thousand pounds.

The club had considered establishing its base at Southampton, but this was thought to be too far from London to make it a success. Croydon was the favoured location—a strange choice given that airships would have been a hazard to commercial aeroplane traffic using the aerodrome. Little more was thereafter heard of the London Airship Club, which never succeeded in operating any airships. Croydon Aerodrome has also long since disappeared, and housing been built on the site. Redford Avenue occupies the place where the airship mast once stood. The iconic Art Deco terminal building, once the gateway to Europe, has fortunately been preserved.

Cramlington Airship Station

The construction of airships had been in the hands of the British government and large arms manufacturers since 1914. But in the late 1920s, a small enterprise which went by the name of 'British Airships'—later changed to 'Airship Development Company'—thought it could revive the fortunes of the small non-rigid airship. The Conservative Party were initially approached to finance the venture, yet the airship staff at Cardington frowned upon this effort. If an airship belonging to the Airship Development Company were involved in an accident, it would reflect unfavourably on the main Empire Development programme, as far as public opinion is concerned. In March 1928, the company considered applying to use the Coastal shed at Pulham in which to build a small airship and for half of No. 1 shed in which to construct a semi-rigid airship. This idea was dropped in favour of the Coastal shed at the abandoned Cramlington airship station, Northumberland. It was inside this building that the *A.D.1* airship took shape.

The *A.D.1* resembled the wartime Submarine Scout, but incorporated recent developments in airship technology. With a length of 138 feet and a maximum diameter of 29 feet, it was advertised as suitable for private flying, passenger flights, instruction, advertising, aerial photography, and surveying. The main revenue was anticipated to come from advertising, for which role it had panels on either side of its envelope measuring 76 feet by 24 feet.

The *A.D.1* airship first flew on 13 September 1929, bearing the registration G-FAAX. The following month it appeared at the Newcastle Air Pageant, where it circled with the engine throttled back and was so quiet that spectators could hear the two crewmen speaking to each other. That summer, it left Cramlington for southern England to demonstrate its capabilities. On this flight the weather deteriorated, so the crew decided to put down at Grantham. It remained here for several days before resuming its journey. On 26 June 1930, it landed at its intended destination, the old RNAS airship station at Capel, Folkestone. A party of men recruited from the Dover Labour Exchange acted as the handling party and hauled it to a specially prepared site in the woods, the same place that airships were taken and hidden in times of air

The small airship *AD-1*, built and flown at the former RNAS Cramlington in 1929. It was used to advertise Carreras and Walter Wilson brands of cigarettes. (*Northumberland Archives/ Woodhorn*)

raids in the First World War. A hole had been dug for the *A.D.1* control car and new mooring blocks installed.

The *A.D.1*'s stay at Capel saw its engine overhauled and advertising banners laced onto the side of its envelope. Although the mooring out site provided good shelter, problems were experienced in taking the airship in and out of the woodland. It was therefore decided to move the *A.D.1* to East Horsley in Sussex, along with its coxswain, an engineer, two riggers, and two pilots. On the night of 14 July 1930, a strong wind blew up from the north and the rain came down in torrents. The *A.D.1* was in danger of becoming dismembered by the elements, so a volunteer ground crew was assembled and moved it to a less exposed location. It remained in the grounds of East Horsley Tower School, moored in the lee of some high trees, until the 25th, when it embarked on a flight over London and circled the dome of St Paul's Cathedral like so many earlier machines. The *A.D.1* later returned to its base at Cramlington, where construction had already begun on the *A.D.2*. In the autumn, the *A.D.1* made a return visit to the former airship station at Capel, Folkestone on 10 September 1930, and later departed for Belgium to advertise a cigarette company. It met a premature demise on 5 October 1930, destroyed by a gale at a mooring out site.

The Airship Development Company went into liquidation not long afterwards, having overestimated the demand for its services. Two airship envelopes were sold to be made into dust sheets for furniture, and the shed at Cramlinton was vacated. It would be over twenty years before another small non-rigid airship was built in Britain. The airship shed at Cramlington lingered on in an increasingly derelict state, until it was finally demolished.

Military Airships Stations

The Armistice ushered in the rapid decline of RAF aerodromes in the British Isles as well as aircraft, including most airship stations. The Admiralty had originally intended to retain four rigid airship stations at either Howden, East Fortune, Cranwell, Kingsnorth, or Pulham. Yet budgetary restrictions soon whittled the choice down to two, as we shall see. Lord Trenchard, responsible for a memorandum on the future of military aviation in Britain, had little time for airships. In the First World War, they had operated in support of the Royal Navy, but this now had little say in the role of military aviation. All military aviation had become the responsibility of the RAF.

RAF East Fortune

RAF East Fortune was the first post-war casualty. Initially, the future had looked bright for this station: unlike most of its counterparts, it had an extensive aerodrome, where pilots were trained in the use of torpedoes to attack ships. It had remained active until the very last days of conflict: on 11 November 1918, East Fortune had three airships on patrol, and a few days later, its airships filmed the surrender of the

German Fleet as it sailed up the Firth of Forth to anchor off at Leith. By the end of 1918, East Fortune still had six operational airships: *R.29*, North Sea *N.S.7* and *N.S.8*, Coastal Star *C*3* and *C*8*, and Submarine Scout Zero *S.S.Z.60*. In March 1919, the rigid airship *R.34* made its first flight from Inchinnan. In the same month, the much smaller North Sea *N.S.11* made the longest flight ever undertaken by a British airship over the sea, covering 1,285 miles in 40½ hours. A course was steered for Denmark from East Fortune, and on reaching the Danish coast, *N.S.11* headed for Heligoland and then onto the Netherlands. It completed the last stage of its journey using just one engine before landing at an aerodrome in England, where it was handled by an untrained party of boy mechanics who had never seen an airship at close quarters.

Many of the personnel at East Fortune were not enthusiastic about the achievements of airships or the retention of the station. Demobilisation was not progressing fast enough for them and a strike was called. After a few stern words from the station commander, order was restored. The *R.34* arrived here on 30 May 1919, after having been long delayed by objections from the CO. There were only 156 personnel to make up the landing party—instead of the 500 required—there was a shortage of gas—as the hydrogen plant was out of order—and the airship shed was occupied by the *R.29*, which was having new gas bags fitted. As soon as the *R.34* was considered airworthy, plans were drawn up for a transatlantic flight. There was some urgency as it was thought the Americans may be the first to make an attempt. The flight was delayed as the Germans were reluctant to sign the Treaty of Versailles. It was feared that hostilities could break out again and the *R.34* would be needed in the new conflict. The *R.29* and North Sea *N.S.7* and *N.S.8* were also put on standby to enforce a possible blockade against Germany.

On 17 June 1919, *R.34* took to the air armed with machine guns. It flew over Germany, Hamburg, and Friedrichshafen to demonstrate Allied supremacy over the skies. By the end of the month, the crisis was over and the *R.34* prepared for its delayed flight across the Atlantic. On the morning of 2 July, the *R.34* was walked out of its shed at East Fortune by a handling party of 550 men. A short time later it took off—next stop, New York. On the tip of its bow it carried the motto *Pro Patria Volans* ('Flying For My Country'). Upon its return, its crew assumed that they would land back at East Fortune, but for reasons unknown were was instructed by the Air Ministry to end the epic flight at Pulham, where it deposited water ballast over most its ground handling party and received a low-key reception. There were rumours that the anti-airship lobby did not want large crowds welcoming the return of the *R.34*, and this was why it was sent to the remote Pulham rather than East Fortune, which was only 20 miles from Edinburgh. The *R.34* was housed in one of Pulham's rigid airship sheds and little further flying was carried out.

Not long after the *R.34*'s Atlantic venture came the unexpected announcement that East Fortune was to close, even though new buildings were still under construction. After an active life, the rigid airship *R.29* was scrapped on site in October 1919. This outcome could not have deviated further from what had been planned for the station just a year earlier—had the war not ended, two rigid airships, two North Sea and no less than ten Submarine Scout Twin airships would have been operational here. There was great hostility in Scotland to it losing its only airship station. On 17 October 1919, *The Scotsman* published a long article arguing the case for East Fortune:

There are three great airship stations in the United Kingdom—East Fortune in Haddingtonshire, Pulham in Norfolk and Howden in Yorkshire. These are the only stations where there is shed accommodation to house such vessels as the *R.34*. Of the three, East Fortune is in the highest state of development. More money has been spent on it than on any of the others and as it stands it is a more valuable property. It has long been regarded as a permanent institution. Since the Armistice many thousands of pounds have been spent to establish it as such. The first threat of extinction came a little over a month ago and costly schemes of further improvement have been stopped half way. The official decision came as a thunderbolt to all concerned. The Government have decided that two of the three stations shall be abolished and, according to their decision, East Fortune and Pulham are doomed to disappear and only Howden to remain. The establishments on the Forth and the Wash will be transferred to Yorkshire. Howden has long been a most unpopular station. It is situated on low lying swampy ground, the surroundings are uncongenial and the living accommodation is of a temporary character. In these respects it is a direct contrast to East Fortune which enjoys an ideal site, a bracing atmosphere and permanent quarters of all excellent description. A more important consideration than any of these is the relative position of the two places to the war stations of The Grand Fleet. The primary purpose of these great airships was co-operation with the Navy. They were to be the eyes of the Fleet. East Fortune's relation to the Firth of Forth makes its relative superiority over Howden in this respect obvious. The strategic pre-eminence of the Scottish aerodrome is indisputable.

To restrict the number of airship stations to one is condemned as a short sighted policy. There are days when flying is impracticable at Howden and practicable at East Fortune and vice-versa. An airship, it is argued, should always have an alternative landing place. Howden possesses one advantage, however, which may have been the deciding factor in determining its continuance. It has an airship shed on the point of completion which outrivals anything at East Fortune. It is stated that the largest shed at East Fortune would be insufficient to accommodate the new type of airship now being built. But expert opinion states that the present shed accommodation at East Fortune could be readily increased and the cost of the extension would be less than the cost of providing permanent quarters at Howden on the lines of those already in existence at East Fortune. In any event, Howden's single asset is in the view of airship experts, more apparent than real. Lighter than air vessels have developed with extra-ordinary rapidity during the war years and it is confidently predicted that the great shed at Howden must become obsolete a year or two hence in the same way as the East Fortune shed, built for the *R.29* and *R.34* within the last three years, has already become out of date.

Questions were also raised in Parliament about the matter. The Parliamentary Undersecretary of State for Air defended the choice of Howden:

I pass to the advantages possessed by Howden over East Fortune. The sheds at Howden lend themselves more readily to expansion in the future. The reason for this is that sheds at East Fortune are of less height than the sheds at Howden. Consequently for airships, without being unduly imaginative, we are entitled to contemplate in the future, the sheds in existence at Howden at the moment, owing to their height, are more suitable for future expansion than those at East Fortune. With regard to the weather conditions at East Fortune, the wind barrage in the mouth of the Forth is a serious difficulty to navigation. When there is a fog in the Forth, the high ground in the vicinity of East Fortune known as North Berwick Law constitutes a serious danger to an airship coming low in order to find the aerodrome and I am sure the noble Earl who may or may not have been up in an airship, knows the immense difficulties of landing when the atmospheric conditions are not as clear as one would like them to be. In view of the great difficulties which accompany the safe landing of immense airships, it is important that the conformation of the surrounding country should be carefully considered, certainly in all cases where there is a question of one locality against another.[1]

But the Earl of Wemyss, who argued for East Fortune, had the last say in the matter:

I think the noble Marquis has made out a case for Howden in some ways, but as a native of the county in which East Fortune is situated, I must enter a protest against his description of my county being a foggy place. I venture to say that it is considerably freer from fogs than any part of Yorkshire. Of course we have sea fogs. I should also like to know whether there has ever been an accident to any airship, large or small when landing in the aerodrome at East Fortune. I think I should have heard of it had there been. I spared your Lordships the reading of this letter which I hold in my hand which gives a most gloomy account of Howden, as a place situated in a swamp and as being altogether unpleasant. I do not know whether that account is true because I have not had it authenticated.

The end came on 4 February 1920. The *R.34* and the non-rigid North Sea *N.S.7* were the last airships to leave East Fortune. A care and maintenance detachment remained on the site, continuing the operation of the wireless station until mid-1920. During the National Coal Strike in 1921, the buildings were again used by the Royal Navy servicemen who were sent to various pits in the Lothians to work the pump and safety equipment. After the strike, the airship sheds were used for storage and the breaking down of 160 million rounds of ammunition for recycling. Once this task had been completed, work began in 1922 on dismantling the airship sheds. About 350 acres of land were sold to the South-Eastern Counties of Scotland Joint Sanatorium Board, which established a tuberculosis hospital in the former air station buildings. In June 1940, the site of the former airship station was requisitioned as a satellite aerodrome for RAF Drem. By the end of the year, hard runways and hangars had been built. The following year, a night-fighter training unit was based here. Coastal Command then took over the aerodrome and also used it for training. The aerodrome closed down shortly after the Second World War, although the runway was lengthened in the early 1950s for possible use by the US Air Force.

East Fortune was never used as a military base again. Most of the land was returned to agriculture. Second World War buildings on the south side of the airfield were preserved and are now home to the Museum of Flight. It contains exhibits from when airships once flew from here and is decorated with a plaque commemorating the epic transatlantic flight by the *R.34*. The airship station itself occupied ground on the opposite side of the aerodrome. Some of its domestic buildings—used by a tuberculosis hospital which has long since closed—have survived into the twenty-first century, albeit in a derelict state.

RAF Howden

RAF Howden, Yorkshire, became the last refuge of operational RAF airships. Its last Coastal airships (*C.5* and *C.9*) and its Submarine Scout Zeros were phased out and replaced by Coastal Star *C*6, C*7, C*9*, and *C*10* in the closing months of the First World War. These were still on strength in early 1919, along with three North Sea airships. The Submarine Scout Zeros were replaced by Submarine Scout Twins *S.S.T.3, S.S.T.4, S.S.T.5, S.S.T.7, S.S.T.9, S.S.T.10, S.S.T.11*, and *S.S.T.12*, which were used to assist with the clearance of minefields in the North Sea. Although the mooring out stations at Lowthorpe and Kirkleatham were shut down, work was still being undertaken to upgrade Howden itself: an underground petrol storage facility was constructed, with mains to the sheds; additional quarters were built for married officers; and more land was acquired. The station perimeter now enclosed 1,500 acres.

In August and September 1919, there were drastic cutbacks to the number of airships in RAF service—almost all the non-rigids, such as the Submarine Scout Twins, were retired. North Sea *N.S.9* and *N.S.16* continued to fly from Howden until the station closed in 1921. While other airship manufacturers—such as Beardmore and Vickers—had closed their doors once they completed their orders, the Royal Airship Works at Cardington were thrown a lifeline. The US Navy had been impressed by the *R.34*'s flight to the USA and wished to acquire a large airship. They would have probably ordered it from the Zeppelin Company, but at that time the Allies had placed restrictions on the building of airships in Germany. The order was eventually placed with the British government, which was eager to keep Cardington in business as well as earn foreign currency. In 1919, a document argued the case for retaining this location as an 'aerial dockyard' in preference to any other:

> [...] it contains a model village and plant for making certain raw materials used in airship construction and, moreover, is already manned by civilian labour and situated in a district very favourable for supplying the type of labour required, and it would only be necessary to erect two non-rigid sheds, for which there is ample room, in order that the station may deal efficiently both in peace and war with non-rigid as well as rigid airships.[2]

Like all the other rigid airships built between 1914 and 1918, the new *R.38* was based on technology gleaned from Zeppelins that had crashed in Britain. It was unfortunate

The large double rigid shed under construction at RNAS Howden, March 1919. One of the partially complete doors is visible to the left of the shed. (*The National Archives*)

The brick electricity-generating house at Howden in October 1919. (*The National Archives*)

that the *R.38*'s particular design had its origins in a high-altitude craft known as the 'Zeppelin Height Climber', designed to fly at heights beyond the reach of allied aeroplanes. Copying this lightweight design eventually had disastrous consequences for the *R.38*, compounded by the fact that the Royal Airship Works did not have the same experience of building airships as companies such as Shorts Brothers or Vickers. In April 1920, the US Navy sent a party of officers and other ranks to train on British airships at Howden, prior to taking delivery of the *R.38*. This did not prevent the government halting all building work on the station in that summer and making many hundreds of its workers redundant. Only a handful were retained to operate the plant and machinery for the training of the Americans, and to service the Rigid Airship Trials Flight still based here. Howden's Coastal sheds were retained for the time being, but would shortly be sold for scrap.

The Americans requested that they be trained in a metal rigid airship such as the *R.33* or the *R.34*, but initially neither was available—they had to make do with the wooden *R.32*. The US Navy personnel stripped and overhauled it, and by August it was ready for its first flight. The *R.34* had been permanently assigned to Howden, and in March 1920, was ready to resume its flying career. On 21 January 1921 it departed on a trial flight heading towards the North Sea. For a time radio contact was lost, which caused some concern back at Howden. The *R.32* was dispatched to search. Eventually communications were restored and the *R.34* was instructed to return to base. By then the weather had deteriorated into thick fog coverage, and to make matters worse, *R.34*'s navigating officer was unsure of his position. While heading inland just past midnight, the *R.34* struck a hilltop on Guisborough Moor, in the North York Moors (the minimum safe height for operating a rigid airship was considered to be 2½ times its length). Fortunately, the *R.34* bounced upwards after its grounding, but its problems were far from over.

Only two of the *R.34*'s four engines were running when the airship was blown out over the North Sea. Eventually it managed to limp back to Howden, arriving at about 3.00 p.m. But despite a handling party of around 400 men, the rising wind prevented it being housed in its shed. Instead, it was decided to moor it out in the open until conditions improved. During the night it was assaulted and dashed against the ground by gales, so that, by morning, its bows were smashed and the hull damaged beyond repair. Much to the dismay of its crew, the decision was made almost immediately to scrap the damaged airship, and this work was underway only three days later. With the demise of the *R.34*, the *R.80* was re-inflated and flew at least four training flights for the US Navy personnel. In July the *R.38* arrived from Cardington, but its stay was short lived, for although the station commander at Howden had requested a temporary mooring mast, its arrival was delayed.

A mooring mast was available elsewhere, however: on 23 August 1921, the *R.38* left Howden for Pulham, where it was to be based until it departed for the USA. As soon as the airship was airborne, the weather deteriorated: fog obscured Pulham such that the *R.38* stayed out all night. Upon its second attempt to dock, the weather had still not improved, so the airship set course to return to Howden. It had just overflown

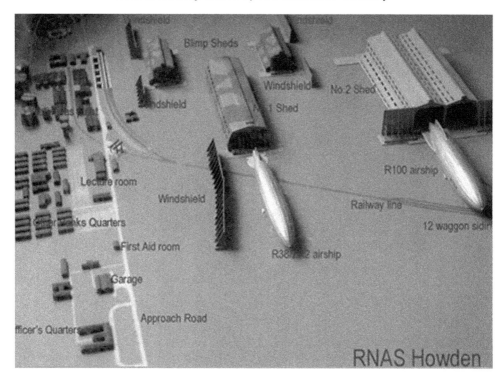

A model of RNAS Howden, *c.* 1921. The *R.100* is featured, but this airship did not emerge from the No. 2 rigid shed until 1929. By this time, many of the other buildings at Howden had been demolished. This model is exhibited in the Yorkshire Air Museum at Elvington. (*Kenneth Deacon*)

The *R.38*, or the *ZR2* as it was designated by the US navy, emerging from the shed at Cardington in 1921. It left here for RAF Howden shortly after its construction was completed. (*Bedfordshire and Luton Archives*)

Hull when disaster struck. David Ernest recounted what he witnessed under the headline 'R.38 Back Crumples Like Paper-Appalling Spectacle':

> I was just in from the Great Central Railway Company's offices, perhaps 300 yards from the Victoria Pier. This was about 5.30. The noise of the engines had caused me to look upwards and there coming through the clouds was a huge airship. She fell into clear view perhaps 1,000 yards up and seemed running perfectly. 'What a beautiful object', was my remark to a tramway man standing near me, and he agreed, for she really was. Two minutes after I first saw her, the ship made a sudden dip and I thought just for a moment that she was going to fly lower so that the inhabitants of the town would be able to see her more distinctly. But almost at the same instant I saw her back crinkle in the middle just like a piece of paper. 'Good God, it has gone', was the exclamation which sprang to my lips and within what seemed no more than a couple of seconds, the ship broke in two and its engines seemed to drop into the river just beneath, one after another.
>
> While the two halves were suspended in the air at least one parachute detached itself from the ship. There may have been more but I saw this one open out and begin a gradual descent. Fifteen or twenty seconds had elapsed from the breaking of the ship when the front part of it exploded with frightful force and a terrible flash of flame. Very quickly afterwards the back half of the ship burst with equal violence. All that was left of the vessel fell flaming straight down from the sky on the River Humber, where it sat like a mass of black smoke and fire. Tugs rushed to the rescue at once and cruised about rendering all the help they could. Ten minutes later, the only part of the *R.38* visible was 50 feet of her stern sticking up slantwise from the water. 'I saw a parachute rock under the force of the explosion and what looked like another parachute fell on the Lincolnshire side of the River.'

Five of the crew who had been in the tail section survived. Forty-four others died. They included one of its designers, Air Cdr Edward Maitland, the Commanding Officer of Howden airship station—he had a long association with airships, and had flown the R.34 across the Atlantic. Almost all of the American crew perished. The official report attributed the disintegration of the *R.38* to structural weakness. Shortly before the disaster, it was seen to perform a number of sharp turns, and these were thought to have caused the airship to break up. The German design on which it was based could withstand violent manoeuvres but only at high altitude. This accident provided airship critics with the necessary leverage to obstruct any further development. Howden closed down a short time later. The last flight from Howden was made by the *R.80*, with the station's new Commanding Officer on board and destined for Pulham. The airship works at Cardington were mothballed. The *R.36* was presented to the Americans in place of the *R.38* but this offer declined.

The *Westminster Gazette*'s Selby correspondent reported that Howden was being taken over by the Admiralty in early August 1922: 'there is very good reason for stating that the airship station will be used for a fleet of six ships about two-thirds the size of the *R.39* class.' The Royal Navy would have been glad of its own air arm, but since the RAF was now in charge of all military aviation, the credibility of this story is questionable.

Howden was soon put up for sale by the Disposals Board. An astonishing approach was made by the Zeppelin Company, which expressed an interest in purchasing the site. Further to this, it announced in May 1923 that it intended to relocate its airship-building activities here. As the Allies at this time had restricted the size of airships that could be built in Germany, this move would have circumvented this regulation. Sir Dennis Burney and Goodyear were in fact planning on setting up a worldwide passenger network with the Zeppelin Company, so any activity undertaken at Howden would probably not have been exclusively German. However, the Air Ministry opposed Zeppelin's move to Britain, leaving the airship sheds to rust. This was not the last time that the Zeppelin Company would express an interest in Howden.

RAF Pulham

For the latter part of war and indeed after hostilities had ended, RAF Pulham concentrated on carrying out experimental work with airships. In late 1918, up to four non-rigid airships could be seen there at any one time, attached to small masts and undertaking mooring-out tests. The installation of the tall Vickers mast 1919 meant that trials with rigid airships could commence—this was the only structure of its type in the country. Parachute development also continued to be undertaken here using the Italian-built *S.R.1* airship. The RAF had received a single example of this semi-rigid airship in late 1918, which flew from Italy to Pulham, stopping several times *en route*. This was the first airship flight between the two countries. The *S.R.1* was nevertheless deflated by the end of 1919.

By 1920, the only non-rigid airship still flying from Pulham was the Submarine Scout Experimental *S.S.E.3*. Like other airship stations, Pulham had an outbreak of dissent when the RAF was perceived to drag its feet over demobilisation. One day in March, many refused to resume work after dinner. The situation was soon defused, but not before a party of Royal Marines was drafted in, lest matters get out of hand. Pulham was once more put on alert when the Germans were reluctant to sign the peace treaty in June 1919. The possibility of renewed hostilities prompted the transfer of personnel from Howden to Pulham, in case the *R.33* needed to be deployed. The crisis blew over in a matter of days, however, and Pulham returned to its experimental work.

July 1919 witnessed the return of the *R.34* to Britain after its voyage to New York. The handling party that greeted its arrival shortly before 7.00 a.m. on the 6th was made up of servicemen from Norwich and numerous local residents. But events two days later tainted this triumph with disaster. North Sea *N.S.11* failed to return to Pulham from 'a routine mine hunting patrol', and in the early hours of 15 July, a large explosion was seen off the coast of Norfolk, not far from Cromer. Mrs G. Hudson of Blakeney bore witness:

The two rigid airship sheds at RNAS Pulham. One was 712 feet long and the other 758 feet. (*Picture Norfolk*)

The rigid airship *R.33* attached to the tall steel mooring mast designed by Vickers at Pulham Airship Station. Although the airship is painted in RAF colours, it also displays the civil registration *G-FAAG*. The *R.33* carried out extensive mooring mast trials here in 1920, enduring wind speeds of up to 80 mph. (*Picture Norfolk*)

I heard an awful explosion and saw a terrific glare. I rushed to the window with my glasses and saw the airship ... while I was watching she suddenly took a header and went down to the sea in flames. Just before she reached the water she exploded again and flaming fragments were scattered about. The mass burnt on the surface of the sea for hours after the explosion.[3]

None of the crew of nine survived. Among them was Capt. Warneford, who earlier in the year had set a world endurance record in the very same vessel, when it made a non-stop 4,000-mile flight from RNAS Longside. It was thought that he may have undertaken this flight in an unofficial attempt to set a new endurance record for airships which was now held by the R.34.

In the summer of 1920, two Zeppelins were delivered to Pulham as part of Germany's post-war reparations. A press article entitled 'Gemany's Leviathian Airship' in the *Southern Reporter* on 8 July 1920 described one arrival on the first day of that month:

The rigid airship, *L71*, the Leviathan of the German Air War Service which has been surrendered to Great Britain, arrived at Pulham about six o'clock yesterday morning, but owing apparently to the airship containing too much gas, it was deemed inadvisable to effect an immediate landing. The ship manoeuvred over the country for some considerable time to get rid of surplus gas and proceeded as far as Norwich, where it arrived a little after nine o'clock. It hovered over the city for nearly three-quarters of an hour, when it headed back to Pulham. There it remained in the air for an hour or two. A rope was dropped and seized by a berthing party of about 300 men. The landing of the giant was carried out without a hitch and the ship was immediately guided into a shed for its reception. The great vessel had been completely camouflaged so far as outward marks were concerned and the design of an iron cross on the stern had been painted over.

Britain was also allocated a Zeppelin shed as reparation, but had little need of it, so it remained in Germany. On 20 September 1920, the Air Ministry ordered that all construction work on airships excepting the *R.38* cease, and much of the Pulham personnel left within the year. On 1 December 1920, the airship station was taken over by the Controller General of Civil Aviation. Around the same time, the government proposed to hand over all service airships and existing bases to any private company wishing to utilise them for commercial purposes. This offer was not taken up. On 1 April 1921, the *Engineering Journal* published an article featuring a comprehensive description of Pulham:

The station occupies an area of 920 acres of flat grass land, of which sheds and other buildings cover about 56 acres, the most important buildings being two large sheds for rigid airships. The larger of these sheds is 757 feet long, 180 feet wide and 110 feet high, so that it can easily accommodate two of the largest airships at present in existence. It is in fact now occupied by the two ex-German airships, *L.64* and *L.71*. These ships appear to be in good condition, except that the gas bags have been removed as being unfit for further service. The dimensions of the second large shed are 710 feet long, 150 feet wide and 100 feet high, while there is another small shed suitable for housing non-rigid airships of the coastal type. There are two hydrogen generating plants, one employing the water gas process and having an output of 16,000 cubic feet per hour and the other operating on the silicol system producing 12,000 cubic feet per hour. Four gasholders are used in connection with the hydrogen plant, three having capacities of 500,000 cubic feet each while the fourth has a capacity of 120,000 cubic feet.

The other equipment includes a gas compressing plant, electrical generating station, wireless telegraphic and telephonic apparatus and a meteorological hut, as well as workshops for engineers, carpenters, fabric workers, riggers, blacksmiths, welders, coppersmiths, etc. Hut accommodation is provided for about 36 officers and 500 men, although only about 200 civilians are employed at present. The station is connected to the Great Eastern Railway by a standard gauge track and is equipped with a light railway system. Good roads connecting the various buildings have also been made.

Despite the continued disbandment of Pulham in 1921, its mooring mast experiments continued. Countless other innovations for airships had been created at this station, but mooring mast trials were considered its most important contribution. The staff of the *Engineering Journal* witnessed the *R.33* being moored to the tall mast by a team of eight men, compared with the 300 to 400 which would have been necessary to place it in its shed. There were now in fact too few personnel at Pulham to form large handling parties, so when the need arose, lorries drove down the road to neighbouring villages to pick up volunteers. There was never any shortage of men willing to hold onto the ropes of a large airship. At night, the mooring mast and attached airship would be floodlit, creating a dramatic sight above the Norfolk landscape.

In April 1921, the *R.33* was joined by the newly completed *R.36*. This had started as a military airship but was converted into a passenger-carrier during its construction. In June it gave a number of demonstration flights to MPs and journalists. To embark, they all had to climb up the external ladder of the 120-foot-high mooring mast, a daunting prospect. The *R.36* performed a new role for an airship, when it undertook traffic control duties for the Ascot Races. The Metropolitan Police took the airship over for the day and used it as a flying control room. Its duties were to remain on station while cars were going to and from Ascot and to keep the police informed by wireless telegraphy of any stoppage or irregularity in the flow of traffic. The airship did not arrive back at Pulham until 11.00 p.m.; its mooring was made with the aid of searchlights.

On 21 June, the *R.36* made another test flight. After flying to the north of England, it arrived back at Pulham not long after 9.00 p.m. The mooring rope was dropped and attached to the mast, but the airship approached far too quickly and the rope caught the bottom of its hull. This caused the *R.36* to jerk upwards. The shock caused the contents of the emergency ballast bags to be released, and the nose pitched up sharply. Damage was sustained to the hull, and it was decided that the airship could

The Rigid *R.36*, attached to Pulham's tall steel mooring mast not long after its arrival at Pulham in 1921. Originally designed for the military, it converted to a passenger-carrying role during its construction at Inchinnan. Beneath the hull is the control and passenger cabin, which was furnished with fifty wicker chairs, tables, and a galley. To emphasise its civilian role, it displays the civilian registration *G-FAAF*. (*Picture Norfolk*)

not remain moored at the mast any longer but had to be housed in a shed as soon as possible. The only accommodation then available was at Howden, because the sheds at Pulham were occupied by the two German Zeppelins and the *R.33*. With the wind now increasing in force, one of them had to be removed to make way for the *R.36*. The choice fell on the *L.64* which shared a shed with the *R.33*; but it refused to be sacrificed, as the handling party could not remove it from its berth. Even when a Fowler ploughing tractor hitched a cable to it, the *L.64* stubbornly remained inside its shed. A drastic course of action was now of the essence, and the *L.64* was broken up where it sat by officers and men armed with axes and saws. Finally, at 2.00 a.m., there was enough room in the shed for the *R.36*. As it was being manoeuvred into position, a gust of wind caught it and it flew against the shed doors, inflicting further damage. With the airship programme by now in decline, it was decided not to repair the *R.36* immediately, but to leave it laid up.

One of the last airships to arrive at Pulham was the *R.80* on 20 August 1921. It had flown from Howden, ferrying the station commander's pets and livestock to their new home. The same month, it was announced that Pulham's—like Howden's—services were no longer required, and that it would be reduced to a care and maintenance state.

Two herculean Fowler BB1 ploughing engines were acquired at Pulham in 1919. One was put to use as a winch for the newly erected tall mooring mast. The other replaced the man-powered windlass used to open the doors of a rigid shed. (*Picture Norfolk*)

After having thrilled enormous crowds at the RAF Hendon Air Show the previous month, the *R.33* left Pulham on 18 August for Cardington, where it was deflated and placed in storage. In March 1922, airships in the hands of the Air Ministry were the *R.80*, *R.33*, *R.36*, *R.37* (incomplete), and the German Zeppelin *L.71*. By the end of the month, all but the Zeppelin were advertised for sale in the newspapers, with or without their bases, sheds, and other equipment. No buyer was found, so they remained in storage at Cardington and Pulham.

13

Airships for Empire, *R.100* and *R.101*

In the 1920s, British politicians decided that an airship service should be established to link the country with the distant lands of Empire. Various schemes were put forward, all of which involved private enterprise. Although the government was willing to let private companies use its surplus airships and associated facilities, it was reluctant to offer financial backing. Circumstances changed dramatically in 1924, when the Conservatives lost power and were replaced by the first Labour administration. Ramsay MacDonald, the new Prime Minister, was an aviation enthusiast in favour of developing passenger airships. He decided that the State ought to take the initiative by re-opening the Royal Airship Works at Cardington, where a new airship—the R.101—would be built at taxpayers' expense. For this reason, the *R.101* is sometimes known as the 'Socialist' airship. A network of overseas mooring towers would also be built along passenger routes by the Air Ministry. But to ensure that the Imperial Airship Scheme was not entirely a state monopoly, the contract to build the second airship—the *R.100*—was awarded to Vickers, which had formed the Airship Guarantee Company for this purpose. This was the *R.101*'s 'Capitalist' counterpart. The revival in airship activity centred on three derelict airship stations—Cardington, Howden, and Pulham.

Pulham Airship Station

On 2 April 1925, the dormant station at Pulham sprang back into life with the return of the rigid airship *R.33* to its old haunt. It had been reconditioned at Cardington, and its RAF markings painted out and replaced with the civilian registration G-FAAG. The *R.33* then began a series of laminar flow tests for the development of *R.100* and *R.101*. Two weeks after its return to Pulham and with only a handful of crew members on board, the airship was moored to the tall steel mast. A strong wind sprang up and as the night wore on, the wind speed increased. Suddenly the *R.33* was wrenched from the mooring mast, tearing a large hole in its nose. It was blown backwards, narrowly missing the doors of one of Pulham's sheds, and taking to the air. The men on board started the motors to try to bring the *R.33* under control. Flt Lt Booth and 'Sky' Hunt climbed on top of the hull and crawled along it to assess the damage, and equipment

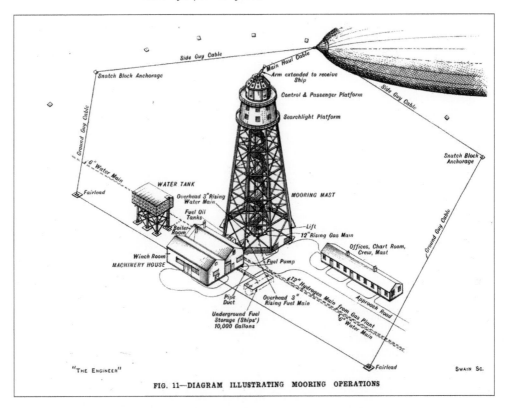

FIG. 11—DIAGRAM ILLUSTRATING MOORING OPERATIONS

Airship mooring operations—a rigid airship approaching a mooring mast. (*The Engineer*)

in the nose was jettisoned overboard. After struggling for nearly 5 hours, the crew managed to halt the drifting airship, which had now been blown far out over the North Sea. Ships were placed on standby should it come down in the water, and at one stage, even German handling parties were ready to assist should the crew decide to proceed to Cologne. Eventually, after 29 hours in the air, the *R.33* managed to limp back to Pulham. Large crowds had come from far and wide to watch and there was no shortage of people willing to assist in handling it, women in fur coats and schoolboys among them. The crew were celebrated as heroes for saving their airship.

After being repaired and fitted with a new metal nose at Cardington, the *R.33* was ready to take to the air again in October 1925. The hull had been adapted to carry a small de Havilland Hummingbird aeroplane, which was meant to function like a small picket boat for an ocean liner, delivering mail and vital goods. The aeroplane could also defend the mother ship if necessary. Only on the third trial flight in December did the small aeroplane manage to reattach itself to a trapeze-like device on the bottom of the airship while both were in flight. Such experiments had already been considered in 1924, when the plans were laid to build the *R.100* and *R.101*.

Although primarily intended to carry passengers and mail, it appears the military potential of giant airships had not been entirely forsaken. The *Dundee Courier* on 15 August 1924 conjectures on the possibilities of a new military role:

The damaged *R.33* arriving back at RNAS Pulham after its involuntary excursion over the North Sea. On the night of 16 April 1925, a strong wind tore the airship from its mooring mast, damaging its nose in the process. The *R.33* narrowly missed hitting one of Pulham's airship sheds as it careered out of control. The small number of crew on board eventually managed to regain control and flew it back to its base. (*Picture Norfolk*)

The chance of using Great Britain's new airships which are shortly to be laid down, as flying aerodromes, has been exercising the minds of Air Ministry experts. This would increase the range of the fighting aeroplanes from 1,000 miles to 10,000 miles or more. Actual experiments have been secretly carried out which demonstrate that an aeroplane can be launched in safety from an airship in flight and can be picked up again at the end of a trip. British airships will fulfil this function of sky aerodromes, Bombers, Fighting planes, scouts and reconnaissance machines will all be carried, ready to be launched at a favourable opportunity. It will be possible to transport a whole squadron of planes halfway round the world and then from a vantage point of comparative safety, to launch them on relatively short flight to scatter death and destruction.

Skilled tradesmen from Cardington were sent to Pulham to make the *R.36* airworthy again. Unlike the *R.33*, it had never left here when the station closed. It was intended to send the *R.36* on a non-stop flight to Ismailia, Egypt, to glean information on the effects of a tropical climate on airship fabric and gas. By August 1925, *R.36* was ready to take to the air again and the flight planned for October, but a miscalculation discovered only after the overhaul had been completed created concern that the airship did not have the necessary lift to reach its destination. The *R.33* was also supposed to make a number of overseas flights to gather information for future passenger airship services. Neither of these plans were put into action. A further blow was dealt to Pulham in January 1926, when the *R.33* crew received notice that their services were no longer needed. This was for reasons of economy, and the *R.33* was no called for for experimental work, besides. But this was not the last of the Pulham airship station.

A few months later, on 11 April 1926, Pulham received an unusual visitor—the *Norge* airship. It had flown all the way from Italy and was heading to the Arctic Island of Spitzbergen. From here, the Norwegian explorer Roald Amundsen intended to launch a flying expedition over the North Pole and then on to Alaska. Several thousand spectators had awaited the arrival of the *Norge*, but much to their dismay, its arrival was delayed over two hours as it circled over the surrounding area before landing, with several false alarms. The crew blamed their difficulties on temperature variations. A landing party of around 150 agricultural workers had been assembled to moor it, but once on the ground, their numbers were swollen by hundreds of members of the public wanting to help, too.

Both the *R.100* and *R.101* were to be based at Cardington upon completion, so additional accommodation was required, especially since there was still only one airship shed. In order to save the expense of building a second shed, it was decided to dismantle the largest shed at Pulham—No. 2—and transport it to Cardington to be rebuilt. This project was undertaken by the Cleveland Bridge and Engineering Company, and by August 1927, No. 2's external sheeting was being removed by a workforce of around 160 men. They were hampered by frequent heavy rain and for much of that month had to wear oil skins. The steel work was then placed in railway wagons and moved to Cardington, where it was re-assembled with an extra 56 feet added to its length and 35 feet to its height. Only rigid airship shed No. 1, which housed the decommissioned *R.33*, was left at Pulham.

In the Second World War, Pulham housed Maintenance Unit No. 53, which stored bombs and explosives for the RAF. On a number of occasions it was the target of German bombers. At the time full of explosives, the airship shed had a narrow escape in February 1941 when a stick of five bombs hit its roof—two of them struck its concrete floor before bouncing through the side walls and exploding. The airship shed was built with detachable panels in its walls in case of a gas explosion. These functioned equally well when two of the German bombs exploded inside the building, falling from their fixtures and greatly reducing the amount of destruction that might have been caused. Despite the raids on the shed, it survived until 1947, when the structure was dismantled for scrap by mobile cranes with 200-foot jibs. Thereafter, most of the site once occupied by the Pulham airship station progressively returned to its original function as arable farmland. There is now little evidence that it once played host to many of Britain's largest airships.

Howden Airship Station

In the years after the closure of Howden as an RAF station, many of its buildings were auctioned off and demolished. By 1924, the smaller, No. 1 rigid airship shed had vanished from the Yorkshire landscape. Only the falling price of scrap metal saved the larger double berth shed from the breaker's axe. In 1924, the Airship Guarantee Company newly formed by Vickers was awarded the contract to construct the 5,000,000-cubic-foot rigid passenger airship *R.100*. With government approval, the company purchased the double rigid airship shed at Howden in which to build it. Indeed, Vickers must have regretted the cancellation of the 900-foot-long shed at Flookburgh, which would have been a far superior facility for this project. In any case, the shed at Howden proved far from ideal, and in 1925, Airship Guarantee had to launch its renovation. Rabbits and foxes inhabited the structure; rubble from the demolished buildings lay strewn around the area; and the door clearance had to be increased by 10 feet to enable the *R.100* to fit in. It took nearly a year to return the shed to a functional state. Early on in the Imperial Airship Scheme, the Air Ministry suggested that both the *R.100* and *R.101* be constructed at Howden, but owing to the small clearance between the airships and the framework of the shed, it would difficult to conduct flying operations from here. Instead Cardington would serve as the base for the two airships when completed although it only had one rigid shed at that time.

As late as 1926, it was thought that the *R.100* and *R.101* would both be ready to operate scheduled services by the end of 1927, with a further two to join in 1929. Many of its design team at Howden moved into bungalows which were once part of the officers' quarters. Overall, the premises were far from satisfactory. There was also a problem in finding skilled workers, given Howden's rural location. Local women from the town and surrounding farms subsequently had to be trained to do many of the tasks; some were employed alongside men in the construction of the main ring frames, though most did simple riveting jobs.

Huge traverse frames were first constructed on the floor then hoisted to the roof. This was repeated with the next frame and so on. The vertical frames were then linked together by horizontal ones. They were made out of duralumin, an alloy of copper and aluminium. Such was the complexity of the framework that it took thirty men three months to varnish for protection against corrosion. Work on the airship was interrupted by industrial unrest and on several occasions strikes were called at short notice.

Both Barnes Wallis and Nevil Shute Norway were involved in designing the *R.100*. The latter, who later became a famous novelist, complained in his autobiography *Slide Rule* that the location was an unwise choice. The air was very humid and the ground often covered in puddles in winter. Even in summer, water was never very far below the surface. Often, the huge shed—which had a floor space of nearly 8 acres—was filled with mist. This caused the materials to corrode, including the duralumin framework of the airship itself. When the temperatures dropped on winter mornings, ice would cling to the *R.100*'s girders, preventing work from starting. As the airship shed stood in an exposed position, it was also feared that its roof might blow off in gale-force winds. Riggers stood by when the elements raged in case emergency repairs had to be made. During a spell of bad weather in January 1929, a horde of rats invaded the building and large quantities of poison had to be used to destroy them.

The reconditioned hydrogen plant stood next to the large airship shed. After many delays, the gas bags were inflated in the *R.100* in July 1929. The airship floated off the ground and its engines were tested while it was still inside the shed. Nevil Shute later wrote that he considered these trials far more dangerous than any flight he later undertook in the airship. In September 1929 the airship's crew arrived, and by November the *R.100* was finally ready to be handed over to the Air Ministry. The airship was allocated the civil registration G-FAAV, displayed in huge letters on its silver side. On the morning of 16 December, *R.100* saw the light of day for the first time as it was gradually extracted from its shed by 500 soldiers from York. Not long after, it soared up into a clear blue sky, never to return to Howden.

Early on in the Imperial Airship Scheme, consideration was given to the building of an airship mooring mast so that the *R.100* could be based at Howden. But this would have entailed considerable expenditure, as the soil at Howden was clay and unsuitable for supporting such a structure, necessitating reinforced foundations, and the government was reluctant to finance this venture for a private company. A further factor against the *R.100* remaining at Howden was the size of the doors of the shed which allowed very little leeway when moving the airship. In windy conditions, there was a danger that the airship may come into contact with the sides of the shed and

The concrete water tower at RNAS Howden, one of the few large airship station structures of to have survived into the twenty-first century. (*The National Archives*)

be damaged. This was why it was decided to house the *R.100* in the second airship shed at Cardington. After its successful flight to Canada, the workforce expected further orders for airships. They waited in vain. Even if the programme had continued, the government was likely to have placed them with the Royal Airship Works at Cardington, making Howden surplus to requirements anyway. The crash of the *R.101* was the final death knell for the Airship Guarantee Company and the long association of Vickers with airships. The design team at Howden was dismissed and works drawn to a close in December 1930.

Cardington Airship Station

Cardington had been used to store airships upon the government's suspension of airship-flying in 1921. The *Dundee Courier* reported the re-opening of the Royal Airship Works on 5 August 1924:

> Cardington, on the outskirts of Bedford, is to be Great Britain's airship station and the appointment of officers to supervise the construction of the new leviathan which has been sanctioned by the Government has just been made. They will proceed almost immediately to Cardington to begin their work. It is not without significance that when the Air Minister was elevated to the House of Lords he took the title of Lord Thomson of Cardington, for Cardington is destined to become the greatest airship centre in the World. It is self-contained, even to its own electric lighting and water systems and there are nearly two hundred little brick houses and flats there. Over a thousand acres of level ground are reserved for landing purposes, making an airship aerodrome that is without equal in the World.

Cardington had changed little since it was first built by the Short Brothers. Now it was about to undergo a radical transformation. In contrast to Howden and Pulham, the government practically threw money at it. The original airship shed was too small to construct the *R.101* in so it was rebuilt and extended, and the rigid airship shed from Pulham re-erected next to it. It was necessary to increase the original Cardington shed's length by 112 feet and its height by 35 feet, but was considered unnecessary to provide doors at both ends of the shed, or to arrange windbreaks beyond the doors, as in the first structure.

The Cleveland Bridge and Engineering Company was commissioned, and began the enlargement of the shed by erecting a 7-tonne steam crane on a 40-foot-high steel stage at one end. This crane was used in turn to assemble another much taller travelling stage, 120-feet-high, with two 10-tonne steam cranes on top running on a double track. The original sliding doors were in four leaves, each of which was operated by means of a capstan. To open them took about half an hour and required the efforts of a large number of men. New doors replaced the originals, which six persons could open in 10 minutes.

The extended shed had a concrete floor that spanned 4¾ acres. The walls were covered in galvanised corrugated sheeting with numerous large windows, so that natural light flooded the interior. Conversely, electric lights in gas-tight fittings and portable floodlights provided artificial illumination. Ventilation louvres ran the full length of the roof to prevent the natural accumulation of gas. Work on the airship shed began in October 1924 and was completed by May 1926, without any serious accidents. The rigid airship shed transferred from Pulham was erected in 1928 also by the Cleveland Bridge and Engineering Company.

The most iconic of all the airship structures was the Cardington mooring tower, completed the same year that work finished on the enlarged shed. A machinery house was located next to its base and contained three steam-driven winches which could haul cable in at the rate of 50 feet per minute. It would have been the first of many mooring masts had the Imperial Airship Scheme come to fruition. Much of the experimental work for it had been undertaken at Pulham, where rigid airships remained attached to the tall slender steel mast for days on end. The tower built at Cardington was a much more elaborate structure.

In November 1926, the *R.33* airship flew from Pulham to Cardington to become the first airship to moor at the new tower. It carried out a series of comprehensive tests, several times attaching and slipping from it, and successfully carried out experiments with parachutes and Gloster Grebes here. It would, however, be another three years before an airship returned to the skies over Cardington.

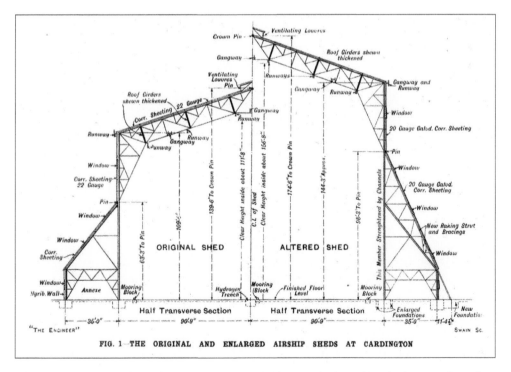

FIG. 1—THE ORIGINAL AND ENLARGED AIRSHIP SHEDS AT CARDINGTON

This diagram shows how the original First World War rigid airship shed was enlarged to facilitate the assembly of the *R.101*. (*The Engineer*)

The large brick-built workshops at Cardington. Most airship stations engaged in the construction of airships had to make do with much less impressive premises. (*Bedfordshire and Luton Archives*)

Airship shed No.1 at Cardington being rebuilt and enlarged for the construction of the *R.101*, February 1926. (*Bedfordshire and Luton Archives*)

With the extension of the original airship shed at Cardington, Britain now had the largest airship shed in the world, in which was going to be built the largest airship in the world. The first structural parts for the *R.101* began to arrive at Cardington in the summer of 1926 and by November, two thirds of its components were finished. Unlike previous rigid airships copied from crashed Zeppelins, the *R.101* was a totally new design. It incorporated many innovative features which resulted in substantial delays, and it was not until June 1928 that assembly finally began. While most of the press published jingoistic articles about the Empire Airship Scheme, some commentators questioned the amount of money being spent on it. One of them was Edward Spanner, who once worked for the Royal Corps of Naval Constructors. Cdr Burney dismissed his objections by pointing out that flying an airship is so different to sailing a ship on the sea that one cannot make the comparison.

The *R.101* eventually emerged from its shed on 12 October 1929 and was attached to the mooring tower. Extra police were drafted into the district to help control the traffic, as hoards of spectators descended on Cardington to catch a glimpse—cars were parked along the roads for 10 miles. Two days later, the *R.101* slipped its mooring cables and made its first test flight, around three years later than planned when the project commenced in 1924. On 21 October 1929, an approaching gale meant the airship had to be returned to the safety of its shed. A handling party was assembled, consisting of 150 RAF personnel from Henlow, fifty unemployed from Bedford, and 200 employees of the Royal Airship Works. The giant airship was then walked from the mooring tower to its shed, a distance of nearly a mile. While this operation was being performed, all traffic on the neighbouring roads was stopped in order that no noise should not interfere with the orders being shouted. By the end of the year, the *R.101* had completed a total of six test flights. Meanwhile its rival, the *R.100*, had been finished and was ready to take to the air, though its first flight was delayed as the *R.101* occupied the sole mooring tower at Cardington.

The *R.100 and R.101*'s journeys illustrate how dependent rigid airships were on their supporting infrastructure, such as the large sheds needed to house them and mooring masts. Their programme of development was dictated by the availability of these structures, and the *R.101* had to be removed from the Cardington mooring mast and placed back in its shed before the *R.100* could make its first flight.

When on 16 December 1929 the *R.100* arrived at Cardington, difficulty was encountered in mooring it. It took three attempts to connect the steel cable dropped from the nose of the airship to the cable from the mooring mast laid out on the ground below. The following day, the airship made a test flight over the surrounding countryside and was then placed in the shed alongside the *R.101*. Early the next year, both airships resumed their test flights. In April 1930, the *LZ-127* Graf Zeppelin paid a brief visit to Cardington. The *R.100* was attached to the mooring mast at the time, so the Graf Zeppelin had to land on the ground. The crews of the *R.100* and *R.101* led the handling party and, once the airship was safely down, crowds of spectators rushed towards it. This was a fleeting visit, as the *LZ-127* departed the same day.

After dark, the mooring mast was illuminated with red and white lights. When an airship was flying, the landing ground would be floodlit while searchlights shone

The *R.100* approaching the mooring mast at Cardington at the end of its maiden flight from Howden. (*The Press Association*)

beams of light into the sky. The *R.100* departed for Canada in the dark at 3.30 a.m. on 29 July 1930. This was the first transatlantic flight by a British airship since the *R.34* flew to New York some eleven years earlier. Two and a half weeks later, the *R.100* returned to a jubilant reception:

> There was a steady stream of traffic towards the landing base during the morning and there was a huge crowd present when the airship was sighted by telescope from the Crow's Nest of the mooring mast at 10.45 a.m. Suddenly, the silver nose appeared through clouds on the south-western horizon. A moment afterwards the *R.100* was lost in clouds for a few seconds. Then it came into sight again, its prow gleaming silver in the sunlight. Its stern was half hidden in the shroud of clouds. Slowly it came nearer until the whole bulk was revealed. When the air monster was within a mile of the tower, with her propellers slowly revolving, she cast down her landing hawser and this was clamped to the similar hawser from the crest of the tower. Thus she was gradually drawn nearer and nearer to her haven. 'What a great triumph of scientific engineering', commented Lord Thomson, the Air Minister, who watched the proceedings from the masthead.

During the summer, the *R.101* undertook a series of test flights as well as appearing at the RAF Hendon Air Display. It was found that it was nose heavy, and its performance well below what was required; it was therefore returned to its shed for major modifications. After being lengthened by the insertion of a new section, *R.101* took to the air again on 1 October 1930 on a test flight.

The *R.100* attached to the mooring mast at Cardington on 26 April 1930. In the background is the *Graf Zeppelin*, arriving on its courtesy visit. (*Bedfordshire and Luton Archives*)

Around 550 men were engaged in taking it out of its shed to the mooring mast and then taking the *R.100* from the shed where it was housed to that recently vacated by the *R.101*. In early 1931, the *R.100* was to be overhauled before resuming flying. With the airship programme well behind schedule, Lord Thompson was nonetheless keen to prove their worth. Although no rigid British airship had ever flown anywhere near the tropics, the *R.101* was earmarked to travel to India even before it had finished its trials. The *R.33* or *R.36* should have acted as pathfinders for such a venture, but were never given the chance to do so for lack of finance.

On 4 October, having made only one test flight since its major modification, the *R.101* detached itself from the mooring mast at and headed to India. The Certificate of Air Worthiness was handed to the captain only minutes before departure. The *R.101* never got beyond France. On a wet and windy night, it crashed into a hillside at Beauvais. Among the forty-eight lives lost were Lord Thompson, Sir Sefton Brancker—Director of Civil Aviation—and Col. V. Richmond—the airship's designer. It was difficult to believe that such a disaster could happen, and implausible explanations were put forward—that the *R.101* had been sabotaged or that it was struck by a meteorite. The exact cause of the crash has never been determined, but the design of the *R.101* is the most often cited. This may well have been a contributing factor, but the weather it encountered early on its flight may equally have destroyed any airship.

The *R.101* on the mooring mast at Cardington. As if to underscore this lost world, teams of horses haul carts with timber along the road in the foreground. (*Bedfordshire and Luton Archives*)

Air turbulence and downdraughts associated with rainstorms were not fully understood until many decades later. The *R.101* disaster was the final curtain for the airship industry. There would not be another flight by a large British rigid airship for the rest of the twentieth century.

14

Imperial Airship Routes

Long before either the *R.100* or *R.101* had flown, work was underway to set up bases from which the giant airships could operate. In the mid-1920s, the Air Ministry sent small parties to Scout out potential sites across the British Empire. At the same time, an extensive investigation was carried out into the weather that would be encountered along the air routes. This work was to be a lasting legacy of the Imperial Airship Scheme. Many of the locations selected to serve as mooring bases of passenger airships had been suggested shortly after the end of the First World War. These facilities were essential not only for disembarking passengers, but for refuelling and re-inflating the airship with hydrogen. Sir Sefton Branker, then Director of Civil Aviation, gave this insight into the influences determining the choice of passenger airship routes:

> It is not so important to avoid great heat or great cold in airship flying as it is to avoid alternations of high and low temperatures. It is also advisable to use routes which do not involve great heights. Very hot days with very cold nights, such as are met with especially in certain regions traversed by high mountain ranges, limit the radius of an airship materially and necessitate the establishment of a greater number of stations where gas and ballast can be replenished, heat causes the gas in the gas bags to expand and when that occurs the surplus gas escapes through the safety valve. Then when the temperature becomes cold at night, the gas in the gas bags contracts, making it necessary to throw out ballast in order to maintain the airship at a proper height. Consequently, in those circumstances, there is a continuous loss of gas and ballast which quickly makes it impossible for the airship to proceed until she is replenished at a station where these two essentials have been previously stored. Hence the importance of avoiding as far as possible regions which are both hot and mountainous.[1]

Towards the end of the 1920s, three large facilities for British airships had been built in Canada, Egypt, and India.

Canada

As dawn was breaking on the morning of 1 August 1930, the *R.100* gradually manoeuvred itself into position to hook up with the mooring mast at St Hubert's aerodrome near Montreal. This was the first and last time a British passenger airship ventured to the lands of the Empire. As testimony to its design, the *R.100* had flown through a storm which few other airships would have survived. The voyage could not have generated a greater interest with the citizens of Canada: as the airship flew over Quebec City, 40,000 or more spectators cheered and waved as it flew overhead. This number was dwarfed by the 600,000 who came to see it at St Hubert, some from as far away as the west coast. 'To the Canadians, the R.100 was a magnificent gesture sent to them by the mother country';[2] every hotel in Montreal was full, and a special railway siding was even built by the Canadian Pacific Railway to transport passengers to the aerodrome.

Around 3,000 people were given the opportunity to go aboard the *R.100*. This was not for the faint hearted, as a gap of around 2 feet between the airship's gangway and the tower platform had to be negotiated. The Air Ministry had not sent the necessary drawings of the gangway or the platform for the airship tower, either, which left the design of the remote-control mooring winches to improvisation. After undertaking a series of local flights over eastern Canada with government officials and senior military officers, the *R.100* departed for Britain on the 13th. Many expected to see it return within a few months.

The planning for this voyage started many years earlier. Maj. Scott and Mr Gibbs covered 5,800 miles by rail and 1,300 miles by road investigating potential sites for an airship base in eastern Canada. Their efforts were concentrated around the major cities. The Connaught Range, a training centre for the Canadian armed forces 10 miles east of Ottawa, was short-listed, but airships could not have used this base while the firing range was in use. On the plus side, the Canadian National Railway ran close by and there were no obstructions that might endanger a landing airship. The main drawback was a lack of land for building an airship shed. Valcartier Camp, 13 miles to the north of Quebec, had a flat area of about 1 square mile. The site was covered with Canadian moss, which gave the ground a smooth surface. The main disadvantage here was that four hills were roughly situated at the four corners of the ground which would produce currents over the aerodrome, affecting the airship during mooring operations.

The mayor of Toronto was very keen to ensure that the mooring mast be located near his city, but the potential sites did not impress Maj. Scott. A visit was also made to the Atlantic coast to investigate the possibility of establishing an airship base there, despite it being so remote. Two sites were inspected near Halifax, but the ground was very rough and the area too restricted, even for a mooring mast, let alone any other large buildings. The same applied to North Sydney and Sydney Mines. The ground here was either too boggy or would have required extensive rock cutting and its removal. Montreal officials showed Scott and Gibbs a prospective site at Maisonneuve Park. It was much too small, but while motoring over the district between Longueuil and St Hubert, the party encountered several areas of ground which were thought suitable. Finally, a triangular area of ground covering 750 acres on the south bank of the St Lawrence River at St Hubert was purchased. In the summer of 1927, construction of a large aerodrome for Montreal began here on what were once ploughed fields. According to the *Montreal Gazette* on 7 April 1928,

The mooring mast at St Hubert, Canada, October 1929. (*The National Archives*)

Chosen primarily on account of its suitability for a terminus of the contemplated transatlantic airship service, this airport will be one of the most efficient on the continent for heavier than air machines when finished. The mooring mast will be erected at the northern corner of the field, furthest removed from the railroad tracks to obviate any danger of locomotive sparks falling in the vicinity of the gas bag. The southern apex of the aerodrome will be occupied by a hotel with restaurant. Space is also being reserved for the erection of an airship shed should it decided that such is necessary.

However, there was one hazard in this otherwise flat area—the spire of St Hubert's Church. Fearing for the safety of his building as well as that of night-time aviators, the priest had a 'fiery cross' installed on top of the spire to make it visible at night. In preparation for the first airships, a small team from the Royal Canadian Navy spent eighteen months training at Cardington. At 205 feet, the steel mooring mast was a few feet taller but otherwise an almost exact copy of that built at Cardington, England, and was constructed by Canadian Vickers. The winch drums for the nose mooring held 2,000 feet of cable. The 143-foot-high platform was fitted with searchlights to illuminate anchorages on the ground and generally assist with airship mooring at night. A lift would take passengers to the top of the mast for embarkation. The mast was painted in a striking black and chrome colour scheme to enhance its visibility, in a similar fashion to the pylons used in the Schneider Air Race. A hydrogen plant was constructed which could supply 60,000 cubic feet of gas per hour, and it was anticipated that one-tenth of the gas of an airship would need to be replenished after a flight across the Atlantic.

After the *R.100*'s visit, the mooring mast was never used again. Had a regular airship service been established to serve Canada, its cold winters may have posed a problem. While a large airship could ride out many forms of weather when attached to its mooring mast, it was still vulnerable to heavy falls of snow and freezing weather, which could make it top heavy and liable to come into contact with the ground. The Premier of New Brunswick travelled from his province to tour the *R.100* when it arrived at St Hubert, and declared that he would strongly support the building of a mast in New Brunswick. It was hinted that this would possibly become the winter terminus for the transatlantic airship service to enable airships to avoid the harsh conditions experienced in the interior of the country. Only sites in Eastern Canada had been investigated as potential airship bases, as it was believed that aeroplanes would provide passenger feeder services from the western provinces to St Hubert. However, by the late 1930s it was decided that St Hubert's mooring mast represented a menace to aeroplanes, and on 13 January 1938, it was demolished using explosives. It was immortalised in the 'Frog' model of the *R.100*, one of the few plastic kits ever made of an airship. St Hubert aerodrome still exists, principally servicing domestic Canadian air routes.

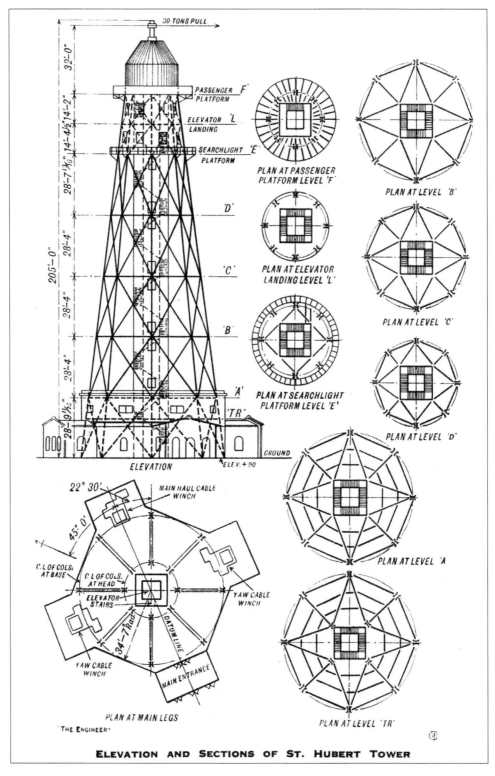

Elevation and sections of the St Hubert tower (or mooring mast) in Canada. Similar structures were built at Cardington, Ismailia, and Karachi. (*The Engineer*)

Bermuda

Had a comprehensive network of routes linking the far-flung colonies of the British Empire been established, it is likely that, in time, Bermuda would have had its own airship base. The island would have been ideally located as a stepping stone for routes to the USA and the Caribbean. In February 1925, the giant American airship *Los Angeles* flew from Lakehurst, New Jersey, to Bermuda in 12 hours. Due to strong winds it could not land and instead dropped its cargo of letters. It then spent several hours circling the island before heading back home. If the flight had gone as planned the *Los Angeles* would have landed and attached itself to the 'special mooring mast' erected on the stern of the fleet oiler *Patoka*. A map of Imperial Airship routes drawn up in 1926 included Jamaica—then a British possession—as a destination for passenger airship services, but no survey was undertaken to investigate possible sites for a base here.

Egypt and Malta

In the first plans for Imperial Airship routes, Cairo was the preferred location for a base in Egypt. By the time the *R.100* and *R.101* were under construction, Ismailia—located halfway up the Suez Canal—was favoured as the first stop for an airship on its way to India. Earlier plans had proposed a number of intermediate airship bases in Europe on the way to Africa, including Malta in the Mediterranean. This idea was resurrected in September 1930, when it was realised that the airship's performance fell below expectations and that, if it was carrying a full complement of passengers, the journey would have to be broken sooner. Funds were provided for the construction of a mooring mast in September 1930, which would presumably have been built on the site selected for an RAF airship station at the end of the First World War. According to one newspaper article, there were plans to eventually build seventeen mooring masts along the route to India, so no airship flying this route would be more than 150 miles distant from one. A proposed airship base at Aden (Yemen) was one nebulous example.

Unlike the airship mast at Malta, the one at Ismailia, Egypt actually was constructed. Six hundred acres of level ground on the edge of the desert were acquired. Landing grounds for aeroplanes had already been established in the vicinity. The 200-foot mooring mast was of similar size and design to that at Cardington and St Hubert, and would be fitted with searchlights that would flash over the desert throughout the night as a navigational aid. A new railway was planned to transport disembarked passengers to Cairo and Port Said. Unlike some other airship bases along the Imperial Airship route, there were no plans to erect an airship shed here, but a silicol hydrogen plant that could produce one million cubic feet of hydrogen per day was completed. The base was under the command of an officer from the Royal Airship Works at Cardington, who had a number of RAF personnel to assist him. Local Egyptians were employed to assist in operating the mooring facilities. In 1929, a request was made by Germany for the *Graf Zeppelin* to use the newly completed mooring mast at Ismailia

The mooring mast at Ismailia, Egypt, August 1926. (*The National Archives*)

on a flight to the Mediterranean. Britain denied the request, as the Air Ministry did not want an airship from a rival power to be the first to use its new mast. A large banquet was to be held on board the *R.101* the following year, when it arrived in Egypt on its next voyage from Cardington, bound for India. This was not to be, for it crashed *en route*. The airship mast at Ismailia was still standing in 1939. An article in *Flight* around that time suggests that the Royal Navy considered using the mast at Ismailia as a base for rigid airships patrolling the sea lanes against enemy surface raiders.

India

While Australia and New Zealand would eventually become the Imperial Airships' final destinations, India was given immediate priority in receiving the first scheduled services. By 1925, Karachi (then in India) had been selected as a terminus in preference to Bombay, because thunderstorms were less frequent there. The site, 13 miles east of Karachi, was near sea level and experienced climatic conditions that would provide extra lift for the airships. The Indian Air Board recommended that a mooring mast was essential for Bombay as well, and that a site for Calcutta ought also to be considered.

The airship base at Karachi in October 1929. The mooring mast is visible on the right and the giant airship shed beyond it. (*The National Archives*)

Work commenced on the airship base at Karachi in 1926. It was to have an airship shed of far grander dimensions than Ismailia—850 feet long and 170 feet tall, high enough to house Nelson's Column—so that it could accommodate the next generation of airships, including the 822-foot-long *R.102*. As there were no major iron and steel works in India at that time, all the components had to be imported from Britain. The steelwork was fabricated at the Germiston Works, Glasgow, and the Armstrong Construction Company was awarded the contract for the shed's construction. On 9 October 1926, the first piece of structural steelwork was hoisted into position in the presence of many distinguished guests. The ceremony was performed by Mrs T. C. Frampton, the wife of the agent of the Armstrong Construction Company. Local labour was used in the on-site construction. Working on such tall structures was not without danger—the senior Indian supervisor, Mackinwalla, fell to his death from the top of the structure early in 1927.

The shed was constructed along the lines of previous airship sheds except that, despite its size and the 4,000 tonnes of milled steel in its structure, the government contract stated it should be capable of being dismantled and erected in another location. This requirement was met by restricting the weight of each assembled piece to a maximum of 12 tonnes. Another departure from standard airship shed design was that it had doors at only one end. Its door frame was also entirely separate from the

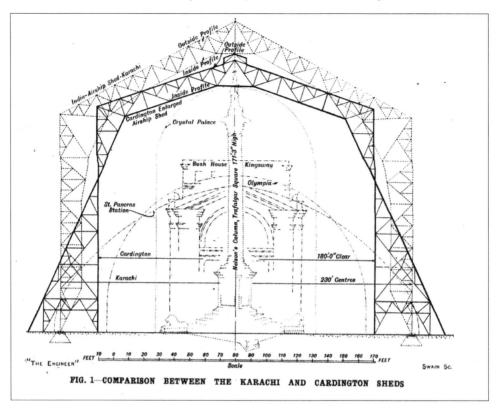

FIG. 1—COMPARISON BETWEEN THE KARACHI AND CARDINGTON SHEDS

A comparison of the Karachi and Cardington sheds. (*The Engineer*)

rest of the structure. A huge girder, 315 feet long, ran across the front of the building, holding the two enormous doors—91 feet wide and 171 feet high—in place. In good weather, the doors could be opened by electric power winches in 8–10 minutes. Once completed, the airship shed was the biggest structure in the British Empire, and dwarfed the surrounding countryside.

The construction of a mooring mast along the lines of that at Cardington was started in 1929 and completed in August 1930. It was not an exact copy, for there was an octagonal complex of buildings around its base. To transport passengers, an 8-mile railway spur was built. Karachi Airport has a railway station which in the 1920s—before the airport was built—was known as 'Airship'. Finally, a hydrogen plant was erected along with gas holders that could store enough hydrogen gas to completely fill the *R.101*. Even before this airship departed on its fatal voyage, some sceptics thought that it would not get beyond Egypt and that Karachi was one mooring mast too far. Meteorologists were of the opinion that the weather was set against a successful flight if the *R.101* were to depart in the autumn as planned. The Director of Airship Development had also urged additional mooring masts be built at Athens and Basra on the Persian Gulf before the *R.101* left Britain.

By 1929, the giant Karachi airship shed and mooring mast were complete. Neither was ever used by an airship of any type. Nonetheless, eighteen men were employed until 1939 to maintain the facility. Until 1934, the giant airship shed served as a

The mooring mast for the airship station at Karachi. This had a similar design to Cardington's, the main difference being that it had a large brick building at its base. (*The National Archives*)

The giant airship shed at Karachi under construction. (*The National Archives*)

sports arena for British soldiers. Sheltered from the blazing sun, two games of football could be played at once. It is also rumoured that the building hosted polo games, too. It finally assumed an aeronautical role when Imperial Airways took it over as an aeroplane hangar and workshop.

In the Second World War, the giant structure was used by both the RAF and US Army Forces for repairing aircraft involved in operations in Burma and Indochina. The US Navy did investigate the possibility of using it as a base for its airships in the closing stages of the conflict, but this idea did not progress any further. On 1 August 1952, Pakistan Aviation issued a tender to demolish the *Kala Chapra*—the 'Black Shed', as it was locally known. The structure lingered on for nearly ten more years before its destruction began in earnest. The steel was used on railway structures and bridges across Pakistan. In the early twenty-first century, the aviation legacy of the site lives on: Pakistan International Airlines has its wide-bodied aircraft hangar close to the grounds once occupied by the giant airship shed.

Rangoon, Burma

Although Australia was meant to be the next destination for Imperial airships beyond India, there were ambitions to extend the network eastwards instead, possibly as far as China. In the 1920s, Burma was a British possession, and investigation into possible sites for an airship base were carried out around the then capital, Rangoon (now Yangon).

Ceylon (Sri Lanka)

The British Airship Mission arrived at the capital, Colombo, on 11 October 1927 to survey possible sites for an airship base. It was speculated that as well as carrying passengers and mail, cargoes of tea, cocoa, and precious stones could also be transported by airship. It was predicted that Ceylon would in time become a junction linking air services to Europe, Australia, New Zealand, and the Far East. The survey mission spent a week travelling around the island, visiting towns such as Trincomalee on the coast and Kandy in the central area—which was to be avoided as a location for airship bases due to its altitude and the undulating nature of the land. The main criterion for a suitable site was the expected meteorological conditions. Other decisive factors were an adequate water supply, convenient access to the commercial centre of the island, and 'the general salubriousness of the district'.[3] The latter condition ruled out areas south of Trincomalee and north of Chilaw, as well as much of the south of the Island, as the malaria prevalent in these regions represented a serious hazard to the European staff of the station.

Exposure to storms was to be minimised, even if this meant the site being some distance from Ceylon's major towns. It was of fundamental importance that airships should maintain a reliable schedule and not be subject to weather delays. There was no experience in operating large airships in tropical conditions, so it was deemed necessary that more meteorological data be obtained before any decision was made. In the meantime, several sites were short-listed, most of which were on the west coast. Negombo and Mount Lavinia were deemed the best options, each a short distance from Colombo. Although land was more expensive here than elsewhere, it was thought that this factor would not influence the final location, as the facility would enhance the economy of Ceylon. An area of around 1,200 acres was recommended, so that in time three or four mooring masts could be erected on it. Each airship required a tower to itself. Contrary to India, construction work on an airship base never was begun in Ceylon.

Cocos Islands (Keeling Islands)

This cluster of twenty-seven small islands—uninhabited until the 1820s—was strategically placed, about halfway between India and Australia in the Indian Ocean. John Clunies Ross settled here and planted hundreds of coconut palms for copra. The Cocos Islands were so isolated that Lt Nixon, who was tasked with surveying the islands in 1927 for possible use as an airship base, had great difficulty in finding a passenger ship that would divert to the archipelago. Ship owners were reluctant to approach the islands for fear of running aground on its reefs, and while transferring to a small boat, Lt Nixon fell into the sea. The most suitable location for an airship mast was deemed to be the West (Ross) Island, 5 miles long and 850 yards wide. The other

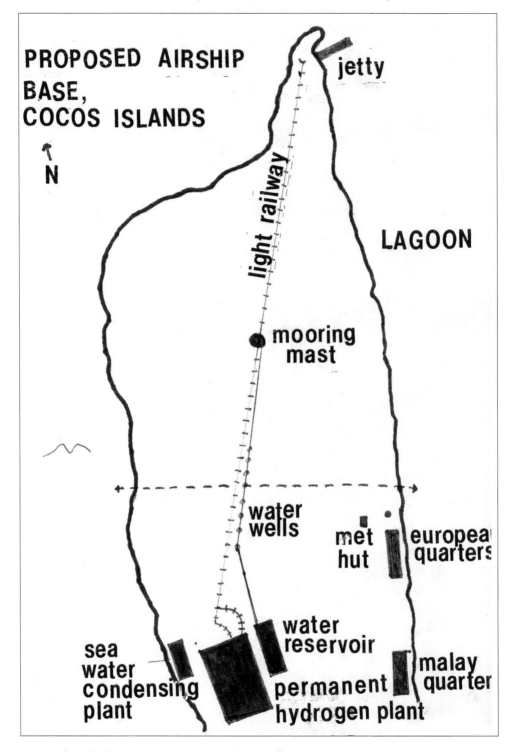

Proposed airship base, Cocos Islands. (*Author's collection*)

islands were either too small or had huts on them. Many cocoa trees would have to be felled for the new airship base. Another problem to be overcome was a supply of fresh water, which was necessary as ballast—sea water was unsuitable because it corroded the fabric of airships. Sinking wells would partially overcome this problem.

Any mooring mast on the West Island would have to be re-enforced to withstand hurricanes, as in 1909 it had been battered by winds of 150 mph. It was suggested that European living quarters, offices, and shops should be positioned facing the cool south-easterly Trade Winds. The type of hydrogen plant for the base would be determined by whether the Cocos Islands would serve for emergencies or as a regular refuelling station. In the former case, a silicol plant was recommended, as this would have been the cheapest method of production. If a permanent base was to be built, the high capital cost and heavy maintenance charges of an iron contact plant would have been justified. Cheap supplies of coke could be obtained from Durban. Finally, an airship base would have attracted tourist traffic. There would have been few more chimerical visions in the 1920s than a large silver airship approaching its mooring mast on a tropical island over a coral sea. Unfortunately, plans for airship base on the Cocos Islands remained just this.

South Africa

The introduction of an airship service was given the same priority in South Africa as it was in India. This was a valuable British colony at the time, renowned for its vast mineral wealth. The Director of Civil Aviation, Sir Sefton Brancker, believed that once a reliable service to South Africa was established, the gold-mining industry would be prepared to send a tonne of gold a day by that route. Tourists would also be attracted by the beautiful scenery and the prospect of big game hunting. In 1904, the press reported that African pygmies at the St Louis World's Fair in the USA were negotiating for the purchase of an airship with which to hunt elephants! The airship mission first set foot in South Africa in April 1927, counting Lt Nixon—who had investigated sites in several other countries—among its party.

Johannesburg was ruled out at an early stage because of its climate and surrounding terrain. A coastal location was preferred, so several sites near Cape Town and Durban were given to inspection. At the former, four sites were noted for their suitability. One was near Milnerton Aerodrome, where it was thought there would be ample room for expansion in the future, including space for an airship repair shed. But it had a number of disadvantages, too: it was 12 miles from Cape Town and there were 800-foot wireless masts in the vicinity. Kraaifontein, a short distance north-east of Cape Town and close to a mainline railway, was another contender, but the airship mission preferred Rietvlei, near the coast. This was not far from Milnerton but had the advantage of being 4-8 miles further away from Table Mountain, a serious hazard in cloudy or foggy weather. There was ample room to erect an airship shed, though high winds at certain times of the year would have proven a problem. Being adjacent to the coast, the airship base could also have been served by flying boats.

At Durban, two possible sites were selected in the surrounding region. The first was at Isipingo, 8 miles to the south; the second was at Groutville, 48 miles to the north which was deemed to be more suitable. The open nature of the land there would enable any approaching storms to be spotted in time and an airship warned in advance. The land was owned by the Charlotte Dale Native Mission and could be obtained at a reasonable price. While Cape Town was the preferred terminus for the Imperial Airship route, Groutville was selected for the first mooring mast in South Africa because an airship flying down the east coast of Africa only had the range to reach Durban. This station would act as a stop-gap on the way to Cape Town.

> The mooring tower which it is proposed to erect in South Africa is of steel lattice work construction, approximately 200 feet high. Powerful winches are installed for the purpose of hauling the airship to her moorings and whilst at anchor, provision is made for pumping water for ballasting purposes, fuel oil and hydrogen gas to the ship. In short, the mast or tower is analogous to a harbour for surface ships and provides a ready means for landing and embarking passengers and freight and for the taking on board of necessary fuel and supplies.[4]

Accommodation quarters were to be constructed for 103 persons. The personnel included thirteen mooring mast crew, eighteen hydrogen plant workers, eight meteorological staff and four wireless operators. Provision was also to be made for housing the crew of visiting airships. 200,000 gallons of water was to be available at any one time.

The airship mission also pointed out to the South African government that a mooring mast in their country was indispensable as an intermediate base for Australian and New Zealand services. An outward trip by airship via India was almost impossible because of the meteorological conditions, whereas, going via South Africa, advantage could be taken of the prevailing west-to-east winds. The South-African administration was apparently persuaded by the airship mission while it was there and placed an order for the mooring mast, its mooring head, and a hydrogen plant, all to be fabricated in England. The Railway Department was given the task of creating the airship station. The airship mission then set sail for Australia. The mooring mast was never built, but the mechanical mast head is rumoured to have made it as far as Aden, where it may have been spotted lying forlorn during the Second World War.

East Africa

While South Africa was going to be the first destination on the African continent to be served by airships flying from Ismailia, there were many other British colonies—Kenya, Tanganyika, and North and South Rhodesia, for instance—*en route*. It was in fact possible to fly the entire length of Africa over British territory. But none of these other countries held the same status as South Africa. Several locations were surveyed with the intention of establishing a number of intermediate airship stations at Mombasa, Zanzibar, and Dar-el-Salaam. All were on the coast, where the weather conditions were less hostile to airship operations than in the interior. Plans were formed to erect two mooring masts at Mombasa.

West Africa

The preferred route by which to traverse Africa from north to south was via the east coast. The main drawbacks of the west coast were that much of the territory was in the hands of foreign powers, and that the weather conditions were less stable. An airship service on this route was also dependent on a Spanish consortium—which included the Zeppelin Company—providing mooring facilities in the Canary Islands. Bathurst (now Banjul), capital of Gambia, then a British colony, was one of the few sites considered on the mainland. More improbably, a couple of remote islands in the middle of the South Atlantic were also surveyed.

In March 1927, a member of the Planning and Organisation Section of the Airship Development Department boarded the SS *Llanstephan Castle* at Tenerife for Cape Town. It stopped on the way at Ascension Island, but no passengers were allowed ashore. The only reconnaissance possible was from the deck of the ship, which found that there would be little chance of finding a suitable site for an airship base in the island's mountainous terrain, even for emergency use only. The next stop was at St Helena, where the situation looked hardly more promising, but at least the surveyor managed to get ashore for 3 hours. Almost the entire 10-mile-long island was occupied by mountains and deep ravines. Only the plains on the road from Jamestown to Longwood provided flat land. It was concluded that St Helena Island was unsuitable; if an emergency landing ground was established here, it was emphasised that it should only be used in extreme cases.

Australia

If everything had gone as planned, airship trials would have been made to Egypt and India in the first half of 1929, to be followed by demonstration flights to Canada and South Africa later in the year. It was predicted that trial flights to Egypt and India would be continued and include a demonstration voyage to Australia and possibly New Zealand in 1930. Regular flights to the antipodes would have to wait for several more years. Still, the airship mission arrived in Australia in June 1927. Their stay in the country was twice as long as planned, in part because the Australian Prime Minister asked the party to give a series of lectures to the public informing them of the purpose of their visit.

Perth and Fremantle were the first regions to be surveyed. The west coast had a high priority, as it would be the first landfall for an airship flying from either India or South Africa. The main factor influencing the choice of a site here were the Darling Hills running parallel to the coast. On the other hand, the airship mission wished to avoid a location next to the sea itself, for it would be exposed to the full force of the winds off the Indian Ocean. The maximum desired altitude was 100 feet above sea level, which would enable an airship to depart with a maximum load—the higher the point of departure, the smaller the load that could be carried. Rockingham stood as candidate, at an advantage due to its ample room for potential expansion. Victoria Park, Queens Park, and Midland Junction were closer to Perth, but the land prices were higher and the sites somewhat restricted in size.

The preferred location was at Jandakot, about halfway between Fremantle and Perth, where over 1,000 acres of scrub and forested ground available. Although a plan showing no less than three airship mooring masts was drawn up, it was intended initially to erect just one, requiring only 130 acres of land. Additional ground would have to be cleared around the landing area to reduce the threat from bush fires. Another point in favour of Jandakot was that the rail line from Fremantle ran past it. This would enable oil and coke to be easily transported from the port to the airship base.

On 12 July, the airship mission departed on board the Australian Prime Minister's personal train for Melbourne. Such was his interest in the Imperial Airship Scheme that he conducted discussions with the British delegation while travelling. At Adelaide, land to the north near Salisbury Aerodrome was thought to meet the requirements for airship operations. Tasmania, although not on the original schedule, was also paid a visit but the mission was not enthusiastic about what it found here. Much of the island was covered by rugged terrain and had few flat stretches, even along the coast. Seven Mile Beach at Hobart was thought to be acceptable, as it could be approached over the sea. Both Sydney and Melbourne were high on the priority as locations for major airship bases. The climate at Sydney was less favourable for operations than either Melbourne or Perth, since it was prone to thunderstorms as well as sudden changes of wind and temperature, and the Blue Mountains to the west caused disturbance to the air currents. The civil aerodrome at Mascot was considered too small, and that at Richmond too close to hills. Finally, a suitable area was found in the Riverstone District near Marsden, which had been cleared of trees and shrubs.

Choice around Melbourne was limited by the hills that flanked it to the north and east. Also, the airship mission wished to avoid a location directly next to the sea. The most suitable areas were found south of Dandenong or to the west between the railway lines to Ballarat and Geelong. There was some concern that the railways may be electrified and the power cables would represent a hazard to airships, so it was a requirement that there should be no overhead electric cables within 4 miles of an airship mooring mast. The area around Cowie and Green Hill were thought most appropriate. A plan was even drawn showing the possible layout of an airship base for Melbourne with three mooring masts and a large two-berthed airship shed. A similar number of masts were proposed for Sydney, but it was initially planned to build only one airship base on the east side of Australia, for which Melbourne was the most likely choice.

If the Imperial Airship route were to extend to New Zealand, Melbourne was better placed to serve it than Sydney. There was also talk of running a further service to Tasmania, possibly by an Australian company, for which Melbourne was, again, ideally placed. The capital city of Canberra was dropped from consideration as a

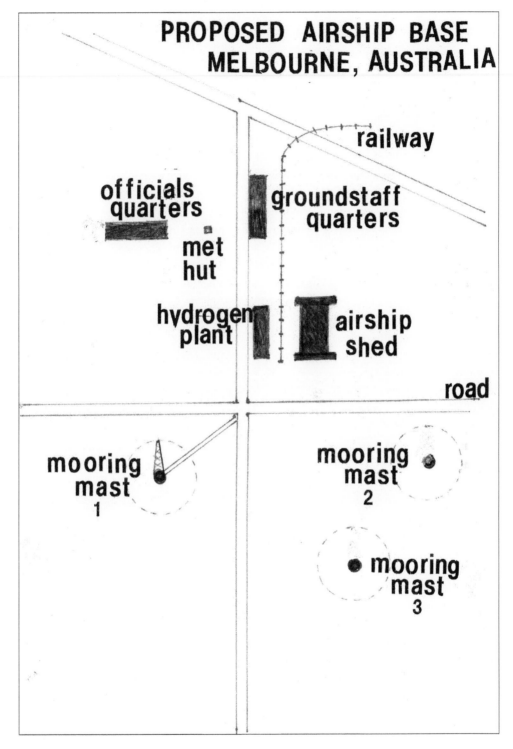

Proposed airship base, Melbourne, Australia. (*Author's collection*)

landing ground at an early stage because it was surrounded by hills. The airship mission then left for New Zealand. Unlike Egypt and India, the proposals never proceeded beyond the planning stage. Melbourne never would become the junction of an airship network.

New Zealand

New Zealand would have been the furthermost destination of the Imperial Airship service. If a comprehensive network of air routes had been developed, it may in time have been extended across the Pacific Ocean, from New Zealand to Canada. The airship mission arrived at the end of August 1927 and spent just over two weeks searching for suitable sites. The South Island was ruled out because of its mountainous nature and sparse population. A number of areas on the North Island, including Hamilton, were examined from the air, and while several large flatlands were observed, they were nevertheless thought too close to the mountains. Wellington was ruled out for this very reason.

Attention was drawn to Auckland, the main population centre. A number of sites here were short-listed, but while they could accommodate a mooring mast, they did not have the room for an airship shed. Eventually, a low-lying plain between the settlements of Bulls and Sanson to the north-east of Wellington was selected, and plans showing the possible locations of three mooring masts as well as a large airship shed drawn up. The airship mission recommended that the following staff be sent for training at an established airship base, fifteen months before the first airship arrived:

One official in charge of base and mooring operation.
Two control men for engine-room telegraphing and signalling.
One mechanical engineer in charge of winch plant and pumps.
One electrician in charge and to become acquainted with electrical gear.
Two hydrogen plant men (foreman and assistant foreman).

To the surprise of the airship mission, a letter was received from the New Zealand Prime Minister a few months later, rejecting the choice of site. He complained that there were numerous electric power lines in the area, and that they would have to be re-laid underground for a radius of 4 miles if the project went ahead. Instead, he proposed two sites a few miles to the north as alternatives. One had already been rejected by the airship mission on the grounds that the surrounding, 100-foot-high sand dunes might have produced air disturbances. Ironically, the Royal New Zealand Air Force constructed Ohakea aerodrome on the land between Bulls and Sanson in 1939, the very land most desired by the airship mission. Today, it still functions as a military aerodrome.

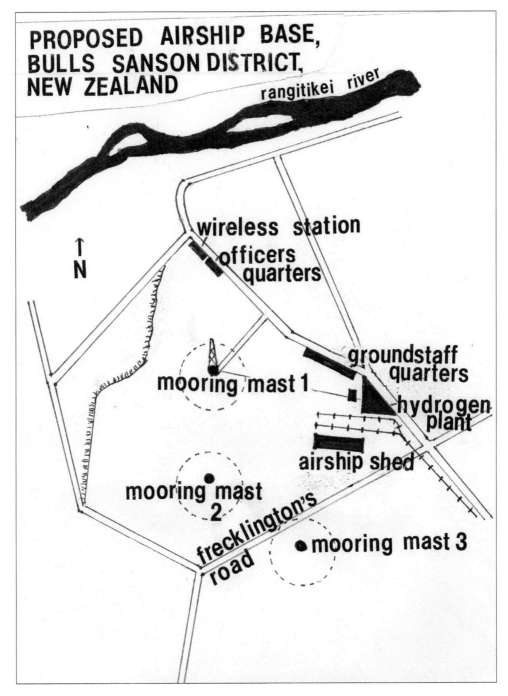

Proposed airship base, Bulls Sanson District, New Zealand. (*Author's collection*)

15

The 1930s and
the Second World War

The crash of the *R.101* in 1930 dealt a major blow to the British airship industry, but despite this disaster, there was still faith in the airship in some quarters. The Chief of the Air Staff suggested that the *R.100* should fly to India in an effort to regain credibility for the Imperial Airship Scheme, but this never went ahead. The Prime Minister still supported funding for development and there was a scheme to retain the *R.100* for experimental purposes to ensure the preservation of specialist skills. But Britain was in the grip of a major recession—the Wall Street Crash had taken place just a year previously—and the government had already spent over £2.35 million on the construction of the two airships. Besides, work had started on a more advanced airship, the *R.102*, at Cardington when the *R.101* crashed. For these reasons, the Committee of National Expenditure ruled against any more state expenditure, and its recommendations had a lasting impact.

The workforce at Cardington was made redundant. In December 1931, dismantlement of the *R.100* still housed in its shed at Cardington began. Hopes of a buyer had come to nothing. Some twenty men were employed in scrapping the Britain's last surviving airship, after which a steam roller ran over the parts to flatten them.

The following article appeared in the *Nottingham Evening Post* in March 1934. It gives an account of the aftermath of the Cardington Airship Works' abandonment in the local community:

Yesterday afternoon I spent in a haunted countryside, among villages still overshadowed by the greatest aerial tragedy in our history. It is now more than three years since the *R.101* left the mooring mast at Cardington on her last voyage. The vast airship works still stretch along the brow of the hill 3 miles outside Bedford. A little below, the hangars where the *R.100* and *R.101* were housed still face the Bedfordshire plain and the mooring mast has not been removed. Outwardly one would say nothing has changed yet the change is tragic and complete. A few years ago the Works employed hundreds of men, most of them from Bedford or from neighbouring villages. They had plenty to do. Offices, sheds and works were full. There was unceasing activity on the hill at Shortstown where since 1917 a red brick village had grown up, side by side with the air station and then suddenly came crushing disaster and the end.

A villager summed up the position in a sentence, 'the tide had gone out', he said, 'and we are left'. During the year that followed the disaster, hundreds of men, mechanics, engineers, workmen of all types lost their Posts. Many of them are unemployed still and it will be a long time before the villages of Cardington and Shortstown recover their vitality. The villages cannot escape from the tragedy for the enormous hangars dominate the district. In a hilly country the slight rise on which the airship works stand would be negligible but in the Bedfordshire Plain it is the most prominent feature of the landscape. As one leaves Bedford on the Hitchen Road the hangars tower ominously on the skyline and Cardington is completely under their shadow.

Cardington Airship Works remained intact in spite of closure. The sheds did not remain empty for long, as in 1932 they were requisitioned to store surplus RAF aeroplanes and a landing ground was prepared. Men were initially bussed from RAF Henlow due to lack of accommodation, but this inconvenience was resolved when some of the old huts at Cardington were brought back into use. In 1934, the work was handed over to civilians. Such was the demand for space that the large brick workshop known as 'the Arcade' was also used for storing aeroplanes. Eventually, over 300 aeroplanes came to be housed at Cardington, with some 3,000 landings and take-offs being recorded in one year. The transfer of the No. 2 Aeroplane Storage Depot to RAF Brize Norton in 1938 eventually saw the planes' departure.

Less fortunate were the rival works at Howden. These was sold to a Mr Mortimer of Knedlington Manor. Over the next few years, he attempted to persuade various parties to develop the site as an aerodrome but was unsuccessful, and in 1933 the large rigid airship shed was sold for scrap. It took nearly two years to dismantle the enormous structure. The railway line was also pulled up, although a number of bungalows which had served as the officers' quarters were retained by Mr Mortimer, who planned to create a garden village. The surrounding land was returned to arable farming. Early in the twenty-first century, Boothberry Golf Course occupied the southern portion of the former airship station. Today, the only surviving structures are a large concrete water tower and a couple of ruined brick buildings which once served as workshops. The memory of Howden airship station has been preserved in a history trail created in the main street of the small town which shares its name.

By the early 1930s, Britain was a country without airships or functioning airship stations. Yet in 1936, a private company proposed to establish a transatlantic airship service there. It was reportedly backed by a powerful British consortium which, according to press reports, was in the process of having a large airship built abroad, presumably in Germany. The company intended to operate a passenger service from Plymouth to New York, for which fares would not greatly exceed the first-class rates of a passenger liner. The spokesman for the company, airship pilot Capt. A. Sinclair, estimated that the airship would take around two days to make the journey, making it a day faster than flying boats that flew via the Azores. Like many grand ideas involving airships, it did not take off.

This was not the first plan to establish a civil airship base at Plymouth. In 1930, Devonport Mercantile Association was investigating ways of regenerating the Dockyard area which had suffered from a reduction in work for the Royal Navy. A letter was sent to Sir Dennis Burney, designer of the *R.100*, enquiring about the possibility of building an airship base here. He replied that the cost of a double airship shed would be £300,000, a mooring mast £75,000, and hydrogen gas plant and gas holder £50,000. Burney also raised practical objections to the project:

> I would very much doubt whether there is sufficient room for the establishment in the Hamoaze, in fact the only ground which appears to be suitable for an airship base is the high land just above Torpoint. If, on the other hand, St John's Lake was filled in it might be possible to put an airship hangar on the level ground so reclaimed, but I should imagine that the draining and filling in would be so expensive that such a programme would be really out of the question.

Burney added to his conclusion that there was little hope of things developing in the immediate future, owing to the difficult financial situation not only in Britain, but in the United States.

Although Britain did not have a single airship after 1931, Zeppelins did occasionally visit Britain or fly overhead on their way to New York. At one stage, it looked as though the Germans might have become the saviours of the ailing British airship industry. In December 1931, Dr Hugo Eckener, head of the Zeppelin Company, paid a visit to the by then abandoned Howden airship construction works. He declared that he was prepared to place his experience at the service of the British government and hoped that some kind of an agreement could be reached, whereby both Howden and Cardington would be leased to build airships for transatlantic service. Around ten years earlier, the same company had already expressed interest in a similar enterprise. Commenting on the size of the airship shed at Howden, Dr Hugo Eckener observed that it would have to be enlarged considerably to accommodate airships of the future.

Early the following year, meetings were held in London with the Air Minister and Col. Deeds, an American financier. It was hoped that a company would be formed in 1932 that would re-launch airship construction in Britain. The proposal came to nothing, probably as a result of the British government's disinterest. And yet, the British public flocked in their thousands to see the *Graf Zeppelin* when it visited Cardington in 1930. It was less than an hour before it took to the air again and headed back to its base at Friedrichshafen, Germany. It returned to Britain the following year.

By 1931, Cardington was being demobilised and the Zeppelin Company had to find an alternative location. On 18th August 1931, *Graf Zeppelin* was moored on the ground at Hanworth Aerodrome, Middlesex (O. S. 1/50,000 map 176 (TQ)115725), with the aid of 200 employees of the London underground railways who had volunteered for this task. Some 50,000 people watched it arrive, and some even found the opportunity to write their names on the silver painted hull of the control cabin. The *Graf Zeppelin* then took twenty passengers on board for a flight around Britain.

Hanworth, or 'London Air Park' as it was known, was a large private aerodrome which opened in 1929. Its clubhouse was a mansion situated in the centre of the aerodrome, surrounded by hangars. It was intended to construct a chain of ten provincial air parks throughout Britain to promote civil aviation. Being situated on the western edge of London, it saw frequent use by private aeroplanes. It also hosted air races and air displays.

The *Graf Zeppelin* rigid airship moored at Hanworth Aerodrome in July 1932 on its third and final visit to Britain. In front of the Zeppelin are the words 'London Air Park', spelled out on the ground in large white letters to enable identification of the aerodrome from the air. (*Aerofilms/English Heritage*)

The *Graf Zeppelin* airship returned for a final visit in early July 1932. When it landed at Hanworth onlookers were treated to a further spectacle, as a Junkers G.38—virtually an enormous flying wing—circled overhead. Few times in aviation history could there have been a more bizarre sight. The *Graf Zeppelin* again made a trip around Britain as well as a short flight over the centre of London. Upon its return back to Hanworth it was escorted by several small aeroplanes. Its visit was not without incident, making news headlines in many newspapers, including the *Western Morning News* on 4 July 1932:

A thrilling incident occurred last night, just before the Zeppelin left for an hour's cruise at seven o'clock, although the thousands in the public enclosure at Hanworth did not realize the danger until it was passed. The breeze suddenly freshened and, as the great ship swung slowly round, one of the mooring ropes being held by about fifty scouts snapped and they were thrown to the ground. The ship's nose rose slightly and she swung slowly round into the wind. A shout of alarm rang out, bringing the officers to the windows of the control cabin. Commands in German were given and swiftly another mooring rope was dropped from a porthole in the nose. The scouts, who were unhurt, seized this and the Zeppelin was once more under control. Almost immediately, further commands were given, the scouts eased up the guy-ropes and the Zeppelin rose.

Dr Hugo Eckener was satisfied that the Zeppelin had never been handled by a landing crew in such a splendid manner as by the Rover scouts and offered places to three of their leaders on the return flight to Germany. Only one took up the offer. At the end of the day, the loudspeakers announced that the *Graf Zeppelin* could be inspected at close quarters. Around 30,000 people surged through the barriers and raced the quarter mile across the grass to it. This was not without risk as, earlier that day, a man had been seen on the landing ground with a lighted cigarette and the Zeppelin was filled with flammable hydrogen gas. The police were instructed to remove anyone seen smoking. When it came for the time for the *Graf Zeppelin* to depart, it rose into the air to the strains of *Auld Lang Syne*. The giant airship dipped her German ensign in salute and pointed its nose for home. This was the last time a large rigid airship would take off from British soil. The aerodrome at Hanworth has long since disappeared; the site remains open ground and the mansion house still stands isolated at its centre.

The 1930s also saw the suggestion that the *Graf Zeppelin* visit Blackpool, and that the landing party of several hundred be drawn from the ranks of the unemployed! Apparently, there was not enough time to make the arrangements, so this idea was dropped. Towards the end of the decade, the threat of war elicited a rapid expansion of the RAF and Fleet Air Arm. Although German submarines again posed a serious menace, there appears to have been little consideration of airships to counteract it, other than in an exchange in Parliament on 17 February 1943. Wg Cdr Hulbert asked the Secretary of State for Air,

> [...] whether he is aware that semi-rigid airships were conspicuously successful in U-boat spotting in the last war and whether consideration has been given to the use of this type of aeroplane at the present time.[1]

The Secretary of State for Air, Sir A. Sinclair, replied,

> I am aware that airships were used in the last war for the purpose referred to and the question of using them in this has been carefully considered. It would not be in the public interest to say more.

Britain's towns and military installations were protected by a large number of barrage balloons, the nearest thing the country then had to airships, and which were similar in size and shape to the non-rigid airships of the RNAS. By the middle of 1940, there were 1,400 of these balloons in the skies over Britain. Appropriately, the former airship works at Cardington had been taken over in 1936 to train barrage balloon crews. Work was also undertaken on the design and development of balloons. By 1938, the former Royal Airship Works was now designated The Balloon Development Establishment. This employed some of the former designers of the *R.101* airship, as well as former crew members of the *R.100*. The former airship sheds were turned over to the manufacture of barrage balloons. At its peak, Cardington was producing twenty-six of them a week. Personnel from outside companies were also trained here, so additional production lines could be founded across the country.

When in the latter stages of the Second World War the threat from the Luftwaffe receded, barrage balloons in turn faded from the national agenda. The No. 1 Balloon Training Unit was finally closed in 1943, by which time it had trained 10,000 operators and a further 12,000 operators and drivers. The Cardington Balloon Establishment continued its research here for many more years until it was transferred to RAF Hullavington, Wiltshire in 1966.

Similarly to the British, the Germans did not enlist airships in their armoury during the Second World War, though there were signs to the contrary in the months leading up to conflict. *Graf Zeppelin II* had a section of its passenger quarters converted to house special radio detection equipment, for instance. Britain was building a chain of radar stations along its coast to provide advanced warning of the approach of enemy bombers. The *Graf Zeppelin II* flew a number of flights along the east coast in an effort to gain information on the large radar masts that were being erected. Between the 2nd and 4th of August 1939, the large airship flew as far north as the Shetland Islands. Not far from Aberdeen it developed unexplained engine trouble and began to drift towards a group of large radio masts. It was chased away by RAF Spitfires sent to intercept it. In spite of such missions, the Germans did not realise the true importance of these radar stations, the 'eyes' of RAF fighters, perhaps because the metal framework of the airship tended to disperse radio signals, making it difficult for the German technicians to interpret them.

Nowadays, airship advocates contend that they could vitally contribute to intelligence gathering and surveillance. But in 1940, this was not the opinion of Herman Goering, commander of the Luftwaffe, who in the spring ordered the two Graf Zeppelins to be broken up for their metal. In May, the giant airship sheds at Frankfurt were demolished so that German bombers could use the airfield. In contrast to European forces, the US Navy had never given up faith in the airship. Despite the loss of three large rigid airships, including the *Akron* in 1933 and the *Macon* in 1935, small blimps continued to be built by Goodyear throughout that decade. At the time of the attack on Pearl Harbor, the US Navy had ten airships in service, and by June 1942, no less than 200 were on order.

The K-class airship became the stalwart of the US airship service. It had a crew of nine, and initially operated along both the east and west seaboards of the USA. Airships were later deployed in the Pacific, and in 1944, Blimp Squadron 14 was deployed to Port Lyautey in French Morocco—this was the first time a non-rigid airship had made a transatlantic crossing. In June 1944, the US Navy airships started patrols in the Straits of Gibraltar to prevent German submarines from entering the Mediterranean Sea. Much of the flying was carried out at night to make up for the reduced effectiveness of patrols by aeroplanes. *K-112* became the first US Navy airship to land in Europe, when it touched down at the RAF aerodrome at Gibraltar on 18 July 1944. Fifty RAF men acted as the handling party. It was joined by a second airship a short time later. The aerodrome was meant to become an emergency landing ground for airships and a mobile mooring mast was erected, but US Navy airships made no further use of this facility.

In the closing stages of the conflict in Europe, the US Navy dispatched a further two airships to Europe. They flew via Bermuda, which would have become a staging post for British rigid airships, had the Imperial Airship Scheme borne fruit. As the threat from German submarines diminished, US Navy airships switched to mine-hunting duties, operating from a number of locations in Italy and Malta. At the latter location, detachment No. 5 had a mooring mast at HMS Goldfinch (Ta Kali), a Royal Navy aerodrome.

There were plans to deploy US Navy airships from mainland Britain, for instance in late 1944, when the Royal Navy requested a squadron of airships for patrol and mine-sweeping duties to protect the south-western approaches of the British Isles. They would have been stationed at the Royal Air Force Coastal Command aerodrome at Chivenor, near Barnstaple, North Devon. A mooring detachment would equally have been made available at RAF St Eval, 6 miles north-east of Newquay, Cornwall. Finally, the maintenance of the US Navy airships would have been carried out in the former airship sheds at RAF Cardington, somewhat reminiscently. The cessation of hostilities abruptly halted these plans, when a maintenance detachment was already on board a ship sailing for Britain and two flight crews were already in the Azores awaiting arrival of their airships.

Not a single ship escorted by US Navy airships during the Second World War was sunk, but it should be noted that they generally operated in areas unlikely to be attacked by enemy aeroplane. The destruction of the Luftwaffe enabled their deployment over Europe in the final stages of the war. The US Navy continued to use airships up until 1962. American interest in the airship has recently been rekindled, however, and in 2013 the US Navy operated one.

16

Modern Times

A 1949 headline in the *Derby Daily Telegraph* once proclaimed, 'Airships to Make Come-Back? Nearly Ready'. Over sixty years later, similar statements still appear in magazines and newspapers. Numerous predictions about the imminent arrival of the large airship have surfaced, but come to nothing. Dr Hugo Eckener, who developed the Zeppelin air services of the 1930s, asserted in the above newspaper article that the business world was ready to invest in airships again. He envisaged a daily non-stop air service between the English Midlands and New York:

> French technicians were all set to build a graceful Paris–London–Midlands leviathan that would capture Atlantic luxury travel. It would have a bathroom in every cabin, a ballroom, cocktail bars and a restaurant serving 100 passengers. An American aircraft company had also publicly announced it had plans for the construction of both cargo and passenger airships. They were going to be 950 feet long and would be able to carry 288 passengers. Britain, with its experience of building 2,400 barrage balloons, had amassed a fund of useful experience and, according to airship experts, could be first in the sky with a fleet of twenty four dirigibles. They will argue that the future will look back with derision at the millions we squander on new runways when an airship needs only a mooring mast to discharge passengers and freight in the heart of a city. They will question whether aircraft have not reached their limit in size and speed.[1]

Two years after this article was published, Britain actually did build an airship, though it was no transatlantic leviathan. Arthur Eveleigh-de-Moleyne had been interested in airships for most of his life. While a young schoolboy at Wellington College, his curiosity was aroused by the airships he would often see overhead from Farnborough. He decided to visit the airship station and was sneaked in by a sympathetic sentry. In Shed-A he saw naval airship *No. 4*, as well as the Parseval airship bought by the Admiralty in 1913, both rigged for flight. In Shed-C there was the diminutive *Willows* and the control cars for *Beta One* and *Beta Two*, *Gamma*, *Delta*, and *Eta*. On a later visit in the summer of 1914, he came across *Gamma*, *Willows*, and the Parseval inflated in their sheds.

At the beginning of the First World War, Eveleigh-de-Moleyne visited RNAS Wormwood Scrubs and befriended Wg Cdr Clive Waterlow. Nearly twenty years later, he took the opportunity to fly on the Zeppelin when it visited Hanworth. His life-long fascination led him to establish the Airship Club in 1948, with the aim of building the first airship in Britain for twenty years. A small team began collecting the requisite parts for this project in a hired shed at Hurn airport, Bournemouth. A control car was constructed here by Alec Leith, who had worked on non-rigid airships in the last war. The airship was then transferred to Cardington for final assembly, where its arrival was met with great enthusiasm by the staff. Some of the construction work on the new airship was actually carried out by the *R.100* crew, as well as two survivors from the *R.101*. Cardington was now an RAF station, but had changed little since the *R.101* had been constructed there in the 1920s. Only the iconic mooring mast had been demolished and its steel reassigned to the war effort in 1943.

The new airship was housed in shed No. 2 and made its first flight on 19 July 1951, whereupon it bore the civilian registration G-AMJH and 'Bournemouth' on its nose—the city council had assisted in financing the project. The airship was supposed to fly over the town once the trials had finished. Future operating sites, including King's Park, had also been investigated. The headmaster of St Peter's School had given the *Bournemouth* permission to use the sheltered sports field as an emergency landing ground. To keep operating costs down, the small airship was going to be housed in the open. Lord Ventry, as Arthur Eveleigh-de-Moleyne was by then known, may have got this idea from his visit to the airship mooring out site at Upton during the First World War. In 1950, *Flight* explained his thinking thus:

The *Bournemouth* airship at Cardington. This small airship, only 108 feet long, made several flights from here in 1951 and 1952. (*Bedfordshire and Luton Archives*)

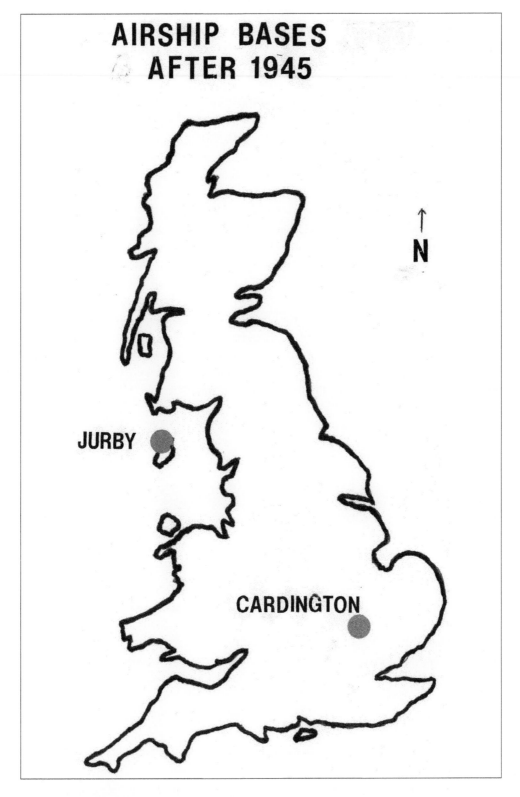

Airship bases after 1945. (*Author's collection*)

One of the most expensive items in the construction of an airship must be the hangar and at the present time it is one which, in a private venture, would be virtually impossible of achievement. Surprisingly, however, an airship is quite amenable to being tethered in the open and we are assured by Lord Ventry that with the aid of a protective screen of trees, a small non-rigid can safely ride out a 70 mph gale if properly picketed. This, therefore, is the plan for the *Bournemouth*. She will be kept inflated and out of doors during all spells of operational activity that promise to be fairly continuous.[2]

Presumably, Lord Ventry was considering using woodland near Bournemouth, where he lived, for berthing the airship. On its first flight, the *Bournemouth* carried a pilot and three passengers. Unfortunately, it was found to be nose heavy and the controls were almost ineffective. Disaster struck on the third trial flight when the airship flew low over the station gymnasium at Cardington. The trail ropes got caught on an obstruction, which caused the airship to come crashing down on its roof, smashing windows in the process. Although no one was seriously hurt, the airship required repairs to its envelope and damaged propeller. These were completed by September 1951, but further modifications were required if it was to obtain a Certificate of Airworthiness.

Trials recommenced at Cardington in 1952. A single-decker bus assisted with mooring and moving the airship in and out of its shed. A total of eight flights were flown that year. The *Bournemouth* made its last flight on 16 August 1952, when it took part in the Battle of Britain celebrations. It flew over Bedford and was in the air for nearly two hours. Most of the early problems with the airship had been resolved and its future looked bright when it was housed in the No. 2 shed at Cardington for the winter. Tentative plans were made to construct a second airship of similar size in response to the huge public interest in the *Bournemouth*. Unfortunately, on 24 April 1953, some of the netting covering the airship came loose and tore away a 'rip panel' (used to deflate the airship in emergencies) causing the envelope of the *Bournemouth* to seriously tear. The front section reared up into the roof of the shed, while the rear end collapsed on the floor. The Airship Club did not have the resources to effect a repair and the *Bournemouth* never flew again. It had been only three months away from concluding its flying tests at Cardington.

A long interlude followed before an airship was again seen in British skies. The first airship to serve with the French military was the *Lebaudy Patrie*. It was built for the French Army by the sugar producers Lebaudy Frères, and first flew in 1907. Sixty years later, a scaled down replica of the airship was built for the 1968 film of *Chitty Chitty Bang Bang*, a children's story by Ian Fleming which revolved around a magical flying Edwardian motorcar. The 140-foot-long Lebaudy replica airship was intended to represent the craft of the fictional villain Baron Bomburst of Vulgaria. But on a test flight it proved unstable, collided with power cables, and had to make a forced landing. After the incident it was fitted with a new envelope. The Lebaudy replica airship was moored in a wooded valley near Turville in Buckinghamshire for most of its career, and before it could fly again, it was wrecked there in a gale. The original Lebaudy airship had met its end in a similar manner.

On the other side of the Atlantic, airships were valued for their commercial role as flying advertising boards and assistance in covering major sports events. Between 1911 and 1978, Goodyear Tire and Rubber Company of Akron, Ohio, built 287 airships, mainly for the US Navy. In the late 1960s, Goodyear had a small fleet of its own airships, which were usually referred to as 'blimps', and regularly operated out of Miami, Houston, and Los Angeles. The European branch of this company decided to establish a similar enterprise. On 10 December 1971, a giant 'Guppy' transport plane arrived at R.A.E. Bedford from Akron. Its cargo was then taken by road to the No. 1 shed at Cardington, where it was assembled into an airship appropriately named *Europa*. Its career almost came to an end before it had begun, when a strong wind tore *Europa* loose from its moorings. It bounded along the ground, eventually coming to rest in a tree in the grounds of Manor Farm, once the home of Maj. Scott of the *R.101*. Fortunately it was not beyond repair and went back into service on 28 June 1972, when it made twelve flights from Cardington carrying a total of sixty-seven passengers. On the following day, a further 111 people experienced the delight of lighter-than-air travel. The *Europa* then spent three weeks at Leavesden Aerodrome, just north of Watford, performing further demonstration flights. Its gondola was capable of accommodating two pilots and six passengers.

An unusual feature of *Europa*—yet typical of Goodyear craft—was the installation of 3,780 lamps on the side of its envelope. These could create a four-coloured sign which was legible from over a mile away. Unfortunately, aerial advertising was at the time banned in Britain and, in any case, the *Europa* spent much of its long life out of the country. A purpose-built shed was constructed for it at Capena, 18 miles from Rome. The airship did later return to Britain to act as a broadcasting platform, namely for the wedding of Prince Charles and Lady Diana Spencer. When operating away from its main base, it was usually attached to a small mooring mast not unlike those used by RNAS airships in the First World War. In 1982, Goodyear decided it could no longer afford to fund its European airship operation and closed the base in Italy. The *Europa* continued to fly until 1986, when it crashed in the south of France while filming a BBC wildlife documentary.

Between 1974 and 1976, a group of enthusiasts constructed Britain's third post-war airship at Cardington. It was just 72 feet long and was named *Santos-Dumont*, after the early airship pioneer. It first flew in 1974, but its career was cut short two years later when it encountered some trees near Old Warden Aerodrome. Around the same time, there were stirrings to resurrect airships for commercial use. Roger Munk, a professional naval architect, undertook a study of how Shell might transport methane from North Africa by airship. He formed a company called Aerospace Developments, to design a carrier for this natural resource. For the construction of this airship, it was intended to erect a new shed and not to re-use old facilities such as Cardington. The US company Birdair was given the brief to design a constructional facility based on the principles of the early airship sheds, employing a cantilevered A-frame system that was 1,800 feet long and 300 feet wide. This would have been, at the time, the world's largest building.

The plans for this giant new rigid airship did not proceed beyond the design stage, partly because of the discovery of North Sea oil in 1972, which reduced Britain's dependency on imported energy sources. Roger Munk persisted in his faith in the airship and his company went on to build the 164-foot-long *AD-500*. It first flew from Cardington, carrying the registration G-BECE, in the spring of 1979, eight years after it was first conceived. After making two short flights, the airship went the same way as many of its predecessors. On 8 March 1979, high winds prevented the *AD-500* being taken back into its shed at Cardington. It was subsequently left attached to its stub mooring mast, and as the wind increased in strength, the airship was badly damaged.

Another two years passed before a replacement appeared in the form of the Skyship 500, G-BIHN. This proved a success, stimulating interest in airships across several continents. In April 1985, Airship Industries was granted Britain's first Air Operator's Certificate for the public carriage of passengers in an airship. On 23 April 1986, Skyship G-BIHN flew Britain's first fare-paying passenger airship flight from Leavesden Aerodrome. The following year, the operation was transferred to the old Handley Page Aerodrome at Radlett, south of St Albans. There were better facilities here for the passengers, including a terminal building with a waiting room. When sight-seeing flights over London ceased, Cardington became the new base for excursions. From here the flights were shorter and mainly over the Bedford area. A total of six Skyship 500s airships were built between 1980 and 1990. The Skycruise concept of sight-seeing proved so successful that an improved airship was produced in the form of the Skyship 600.

Ambitious plans for rigid airships were formulated in 1980. One was the Skyship *R.40*. It was to be 600 feet long and resembled the *R.100* airship in shape. A second design was the *R.150*, which would have been 571 feet long and totally metal-clad on the outside. Redcoat, a British air cargo airline based at Manston Aerodrome, Kent, ordered four of the *R.150* airships with a view to a further ten, but unfortunately went out of business in 1982. Airship Industries abandoned their work on rigid airships. Despite the success of the Skyships, Robert Munk's company often struggled financially. It received cash injections from a number of investors, which resulted in several name changes; but after producing seventeen new airships and operating them in Europe, North America, Australia, Japan, and South Korea, the company was finally wound up in 1990. Its airships fly on.

Military interest in airships blew hot and cold. The Ministry of Defence purchased a Skyship 600 and based it at the Defence Test and Evaluation Airfield at Boscombe Down. It bore the military designation *ZH762*, but was less formally known as the *Prince of Wales*. In May 1995, it ruptured its envelope while being moored to its mast. Later that year, questions were asked about its running cost in the Houses of Parliament. It was eventually sold in 1998 after the completion of the trials.

There were other attempts in the late twentieth century to resuscitate the airship industry. Strangely, their focal point was not Cardington, but the Isle of Man. A breakaway company from Airship Industries named Wren Skyships, after its founder Maj. Malcolm Wren, was formed with the intention of continuing to develop the large rigid metal-clad airship. According to a 1985 *Flight* article, the company announced that it was going to commence construction of airships in Scotland the following year. Two sites had been short listed to this end, Prestwick Airport and a closed steel mill at Glengarnock, near Kilbirnie. It was projected that 66 examples of its *RS.1* rigid airship would be produced over the next decade. These would be 420 feet long and have a 27-tonne payload, and would mainly accrue demand among specialist air companies. Other potential roles for this large airship included supplying materials for remote construction projects, transporting timber, and maritime surveillance. A peak production rate of thirteen airships a year was predicted to occur in 1991 and with 2,000 workers employed. Wren Skyships did not set up a construction facility in Scotland and never produced a *RS.1* rigid airship, as the anticipated grant from the Scottish Development Agency never materialized. Instead, it established its base on the Isle of Man.

A unique design of the production facility for the *RS-1* was proposed by Christopher Dean Architects of London, but was not taken up. Instead, a fabric-covered steel-arched shed (300 feet long, 143 feet wide, and 73 feet high) was completed in 1987 for the Wren Advanced Non-Rigid (ANR) airship. It was built at the disused RAF Jurby airfield (O. S. 1/50,000 map 95, (SC) 362986) on the northern tip of the Isle of Man. The intention was to complete the ANR airship by the end of 1988, but the project fell behind schedule due to envelope trouble. The company went out of business in the early 1990s without ever flying a single airship. Its airship shed was demolished and its base converted into a go-kart circuit.

The end of the twentieth century nevertheless saw a number of small structures built to house airships. A fabric-covered steel framed shed for helium-inflated airships was constructed by Thunder and Colt in 1987 at Rednal Aerodrome near Ostwestry, Shropshire. This company, too, suspended its operations a few years later. Another similar structure was built at Halfpenny Green Aerodrome in the West Midlands for use by Virgin Lightships. In 2004, Lightship *A60* was assembled and flown from Cardington. Unfortunately, such activity had now become a rare event. For the first time since the visit of the *Graf Zeppelin* to Hanworth in the 1930s, a Zeppelin returned to the skies over London in the summer of 2008 and flew a series of sight-seeing flights from Damyns Hall Aerodrome near Upminster. The airship also paid a visit to Cardington. It was a very much smaller craft than its antecedents, measuring 246 feet in length, and had seats for only twelve passengers. It was one of a number of new non-rigid airships built by the original Zeppelin Company.

Meanwhile, the former Royal Airship Works at Cardington had long been converted into an RAF station. This has also seen use by the Department of the Environment, and for a time by the RAF Museum for storing historic planes. When the RAF relinquished its facilities at Cardington, the site became subject to commercial pressures. There had been few changes to the complex before the end of the twentieth century, but since then, the erstwhile workshops and accommodation blocks have been demolished and houses put up in their place.

Only the two enormous airship sheds and the iconic red brick administrative building dating from 1917 remain. In early 21st century, shed No. 1 still functions

The Coastal shed at Cramlington in the late 1960s, shortly before demolition. Most other British airship sheds of the First World War had vanished by 1939. (*Northumberland Archives /Woodhorn*)

in its traditional role, housing visiting airships, although none are built here. A new role has been found for shed No. 2, which is now the largest film studio in Britain. Films made here include *Chitty Chitty Bang Bang* (1968), *Zeppelin* (1971), and *Sky Captain and the World of Tomorrow* (2004), though its best known creation is probably the Batman trilogy—*Batman Begins* (2005), *The Dark Knight* (2008), and *The Dark Knight Rises* (2012). The two enormous airship sheds, which still tower over the Bedfordshire landscape, are the largest structures of their kind outside the USA. Their national significance has only recently been acknowledged. In 2013, the No. 1 shed—Cardington's first—was subject to an extensive renovation. While the structures themselves will be preserved, the construction of houses in their immediate vicinity may curtail future operations by airships.

Attempts to resurrect the British airship industry have not completely failed. In 1995, former employees of Airship Industries founded a successor company, the Advanced Airship Technologies Group. On 28 March 2002, it flew the *AT-10* airship, which it had built at Cardington. This was the first and last creation of this short-lived company. Its assets were acquired by an Italian-British consortium and the new business was re-named the Skycat Group. This in turn was acquired by a new British firm, Hybrid Air Vehicles, which won a contract to develop three advanced airships for surveillance duties in conjunction with Northrop Grumman. Only one example was flown (in the USA) before the project was cancelled by the US Department of Defence in 2013. Hybrid Air Vehicles re-acquired the single flying prototype, which resembled a cross between a flying saucer and a traditional rigid machine. Britain once again had a large airship in its skies.

In early 2014, Hybrid Air Vehicles' airship, now named the *Airlander 10* was re-assembled in Cardington shed No. 1. At 305 feet, it is the longest flying machine in the world, exceeding the length of the Boeing 747 and the Airbus A380 by 60 feet. Unlike the previous large airships which once occupied Cardington, sixty per cent of its lift is provided by helium, not hydrogen—the remaining lift comes from its wing-shaped hull. *Airlander 10* has the ability to carry 10 tonnes of cargo, and an even bigger version is on the cards. Being able to land vertically, it can transport goods to remote locations without the need for a runway or vast handling party, as was the case in the past. This hybrid airship requires a crew of only two, and is considerably cheaper to operate than an aeroplane or helicopter.

Appendices

Appendix 1. Further Images

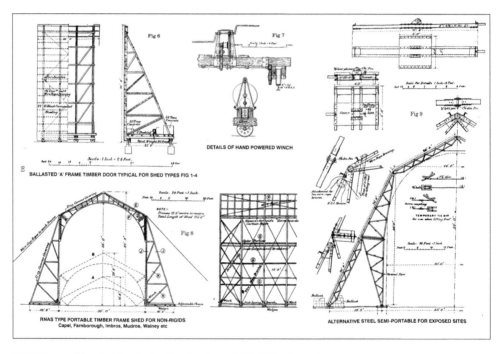

RNAS portable airship sheds. (*Institution of Civil Engineers*)

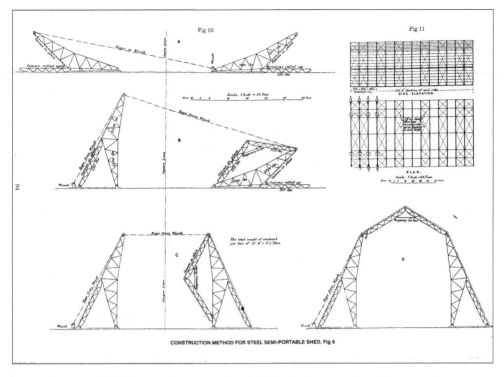

Construction method for a steel, semi-portable shed. (*Institution of Civil Engineers*)

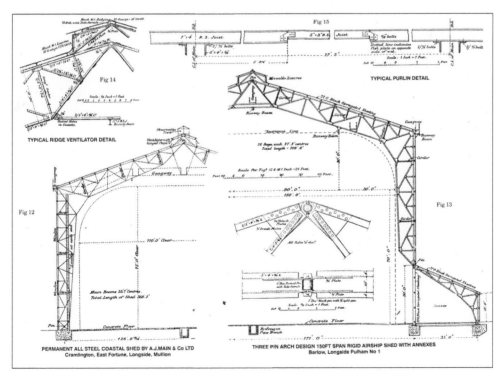

Permanent all-steel Coastal sheds. (*Institution of Civil Engineers*)

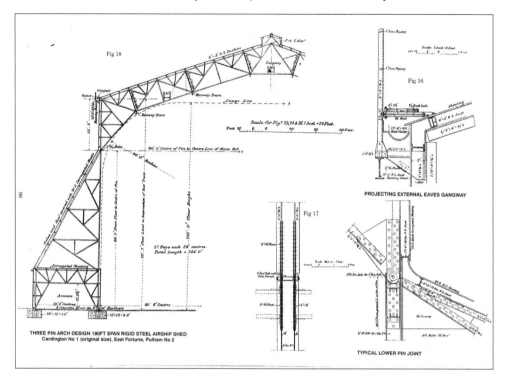

Three-pin arch design a 180-foot Rigid steel shed. (*Institution of Civil Engineers*)

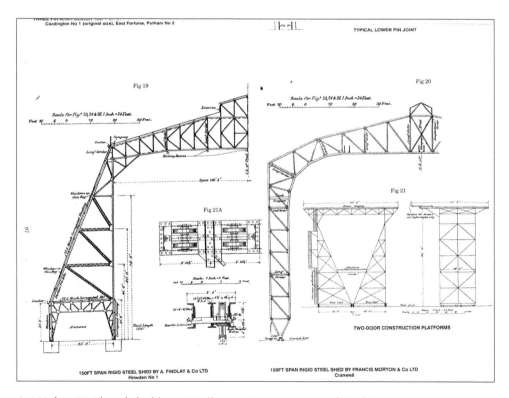

A 150-foot Rigid steel shed by A. Findlay & Co. (*Institution of Civil Engineers*)

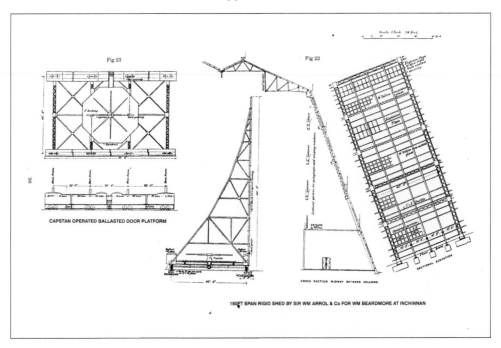

A 150-foot Rigid shed by Sir William Arrol & Co. for Beardmore at Inchinnan. (*Institution of Civil Engineers*)

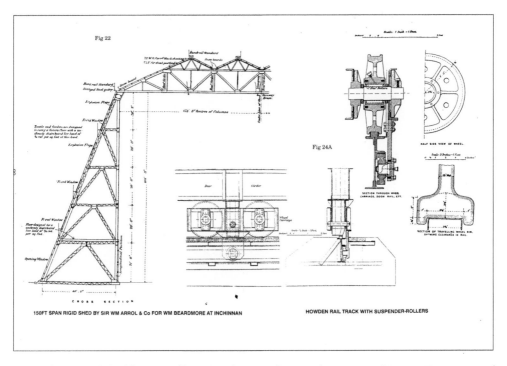

A 150-foot Rigid shed by Sir William Arrol & Co. for Beardmore at Inchinnan. (*Institution of Civil Engineers*)

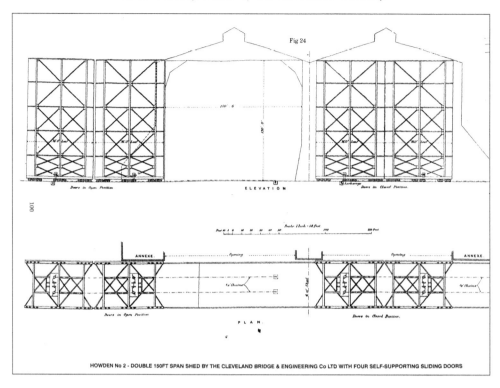

Howden No. 2. A double 150-foot shed by Cleveland Bridge & Engineering Co. (*The Institution of Civil Engineers*)

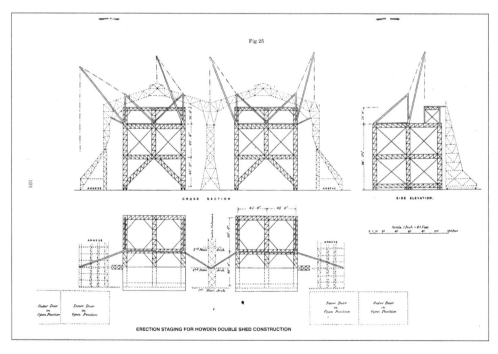

Erection staging for the Howden double shed construction. (*The Institution of Civil Engineers*)

Appendix 2. Deployment of RNAS Airships—1 February 1917

STATION	SUBMARINE SCOUT	COASTAL
Anglesey	4	0
Barrow	2	0
Caldale	2	0
Cranwell (training)	2	1
East Fortune	0	4
Folkestone	6	1
Howden	0	4
Kingsnorth	5 (under construction)	2 (under construction)
Longside	0	4
Luce Bay	4	0
Mullion	0	3
Pembroke	2	2
Polegate	6	1
Pulham	0	3
Wormwood Scrubs	3 (under construction)	0 (under construction)

Pilots Qualified 88
Pilots under Training 33

Appendix 3. Deployment of RNAS Airships—January 1918

STATION	SERIAL NO.	TYPE	STATUS
Anglesey	S.S.25	Submarine Scout	On strength
	S.S.P.1	Submarine Scout Pusher	On strength
	S.S.P.5	Submarine Scout Pusher	Repairs
	S.S.P.6	Submarine Scout Pusher	Rigging
Caldale (airship station closed)	S.S.41	Submarine Scout	Deflated
Capel	S.S.Z.1	Submarine Scout Zero	Repairs
	S.S.Z.4	Submarine Scout Zero	On strength
	S.S.Z.5	Submarine Scout Zero	On strength
	S.S.Z.18	Submarine Scout Zero	Rebuilding
	S.S.Z.26	Submarine Scout Zero	On strength

Cranwell	No. 6	Parseval	Awaiting acceptance
	S.S.28	Submarine Scout	Rebuilding
	S.S.29	Submarine Scout	Training
	S.S.30A	Submarine Scout	Training
	S.S.31A	Submarine Scout	Rebuilding
	S.S.37	Submarine Scout	Training
	S.S.39A	Submarine Scout	Training
East Fortune	R.24	23-class Rigid Airship	On strength
	C.25	Coastal	On strength
	N.S.1	North Sea	Deflated
	N.S.4	North Sea	On strength
Howden	R.9	Rigid Airship	On strength
	R.25	23-class Rigid Airship	On strength
	No. 5	Parseval	Awaiting acceptance
	No. 7	Parseval	Awaiting acceptance
	C.4	Coastal	On strength
	C.19	Coastal	On strength
	C.21	Coastal	On strength
Kingsnorth	C.1	Coastal	Experimental
	C.11	Coastal	Rebuilding
	C.12	Coastal	Deflated
	C.24	Coastal	Rebuilding
	N.S.1	North Sea	Rebuilding
	N.S.2	North Sea	Rebuilding
	N.S.5	North Sea	Rebuilding
	N.S.6	North Sea	Rebuilding
	S.S.14	Submarine Scout	Rebuilding
Longside	C.7	Coastal	Inflating
	C.10A	Coastal	On strength
	C.14	Coastal	On strength
	C.18	Coastal	On strength
Luce Bay	S.S.23	Submarine Scout	Not ready
	S.S.Z.11	Submarine Scout Zero	On strength
	S.S.Z.12	Submarine Scout Zero	On strength
	S.S.Z.13	Submarine Scout Zero	On strength

	S.S.Z.20	Submarine Scout Zero	Rigging
Mullion	C.2	Coastal	On strength
	C.9	Coastal	On strength
	C.23A	Coastal	On strength
	S.S.Z.14	Submarine Scout Zero	Awaiting spares
	S.S.Z.15	Submarine Scout Zero	On strength
	S.S.Z.20	Submarine Scout Zero	Awaiting envelope
Pembroke	C.3	Coastal	On strength
	C.5A	Coastal	On strength
	S.S.Z.16	Submarine Scout Zero	Not ready
Polegate	S.S.9A	Submarine Scout	On strength
	S.S.Z.6	Submarine Scout Zero	On strength
	S.S.Z.8	Submarine Scout Zero	On strength
	S.S.Z.9	Submarine Scout Zero	On strength
	S.S.Z.19	Submarine Scout Zero	Deflated
Pulham	R.23	23-class Rigid Airship	On strength
	C.14A	Coastal	On strength
	S.S.35	Submarine Scout	Experimental
	S.S.Z.3	Submarine Scout Zero	Experimental
	S.S.14A	Submarine Scout	On strength
Walney Island	S.S.32A	Submarine Scout	Repairs
	S.S.36	Submarine Scout	Experimental
Wormwood Scrubs	S.S.16	Submarine Scout	Rebuilding
	S.S.20	Submarine Scout	Rebuilding
	S.S.24	Submarine Scout	Rebuilding
	S.S.40	Submarine Scout	Rebuilding
	S.S.43	Submarine Scout	Deflated

Appendix 4. Deployment of RNAS Airships Overseas

STATION	SERIAL NO.	TYPE	STATUS
Kassandra	S.S.7	Submarine Scout	Awaiting spares
	S.S.8	Submarine Scout	Awaiting spares
	S.S.17	Submarine Scout	On strength
Mudros	S.S.3	Submarine Scout	Awaiting spares
	S.S.19	Submarine Scout	Awaiting spares

Appendix 5. Rigid Airships Under Construction

STATION	MANUFACTURER	SERIAL NO.	TYPE
Barlow	Armstrong Whitworth	R.29	23X-class
		R.33	33-class
		R.35	33-class
Cardington	Shorts	R.31	31-class
		R.32	31-class
Inchinnan	Beardmore	R.27	23X-class
		R.34	33-class
Walney Island	Vickers	R.26	23-class
		R.37	33-class

Endnotes

1. The Airship Pioneers

1 'King Solomon's Airship—the Art of Flying in the 10th century B.C.', *Dundee Evening Telegraph, 28 February 1923.*
2 'Francesco Lana de Terzi, Father of Aeronautics', on *www.faculty.fairfield.edu.*
3 Dudley, Ray, 'The Dr. F Alexander Barton Airship Story', *Dirigible*, 14.3 (2003), p. 20.
4 Bennet, J., 'London's First Airport', *Dirigible*, 55 (autumn 2008), pp. 11-12.
5 *ibid.*

2. Military Airship Bases before the First World War

1 Walker, Percy, *Early Aviation at Farnborough-Balloons, Kites and Airships*, (London: MacDonald, 1971), p. 53.
2 'Englishman's Unique Invention', *Dundee Courier*, 13 September 1913, p. 3.
3 *Dundee Evening Telegraph*, 22 May 1911, p. 3. See Roskill, Capt. S. W. (ed.), *Documents Relating to the Naval Air Service vol. 1, 1908-1918* (London: Spottiswood, Ballantyne and Co., 1967)
4 Bible, Tina, *Kingsnorth Airship Station* (Stroud: The History Press, 2013), p. 61.
5 Roskill, p. 143.
6 *ibid.*, p. 122.
7 *ibid.*, p. 143.

3. RNAS Airship Stations in South-East England

1 Mowthorpe, Ces, *Sky Sailors—The Story of the World's Airshipmen* (Stroud: Sutton Publishing, 1999), p. 30.
2 Golightly, M. J., 'RNAS Airship Memories', *Flight*, 10 June 1960, pp. 803-804.
3 'Airship Sheds, Rye', 20 November 1918, vol. 110 c347 in *Hansard* (hansard. millbanksystems.com).

4. RNAS Airship Stations in South-West England

1 'Monthly Return of Items of Information: Airship and Kite Balloon Services', May 1918, The National Archives, p. 56.
2 *ibid.*, p. 55.
3 'Additional Airship Stations, Memo from C and C Portsmouth to Director of Air Services', *Dirigible*, 15. 2.
4 *ibid.*, p. 5.
5 28 October 1919, vol. 120 cc 488-9w in *Hansard* (hansard.millbanksystems. com).

5. RNAS Airship Stations in East England

1 'Instructions to Pilots', memo from RNAS Pulham to Commodore at Lowestoft, 19 May 1917, The National Archives.
2 'Report by Captain of Airship C.27', to Commanding Officer at RNAS Pulham, 1 May 1917, The National Archives.
3 Correspondence on the Admiralty's reply to complaints, Whitehall, 19 July 1917, in RNAS Pulham Records.
4 Correspondence on suspicious people near Pulham, November 1917, RNAS Pulham Records.
5 Mowthorpe, Ces, 'RNAS Lowthorpe Airship Mooring-Out Site', *Cross and Cockade*, 27.1, p. 43.

6. RNAS Airship Stations in Wales

1 Johnston, Ernest, *Airship Navigator* (Stroud: Skyline, 1994).
2 Gamble, H., 'Life in Blimps', *Cross and Cockade*, 19.3, p. 148.

7. RNAS Airship Stations in Scotland

1 Lowry, Adml, 'General Report on East Fortune Naval Air Station', January 1916, The National Archives.
2 Wind Barrage at East Fortune Airship Station, Air 23-9384, The National Archives.
3 'Monthly Return of Items of Information: Airship and Kite Balloon Services, Longside', The National Archives, p. 3.
4 Operational Reports, R. N. Airship Station, Longside, 21 April 1917.
5 Turpin, Brian, 'Coastal Patrol Airships', *Cross and Cockade*, 15.3, p. 128.
6 'Report by Cdr Roland C. S. Hunt, on sites for a Coastal Airship Station at Scapa Flow', 19 April 1916, The National Archives.

7 'Monthly Return of Items of Information: Airship and Kite Balloon Services, Kirkwall', November 1916, The National Archives.

8. RNAS Airship Stations in Ireland

1 Warner, Guy, 'The First crossing to Ireland by Airship', *Airships over the North Channel* (Newtownards: April Sky Design, 2005), p. 22.
2 'Proposed Airship Station in the Vicinity of Dublin or Kingston', 1917, The National Archives.

9. RNAS Overseas Airship Stations

1 Roskill, p. 122.
2 'General Description of Naval Airship Station, Dunkirk' (booklet), 1915, The National Archives.
3 *ibid.*
4 Mowthorpe, p. 1.
5 *ibid.*
6 *ibid.*
7 Goddard, AM Victor, 'The Black Ship', *Cross and Cockade*, 13, p. 159.
8 'Report of Commanding Officer of Airship Station, Kephalos Bay, Imbros, General Comments', 1915, The National Archives.
9 'Memo by Vice Admiral, Malta', 20 December 1915, The National Archives.
10 'Director of Air Services Memo', January 1916, The National Archives.

10. RNAS Training and Airship Construction Stations

1 MacMillan, Norman, *Sir Sefton Brancker*, (London: Heinemann, 1935), p. 45.
2 Farnborough Naval Airship Station Airship Log Book, 1 January 1914 to 23 September 1915.
3 Request for three S. S. Airships to be permanently based at Kingsnorth Air Station, September 1915, The National Archives.
4 Roskill, p.178.
5 Mowthorpe, p. 21.
6 *Hull Daily Mail*, 25 July 1917, p. 2.

11. Rigid Airship Construction Works

1 'The Construction of the Navy Dirigibles by Vickers', *Dirigible*, 5.11, No. 2, pp. 6-9, as published in *Aeronautics*, 1914.

2   *Manchester Courier and Lancashire General Advertiser*, 26 September 1913, p. 7.

3   Whale, George, *British Airships, Past, Present and Future* (McLean, Virginia: Indy Publishing, no date), p. 67. [reprint]

4   'Mr. Henry Ford's Scheme for Mass Production', *Nottingham Evening Post*, 28 March 1925.

5   'Yorkshire Airship Works Closed Down', *Yorkshire Evening Post*, 1 September 1919, p. 7.

6   'Airships at Inchinnan', *Dirigible*, 5.11, No. 2, quoting the *Beardmore News*, March 1919.

7   'Bedford, Site for Airship Shed, Director of Works, Minute Sheet', 1916, The National Archives.

12. The Early Post War Years

1   *The Scotsman*, 31 October 1919.

2   'Airship Construction Policy Extract from Board Minutes', 16 January 1919, The National Archives.

3   'Airship's Catastrophic End', *Western Daily Express*, 25 August 1921, p. 8.

4   *Dundee, Perth, Forfar and Fife's People Journal*, 19 July 1919, p. 6.

14. Imperial Airship Routes

1   MacMillan, p. 415.

2   Pirie, Gordon, *Air Empire, British Imperial Civil Aviation 1919-39* (Manchester: Manchester University Press, 2009), p. 131.

15. The 1930s and the Second World War

1   17 February 1943, vol. 386 cc 1713-4 in *Hansard* (hansard.millbanksystems. com).

16. Modern Times

1   *Derby Daily Telegraph*, 5 October 1949.

2   'A British Airship Again', *Flight*, 16 November 1950, p. 420.

Bibliography

Public Records Office, Kew

Air 1-108-15-9-291 Capel Airship Station-Patrols

Air 1-240-15-226-69p Daily Reports of Operations, RAF Stations—Airships

Air 1-420-15-246-5 Reports etc., Airship Stations in Scotland

Air 1-420-115-246-5 Longside Airship Station, Sept.–Nov. 1918

Air 1-437-15-297-4 R.N. Airship Station, Pulham, 20 Oct 1915 – 13 August 1919

Air 1-147-15-67 Employment of Airships with the Expeditionary Force

Air 1-619-16-15-351 Admiralty Airship Station at Pulham

Air 1-640-17-122-209 Proposal for Increase in Number of Available Airships at Pembroke Airship Station

Air 1-641-17-122-215 Suggested New Scheme of Aerial Patrol on the East Coast

Air 1-625-17-2 General Description of Naval Airship Station Dunkirk, Jan 1915

Air 1-645-17-122-329 Request for Three S.S. Airships to be Permanently Allocated to Kingsnorth Air Station for Patrol Duties, Sept. 1915

Air 1-656-17-122-547 British Rigid Airship Identification Numbers

Air 1-672-17-134-16 Airship Station at Capel

Air 1-718-31-2-1 Airship Services, Items of Information, 1 January 1916–31 March 1916

Air 1-719-31-2-6 Airship and Kite Balloons, Items of Information, 1 April 1917–30 June 1917

Air 1-718-31-1-1 Airship Services, Items of Information, 1November 1917–30 November 1917

Air 1-718-31-2-2 Airship Services, Items of Information, 1 April 1916–30 June 1916

Air 1-718-31-1-4 Airship Services, Items of Information, 1 February 1918–28 February 1918

Air 1-718-31-1-3 Airship Services, Items of Information, 1 January 1918–31 January 1918

Air 1-718-31-1-5 Airship Services, Items of Information, 1 March 1918–31 March 1918

Air 1-718-31-2-3 Airship Services, Items of Information, 1 July 1916–30 September 1916

Air 1-718-31-1-2 Airship Services, Items of Information, 1 December 1917–31 December 1917

Air 1-2103-207-30-33 Complements of Airship Stations

Air 1-2307-215-19 Selby Airship Works—Photos, 1916

Air 1-2309-215-21A and 21B Inchinnan Airship Station—Photos

Air 1-2314-222-1a Airship Service General History Royal Naval Air Service Operation Reports

Air 1-2314 222 1b Royal Naval Air Service Operational Reports

Air 1-2314-222-1c Royal Naval Air Service Operational Reports

Air 1-2636 Proposed Airship Building Programme

Air 1-2681 Farnborough Naval Airship Station, Airship Log Book

Air 1-452-15-312-26V Selection of an Airship Base in South Africa

Air 2-14 Cardington Airship Works transfer from Shorts to the Admiralty

Air 2-41 Particulars of Floating Airship Hangar designed by Major Stansfield

Air 2-138 Transfer of Airship Stations to Air Ministry, 1919

Air 2-168 Drafts, Memos, Minutes, and Copies of Correspondence on Work on Rigid Airships. Construction of Airship Establishment and Airships C. Burney Scheme 1917–1919

Air 2-197 Mr Mo O'Gorman's Proposals for an Airship Factory and Programme of Work for 1909–1910

Air 2-259 Leases of Marsa (Malta) Airship Station Land

Air 2-303 Report by Major Scott on visit to Canada and United States regarding an Airship Base

Air 5-1036 Notes on the Selection of an Airship Station

Air 10-859 State of Development of Airship Service, 1 January 1918

Air 11-196 ADI Airship

Air 11-224 vol. VII, Views of Airship Stations

Air 11-227 Egypt Airship Base Photos

Air 11-229 St Hubert Airship Base Photos

Air 11-230 India Airship Base Photos, Book 1

Air 11-231 India Airship Base Photos, Book 2

Air 11-252 Examination of Sites

Air 59-4 Photos of Airship Stations

Air 59-6 Photos of Howden Airship Station

ADM 116-1335 Development of Airship Service since 1914—Disposition of aircraft and airships

ADM 137-4125 Zeppelin Airship Stations

ADM 1-8524-128 Airship Stations at Kingsnorth and Wormwood Scrubs

ADM 1-8530-197 British Rigid Airships—Orders and Requirements

CAB40-152 Rigid Airship Sheds, Supply of Steel

DSIR 23-806 Visit to R.N. Airship Station, Kingsnorth

DSIR 23-348 Illumination of Airship Sheds

DSIR 23-10314 Airship Mooring Masts

DSIR 23-2109 Airship Guarantee Company's and Air Ministry's Types of Mooring Mast

DSIR 23-9384 'Wind Barrage' at East Fortune Airship Station
MUN 4-440 War Priorities Committee

British Aerospace Library, Farnborough

Lord Ventry's Papers:
'Proposed Allocation of Airships For Home Water, 1918–1919'
Various papers relating to 'Shed Erection and Hut Accommodation' at various airship stations

Books and Pamphlets

Abbott, Patrick, *The British Airship at War: 1914–1918* (Lavenham: Terence Dalton, 1989)

Abbott, Patrick and Nick Walmsley, *British Airships in Pictures, An Illustrated History 1784–1998* (Isle of Colonsay, Argyll: House of Lochar, 1999)

Airship R.100 (Howden: Airship Guarantee Company) [promotional brochure]

Asquith, Tom and Kenneth Deacon, *Howden Civic Society* (Howden, 2006) [leaflet]

Bilbe, Tina, *Kingsnorth Airship Station* (Stroud: The History Press, 2013)

Brancker, Sir Sefton, *Norman MacMillan* (London: William Heinemann, 1935)

Brock, Deric, *Wings over Carew—RNAS Pembroke/Milton* (Tenby: RAF Carew Cheriton, 1989)

Brooks, Peter W., *Zeppelin: Putnam Aeronautical Books* (London: Conway Maritime Press, 1992)

Castle, Ian, *British Airships 1905–30* (Oxford: Osprey Publishing, 2009)

Chamberlain, Geoffrey, Airships Cardington (Lavenham: Terence Dalton, 1984)

Chorlton, Martyn, 'Vickers Company Profile 1911–1977', *Aeroplane Monthly* (2013)
Christopher, John, *Balloons at War—Gasbags, Flying Bombs and Cold War Secrets* (Stroud: Tempus, 2004)

Christopher, John, *Transatlantic Airships—An Illustrated History* (Marlborough: The Crowood Press, 2010)

Connon, Peter, *In the Shadow of the Eagle's Wing—The History of Aviation in the Cumbria, Dumfries and Galloway Region, 1825–1914* (Penrith: St Patrick's Press, 1982)

—*An Aeronautical History of the Cumbria, Dumfries and Galloway Region, Part 2: 1915-1930* (Penrith: St Patrick's Press, 1982)

Cooksey, Peter G., *The RFC/RNAS Handbook* (Stroud: Sutton, 2000)

Corser, W. J. L., *Wings on Rails* (Fleet Hargate: Arcturus Press, 2003)

D'Orcy, Ladislas, *D'Orcy's Airship Manual, 1917* (Milton Keynes: Lightning Source, 2011) [reprint]

Dawson, Leslie, *Wings over Dorset* (Wicanton: Dorset Publishing at Wincanton Press, 1983)

Dean, Christohpher (ed.), *Housing the Airship* (London: The Architectural Association, 1989)

Deacon, Kenneth, *Howden's Airship Station* (Howden: Langrick, 2003)

Elliston, R. A., *Eastbourne's Great War 1914–1918* (SB Publications, 1999)

'Airships' in *Encyclopaedia Britannica, vol. 1* (London: William Benton, 1963)

Fife, Malcolm, *Scottish Aerodromes of the First World War* (Stroud: Tempus, 2007)

Hamlin, John F., *Peaceful Fields—A Directory of Civil Airfields and Landing Grounds in the United Kingdom 1919–1939* (Peterborough: GMS Enterprises, 2007)

Paul, Francis, *British Military Airfield Architecture—From Airships to the Jet Age* (Patrick Stephens, 1996)

—'RN Air Station Howden—An Assessment of its Buildings', *Airfield Research Group* (www.airfieldresearchgroup.org.uk/wp-content/uploads/2012/06/RNAS-Howden.pdf)

Gilpin, Leslie R., *The Ulverstone and Lancaster Railway* (Pinner: Cumbrian Railways Association, 2008)

Grieves, Keith (ed.), *Sussex in the First World War* (Lewes: Sussex Record Society, 2004)

Hayes, Karl E., *A History of the Royal Air Force and United States Naval Air Service in Ireland 1913–1923* (Dublin: Irish Air Letter, 1988)

Higham, Robin, *The British Rigid Airship 1908–1931* (London: G. T. Foulis, 1961)

Hume, John R., *Beardmore, The History of a Scottish Industrial Giant* (London: Heinemann, 1979)

Jane, Fred T., *Jane's All the World's Airships 1909* (Newton Abbot: David and Charles, 1969) [reprint]

Jamison, T. W., *Icarus over the Humber—The Last Flight of Airship R.38/ZR-2* (Hull: Lampada Press and University of Hull Press, 1994)

Johnston, E. A., *Airship Navigator* (Stroud: Skyline, 1994)

Johnston, Ian, *Beardmore, The Rise and Fall of a Clydeside Shipyard* (Clydebank: District Libraries and Museums Department, 1993)

Kinsey, Gordon, *Pulham Pigs, A History of an Airship Station* (Lavenham: Terence Dalton, 1988)

London, Peter, *Aviation in Cornwall* (Tunbridge Wells: Air-Britain, 1997).

—*U-Boat Hunters—Cornwall's Air War 1916–19* (Truro: Dyllansow Truran, 1999)

Mather, Guy (ed.), *Royal Naval Airship Station, Polegate: A Souvenir, 1914–1919*, (Eastbourne: Whale-Back Press, 2009)

McKinty, Alec, *The Father of British Airships—A Biography of E. T. Willows* (London: William Kimber, 1972)

Meager, G., *My Airship Flights* (London: William Kimber, 1970)

Mowthorpe, Ces, *Battlebags—British Airships of the First World War* (Stroud: Sutton, 1995)

—*Sky Sailors* (Stroud: Sutton, 1999)

Peake, Norman, and Jocelyn Rawlence, *The Story of Pulham and its Airships* (Pulham: Pulham Market Society, 1989)

Phillips, Alan, *Defending Wales: The Coast and Sea Lanes in Wartime* (Stroud: Amberley, 2010)

Philpot, Wg Cdr Ian M., 'The Trenchard Years 1918–1929' in *The Royal Air Force— An Encyclopaedia of the Inter-War Years*, vol. 1 (Barnsley: Pen and Sword Books, 2005)

Pirie, Gordon, *Air Empire—British Imperial Civil Aviation 1919–1939* (Manchester: Manchester University Press, 2009)

Rosie, George, *Flight of the Titan—The Story of the R34* (Edinburgh: Birlinn, 2010)

Roskill, Capt. S. W. (ed.), *Documents Relating to the Naval Air Service vol 1, 1908– 1918* (London: The Navy Records Society, 1969)

Pratt, Derrick, and Mike Grant, *Wings Across the Border—A History of Aviation in North–East Wales and the Northern Marches*, vol. 1 (Wrexham: Bridge Books, 1998)

Rowland, Patricia, *The Impact of the First World War on Winder Moor, Flookburgh, A research project for Postgraduate Diploma in Lake District Studies* (University of Lancaster, 2009)

Sbatier, J. (translated by), 'Large German Airship Stations', *L'Aéronautique*, March 1921 (Provo, Utah: Repressed, 2012)

Shock, James R., *American Airship Bases and Facilities* (Edgewater, Florida: Atlantis Productions, 1996)

Simmons, Geoffrey, *East Riding Airfields 1915–1920* (Manchester: Crecy, 2009)

Shute, Nevil, *Slide Rule* (London: Vintage Books, 2009)

Treadwell, Terry C., *The First Naval Air War* (Stroud: Tempus, 2010)

Treadwell, Terry C., and Alan C. Wood, *Airships of the First World War* (Stroud: Tempus, 1999)

Thorsby, Robert C., *Glamorgan Aviation* (Stroud: Tempus, 2002)

Walker, Percey B., *Early Aviation at Farnborough—Balloons, Kites and Airships* (London: MacDonald, 1971)

Warner, Guy, *Airships over the North Channel—Royal Naval Air Service Airships during the First World War* (Newtownards: Guy Warner, 2005)

—*Airships over Ulster—Royal Naval Air Service Airships during the First World War* (Newtownards: Guy Warner, 2012)

Watson, Nigel, *The Scareship Mystery: a Survey of Phantom Airship Scares 1909– 1918* (Corby: Domra, 2000)

Whale, George, *British Airships: Past, Present and Future* (Princeton University: John Lane, 1919)

William, T. B., *Airship Pilot No. 28* (London: William Kimber, 1974)

Magazines and Periodicals

Abbott, Patrick, 'A.D.1.Airship', *Dirigible*, 5.4 (Winter 1994–95)

—'Two Victorian Airships', *Dirigible*, 8.28 (Summer 1997)

—'The Spencer Airships—A Reappraisal', *Dirigible*, 13.3 (Autumn 2002)

'Aeronautics, The Construction of the Navy Dirigibles by Vicker' (first published in 1914), *Dirigible*, 13.1 (Spring 2002)

Bennett, J. D., 'London's First Airport', *Dirigible*, 55 (Autumn 2008)

Berry, Peter, 'East Fortune Airfield', *Airfield Review*, 77 (December 1997)

Bunyan, Ian T., 'Non-Rigid Airships at East Fortune During World War I', *Transactions of the East Lothian Antiquarian and Field Naturalists' Society*, 21 (1991)

Collyer, David G., 'When Airships Flew at Capel', *Kent Life*, 1 June 1975

Mick Davis and Bill Morgan, 'Gazetteer of Flying Sites in the UK and Ireland 1912–20', *Cross and Cockade International*, 41.1 (2010)

Dudley, Ray, 'The Dr. F. Alexander Barton Airship Story', *Dirigible*, 14 (2003)

'The Karachi Airship Shed', *The Engineer*, 24 December 1926

The Engineer, 4 March 1927, 11 March 1927, 18 March 1927

'Airship Mooring Gear', *Engineering*, 8 April 1921

'The Passenger-Carrying Airship R.36', *Engineering*, 15 April 1921

Fortier, Renald, 'The R.100 in Canada—Photo Essay Collection', *National Aviation Museum of Canada*, 1999 (www.aviation.technmuses.ca.)

Hutchinson, Iain, 'Airships at Inchinnan', *Dirigible*, 11.2 (Summer 2000)

Humpreys, Roy, 'Adventures with airships over Capel', *Bygone Kent*, 28 (Sept/Oct 2007)

Greenstreet, E. C., 'The Evolution of R.A.E. Farnborough', *Dirigible*, 5.3 (Autumn 1994)

—'The Airship in World War II', *Dirigible*, 7.1 (Spring 1996)

Kender, Martin, 'Gallipoli—The Airship Expeditionary Force in the Eastern Mediterranean', *Dirigible*, 6.1 (Summer 1995)

Jarrett, Philip, 'Dagenham Days—A History of the Aeronautical Society's Flying Ground', *The Aeronautical Journal*, 74 (February 1970)

Jackson, F. W., 'A War-Time Disaster on the Downs', *Sussex County Magazine*, June 1932

Lawson, Alistair, 'HMA No. 9', *Dirigible*, 16.1 (Spring 2005)

Larmuth, Luke, 'Hamilton, Airship Sheds and their Erection' and 'Informal Discussion', *Minutes of Proceedings (Institution of Civil Engineers) Part 2*, 212 (January 1921)

MacDougall, Phillip, 'From Airship Station to Oil Refinery', *Coast and Country*, 8.3 (June 1979)

Mowthorpe, Ces, 'The Airship Constructional Works at Barlow, East Yorkshire', *Cross and Cockade*, 17.3 (1986)

—'Howden Airship Station 1916–1930', *Cross and Cockade*, 10.4 (1979)

Peake, Norman, 'The Vickers 'Parseval' No. 4', *Dirigible*, 13.2 (Summer 2002)

Provan, John, 'The German Airship Sheds', *W.W.1. Aero-Journal of the Early Aeroplane*, 141 (1993)

'The St Hubert Airship Mooring Tower', *The Engineer*, 28 March 1930

Turpin, Brian J., 'Imperial Airships—A Short Lived Dream', *Aeroplane Monthly*, July 1974

—'Imperial Airships, part 2', *Aeroplane Monthly*, August 1974

—'The Polegate Incident', *Aeroplane Monthly*, May 1978

—'Coastal Patrol Airships 1915–1918, Part 2', *Cross and Cockade*, 15.3 (1984)

Walbridge, Steven, 'The Royal Naval Airship Stations of Dorset', *Dirigible*, 15.2 (Autumn 2004)

Walmsey, Nick, 'Stanley Spencer and Mellin's Airship No. 1', *Dirigible*, 8.4 (Winter 1996/97)

—'An Expensive Mistake: The Rise and Fall of the Croydon Airship Mast', *Dirigible*, 11.1 (Spring 2000)

—'R-36—Harbinger of the 1924 Airship Programme', *Dirigible*, 11.1 (Spring 2000)

Whale, Maj. G., 'The Future of the Commercial Airship', *Conquest*, June 1920

Williams, T. B., 'Recollections of an Airship Era', *Country Life*, 6 May 1971

Wright, Peter, 'The RNAS Airship Service and the Air Construction Corps, The RNAS Airship Service and the Air Construction Corps, Part 1', *Cross and Cockade*, 32.4 (2001)

—'The RNAS Airship Service and the Air Construction Corps, Part 2', *Cross and Cockade*, 33.1 (2002)

—'The RNAS Airship Service and the Air Construction Corps, Part 3', *Cross and Cockade*, 33.2 (2002)

Websites

The Airship Heritage Trust

British Newspaper Archive

Flight Global Archives

Google Earth (for current state of airship base sites)

Orkney

The Military History of Slindon—Slindon Estate at War (slindonatwarmyblog.wordpress.com)

Shortstown

Walney Island

Suggested further reading

Cross and Cockade—this quarterly magazine is published by the First World War Aviation Historical Society and sometimes features articles on airships (www.crossandcockade.com)

Dirigible—The Airship Heritage Trust publishes this magazine three times a year. It also has an informative website with extensive histories on a large number of airships (www.airshipsonline.com)